Praise for *Citizen Cash*

"This is an important reassessment of one of American music's greatest performers, revealing a complex artist of the first magnitude who used his art and empathy to parse for him the contradictory times he immortalized in his work."

—KEN BURNS, filmmaker

"Michael Stewart Foley has written a book about Johnny Cash, and I cannot think of a better match of an author and subject. Foley shows how Cash's deep reserves of empathy and insight made him an artist for his time (and ours). This book will change how you think about Johnny Cash."

—JOHN MCMILLIAN, professor of history at Georgia State University and author of *Beatles vs. Stones*

"In this compelling biography, Michael Stewart Foley recovers the 'Man in Black' as a prophetic political voice who used his microphone to plead the case of ordinary Americans, criticize the powerful, and prod his listeners to envision a better world. He shows how Johnny Cash combined empathy and entertainment, bringing together religion, a country vernacular, and lyricism to challenge injustice and inequality in a country that he loved. This is a moving, important book."

—THOMAS J. SUGRUE, New York University

"Certain old-timers in Nashville talk about Johnny Cash with a particular and complex form of respect. I had to read this book to find out why and am left with my own respect for its author."

—BEN RATLIFF, author of *Every Song Ever*

"From the New Deal to the Nixon presidency, Michael Stewart Foley weaves Johnny Cash into the historical fabric of the twentieth century. With his usual sharp insight and keen eye for storytelling, Foley artfully crafts *Citizen Cash* as a biography, a music history, and a cultural diagnosis. Political currents ripped left and right in Cash's America, but the iconic singer navigated the roiling waters with a common-sense empathy for the underdog and suspicion of the powerful. Foley gives us Cash the 'public citizen,' a ballast for the nation as it came together and then came apart."

—ROBERT O. SELF, Brown University

"History is written *for* an era as much as about one, and historian Michael Foley has given us a Johnny Cash that speaks to our divided nation. Foley's Cash offers a 'politics of empathy' that transcends political division; he is a man shaped by the particulars of history, but also a man capable of change. Foley beautifully combines historical biography with his knowledge of Cash's music and its context. This is masterful work!"

—BETH BAILEY, author of *Sex in the Heartland*

"*Citizen Cash* is a big-hearted book about a big-hearted artist making his way through a complicated nation. A refreshing, healing examination of what Michael Foley calls Cash's 'politics of empathy.' In Foley's compassionate take on the Man in Black, we get an earthy sense of public citizenship that was as deep as the man's voice. Read it and feel better about who we are as a diverse people in a troubled land."

—JEFFERSON COWIE,
author of *Stayin' Alive: The 1970s and the
Last Days of the Working Class*

"Most of us remember Johnny Cash as a country music star, a celebrity who projected a loner, outlaw persona. Michael Stewart Foley has done an excellent tear-down of that image by focusing on a key virtue of Cash—his immense empathy for the underdog. Foley draws our attention to the many complexities of Cash—a man full of religious faith, memories of a troubled family, and a fear of what wars can do to the people who fight them. *Citizen Cash* shows us a man who made empathy into art while responding to the historical crises America faced during the late 1960s. Well done, and a fun read as well."

—KEVIN MATTSON,
author of *We're Not Here to Entertain*

"What does it mean to be a political artist? For an artist to 'be political'? In a timely and finely researched meditation on Cash's takes on incarceration, Native rights, racism, and the war in Vietnam, Foley embraces the messiness of politics in public. We get Cash the researcher, Cash the documentarian, Cash the curator, and Cash the empath. We get a book that re-establishes Cash as a fascinating prism for looking though some of the most urgent issues still haunting American political life."

—JOSH KUN, author of
Audiotopia: Music, Race, and America

CITIZEN CASH

CITIZEN CASH

THE POLITICAL LIFE AND TIMES OF JOHNNY CASH

CASH

MICHAEL STEWART FOLEY

BASIC BOOKS

New York

Basic Books
Hachette Book Group
1290 Avenue of the Americas, New York, NY 10104
www.basicbooks.com

Printed in the United States of America

First Edition: December 2021

Published by Basic Books, an imprint of Perseus Books, LLC, a subsidiary of
Hachette Book Group, Inc. The Basic Books name and logo is a trademark
of the Hachette Book Group.

The Hachette Speakers Bureau provides a wide range of authors for speaking events.
To find out more, go to www.hachettespeakersbureau.com or call (866) 376-6591.

The publisher is not responsible for websites (or their content) that are not owned
by the publisher.

Print book interior design by Jeff Williams.

Library of Congress Cataloging-in-Publication Data
Names: Foley, Michael S. author.
Title: Citizen Cash : the political life and times of Johnny Cash / Michael Stewart Foley.
Description: First edition. | New York : Basic Books, 2021. | Includes bibliographical
    references and index. |
Identifiers: LCCN 2021015580 | ISBN 9781541699571 (hardcover) | ISBN
    9781541699564 (ebook)
Subjects: LCSH: Cash, Johnny—Criticism and interpretation. | Cash, Johnny—
    Political activity. | Cash, Johnny—Political and social views. | Country music—
    Political aspects—History—20th century.
Classification: LCC ML420.C265 F65 2021 | DDC 782.421642092—dc23
LC record available at https://lccn.loc.gov/2021015580

ISBNs: 9781541699571 (hardcover), 9781541699564 (ebook)

LSC-C

Printing 1, 2021

In memory of my brother,
Kurt Michael Foley

Everything is political. It just sounds worse if you call it political. I mean, we're talking about life and death and the things that matter.

—KRIS KRISTOFFERSON

He had great feeling for the downtrodden and for those who were marginalized from society. He had empathy for the suffering of others . . . all his political views came from that empathy.

—ROSANNE CASH

Contents

Introduction

The only time I've ever set foot in a high-end auction house was to see the estate of Johnny Cash and June Carter Cash sold off in 2004 at Sotheby's. As an early career historian, working at a public university in the most expensive city in America, I could never hope to afford to take home a prized country music artifact. But I was there for research.

The cavernous, half-empty auction hall reminded me of a federal courtroom just before the start of a trial. People got serious quickly. Bidders were well prepared, having scoured the catalog and toured in advance the de facto museum exhibition of Cash artifacts that Sotheby's had hosted over the last several weeks. This ain't no yard sale, I thought. But, really, what kind of insight was I going to get on Cash by watching well-to-do fans bid on one pair after another of his cowboy boots? I considered leaving.

Before I could push my chair back, a handsome middle-aged couple came in, practically breathless, and sat down next to me. Turns out they had just gotten married and were looking to score a piece of country music history. When the woman asked me what I planned to try for, I somewhat sheepishly admitted to being there not as a bidder but as a historian. That piqued her interest, so I told her a little about my work on the Vietnam War. I started to say that Cash's 1969 Madison Square Garden concert had drawn my attention, not only as a fan but also as a historian, because Cash had spoken about the war and about peace from the stage. She abruptly cut me off: "But anybody who knows anything about Johnny Cash knows he was a Republican, right?" she challenged. "I mean, he was a *patriot!*"

"Yes, he *was* a patriot," I replied, but I pointed out that some people think he was pretty liberal, what with that whole wearing black "for the poor and the beaten down" line from "Man in Black."

"Oh, sure," she replied, "he was a *Christian*—he cared about people. But he was definitely a Republican. You've heard 'Ragged Old Flag,' right?" We debated in friendly fashion for a couple of more minutes, with me trying to explain how not all Johnny Cash fans hear the same message in a song like "Ragged Old Flag," until her new husband returned to drag her off to look at some of June Carter's jewelry.

That passionate Johnny Cash fan at Sotheby's—I never got her name—may not have thought much of my research project, but she had done me an enormous favor. She had gotten me thinking about why no one really wrote about Johnny Cash's politics—at least, not in a way that made sense of it. How *could* we explain such a wide range of political identification with Cash, with self-defined liberals and conservatives claiming him in equal measure? And why do most observers describe his politics as inconsistent, even paradoxical?

What I've learned over the last sixteen years I've spent thinking about these questions is that Cash's politics can seem at first like a moving target in a hall of mirrors. Most of the time there appears to be multiple Johnny Cashes, each one trapped in its own web of mythology. Most famously, there is the redeemed sinner Johnny Cash, the one familiar to anyone who saw Joaquin Phoenix play him in the Hollywood biopic, *Walk the Line*: an Arkansas farm boy who comes out of poverty to enjoy fantastic success alongside fellow Sun Records star, Elvis Presley, only to engage in years of drug-fueled self-sabotage that destroys his marriage and nearly kills him before, by the grace of God and June Carter, he gets his shit together, records a live album at Folsom Prison, and becomes a superstar. It's the classic rise-fall-rise narrative, with all of the ingredients of a big-budget feature-film version of a VH1 *Behind the Music* episode.

But there's also the "walking contradiction" Johnny Cash: "partly truth and partly fiction," to quote his friend Kris Kristofferson, who wrote those lines in a song about himself, only to have Cash and others assume they were about Cash. This myth is especially hard to untangle when Cash's politics come up, given that he *did* seem to contradict himself by both opposing the Vietnam War and expressing support for President Richard Nixon's handling of the war. Or that he supported civil rights, but also spoke of the courage of Confederate soldiers. Or given that he was a God-fearing Christian family man who felt more comfortable in a prison playing to his "fellow miscreants." And so on and so on.

And then there is the blank-screen Johnny Cash: the one on whom we project our own identities, political and otherwise. Like my auction debate partner, we fans have a habit of finding something in Cash's lyrics and image that resonates with us and assuming that he is just like us in every other way. Or we see him as his own son claims to: "nonpolitical, and a patriot with no public political party affiliation."[1] But that's just another of the Johnny Cashes, the one who brings everyone together, who would not risk alienating any segment of his audience by embracing a political identity. He could not be a contradiction because he was "nonpolitical."

No systematic analysis of Cash's actions can conclude that he was "nonpolitical." Johnny Cash not only devoted much of his career to the pressing political questions of his lifetime, but he was also remarkably consistent in the way he did so. If it has been difficult to read him all these years, it has been because we have been looking at him through the wrong lens. In 1971, when Cash stood at the peak of his popularity and influence, the political scientist Robert Levine reported on American citizens behaving in ways experts labeled contradictory. "Voters and citizens are individuals," Levine cautioned, "holding views that *they* believe to be consistent and changing their views along lines they believe to be consistent even though political theorists may not agree." It made little sense, therefore, to insist on using binary labels to categorize Americans into this or that political group—liberal or conservative, hawk or dove, patriot or protester—but you wouldn't know it from the way we talk about American politics. Like most Americans, then and now, Johnny Cash did not experience politics ideologically, or participate in political discourse in ways that would satisfy an ideologue. But that doesn't mean that his stances were not based upon deep reflection or intellectual sophistication. Quite the contrary.[2]

Johnny Cash practiced what I call a politics of empathy. He came to his political positions based on his personal experience, often guided by his own emotional and visceral responses to the issues. In the same way that social movement theorists have written for years now about the role of emotion and storytelling in mobilizing for one cause or another, Americans often engage political questions on the basis of feeling, not doctrine. It makes no sense to apply a one-size-fits-all standard to explaining a person's politics when we know that we are *not* all one size—that our personas, political and otherwise, are forged in the crucibles of our own experiences. Naturally, that makes it hard on those who set or accept the parameters of normative political categories. Johnny Cash seemed unintelligible (or illegible) only insofar as his observers tried to apply conventional political labels to him. As soon as we throw those terms away, though, Cash comes into view as one of the most deeply engaged political artists of his age.[3]

To be sure, to approach political questions only from the perspective of one's own experience would be pretty limiting. Our knowledge and understanding may derive partly from our own experience, but most of us need to draw on other sources to supplement it. Johnny Cash may have seen Black convicts chained together, building the roads or levees in Mississippi County, Arkansas, but he was a white Southerner who had never worked on a chain gang. He may have thought for a long time that he had some Cherokee DNA in his bloodline, but he had never been forced, with his people, off his land or otherwise betrayed by the federal government. He had been locked up overnight a handful of times but had never been sent to prison. And he served in the Air Force, but not in Vietnam. Yet, he wrote and spoke movingly about all of these things—racism, Native rights, prison life, and the Vietnam War, among other subjects—because he possessed the documentarian's unwavering fascination with social realism. He obsessively researched the subjects of the concept albums that he recorded in the early to mid-1960s, trying, as he later recalled, "to get at the reality behind some of our country's history." In each case, he came to these matters initially at the prompting of his own experience, but he was not satisfied until he felt like he understood the actual lives of those he studied. Cash thus followed a well-established folk music tradition, like that embodied by singers such as Odetta (of whom he was a great fan) or Peter La Farge (who was his friend), that insisted on authenticity and truth-telling. But he got there largely on his own, not through the inducements of the cultural left we associate with the 1930s and beyond. Nothing influenced him as much as the field recordings of John and Alan Lomax. Those recordings, especially *Blues in the Mississippi Night* and the *Southern Folk Heritage Series*, which captured not only the voices of singers such as Big Bill Broonzy and Vera Hall but also the background sounds of prison life, levee camps, Cajun bayous, and Appalachian hillbilly stomps, transported Cash to other worlds, opened them up enough that he could better relate to, and empathize with, the people they documented. As an artist, Cash acted like the best documentarian photographers—Dorothea Lange, Walker Evans, Gordon Parks, each of whom preserved the

5

dignity of their subjects, no matter how poor or desperate their circumstances. That same commitment to the empathy of social realism anchored Cash's public citizenship. It also made him a curator of the American experience itself.[4]

By uncovering Cash's politics of empathy over his lifetime, *Citizen Cash* charts the development of one of America's foremost public citizens. Particularly in the 1960s and 1970s, when the term "public citizen" was most associated with the crusading consumer advocate Ralph Nader and the nonpartisan, nonprofit organization he founded of the same name, Johnny Cash, widely regarded as the "rough cut king of country music," used his standing in American culture to try to make a difference on the most pressing public issues of the day. But unlike Nader, he was not much of a crusader. He had to grow into the role, becoming increasingly comfortable across the 1960s until, by the time he got his network television show in 1969, he had secured his standing as a prominent political artist. Cash, without really intending it, fashioned a new model of public citizenship, based on a politics of empathy. It's an approach that's relevant in our own times and yet has been largely misunderstood because it's not as straightforward as electoral politics. Instead of toeing a party line, it looks more like following a series of dance steps only the dancer knows.

We can understand Cash's politics best through his work—his concept albums, his live performances, and especially the appearances on his televised variety show. *The Johnny Cash Show*, airing weekly on ABC from 1969 to 1971, became his primary pulpit for addressing political questions facing a polarized nation. Some weeks, he would use a monologue toward the end of an episode to speak directly to an issue; other weeks, a duet with a guest artist provided an opportunity to weigh in on another topic. Frequently, he employed his Americana-tinged "Ride This Train" segment to draw viewers into a subject that often he framed in political terms. For the three seasons it aired, the show was a hit.[5] The politics of empathy Cash practiced clearly appealed to a vast, diverse audience. "The young like him because he has the ring of authenticity and supports social causes," *Life* reported, and "for people over 30 he sounds a note of sanity in a mixed-up musical world—they can tap their feet and understand his words." Cash's records outsold the Beatles, and his life was the subject of a documentary film, five mass-market biographies, and countless magazine profiles. He seemed as permanent in American life as the Lincoln Memorial.[6]

Cash's politics of empathy should not seem so illegible, either, because it reflected certain timeworn American ideals. It was fundamentally democratic and inclusive. He never trafficked in grievance and rarely expressed bitterness when he related to others. Since he based his politics primarily on his experiences, his empathy could take different forms—at times, deeply personal and intimate, at others, more like a kind of solidarity; on still other occasions, it came from a determined effort to understand the lives of others with whom he had no shared experiences. "I have a feeling for human nature in difficult situations," he said about a year before he died. "Don't know why, but I always have." In its inclusivity, Cash's empathy went beyond the limits of ideology—it was supra-partisan.[7]

Johnny Cash was not some kind of ideal American citizen (whatever that might be). There were times in his life, particularly when his drug addiction had such a grip on him, when he behaved like a pretty poor excuse for a citizen. And one could argue that even when he reached the top of his public citizen game on his television show, he could have done better—been more forceful on certain issues, less trite on others, and more inclusive of certain groups. Still, he tried, earnestly, to use his public standing for the public good, which is not always easy for a prominent celebrity or entertainer to do. Too frequently, the public reacts to the politically engaged artist or actress with disdain, taking them to be a sanctimonious abuser of their privileged place in public life. "Stick to singing!" or "Go back to acting!" The idea that fame makes people less qualified to speak on political issues is connected to the misplaced expectation that everyone—all of us—should have a coherent politics, identifiable, and easily labeled, especially if we are going to open our mouths and share an opinion. But in the same way that a truck driver, teacher, or doctor expects to be able to do their job and also fulfill their duties as citizens, why shouldn't an artist, actress, or musician do the same? "A nation's artists and musicians have a particular place in its social and political life," Bruce Springsteen has observed. The fact that Springsteen has, in his words, "tried to write songs that speak to our pride and criticize our failures," suggests that he studied Johnny Cash closely, for Cash, like Woody Guthrie before him, modeled that kind of citizenship before Springsteen ever picked up a guitar. How Cash got to be that kind of citizen and embodied a singular form of citizenship is the subject of this book.[8]

Throughout *Citizen Cash*, Cash's life itself serves as a text through which we read the story of America at a particular time, from the Great Depression of the 1930s to the new century, but the most attention is given to the "civil war" years of the 1960s. Cash's music and television appearances, statements from the stage and to the press, lyrics recorded on vinyl, album liner notes, and other sources chart the making of Johnny Cash, American citizen. *Citizen Cash* places the Man in Black in historical context as previous biographies have not; this book is as much about the political life of the nation as about the political life of Cash. It takes us back to a time of political polarization, when the country seemed to be coming apart, and (re)introduces us to an artist who, as the nation's most prominent public citizen, transcended it all.[9]

1

A New Deal
for the Cash Family

The *Johnny Cash Show* debuted on ABC as a replacement series in June 1969, at the start of a summer best remembered for the first moon landing and a music and arts festival at a little place called Woodstock. At thirty-seven, Johnny Cash had not yet reached middle age, but to some viewers he and his show seemed to come from a time before shiny rockets took men into space, before the nation's youth formed a counterculture unrecognizable to their parents. One reviewer wrote that the show's sets looked "like old calendars," while another said that, "at this uncertain juncture" in American history, Cash looked like the "lost American," walking "out of yesterday . . . when yesterday looks very, very good." In fact, *The Johnny Cash Show* presented a much more nuanced, multivalent cross section of American life in that first season than these write-ups suggest, but it's not hard to see why reviewers could not get past seeing Cash as a messenger from days gone by.[1]

Not only did Cash's wardrobe make him seem like a Jacksonian-era statesman or a Mississippi riverboat gambler, but from early in the show's run, he introduced a regular segment designed to take viewers on journeys into the American past. He called it "Ride This Train." The idea came from his 1960 concept album of the same name and, over the course of the show's run, it proved to be one of the main vehicles for Cash's public citizenship. Each segment began with the same footage of an old iron horse lumbering around a mountain bend, smoke billowing from its chimney, as Cash sang, "Come along and ride this train," over the lonesome sound of the train whistle. Cash would then sit with his guitar on a primitive set meant to evoke an old railway station and invite us along to see a world beyond our own, acting like a park ranger of our national heritage. He might tell stories in word and song of cowboys in the Old West, or circuit-riding preachers in the South, or truckers moving freight at the dawn of the 1970s. By design, he asked viewers to put themselves in the shoes of other Americans, to imagine the often difficult, challenging lives of those he profiled.

In two episodes of *The Johnny Cash Show*, one preceding Woodstock and the other following, Cash used the "Ride This Train" segment to transport his audience to the Great Depression, mixing anecdotes of his own family's experience with compassionate commentary on America's working poor. He would return repeatedly to these themes over the next two years, but these two early episodes especially captured the way Cash would, in story and song, draw from his own experience in practicing a politics of empathy.

The first aired on August 2, 1969. Cash took us to a "hobo jungle" in 1930s Fordyce, Arkansas, near his birthplace in Kingsland. His father, Ray Cash, had hopped freight cars from Fordyce to Memphis at various times in 1932 and 1933. Like untold thousands of other men, Ray rode the rails looking for work to feed his growing family during the worst years of the Depression. Johnny, born in February 1932, told viewers that, at best, the trip to Memphis might have landed his father a job cutting cord wood. "It was hard work," he said, "but it was honest." And that was the message of Cash's first televised reflection on the Depression: hard work is to be admired, and hobos are not to be disparaged. "He wasn't a bum," Cash said of his dad, "and he didn't know anybody that was." Everyone in that hobo jungle "had to work, and if you didn't work, you didn't make it." Sometimes, he noted, "the pickin's were mighty lean, and at times, were almost unbearable." On one trip to Memphis, Cash recounted, fellow rail riders pulled Ray off the top of a freight car, nearly frozen to death. Over the course of the next six minutes, he played parts of "Wrinkled, Crinkled, Wadded Dollar Bill," "One More Ride," and Jimmie Rodgers's "Hobo Bill's Last Ride." The segment is tight, neatly edited, and conveys a simple premise about the working poor that defied caricature, for these were tales of men—including Cash's own father—risking their to lives to support their families.[2]

A little more than a month later, Cash appeared in a black shirt, a blue bandana tied around his neck, inviting the public to ride this train to the town where he grew up, Dyess, Arkansas. Over film images of a hardscrabble farm, he spoke of cotton farmers dreaming of a big crop. The footage—of broken down cars and a plow stuck in the dead earth, of dogs drinking water out of tires laying on the ground and ragged-looking pigs, goats, and chickens roaming the yard—painted a bleak picture of family farm life. Back on stage, Cash pulled out a couple of cotton bolls for the audience to see. Holding them up for the camera, he described how a cotton gin removes seeds and explained what "fair to middlin'" meant as a grade of cotton. Back in Dyess, he recounted, if a small-patch farmer had a good crop, he might be able to buy some new shoes, store-bought bread, maybe some new clothes. Cash's father always told the kids that things would be better "come pickin' time"—a familiar phrase to longtime fans who knew Cash's song "Pickin' Time," from the 1958 album, *The Fabulous Johnny Cash*. As such, Cash brought the working class into the living rooms of American television viewers who were then living through arguably the best economic run in American history. It's no wonder that so many commentators seized on the idea of Cash as a man stepping out of simpler, bygone days, here to remind us of universal maxims of the dignity and decency of hard work and supporting one's family.[3]

Cash and his record labels had, for many years, cultivated this image. The sleeve notes to nearly every LP he put out on Columbia in the first half of the 1960s mention Cash's precarious early years in Dyess. By the late 1960s and early 1970s, nearly every article, several book-length biographies, and a full-length documentary film essentially retold the same stories of his perilously uncertain upbringing. "If I hadn't grown up there," he told one biographer, "I wouldn't be what I am now. It was the foundation for what I became." To any long-standing Cash fan, it made sense that Cash would recite tales of the times that formed him.[4]

But the trouble with distilling a "good old days" message from Cash's stories of his youth is that critics pretty quickly found themselves trafficking in nostalgia and missing what Cash was actually up to. While these writers positioned him as the embodiment of the so-called good old days, Cash saw himself as not so much a celebrator as a documentarian. Sure, in those "Ride This Train" segments, he sometimes reflected on his experiences—or those of others—positively, but he never shied away from documenting the pain and suffering. He presented his weekly journeys into American life in much the same way as Dorothea Lange and Walker Evans, the social realist photographers, presented portraits of the down-and-out during the Great Depression. Cash developed his own social realist eye over many years, through a myriad of influences, but none were more important than his Arkansas boyhood. If we could "ride this train" back into northeastern Arkansas in the 1930s, to witness both the sorrow and the dignity among the working poor in and around Dyess, we'd see the origins of Cash's public citizenship and an empathy rooted in solidarity.

★

FREDERICK JACKSON TURNER famously declared the closing of the American frontier in 1893, but he must have overlooked Arkansas. For, as late as the 1940s, a young Johnny Cash could have reported from northeastern Arkansas all the signs of frontier life. Much of Mississippi County, where the Cash family arrived in 1935, joining hundreds of other white settlers, like pioneers crossing the plains, remained untamed. For more than a century, the densely wooded swamplands of the northern Mississippi River Delta had sheltered escaped slaves and outlaws, and plantation owners maintained their frontier plantation system—a holdover from slavery—under threat of violence. Guns remained a part of everyday life, carried by both whites and Blacks, sometimes for hunting, sometimes just for killing. Lynchings, and the threat of lynching, if no longer frequent, still enforced a frontier order—a white supremacist frontier order. Northeastern Arkansas in the 1930s is where the Deep South intersected with the Old West, like a crossroads in a boneyard.

Cash's home kept its frontier identity for so long in large part because of the New Madrid earthquakes that shook southeastern Missouri and northeastern Arkansas from December 1811 through February 1812. Thousands of earthquakes rocked the region, but three measured stronger than 8.0 on the Richter scale and were especially damaging. As far away as Boston and Quebec the earth shuddered, but in the upper Mississippi River Delta, the land literally sank, as if the region was the center of a cake removed too soon from the oven. To this day, much of northeastern Arkansas is referred to as "the sunken lands." The rest of the American frontier may have kept sprawling westward, but this one section of it dropped from the horizon to linger where Johnny Cash later grew up.

Cash's Arkansas frontier did not fit the storybook image of cowboys and Indians. The Native peoples who lived there at the time of the earthquakes—Cherokee, mostly—took the violence of the quakes as an ill omen and migrated west to the Arkansas River, north of Little Rock.[5] And instead of cowboys roaming the range,

13

slave owners staked their claim. Enslaved African Americans cleared swamps and drained the land, leaving behind the thick, rich alluvial soil ideal for growing cotton. No one capitalized on this exploitative frontier plantation system more than Robert E. (Lee) Wilson, who built an unrivaled "Delta empire." By the time the Cashes arrived in Dyess, the neighboring town of Wilson, Arkansas, named for its patriarch, had become the largest cotton producer in the United States, with fourteen plantations spread across fifty thousand acres of Delta loam—an empire, like all empires, built on the backs of the oppressed. Sharecroppers had long ago replaced the enslaved when Johnny Cash grew up nearby, still living precarious frontier lives.[6]

Even before the Depression, therefore, most folks who grew up in Mississippi County knew they were starting life truly from the bottom of the sunken lands. Whereas more than half of all Southern farmers (25 percent of all Southerners, or more than eight million people) were tenants or sharecroppers in 1930, 90 percent of farmers in Mississippi County were stuck in an endless cycle of debt, eking out a living on land that wasn't theirs. As New Dealer Lorena Hickok said, it was "a form of slavery in all but name."[7]

In Arkansas, the Depression came as the knockout punch following the devastating one-two combination of the 1927 flood (which drove forty thousand people from their homes) and the 1930–1931 drought. As temperatures reached as high as 110 degrees and rainfall dropped to its lowest levels on record in the summer of 1930, it seemed as if the devil himself had pulled hell up through the crust of the brittle earth and set up shop in Arkansas. When the price of cotton continued to plummet in the face of growing international competition, even the big planters fell deep into debt.[8] In popular memory, desperate Arkies and Okies piled all of their belongings into their jalopies and made for the promised land of California, yet in reality, most Arkansas tenants and croppers stayed behind, desperate for relief. As the region shuddered from the cascade of shocks brought by the Depression—bank closings, layoffs, and waves of evictions—Arkansans looked to their government officials for help, but got nothing. Echoing President Herbert Hoover, the state's senior United States senator, Joseph T. Robinson, advocated a "sit steady in the boat" solution to the crisis—a lot to ask of people who are homeless and starving. One British journalist reported that she had "traveled over most of Europe and part of Africa, but I have never seen such terrible sights as I saw yesterday among the sharecroppers of Arkansas." When food riots broke out at Red Cross relief sites across the state, it surprised no one. "Unless something is done for the American farmer," Edward A. O'Neal, president of the American Farm Bureau Federation, warned the incoming Roosevelt administration, "we will have a revolution in the countryside in less than twelve months."[9]

Roosevelt pushed through two pieces of landmark legislation, the Emergency Farm Mortgage Act and the Agricultural Adjustment Act (AAA), that allowed planters to remortgage their farms and raised prices through a coordinated crop and livestock reduction program. Unscrupulous planters gladly took the AAA payments, but then took acreage worked by tenants out of production. Tenants were evicted, as if the point of the new law was to plow under workers, not cotton. In fact, AAA rules required that tenants and sharecroppers share in the payments with the big planters—but as the checks went directly to the planters, few tenants or sharecroppers saw a dime. According to one estimate, planters pocketed 90 percent—leaving tenants and croppers to apply for relief. But no amount of relief could raise the evicted back even to the meager level of existence they had known living on the plantations. The new rural homeless lived in makeshift shacks, clad in tattered clothes that no longer fit their malnourished figures, tending unwashed infants and toddlers wearing improvised diapers, or going bare bottomed—these were everyday scenes along the roads that ran past the plantations. As the administration experimented with new programs to help farmers (including a plan to resettle sharecroppers like the Cashes in new agricultural colonies), others began to organize.[10]

In fact, in July 1934, just as government builders began clearing the land where the Cash family would settle the following year, eighteen tenant farmers—eleven white and seven Black—met in Tyronza to found the Southern Tenant Farmers Union (STFU). The STFU posed an immediate threat to the planters of northeastern Arkansas, in part because it united Black and white tenants and croppers, defying an economic system that counted on easily exploited labor and a cultural system that depended on racial hierarchy. The union grew rapidly as it rallied tenants to the cause of direct AAA payments—bypassing the planters—and an end to evictions (which conservative estimates put at somewhere between "half a million and a million" throughout the South). By the end of 1935, some twenty-five thousand to thirty thousand tenants had joined the union.

Earlier that same year, when the Cashes finally got to Dyess, sandwiched between Tyronza and Wilson, the state of Arkansas seemed on the brink of class war.[11] Police charged STFU organizer, Rev. Ward Rogers, with "anarchy, attempting to overthrow and usurp the government of Arkansas, blasphemy, and barratry" for suggesting that he could lead a group of tenants and croppers in lynching certain planters. Several weeks later, when Socialist Party leader Norman Thomas spoke to an STFU crowd at Birdsong, about twelve miles south of Dyess, sheriff's deputies pushed him off the speaker platform, with one calling him a "Gawd-damned Yankee bastard," and ran him out of town. As the Cashes got settled in their new home, towns in Poinsett and Mississippi Counties passed ordinances banning union meetings, planters evicted anyone suspected of joining the union, and, in what almost every observer has called a "reign of terror," planters and police "harassed, beat, and jailed union members," breaking up clandestine meetings by shooting into them, even if the gatherings were held in churches. Eventually, in response to the violence, the STFU had to move its headquarters to Memphis. Union organizers started crossing back into Arkansas as if they were bootleggers, moving only at night, crawling along back roads, and outracing night riders and their police buddies back to the nearest bridge across the Mississippi.[12]

In September 1935, just as the Cashes prepared for their first cotton harvest, the STFU made its boldest push by calling a sharecropper strike. Nearly five thousand tenants and croppers stayed out of the fields, prompting some violence and intimidation from the planters but, in the end, winning a temporary victory: higher wages. Once the cotton crop had been picked, though, planters started mass evictions again, just a few months after the strike. Roadside encampments of the evicted spread like a rash.[13]

Although President Roosevelt did little to address the STFU's rightful complaints, his administration could still boast that it introduced more measures than Hoover ever did to minimize suffering in Arkansas. The Works Progress Administration put people to work building 16 hospitals and 297 schools, and thousands of miles of road throughout the state. The Civilian Conservation Corps employed thousands of teenage boys on environmental protection projects at more than one hundred camps across the state. Most importantly, the Federal Emergency Relief Administration (FERA) (and later the Resettlement Administration or RA) established several "colonies" for transplanted tenants and sharecroppers in Arkansas. The very first, and perhaps most ambitious of these projects, had brought the Cash family to Dyess in March 1935, when young J. R. Cash was three years old.[14]

Dyess could be found on no map of Arkansas in 1934 because it did not yet exist. As Colonization Project No. 1, Dyess grew quickly out of the "gumbo" soil of northeastern Arkansas and was in part a response to the political unrest and class conflict there. Instead of letting the crisis devolve further into a protracted frontier guerrilla war between planters and the evicted, the FERA planned to relocate poor farmers to good land and advance them the money to pay for twenty acres and a house. Farmers' crop yields would then fund the repayment of these loans at reasonable rates. Rather than try to crack down on the STFU or other "agitators," Henry Wallace argued that the "American way" to maintain order is to give "dispossessed people a stake in the social system." (Of course, "dispossessed people" did not include Black farmers, who were not allowed to apply for a home and farm in Dyess; the town may have been the product of a new vision, but that vision did not extend much beyond the local context in which it emerged.) It was a noble aim, but measured against its stated goal of trying to help half a million families (including thirty thousand in Arkansas alone), the resettlement program's ultimate relocation of only five thousand families seems a bust. The government simply lacked the money to do more. But through a combination of luck and hard work—FERA administrators preferred applicants who knew cotton farming from experience and had a good work ethic—Ray Cash made his family one of the almost five hundred families that made it to Dyess.[15]

When the Cashes arrived at their brand-new home, they settled into a work-in-progress community. The sixteen-thousand-acre colony was still densely vegetated; the land had never been worked. One thousand four hundred workers from the relief rolls came to clear the land and build the first administration buildings, dig drainage ditches, lay roads, construct bridges, and erect hundreds of modest farm cottages: 277 by mid-1935, and 490 by January 1936. Even without the advantages of later prefabrication techniques, the relief rollers worked very quickly. A ten-man crew could frame a five-room farmhouse in sixteen hours. A seven-man crew could construct a barn in six hours. Dyess was being built almost overnight.[16]

THE STORY OF the Cash family's move to Dyess is so well-known to Cash fans it has entered the realm of myth. But its mere celebration obscures the function Dyess played in Cash's later citizenship, for in and around Dyess, he bore witness not only to a work ethic that comes only from working the land, but also to real suffering—and was formed by a culture that recognized and honored both.

During his lifetime, Cash consistently spoke of Dyess as a kind of "Promised Land." In interviews and in his two autobiographies, he recounted how, in March 1935, his family drove 250 miles along muddy winter roads from Kingsland, where he had been born, to Dyess, where he grew up. "It's not far now," he noted in 1980, "but to us it seemed like the other side of the world." In a scene that could have been conjured by Frank Capra, Cash claimed that he sang "I Am Bound for the Promised Land" as a three-year-old huddled in the back of a flatbed truck, nestled next to all of the family's worldly possessions. When they arrived at Number 266 on Road Three in Dyess, they found a newly constructed five-room house: two bedrooms, a living room, a dining room, and a kitchen. A front and back porch graced the single-floor home, and it came with "luxuries untold": a barn, a chicken house, a smokehouse, and an outhouse. The home had a bathroom (though no toilet) and a deep well from which water could be drawn for the weekly baths. "There was no running water, of course, and no electricity," Cash recalled. "None of us even dreamed of miracles like that." Given that the Cashes could just as easily have found themselves crammed into a makeshift shack, like so many other down-on-their-luck sharecropper families, cast off like excess ballast on the Mississippi County roads that brought them to Dyess, the house alone was miracle enough.[17] Ray and Carrie Cash felt truly blessed to be offered a chance in this Arkansas jungle land. "It gave our family a new start," Ray told one of his son's biographers. No longer sharecroppers, he recalled, "we felt more free . . . we felt ourselves equal with everybody."[18]

The previous fifteen years had been tough on Ray Cash and his young family. The drop-off in their prospects had come quickly. As late as 1850, Ray's grandfather owned 140 acres of land in Georgia, but Ray's father, who had moved to Arkansas as a child, put more energy into being a circuit-riding preacher than into farming. By the time he died in 1912, Ray, then fifteen and a high school dropout, was left with little inheritance. Adrift, he joined the Army, serving on the Mexican border and later in France. When he returned to

Arkansas in 1919, his economic prospects looked no better. Although he married Carrie Rivers and began a family, Ray spent the years between the Great War and the Great Depression scraping by, mostly sharecropping, but also picking up odd jobs to feed the family. For her part, Carrie brought few material resources to the couple's union. Her father, John L. Rivers, made a living as a small-scale farmer, but his real passion was volunteering as a music teacher at his church. Carrie inherited his love of music—which she passed on to her children—but not much else.[19]

Still, Johnny Cash's parents acted as models of perseverance, and they were game for hard work—qualities of character that the Resettlement Administration sought in choosing its colonists. Like all new arrivals, the Cashes were not only rewarded with twenty acres of land, which they needed to clear themselves, but also a mule, plow, and other equipment for tilling the soil; seed to grow their own gardens; and feed for the mule—all as loans that would have to be paid back. "Rural rehabilitation is not a program of public charity," said one FERA field service supervisor. "Beneficiaries are expected to give their notes for repayment in full for both subsistence and capital advances." And, indeed, in later years, Cash loved to recount the epic tales of his father and older brother Roy, then almost fourteen, taming those twenty acres. They hacked away from sunup until sundown, fending off bobcats and poisonous cottonmouths and rattlesnakes, draining the land and blowing up stubborn tree stumps. In the first year, they could only clear three acres before planting, but autumn brought a harvest of three bales of cotton—enough to pay their debts and make the first installment of $111.41 on the farm. When a wildcat kept eating their chickens, Ray waited out in the chicken coop one night and killed it with his shotgun. People came from all over Dyess to see the cat's hide, which was big enough for young J. R., older brother Jack, and younger sister Reba to lay in all together. After three years of working those twenty acres, Ray paid off the loan and took the deed on their farm in January 1938.

This also made him a shareholder in the Dyess Colony Cooperative, which, by selling the colony's entire yield of cotton in bulk, guaranteed the best price and most profit for all Dyess farmers.[20]

Dyess's cooperative nature (and the fact that the whole enterprise had been initiated by the federal government) often led Johnny Cash to tell interviewers that he "grew up under socialism"—a transgressive statement perhaps made only for transgression's sake, but nevertheless provocative given that he made it in the midst of the long Cold War. But although some planters did, indeed, criticize the resettlement colonies as socialist, the label simply didn't fit. The very premise of the program sought to help landless farmers become landowners—owners of private property—and each family farmed their land as an individual family, not in collectives. The idea of farmers getting together, bundling their crops and holding them until they could get the best price, had been around since the Granger movement and Farmers' Alliance of the late nineteenth century—that is, among yeoman farmers unfamiliar with *Das Kapital*. Rather, the Dyess Colony credo had more in common with the most romantic Jeffersonian ideals of an agrarian republic than it did with Marx.

But Cash was right that the community was cooperative. In practice, its distinctive character could be seen most obviously in the center of town, where one found not only the cooperative store but also a cooperative cannery and cotton gin. At the cannery, Carrie Cash joined other women, canning the food crops they grew alongside their cotton so that everyone would have enough food for winter. Each family would take back eight out of ten cans, leaving the rest for sale; any end-of-year profits would be divided equally. The Cashes appreciated the sense of solidarity that being equal in struggle brings. "So many of our neighbors were in the same category as we were," Ray recalled years later. "Not destitute, because we were never destitute, but needy." Johnny agreed. "Everybody was in the same boat there," he told one interviewer in 1980, as the nation prepared to elect Ronald Reagan president. "Everybody knew that the man down the road next to them didn't have any more or less money than he had. . . . Nobody had a lot of money, but everybody had a little—and we got by." On the eve of the "greed is good" 1980s, Cash sounded transgressive again.[21]

But Dyess impressed First Lady Eleanor Roosevelt for much the same reasons. On June 9, 1936, when Johnny Cash was four and a half years old, the First Lady paid a visit to Dyess, followed by a Pathé newsreel crew, which guaranteed that theater audiences all over America saw images of the tiny town. Roosevelt visited one family's home to see what a typical Dyess homestead looked like. She stopped by the Community Center and toured the library, club rooms, and recreation hall. The 226 members of the Dyess 4-H Club, the largest 4-H Club in the world, greeted her by standing and singing, "How do you do, Mrs. Roosevelt," to the First Lady's delight. Smiling broadly, she told the group she hoped to see some of them in Washington one day. But the big event came when she addressed a crowd of 2,500 people at the dedication of the new Administration Building. "I don't suppose you realize the interest with which we in Washington have been watching your experiment here," she wondered aloud to the crowd. "We believe that the unfortunate people of this country would rather work out their own salvation than accept charity." Dyess proved it, she said. Following her remarks, she shook hands with every single person present, including little J. R. Cash and his family (though years later, Cash's boyhood friend, J. E. Huff, recalled that Mrs. Roosevelt tousled his and J. R.'s hair). Following a chicken dinner at the Dyess Café—with young J. R. and family watching through the window—Roosevelt visited the hospital and cannery before being driven back to Memphis to meet the president's train. The visit made a strong impression on Cash who, even as a boy, appreciated the significance of the First Lady coming to his little community. But more than the pomp and circumstance of political celebrity, Cash responded to her message that every American deserves a fair shake—an equal chance to "get by" on their own. Equality of opportunity, he remembered years later, produced a kind of harmony of life to be cherished.[22]

In reality, Dyess administrators worked hard to promote that community harmony, often by tightly managing colony life. In addition to the chief administrators, a home economist named Mrs. Fern Salyers and a farm manager named Jake Terry influenced the day-to-day lives of colonists most directly. For one thing, Salyers and Terry had the most say in whether colonists could stay or go following their two-year probationary period. Terry approved feed, seed, and capital items, and provided instruction on planting not only cotton but food crops for the family and feed for its animals— typically a mule, a cow, one brood sow, and chickens. He advised on soil improvement and how to plow the difficult gumbo soil. For her part, Salyers, a stern woman who criticized some early settlers for coming to Dyess expecting "they would find Santa Claus" giving them everything they needed, taught self-sufficiency. She assisted farm wives in coming up with monthly household budgets (which only she could approve), issuing subsistence checks or coupons for use at the co-op store. She determined a family's clothing and household good needs, and then added the costs to the budget. Salyers also taught certain skills, notably canning, sewing, and quilting (Carrie Cash kept a quilting frame tied to the living room ceiling, from which it could be retrieved when she had time to work on such things). On at least one occasion, the home economist spoke to a group of colony women about basic hygiene, giving tips for simple, inexpensive solutions like brushing one's teeth twice a day with "soda, salt, charcoal"; taking weekly baths with soda and ammonia; and washing hair at least twice a month with "soft water, soda and vinegar as a rinse." Underwear, she pointed out, helpfully, should be changed every day.[23]

Colonists did not always welcome this level of oversight, even if well-intentioned. They bitterly resented Terry, in particular, for being overbearing and imperious, for acting like a plantation overseer riding herd on his sharecroppers. Ray Cash disliked him so much he named five-year-old J. R.'s adopted stray mutt "Jake Terry." He later shot that dog (perhaps driven less by hatred for Terry than by anger with the dog for eating food meant for the pig).[24]

The close supervision by administrators hinted that life in Dyess remained uncertain, as if colonists, left on their own, probably would not make it. Any number of hazards—from floods to droughts to pests to human error—could result in crop failure, but what could one do except work hard? The Cashes, like all of the Dyess families, worked six days a week, from sunup until sundown—or, as some said, "from can to can't"—taking only Sundays off (later, after finding some stability, it seems they would also sometimes take Saturday afternoons off). Plowing, planting, and hoeing took place in late winter, springtime, and early summer. Picking time came in the fall, lasting from October to December. "Daddy taught us many things," Cash recalled in his first autobiography, "but a most important lesson was that hard work is good for you." At just four years old, he began carrying water to his father and older siblings, Roy and Louise, "as they worked the cotton." By the time he was eight or ten (stories varied), he worked in the fields, too, while his younger sister Reba carried the water. "We learned it was not only our obligation, but our privilege to make the cotton crop" for the whole community, he remembered.[25]

The Cashes were Southern Baptists, but from the way they spoke about laboring in the fields, one would think they were early New England Calvinists, believing that a state of grace could be achieved only through unrelenting toil. Every day, Carrie Cash, the most devout of the family, would make breakfast, clean up, and be in the field by 7:00 a.m. At 11:00 a.m., she would go back to the house to prepare the noontime meal for everyone. She would then work from 1:00 p.m. to 5:00 p.m. in the fields before returning to make the family supper. The work may have been gendered, but everyone did their part. They called August, the hottest month of the year, "laying by time," but that did not mean a suspension of labor. It meant only that work in the cotton rows stopped until harvest time. Meanwhile, as the sun beat down on the sunken lands, and squadrons of dragon-flies outran flocks of red-winged blackbirds, the Cash family picked the corn, alfalfa, and soybeans, canned the winter foodstuffs, cut and hauled the hay, and chopped enough wood to fire the cook-ing stove through the winter. This seasonal rhythm defined Johnny Cash's life until he graduated from high school in 1950. When he told these stories years later, in song or in interviews, Cash did not romanticize the work itself—he left no doubt just how physically difficult it could be—but the honesty of doing the work, earning a working-class identity, he made clear, could be a source of pride.[26]

And yet, there could be no denying that for years the Cash fam-ily remained poor. Until about 1948, Cash later told his sweetheart, Vivian Liberto, in a letter from his Air Force posting in Germany, the family had nothing. "As a matter of fact, we were in misery part of the time," he wrote. Thanks to being selected for resettlement, the family never had to join the relief rolls, but "every penny had to go to essential things." Cash told one reporter in 1970 that if they were running short of food, "my Daddy would give me a gun and two bullets, and he expected me to come back with two rabbits." They rarely had cash—actual US currency—because the subsidy pay-ments they received from the Dyess cooperative came in the form of "doodlum," a kind of scrip not unlike those used in coal mining country, which could be spent only at the company co-op store. One of the highlights of young J. R.'s life was when the family brought in a good crop and, after Ray paid all of his debts, came home with "a half-block of cheese, baloney, and store-bought bread." His father often sought additional work clearing timber and drainage ditches in winter, and his mother at one point sold magazines for extra money. She famously took in washing to earn enough to pay for singing lessons for J. R. (which he did not need), and she traded the wildcat hide to a door-to-door salesman for a set of encyclopedias.

The family never got electricity or running water out on Road Three. And only in 1947 could they finally afford to buy a twelve-year-old Ford, the windows of which soon shattered, rattled to bits from the shaking caused by riding over the rocky country roads.[27]

The toll that all of this took on Ray manifested itself in ways it often does in working-class men struggling to provide for their families: heavy drinking and at least the threat of violence. Cash described his father to Vivian as "hard-hearted and cruel" in those years. Not only did he kill J. R.'s dog, but when Carrie, presumably exhausted after five years of struggling to survive in Dyess, said she wanted to move back to the hill country near her family in Kingsland, he exploded in a drunken rage. Only the intervention of Jack, J. R.'s older brother by two years, but still a child at ten, stopped their father from beating their mother.[28]

In later years, Cash emphasized the idyllic moments of his childhood over any looming violence or alienation. He told tales of growing up swimming and fishing in the Tyronza River, which cut through Dyess, venturing out with others to the Blue Hole or up into the town's water tower to swim, as if his youth drew equally from Steinbeck and Mark Twain. He and Jack liked to play a dangerous summer game of searching for cottonmouths sunning themselves in the willows and smacking them out of the trees with long branches. He remembered drying peanuts from the fields in the barn with Jack, roasting and bagging them to sell outside the Dyess movie theater, "a nickel for a small bag, a dime for a big one." Cash even turned the devastation wrought by the January 1937 Mississippi River flood, which cost the Cashes their cow and beehives and left their house full of mud, chickens, eggs, and pig shit, into a variously unnerving and whimsical hit song, "Five Feet High and Rising." Had the flood hit at any other time, from two to ten months later, it would have wiped out the year's cotton yield. Fortunately, by coming in January, it laid down a thick layer of new loam that produced a bumper crop in the fall. To some residents, it seemed their faith in God had been rewarded.[29]

Faith and social life held the Cashes and the colony together. In the early years, the *Dyess Colony Herald* newspaper featured articles urging people to make friends and to join this or that church or prayer meeting. In a town where eventually everyone knew everyone, the newspaper's details of residents' comings and goings read like a police surveillance report. One issue from July 1936 featured "Lepanto Road News" (meaning Road Three) and noted that young Roy and Louise Cash had been sent off to visit their grandparents, the Rivers, in Kingsland, and that Ray and Carrie spent the day in Marked Tree. The following week, it noted the kids' return, accompanied by Grandma Rivers. Presumably, editors intended for this level of detail to facilitate everyone getting to know one another. One wrote a column called "Friendship" in the summer of 1936, acknowledging that everyone in Dyess, having come from elsewhere in the state, feels like an outsider at times. He counseled speaking to neighbors and offering a nod and a smile to fellow residents. If everyone followed these simple guidelines, they would be "happy, contented, and very reluctant to leave the sheltering and protective arms of a new hope—the ever-extending friendship and unity of the Colony." Perhaps the columnist made these remarks because the colony had already lost a number of settlers, many of whom either could not or would not do the work required (or hoped yet that Santa's sleigh would run over Fern Salyers, the home economist). Or perhaps they felt duped.[30]

The many church services, prayer meetings, and revivals that sprang up in the colony's early years did more to build community cohesion than the feeble admonishments of a few booster colonists, though in the beginning, there were no churches. In the first couple of years, settlers used Sawmill Number 6 for interdenominational Sunday school and a livestock barn for church services. Later, services moved to the newly constructed Community Center, and Sunday school to the auditorium at the elementary school. Baptisms took place in the Blue Hole of the Tyronza, and revival meetings popped up in residents' homes. One newspaper notice mentioned a revival in one home out on Road 10-A that was so successful that its resident planned Thursday night prayer meetings every week. Evangelists from Moody Bible Institute in Chicago came to Dyess, accompanied by the Calvary Male Quartet. A November 1935 survey revealed that most colonists were either Baptist or Methodist, but Cash mostly recalled going to Sunday services at the Road Fifteen Church of God that he found terrifying. He remembered the preacher breathing fire and brimstone down on the congregation, parishioners writhing on the floor, trembling, while others raised their hands in praise—only snakes and speaking in tongues were missing from this fever dream of God's holy light. Despite his own fear, Cash reported, his Methodist mother always emerged happy, and he himself began to appreciate the music. Songs, he decided, were a kind of prayer, a way of talking to God—a "telephone to heaven, and I tied up the line quite a bit."[31]

For a group of people who felt tested, like Job, day in and day out, the religious encounters with their fellow citizens must have been cathartic. On the other hand, the brutally difficult labor on the farms, the dire predictions of hell and damnation at church, and the close supervision of government bureaucrats everywhere could just as easily create the impression of a latter-day frontier dystopia from which there could be no escape. Cash never spoke of it in those terms, exactly, but over time, a growing number of settlers felt like they had been lured not to the Promised Land but into some kind of frontier purgatory, passage from which seemed increasingly unlikely.

For years, Resettlement Administration officials had been painting a picture of Dyess's future in the brightest colors, but by 1940, many colonists were kicking themselves for having believed it. "Never again need you be assailed by the terrible fear that you and your family will have no roof over your heads, nor that stark hunger will overcome you," the chief RA administrator in Dyess, Lawrence Westbrook, had told a colonist meeting in 1936. "There is more real security here in the little homes that you live in than there is in the finest mansion in the most fashionable and arrogant residential section of Memphis." And the national press seemed convinced, too: compared to all of the sharecropper shacks outside of Dyess, colony homes looked like "debutantes in the slums." But after five years, too few farm families in Dyess experienced the promised sense of security, let alone felt like the belles of the ball. Despite the cooperative bundling of cotton for sale out of Dyess, the price for the staple crop had not sufficiently improved, and as the soil tired, it became increasingly difficult to just get by on twenty acres. Even Ray Cash, who had at least been able to take the deed of his home in 1938, started to look for ways to buy another twenty acres so that he could stay afloat. By April 1938, 39 percent of the 649 families who had lived in the colony since 1934 had given up and moved away; the attrition rate reflected discontent within this corner of the sunken lands.[32]

Just as a new world war erupted in Europe, a large number of Dyess colonists organized to demand a redress of several key grievances. First, they complained that the path to owning their farms seemed like a shell game. When families completed their two-year probation period, they received a sales contract to buy the land and home where they worked and lived, but often at a price they considered much too high. Many had objected that, when they first arrived in Dyess, their contracts did not specify the exact cost of their farmsteads, nor how much time they had to pay them off. The problem started with false expectations and poor communication from the Resettlement Administration. The colonists knew that the federal government had purchased the original sixteen thousand acres for two dollars and fifty cents an acre, and many of them concluded— an assumption never clearly corrected by administrators—that they would be able to purchase their farmsteads from the government for the same two dollars and fifty cents an acre. But the sales contract they received put the price at something closer to one hundred dollars an acre, a reasonable number given all the improvements made by the agency: roads, bridges, drainage ditches, community build-ings and services, and the colonists' own houses. Yet the ultimate price was so far off from what was expected that it outraged many of the settlers.[33]

There were more daily grievances that rankled. Colonists were also fed up with being forced to use doodlum to pay inflated prices at the co-op store. Dyess folks were not stupid: they knew that twenty-one dollars in doodlum for a ton of hay was far more than the twelve dollars they would pay elsewhere if they had cash. Like the miners who complained of having to use scrip at the company store, or sharecroppers who resented using "brozeen" at the Wilson plantation store, Dyess colonists felt cheated. And doing battle with Jake Terry, who cussed at them like they were his sharecroppers, was another common point of tension. "Free men from the hills of Arkansas are not accustomed to such treatment," observed H. L. Mitchell of the STFU. It felt to the colonists like, after hold-ing up their end of the bargain—clearing the land, toiling under the brutal Delta sun, playing by all the rules—the government did not deliver the promised New Deal. Being treated as second-class citizens—by Terry, by the co-op store, by the administrators who moved the mortgage goalposts—seemed like a new version of the same Old Deal.[34]

Consequently, when the dissidents organized two mass demon-strations at the Osceola courthouse to call attention to being overcharged for their farms, the STFU rallied to their cause. The STFU had remained a potent political force in the years since the 1935 sharecropper strike, but it had also continued to face violent repression. In May and June 1936, planters responded to another strike, in which five thousand sharecroppers withheld their labor, with arrests, intimidation, and beatings. And when Little Rock pas-tor Claude Williams and Memphis social worker Willie Sue Blagden went to Earle, Arkansas in June of that year to investigate the beating and alleged disappearance of a Black sharecropper, Frank Weems, six well-dressed men forced them into a waiting car, drove them to the woods, and flogged them. They were released, but photos of Blagden's bruised thighs appeared in newspapers all over the country. So one can imagine that the colonists in Dyess might think flirting with the STFU could bring more trouble than it was worth. But by 1939, enough were fed up that they formed STFU Local No. 29, which grew rapidly.[35]

Led by Dyess colonist Floyd Slayton, Local 29 recruited almost 200 of the colony's remaining 328 families into the STFU by February 1940. The STFU-aligned colonists pushed for a more "democratic operation," which meant winning collective bargaining rights. They wanted to bargain equally with the Farm Security Administration (which had superseded by now the Resettlement Administration) on their loans and repayment terms, on settling debts, and on future plans and personnel. At one point, Slayton also suggested that the usual cooperative arrangement be replaced by a more flexible one in which individual farmers could take out loans "for crop furnish"—planting costs—but then "trade where they please and do their Gining [sic] likewise." In effect, they wanted to abandon the government's cooperative scheme and take their chances on their own bundling and selling of the cotton yield. H. L. Mitchell brought the STFU demands to administrators in Washington who encouraged the colonists to elect an advisory committee that could consult with colony management "on matters of mutual concern." When the elections were held, STFU members won five of the eight seats and urged the other three to join the union, too—but advising was hardly the same as collective bargaining, and little came of their efforts. Within a few months, membership in Local 29 dropped off precipitously, with too few farmers able to pay the monthly dues. Slayton wrote a long Hail Mary memo to the Farm Security Administration, "exposing" numerous examples of alleged "extravagance, mismanagement and wastefulness if not actual graft" on the part of colony administrators over the years, to no discernible effect. As membership in the union fell, so, too, did the population of Dyess.[36]

Local 29's membership records were not always complete and did not often detail individual names, but where they did, they do not include the name Ray Cash. It is possible that Cash joined the STFU—he certainly disliked the way Jake Terry treated him—but it is also possible, perhaps more likely, that he did not. He had taken deed of his farmstead in January 1938, early compared to most, achieving the kind of independence promised by colony agents. If he had complaints about the ultimate cost of his property, there is no record of it. And later, he benefited from the high attrition rate when he acquired another twenty acres from a vacating neighbor. That may be why Johnny Cash said, forty years later, that he did not remember "seeing any real trouble in the community." At only eight years old in 1940, he may not have even been aware of colony controversy if it did not touch his family directly.[37]

At the same time, if the tumult within the community of Dyess passed young J. R. by, he did not miss the deprivation all around him, a level of poverty worse than even his family suffered. On any trip out of town, to Blytheville or Osceola or Tyronza, the Cashes would have passed numerous sharecropper shacks, mostly for landless farmers working the big plantations. As an adult, Cash often told the story of living "across the road" from a three-room shotgun shack inhabited by a rotating cast of sharecroppers working the Stuckey plantation.[38] Cash told one journalist a harrowing story about a sharecropper father who had to bury a deceased baby in a ditch, and another about a six-year-old who confessed to poisoning her father. He said that Ray would not let the Cash children play with the sharecropper children sometimes because they had lice. The "dire poverty" he saw in the sharecroppers—whom he never identified as either Black or white—made a deep impression on him. "They'd come with rags on their backs and maybe a skillet tied to their wagon. Mostly they just walked in." Compared to their shack, it seemed like the Cashes lived in a "big house." As he later recounted in "Christmas as I Knew It," a song on his 1963 album, *The Christmas*

Spirit, he and his brother Jack brought gifts of coal oil and hickory nuts to the nearby sharecropper shack even though his own family, owing to a bad year for cotton, had little to share. Later on the album, Cash put some of the Edna St. Vincent Millay poem "The Ballad of the Harp-Weaver" into song, describing an impoverished mother and son living like those sharecroppers he had seen, so cold that at night they needed to burn chairs. As the boy cries to sleep on Christmas Eve, he dreams of seeing his mother sitting in their lone chair, playing a harp, singing as she weaves clothes for him. When he awakes in the morning, his mother has frozen to death, but piled up beside her were "the clothes of a king's son, just my size." The poem and the song are meant as a Christmas miracle story, but the origins came from Cash's own experience and witness of poverty. He understood that although his own family suffered poverty, they were better off than those sharecroppers.[39]

Later, in an age marked by affluence and a dramatic expansion of the American middle class, Cash consistently returned to these themes of poverty and the working poor. On the first of his concept albums, *Songs of Our Soil* (1959), Cash recorded "The Man on the Hill," a song about a family so poor that it cannot make ends meet and has to turn to a planter for help. The situation is so desperate it seems clear that it is about a sharecropper, but in a twist that makes it obvious that Cash was thinking of his own father, the lyrics describe the farmer not being able to harvest enough out of twenty acres and needing more land. The song clearly conveys how deeply young J. R. Cash absorbed the precarious experience of farming in Dyess, as the family teetered on the edge of sharecropper-like poverty. By the end of the song, Cash muses that maybe the "Man on the Hill" of the title—the planter—will help the family in the end, because if they die, who will pay the "dyin' bills"? In 1965, when Cash recorded "All of God's Children Ain't Free"—a song widely misinterpreted as primarily a civil rights song (indeed, it is incorrectly thought to be his *only* civil rights song)—he focused, in fact, on *the poor* not being free. The song mentions the "poor man with no land" and the "man done wrong" and could be referring to a sharecropper shack as a penitentiary—either one is a place where a man, as Cash saw in those sharecroppers across the road, is trapped.[40]

It is no wonder that Cash emerged from this period of his life with a deep appreciation for Franklin Roosevelt and the New Deal that had given his family a second chance, one chance more than those sharecroppers got. "Dyess Colony was our salvation," he later recounted. Without it, he mused, the Cash family would probably have been "following the wheat crop and going to the dogs like the others." It seemed to Cash that resettlement of the landless poor was one of the things America did right, if not completely. His family received the government help it needed, and was grateful for it, but why not everyone? Through no fault of their own, but only through chance and circumstance, did the neighbors across the road fare worse than the Cash family. Even as Cash came away from the experience with a reverence for FDR and the role of the president, even as the New Deal established a standard to which he would always hold his country, he understood that there remained unfinished business—that America could always do better.[41]

Once Columbia Records gave Johnny Cash the freedom to record what he wanted in the early 1960s, his artistic identity increasingly reflected both his admiration for hard work and his empathy for the struggling, working poor. In part, his deep knowledge of and fascination with folk music drove some of his work in those years, particularly when he made a series of concept albums. Still, none of that work would have been possible had he not experienced his Arkansas boyhood in the way that he did, as witness to the working poor's struggles to survive. Across the decade of the 1960s, in the midst of America's thirty-year peak of prosperity, Cash insisted that his audience not forget or ignore what Michael Harrington called "the Other America," the parts of the country where their fellow citizens still skated on the thin ice of survival. Other country music stars, notably Merle Haggard and Loretta Lynn, plumbed similar themes, often through their personal stories, but no artist of any musical genre so consistently tied his public citizenship to honoring the dignity of, and expressing solidarity with, the working poor.

On the two albums that followed *Songs of Our Soil*, as well as on a number of singles, Cash further emphasized his empathy for those who did physical labor. Cash introduces Merle Travis's "Loading Coal," the first song on *Ride This Train* (1960), by saying he's going to tell a story kids don't learn in school. In character, he describes waiting with his mother for his father to come home from the mine, "nothing clean but the whites of his eyes," and admiring the man so much he could not wait to grow up and join him at work underground. The song is upbeat, but not so upbeat that it ignores the poverty of the miners who can never get their hands on cash because they were paid in scrip. Even the prospect of a strike is taken in stride. Though he knows they'll go hungry, he is confident they will get "a nickel more a ton for loading coal." These are not the words of an agitator or even a union foreman; they are the words of a rank-and-file miner, the same kind of man Cash knew in the cotton fields. *Ride This Train* also features a trip to Roseburg, Oregon, to hear Leon Roger Payne's tribute, "Lumberjack," but Cash's close identity with manual labor really crystalized on the 1963 album, *Blood, Sweat and Tears*, which features a cover image of Cash holding an enormous miner's pick over his shoulder and a kerosene lantern in his hand. This album has been widely misread as merely an album of work songs, but the tributes to the manual laborers, both famous (John Henry and Casey Jones) and nameless (the convict laborers and oil field roughnecks) presented an alternate version of America in the midst of the glitz, glamour, and prosperity of the Kennedy years. As with his numerous manual-labor-themed singles—"Pick a Bale of Cotton," "Dark as a Dungeon," "Hammers and Nails," "Cotton Pickin' Hands," "Bottom of the Mountain," to name a few—and other album tracks such as "In Them Old Cottonfields Back Home" and "Call Daddy from the Mine," the songs on *Blood, Sweat and Tears* are meant, in part, to document the social realism of hard work, portraying their subjects as symbols of strength and endurance in the face of overwhelming adversity. As much as Dorothea Lange's and Walker Evans's photos captured both the suffering and dignity of their Depression-era subjects, Cash's songs (and interpretations of others' songs) reflect a desire to put the same social reality before his comfortable record-buying public. He understood that not everyone had experienced these struggles—or witnessed others who had—the way that he did as a boy, but he saw it as his responsibility to use his art to remind Americans, in a time of affluence, of how the other half lived.

Cash's consistent expression of this form of empathy—an empathy rooted in solidarity with the poor—meant that no longtime fans would have been surprised to find Cash exploring the same themes on his network television show. "You know, the rewards for a hardworking man are often very small," he said in a monologue at the end of an early episode in the summer of 1969, as he introduced the Eddie Noack song "These Hands." To raise a family and to build a home, the song suggests, are the rewards that matter, rewards within reach of the hardworking man. A week later, he began his end-of-show monologue by saying that he was "proud of a lot of my folks just for being the good, simple, hardworking people they were," as he introduced his own "Lead Me Father." In other episodes, he devoted his "Ride This Train" tributes to coal miners, lumberjacks, and truckers, using contemporary film footage, showing the men at work, laboring in difficult conditions. These were not historic images, but film shot in 1969 and 1970, further social realist documentation to remind viewers that despite the massive postwar expansion of the middle class, the working class remained the backbone of the nation. At times, this kind of identification with the "forgotten man" would lead political figures to try to claim him, but for Cash there was nothing partisan about the forgotten man.

He preached no doctrine or ideology, though, of course, he was not being apolitical. It's just that his politics were defined by empathy, nothing else.[42]

If some of Cash's television presentations of working people came off as celebrations of muscle and sweat, of a particularly masculine form of citizenship, the ones that emphasized the working poor—the sharecropper, the hobo, the small-patch cotton farmer barely getting by—were more sensitive, more nuanced. In the second season of the show, several episodes aired between February and the end of April 1970 that conveyed his empathy for the working poor best. In the first of these, Cash invited viewers to "Ride This Train" to the Mississippi Delta, to the land of "King Cotton," to see a cotton plantation. "Though the land is rich," Cash intoned, "to many, life is pretty hard." He described sharecroppers living in a shotgun shack, saying that one could work for thirty years and wind up, still, with only that hovel, as he segued into singing Harlan Howard's "Mississippi Delta Land." The lyrics describe the cotton plantation robbing the narrator of his youth, rewarding him only with "a one-room shack." But perhaps most personal to Cash was the line, "There ain't no future for the man that works but never owns the land." As Cash finished singing, he talked about what had been lost in the last forty years, saying that whereas the cotton in the Delta used to be grown by cotton farmers "like my people" who earned "everything they got in life" by "the sweat of their brow and the ache in their back," now in 1970, "big business" owned most of the land, mechanizing the farms, and replacing "the calloused and burr-torn fingers—the human hands—that were once there." The small-patch cotton farmer, he concluded, cannot compete with these "big farms." The segment includes tales of agricultural workers giving up and moving north to seek factory jobs (as he sings Bobby Bare's hit, "Detroit City"), and concludes back in Dyess, as he spoke of his sister Louise leading the family in song to keep "us all cheered up" through the work day.

Few moments in his career captured so perfectly Cash's solidarity with hardworking, struggling people. In this single segment, he brought to an American audience that numbered in the millions the stories of sharecroppers and small cotton farmers—people who could find beauty in singing in the fields and in the setting sun—while also critiquing big business for driving those folks away from working the land.[43]

Two weeks later, Cash brought viewers back to an urban "jungle" a second time, to follow "the American drifter, the hobo." He reminded the audience of how thousands of people, including his father, hopped trains looking for work during the Depression, that they were hobos and not bums. And then, over footage of a modern-day drifter walking down alleys, along the rails, with a bag in hand, he sang a favorite, Kris Kristofferson's "Sunday Morning Coming Down," complete with the "wishing, Lord, that I was stoned" line. With this choice of song and its modern lyrics, Cash deftly gave this aimless man historical roots, but also made clear that he remained part of the fabric of 1970s America. Cash closed by speaking directly to the drifters ("Can any of you hear me out there?" he asked into the camera, as if he knew the drifters did not own their own televisions), telling them to "go ahead and wander where you will," but to know they would not find answers in the bottle or in drugs ("Take it from me, I know—I've been there," he said as the camera zoomed in for a close-up). Instead, finding a sense of belonging comes from being in a place where one finds "love from those around" him. Cash sometimes got grief for leaning too much on the Depression and not speaking enough of the down-and-out in his own times, but in these segments he answered such charges with sensitivity and understanding.[44]

Toward the end of the show's second season, Cash returned to the rural working poor, but this time with an admonishment for his audience to help the destitute. He said that a sharecropper does not have time to care about "what might be happening in Washington" because he is more concerned with whether it is going to rain or not, whether his crop will yield enough to make ends meet. In Dyess "thirty years ago," when he was just a boy, he recalled being in the same boat, with "nickels and dimes" saved for necessities. "We never had money to spend on things we didn't need," he remembered, before singing an early version of "Country Trash" (in which he used "poor white trash" throughout instead of "country trash"). "Yes, sir, a lot of us have known poverty," he said in conclusion, "and some of us still do, but wealth has nothing whatsoever to do with the character of a man." He urged his audience not to be "too slow" in offering to help a neighbor who might be going through similarly hard times. He is just like the rest of us, Cash implied, with his own "hopes and dreams," and although "times may be looking down for him today," some neighborly encouragement might be all he needs to "see him through."[45]

Interestingly, in all of these expressions of empathy for the working poor, particularly in those that drew upon his experience during the Great Depression, Cash never took the opportunity to praise Franklin Roosevelt and the New Deal. To do so would undoubtedly have been seen as partisan, of course, but giving too much of a role to government in these documentary tales would also have undermined his social realist mission. As Cash engaged with social and political issues, as he quietly made himself one of America's foremost public citizens, his politics of empathy—of modeling empathy and calling on his fellow citizens to likewise empathize—relied upon documenting American life, warts and all. He sometimes called upon government officials to act in response to one issue or another, but in recounting his own witness, his own experiences—what he saw with his own eyes—he signaled how he wanted his audience to feel. He might gently prod you not to be slow in helping a struggling neighbor, but mostly he wanted the stories he told in song and on television to move you.

2

Patriotic Chores

J ohnny Cash expected a lot from his television audience. He understood that he was there to entertain, of course, but he also
engaged viewers like no other variety show host, asking that they
think beyond themselves, directing his viewers' attention to the hard
lives of other Americans. He tried to show those lives up close, to
make them real, so that viewers would learn how it felt to be someone else.

At times, just as he called upon his television audience to think
of a neighbor going through hard times, he invited his audience to
reflect upon the lot drawn by those who serve their country. In an
early episode, he asked viewers to come along and ride on a troop
train making stops all over the country—from San Antonio, Texas,
to Augusta, Maine—carrying boys leaving farms and cities to "fight,
defend the nation, the land, and principles." As a start to a "Ride
This Train" piece, it seemed like straightforward patriotic fare, meant
to honor those who, like Cash and other men in his family once did,
boarded trains that took them to basic training.

But then Cash pulled the switch and sent the train down an
unexpected spur as he began singing his 1962 song, "The Big Battle."

The song describes a young soldier being chided, gently, by a commanding officer for thinking that the battle they had just fought had ended there on the battlefield. The "big battle," the more experienced warrior says, comes after the killing, in the hearts of people who suffer the loss. The commanding officer points to the young soldier's friend, Jim McKinney, lying before them, and asks the soldier if he would like to be the one to bring the news of Jim's death to his wife. The veteran officer, experienced in such matters, anticipates the coming struggle for every "mother and sweetheart and wife" who "will grieve for the rest of their lives."

The expectation of unrelenting sorrow described in "The Big Battle" is essential to understanding Cash's—and many other Americans'—stand on American war-making five years into the Vietnam War, but his comments in wartime were never so straightforward. He had not merely jumped, in a matter of minutes, from paying tribute to draftees on a troop train to then emphasizing that some of them would surely die. Instead he coupled the pain of wartime loss with admiration for the troops, making it clear that, for him, one could not feel one way without simultaneously feeling the other. You could admire and respect the troops for their service, but you had to brace for the inevitable suffering that killing would bring to American communities and families. And you might see the battle deaths of these young men as a tragedy or a waste of life, but you nevertheless needed to pay tribute to their service and sacrifice. He tolerated no oversimplification. Applying his social realist frame to military service, he highlighted dignity, honor, and sorrow as elemental truths.

In fact, as Cash segued out of "The Big Battle" in that early episode, he reminded viewers that 180 men defended the Alamo against 5,000 troops in the Mexican Army, "and they fought to the death." Unlike in later performances, Cash did not draw explicit parallels with the Vietnam War; he simply sang "Remember the Alamo" in a way that honored the sacrifice of the nation's servicemen. "In the history of the world, there's only been something like two hundred years of peace," Cash reported into the camera. As nations became more powerful, and "the wars seem to get longer," he lamented, peace starts to feel like "a distant dream." "But you know something?" he asked the audience. "It's a beautiful dream, the dream of peace." And then he began singing an old Ed McCurdy folk song more associated with the likes of Pete Seeger than with Cash's repertoire. "Last night I had the strangest dream I've ever known before," he sang, "I dreamed that all the world agreed to put an end to war." Between "The Big Battle," "Remember the Alamo," and "Last Night I Had the Strangest Dream," Cash had somehow managed to honor those who fought the nation's wars while unflinchingly portraying the costs to those who lost their loved ones at war. He concluded with a plea for peace. He spoke not simply as a hawkish supporter of national defense, or only as a dove, opposed to war, but as a man who had served his country and had also experienced devastating personal loss during wartime.

That same night, one of his musical guests, The First Edition, performed their minor hit, "Ruby, Don't Take Your Love to Town." It is possible that Cash decided to tailor the "Ride This Train" segment to wartime themes because he knew that The First Edition, a hip pop-country group led by a young Kenny Rogers, would play this song. "It wasn't me who started that crazy Asian war," Rogers sings in character, but he did his "patriotic chore," anyway, and went off to fight. For his service, he is now disabled and tormented that Ruby, his girl, is finding love elsewhere. This song probably resonated with Cash because the feeling he had for wartime came, in part, from what he heard on the radio during World War II and the Korean War, when patriotic songs mixed with the pain of lost love. Johnny Cash's wartime experiences combined all of these things: patriotism and citizenship, entangled with devastating grief and sustained anxiety. As he moved from adolescence during the Second World War to adulthood during the early Cold War, Cash endured all these things: tragedy, heartache, service, and sacrifice. That mix did much to shape the empathetic approach with which he later engaged questions of war and peace as a prominent public citizen.[1]

YOUNG J. R. Cash heard the news of the Japanese attack on Pearl Harbor while visiting his brother Roy's home in Trumann, in next door Poinsett County. Like most little brothers, J. R. looked up to his older brothers, Roy and Jack. Roy impressed him especially because he played in a band, the Dixie Rhythm Ramblers, which had once performed on KLCN Radio in Blytheville. When the United States entered the war, Roy and the other Ramblers signed up, not unlike Ray Cash had done during the First World War. Of all the Ramblers, only Roy returned.

As folks migrated to defense plant jobs elsewhere in Arkansas and out of state, and the extreme deprivation that Cash remembered from his youth faded a bit during the war years, there remained an existential pall. The federal government poured half a billion dollars into wartime production facilities in Arkansas, beginning a process of economic transformation that moved the state toward modernization and prosperity—part of a wider "Cotton Belt to Sunbelt" phenomenon. Meanwhile, the military's use of two major training camps at Little Rock and Fort Smith, plus four airfields (including one in Blytheville), and two Japanese American prison camps at Rowher and Jerome changed the character of Arkansas practically overnight—it was now a wartime state. The war, distant though it may have been in Europe and the Pacific, affected every community. In Dyess, the acrimony of the previous couple of years gave way to a collective project to support the war effort. Families expanded their livestock and foodstuffs production as acts of citizenship. As early as May 22, 1942, the *Osceola Times* praised Dyess citizens for setting "a patriotic example that our entire county, or better, our entire state, may well follow." At least two hundred Dyess men went to the armed forces recruiting centers and signed up.[2]

As Cash's brother and others joined the military, as the Office of Price Administration set up rationing schemes and called for the conservation of various materials, and as radio ads called on Americans to buy war bonds, ten-year-old J. R. could already feel the touch of the war. Years later, he described writing some of his first stories—"some terribly bloody war stories" that were never published—while still in grade school, and performing in various school plays, always in the lead role. Of course, he and Jack kept on working the cotton crop, swimming and fishing in the Tyronza, and smacking cottonmouths when they could, so boyhood carried on. And it was not as though the war brought prosperity to Dyess; different members of the family still picked up extra work where they could to help make ends meet. As he entered adolescence, Cash began to get a sense of how war, something he had heard about before only in stories, could shift American society in dramatic ways, how it could reach his own community, his own family.

Evidence of wartime America came to J. R. primarily through the radio. Ever since Ray used a bit of his FERA loan money to buy a battery-powered radio through the Sears and Roebuck catalog that first spring in Dyess, Cash thought of it as a lifeline, tossed to him on a sea of hardship by the father whom he thought of as "hardhearted and cruel." As Cash's daughter Rosanne later recounted, "music was survival," and the boy heard it in church, in the fields, and on that radio. In all of the popular biographies of Cash from the 1960s through the 1990s, he and his chroniclers recount the way that listening to the radio marked the rhythm of the work day and the work week: coming in from the fields for "dinner" at midday, laying on the cool linoleum floor of the kitchen, and listening to Smilin' Eddie Hill's *High Noon Roundup* on WMPS out of Memphis and, later, at 6:00 p.m., the *Suppertime Frolic* on WJJD out of Chicago. On Saturday nights, at a twirl of the dial, he could listen to the *Grand Ole Opry* on WSM out of Nashville, the *Renfro Valley Barn Dance* on WCKY in Ohio, and the *Wheeling Jamboree* on WWVA out of West Virginia. At other times, he tuned in to border radio stations like XERL in Del Rio, Texas, or some of the more local stations playing so-called race records—the industry term at the time for music (whether blues, jazz, rhythm and blues, or gospel) recorded by Black artists, intended for Black listeners—where he could hear Sister Rosetta Tharpe, Big Bill Broonzy, or Pink Anderson. Among country stars, he loved Roy Acuff, of course, but older songs by Vernon Dalhart and Jimmie Rodgers moved him most. Years later Cash told journalist Robert Hilburn that he found something "uplifting" in Dalhart's "The Prisoner's Song" and Rodgers's "Hobo Bill's Last Ride"—a song about a man dying, frozen to death in a boxcar—because "someone cared enough about troubled people to write songs about them." He also remembered that "it was a real privilege and a treat to hear a Christmas carol" on the radio in Dyess, a place too fire and brimstone to be confused with a Currier and Ives winter scene.[3]

If radio widened Cash's perspective beyond little Dyess, it also brought him constant reminders of the war via what one scholar has called "hayloft patriotism." As a devoted listener to the *National Barn Dance*, live on Chicago's fifty-thousand-watt WLS, Cash would have heard Red Foley, Patsy Montana, Lulu Belle and Scotty, Louise Massey and the Westerners, and many others. Throughout the war years, the *Barn Dance* cast presented numerous war-themed broadcasts, and listeners heard reports on the cast's war bond drives, USO tours, and performances for the troops. Rather than charge a typical ticket price for their war bond shows, the *Barn Dance* asked audience members to exchange scrap metal and scrap rubber for a seat (in time, government officials credited the *Barn Dance* with collecting $3 million in scrap materials for use in the war). In 1944, when Red Foley's version of Bob Wills's "Smoke on the Water" appeared for twenty-seven weeks on *Billboard*'s list of "Most Played Juke Box Folk Records" and eleven weeks on its chart of "Most Played Juke Box Records," Cash, who would later become friends with Foley, no doubt listened attentively. In time, the *Grand Ole Opry*, which moved to the Ryman Auditorium in Nashville in June 1943, similarly saw its audience grow until it was a national sensation. So many troops came to *Opry* shows before shipping out, and they brought the *Opry* with them to bases around the country and around the world (enough that it is said that when Japanese units taunted the Americans in island-to-island fighting, they not only shouted "To hell with Roosevelt! To hell with Babe Ruth!" but also "To hell with Roy Acuff!"). World War II not only nationalized country music, it internationalized it. And J. R. Cash, who dreamed of one day joining the *Opry* cast, listened to it as it happened.[4]

As he tuned in to American wartime culture on the radio, no one made an impression on Cash more than Gene Autry. Cash often recalled at length how much Autry meant to him as a movie star and a man—even writing a song, "Who's Gene Autry?" (1978), for his son John Carter Cash, explaining that to a poor country boy, Autry "made the world look better." Early in his career, Autry had taken a stand on behalf of working people when he recorded "The Death of Mother Jones" only months after the labor organizer had died. Later, and much more prominently, Autry became a kind of "New Deal cowboy," promoting Roosevelt administration policies in his films. In 1939's *Rovin' Tumbleweeds*, for example, Autry's character wins election to go to Washington and push for major public works projects, dam building, and flood prevention, as well as for resettling the landless refugees of the Depression. One can imagine how Cash—who saw his first Autry film in 1937—would have seen the Singing Cowboy seemingly on the same side as all of the hardworking folks in Dyess.[5]

During the war years, Gene Autry carried his own public citizenship forward in support of the war, particularly on radio. In July 1942, Autry used a live broadcast of his syndicated Sunday radio show, *Gene Autry's Melody Ranch*, to be inducted as a technical sergeant into the US Army Air Forces. Millions of radio listeners tuned in. Even as he made $600,000 per year, Autry gave it all up to fly cargo planes over the Himalayas. Wrigley's, the chewing gum company, yielded its Doublemint sponsorship of *Melody Ranch* to the

Army Air Corps, which now broadcast the show as the *Sergeant Gene Autry Show*. Jack and J. R. were still too young to follow Autry and big brother Roy into the service, but the Singing Cowboy urged kids their age to save their nickels and dimes to buy stamps, which could be exchanged—once they filled a book with them—for war bonds. It is hard to imagine that the Cash boys, who did not have two nickels to rub together, could ever save enough for a war bond, but as Boy Scouts, they certainly participated in scrap drives to support the war effort.[6]

Despite Gene Autry's sincere calls to service and good citizenship, country music radio did not always distinguish itself with such wholesome patriotism. The most popular song of the era may have been Arkansan Elton Britt's call to heroism, "There's a Star Spangled Banner Waving Somewhere"—the first country music record to be classified as a gold record—but singers such as Denver Darling and Carson Robison produced a rash of more jingoistic work. Darling recorded and released "Cowards over Pearl Harbor" even before Christmas 1941 and a few months later put out "The Devil and Mr. Hitler." Robison's racist "We're Gonna Have to Slap the Dirty Little Jap (and Uncle Sam's the Guy Who Can Do It)" reflected a climate in which few stood up for the Japanese Americans who were summarily rounded up and put in "internment" camps for the duration of the war. As if they were trying to outdo one another, Darling put out "Get Your Gun and Come Along (We're Fixing to Kill a Skunk)," while Robison recorded "1942 Turkey in the Straw," which turned the old folk song into a triumphal tune about destroying a monkey, baboon, and rat (stand-ins for the Axis powers). That you can find no mention of any of these songs or artists among Johnny Cash's interviews or writings says, perhaps, that even as a kid, he could tell the difference between a stupidly crude and nationalistic composition and something more subtle and affecting, on themes that his own wartime music would explore.[7]

Over time, the Second World War produced in country music a new genre of songs about pain and loss, of separation, loneliness, and, ultimately, heartbreak—feelings the Cash family experienced firsthand during the war. In "Silver Dew on the Blue Grass Tonight" and "Why Do You Cry, Little Darling," Bob Wills and Maybelle Carter, respectively, wrote about young women left behind by their sweethearts who have gone off to war. Carter's young woman acknowledges that her love is fighting for his "country true," and that there are many poor girls crying like she is, but in stiff-upper-lip fashion, she promises to kneel by her bedside every night "and ask God to guide you each day/back to your sweetheart that's waiting."[8]

Cash's own sister Louise experienced exactly the torment described in this genre of country music songs. Eight years older than J. R., Louise grew up teaching songs to her younger siblings in the cotton patch. When the Japanese attacked Pearl Harbor, Louise's high school sweetheart, Joe Garrett, signed up for the Navy and went off to fight in the Pacific. News soon came that the Japanese had sunk Garrett's ship, the USS *Houston*, on March 1, 1942, off Jakarta, Indonesia. Devastated, Louise assumed that he had been killed with the rest of the crew. No reports ever came suggesting otherwise and, after three years, Louise married another man. One evening, after the war had ended, as J. R. sat on the steps of the church in Dyess waiting for the second Sunday services to begin, a much thinner Joe Garrett stepped out of a car. "I had no idea who he was," Cash recounted in his second autobiography, but Garrett reintroduced himself and ended up having dinner with the Cashes out on Road Three that evening. He told them the Japanese had pulled him out of the water and, for three years, held him in a prisoner of war camp in Thailand. He was one of only 291 sailors and Marines out of a crew of about 1,100 to survive the *Houston*'s sinking. Crushed to learn from Ray and Carrie that Louise had married, he grew hopeful when they said she was already suing for divorce. The two revived their romance and eventually married. The whiplash of emotion, right in his own family, taught Cash something about the uncertainty of war, that for all of the evident patriotism and valor, the costs of war came in many forms.[9]

Cash did not learn of Joe Garrett's prisoner of war story until after the war's end, but he could not have missed the stories of wartime prisoners all around him. For one thing, the War Relocation Authority (WRA) imprisoned upward of seventeen thousand Japanese Americans in "internment" camps of about ten thousand acres each in Rowher and Jerome, making them "the largest cities in southeast Arkansas south of Pine Bluff." The camps were about two hundred miles south of Dyess, but the sudden arrival of these prisoners caused reverberations throughout the state. WRA director Dillon Myer and other officials tried hard to create the impression that "internees" (most of whom were American citizens) were not, in fact, being treated as prisoners, held unconstitutionally without due process. Consequently, WRA officials drafted conscription-age Japanese American prisoners into the military and allowed the younger boys to establish Boy Scout troops in the camps. Jack and J. R. Cash, both Boy Scouts belonging to a troop in Dyess that often camped in the Ozarks, would undoubtedly have learned of the controversy surrounding the Rowher and Jerome Scouts. When Japanese American Scouts from both troops planned to camp on the Mississippi, invitations went out for other troops in the state to join; only one group from the white council dared to go. Cash grew up around prison work gangs, but learning that boys his own age had been taken from their homes on the West Coast and imprisoned in Arkansas—that was something else altogether.[10]

In the meantime, the news of thousands of German prisoners of war working the fields of Mississippi County plantations could not have escaped the Cashes either. A significant labor shortage in northeast Arkansas had arisen when so many men rushed to enlist in the armed forces and sharecroppers migrated to better wartime jobs in the cities and outside the state. That made planting, tending, and harvesting the tens of thousands of acres of crops in the region difficult. During the Depression, after some of the big plantations had taken cotton acreage out of production, they replanted it with soybeans. Wartime demand for oil substitutes meant that demand for soybeans skyrocketed, but the plantations struggled to find enough labor. They turned increasingly to Mexican laborers and German prisoners of war.[11]

By 1943, planters could apply to set up branch prison camps on plantation land, hold prisoners of war, and put them to work in the fields. The branch camps drew from larger POW base camps at Camp Robinson and Camp Chaffee, which held mostly German soldiers from General Erwin Rommel's Afrika Korps. In time, Mississippi County became home to eight such POW branch camps, including in Blytheville, Osceola, and, just south of Wilson, along the Mississippi River in Bassett. Nearly two thousand German prisoners "saved the day" in the fall of 1944, harvesting more than six thousand bales of cotton and untold quantities of soybeans, while also maintaining drainage ditches, tending work animals, and working other related crops.[12]

Plantations also considered bringing Japanese American prisoners from Rowher and Jerome to work the fields, but regional power brokers rejected the idea. If Japanese Americans stayed in Arkansas after the war, they worried, "instead of having one racial problem we will have two." Even so, when the war ended, and the German prisoners were repatriated, one Wilson plantation tried to entice Japanese Americans from Rowher and Jerome, pledging to house their new sharecroppers and furnish them with everything they needed to make the crops on a loan basis. They promised that Japanese Americans and their children would be treated better than African Americans, allowing them to ride plantation school buses to white schools. Although the Arkansas legislature had passed racist legislation to deny long-term rental or ownership of land to Japanese Americans, the plantation forged ahead; by early 1946, nearly one hundred recruits from Jerome and Rowher lived in Wilson.[13]

All of these wartime experiences—from the alternating themes of patriotism, jingoism, and heartache in country music to the human cost of war on display in the Mississippi Delta—turned young J. R. Cash's world upside down. But the most disruptive event hit closer to home. In an especially cruel twist of fate, the Cash family lost a son during the war years—just not the one who went to war. Jack, older than J. R. by three years, and by all accounts the younger Cash's best friend and biggest influence, died following a freak accident working in a woodshop, when a fence post unexpectedly jerked him onto an unguarded rotating saw blade, cutting him from sternum to groin. When Jack died, eight agonizing days after the accident, J. R. lost his closest role model and playmate, if not to violence, exactly, then violently.

The circumstances surrounding Jack's death are well-known, but what is often underemphasized is that Jack died supporting his family during wartime. We have long been led to believe that the war years lifted the country out of the Depression, transformed the national economy, and began a massive redistribution of wealth that, in time, built the mid-century American middle class. In Dyess, however, little had changed from 1939 to May 1944, when Jack died. The Cashes still did not have enough money to buy a car or to afford electricity in the house. The cotton crop yield had decreased as the minerals in the soil depleted, necessitating Ray's purchase, on credit, of extra acreage. Americans who did do better during the war tended to work in industry, with union-won protections and, with so few consumer products available, socked away hundreds of billions of dollars in savings accounts. The Cashes were not among them. When J. R. had tried to convince Jack to go fishing that Saturday, the older boy considered it, but went to work instead, he said, because the family needed the money.

The impact of Jack's death on J. R. is impossible to overstate. Everyone in Dyess loved Jack. He was probably the most popular of all of the Cash children: bright, charming, and good. As a paperboy for the *Memphis Press-Scimitar*, he was known to everyone in town. He carried a small Bible with him everywhere and stayed up reading it while his younger brother had his ear pressed to the radio each night. Cash, just twelve years old, had stepped forward to be saved at church just a few months earlier in large part because he had been inspired by his older brother. "After Jack's death, I felt like I'd died, too," Cash wrote in his 1997 autobiography. "I just didn't feel alive. I was terribly lonely without him. I had no friend." But in 1966, only twelve years after Jack's death, when Cash spoke to Dixie Deen, editor of *Music City News*, he told her that after Jack's death, he was, in fact, "born the first time—that was when I started to being born." In his loneliness and sorrow, Cash wrote his first poems, first songs, and in another year or so, began singing. Jack's death, he suggested to Deen, set him on his creative path. He had died with Jack, but also started to being born.[14]

Whether Cash died or was born the first time when Jack died, either metaphor will do to illustrate how profoundly the experience shaped him and his later public citizenship. He could never shake the memory of Jack's bloody clothes, his belt sawn in half, shown to him by his father in an ill-advised trip to the smokehouse behind their home. Not only would the untimely deaths of friends cause him to recall these smokehouse memories in later years, but so, too, would the deaths of young people he did not know, who went off to fight and died for their country. Meanwhile, Cash witnessed things in the moments just before Jack died that he could not explain in earthly terms. "If ever a boy was Godly, he was," Cash told Deen. As Jack seemed to fade in and out of consciousness, he told his mother that he hated to leave her, "but you should not grieve for me because it's such a beautiful place." The family watched their son and brother die "in such bliss and glory," Cash wrote in his first memoir, "that it was like we were almost happy because of the way we saw him go. We saw in our mind's eye what he was seeing—a vision of heaven." They buried him in Bassett, in a cemetery on Highway 61, across the road from a German POW camp, under a small headstone inscribed with a Boy Scouts insignia and the slogan "Be Prepared." In much larger script, the stone says, "Meet Me in Heaven."[15]

The day after the funeral, back in the fields, though, the heart-break proved overwhelming. "I watched as my mother fell to her knees and let her head drop onto her chest," Cash later recalled. "My poor daddy came up to her and took her arm, but she brushed him away. 'I'll get up when God pushes me up!' she said, so angrily, so desperately." Rather than take away "too romantic an impression" of his upbringing, Cash instructed readers of his 1997 autobiography, "remember that picture of Carrie Cash down in the mud between the cotton rows on any mother's worst day." As the long, hot summer wore on, Cash remembered that his mother's anguish became "no less bearable."[16]

His future identification with those who suffered their own mother's (or father's or sister's or brother's) worst day defined how Cash engaged with prisoners, soldiers, oppressed minorities, and their families. It shaped how he responded to policymakers driven by knuckleheaded ideology when they should have been driven by more human concerns—he had little patience for powerful people who trafficked in abstract nonsense when common sense, born of experience, would better serve everyone. Anything governments might do, he later said, "is not worth two cents unless you care for people."[17]

BY ALL ACCOUNTS, in the years following Jack's death, J. R. Cash became more serious, more reflective, and more of a dreamer. He still had to work on the farm six days a week, practically all year round, and when he turned fourteen, he spent parts of his summers carrying water to the levee gangs cutting the banks. Although he also earned three dollars a week as a janitor at his church during his high school years, it was not enough to buy a car, and without a car, he could hardly buy a date with a girl. If he could scrounge up some spare change, he would hang around at Ma Woods's Café in the Dyess town center and play the jukebox for a nickel a song. He tried to go to the Cotton Carnival in Memphis each year, though he later told one of his daughters that he never had more than five dollars saved up to spend there. With a social life limited by work, Cash spent time reading and writing poems and songs, listening obsessively to the radio. When he carried those water buckets to the levee crews, he sometimes hopped into the supervisor's truck just to listen to the radio. If the war had brought the world to Arkansas, radio still had the power to carry Cash outside of Dyess, to Memphis and beyond, where he began to imagine making it on the airwaves himself. Cash would "always think of and talk about things that were up in the air," his boyhood friend A. J. Henson later remembered, thinking about things "the rest of us didn't think about."[18]

On the radio, Cash heard country music artists wrestle with the immense and fearsome power of America's new weapon of mass destruction, the atom bomb, by writing gospel songs. The Buchanan Brothers' "Atomic Power," written by Fred Kirby and released in 1946, describes atomic power as God-given, and although it urges against its violent use, the lyrics sound a warning about the bomb's destructive power. "Be careful," it warns listeners, with how you work with "the power of God's holy hand." When *Billboard* declared it "the Greatest Folk Song in Twenty Years," "Atomic Power" inspired a wave of covers and copycats in the late forties and early fifties. The Buchanan Brothers' later hit, "There Is a Power Greater than Atomic" and Lowell Blanchard and the Valley Trio's "Jesus Hits Like an Atom Bomb" are only among the more famous gospel songs to dwell on this awesome and terrifying technological advance. A teenage boy might find comfort, under the circumstances, in the harmonies of his favorite singers—or in their admonitions to just put one's trust in the Lord.[19]

In 1947, the biggest event in Dyess since Eleanor Roosevelt's visit happened when Cash's heroes, the Louvin Brothers (who, five years later, would record their own apocalyptic gospel song, "The Great Atomic Power"), came up from Memphis with the whole cast of

Smilin' Eddie Hill's *High Noon Roundup*. Cash hung around the high school auditorium all day, waiting for the Louvins' arrival. When they pulled in, Cash, despite being utterly starstruck, managed to talk to Charlie Louvin, directing him to a restroom. When he saw Louvin eating soda crackers, he asked if they were good for his throat. "No," he replied, "but they're good for your belly if you're hungry." Louvin asked Cash if he had any requests, and Cash said he sure would appreciate it if they would play "I'll Have a New Body (I'll Have a New Life)" for his mother who would be listening from home to the radio broadcast. As Cash sat in the front row, his idols dedicated the song to "J. R.'s mother." After the show, Charlie waved goodbye. "I didn't even feel the gravel on my bare feet that night when I walked the two-and-a-half miles home in the dark," he remembered, "singing all the songs I'd heard from the stage." In the coming years, as the Louvin Brothers became even bigger stars, their music, too, showed Cash what politically engaged art could look like.[20]

On May 19, 1950, when Cash graduated from high school, the United States found itself trying to contain communism at home as much as abroad. In the wake of the Soviets detonating their first atomic bomb the previous autumn, and the Truman administration "losing" China to communism, Alger Hiss, a former Department of Agriculture administrator and a Southern Tenant Farmers Union sympathizer, went on trial for perjuring himself in congressional testimony; he had claimed not to know Whittaker Chambers, an admitted former communist. The jury found Hiss guilty in January 1950. Meanwhile, in February and March, Senator Joseph McCarthy began making allegations that communists had infiltrated the State Department. He produced little proof but put fear in the hearts of anyone who had ever thought, perhaps in the 1930s, when American capitalism looked like it might not survive, that communism or socialism were viable alternatives. By the end of March, Herb Block, the *Washington Post* cartoonist, had coined the term "McCarthyism."

Meanwhile, British authorities had arrested an atomic physicist named Klaus Fuchs who, in turn, implicated several Americans for participating in a spy ring that fed atomic secrets to the Soviets. By June and July, the FBI had arrested alleged American members of that spy ring, David Greenglass and Julius and Ethel Rosenberg.

For his part, on his graduation day in May, Cash looked ahead to a future no less uncertain than when he started high school. "There was nothing at home," Cash later recalled. "Our land was exhausted, producing barely half a bale of cotton to the acre" (compared to the 1937 post-flood harvest that yielded two bales per acre). He did not have the money for college and any musical talent he possessed remained too raw to go to Memphis and try to get on the radio. Enrollment in a college or university would have spared him worrying about what his local draft board might do, but in an intensifying Cold War, his inevitable classification as 1-A (eligible for call-up) had to weigh on his mind. That spring, President Harry S. Truman and Congress were debating a range of proposals related to national defense and peacetime preparedness, including whether or not to extend the draft for another two years. Most draft-age men knew the draft could be evaded legally by taking jobs in key industries—doing work that a draft board might decide qualified as "in the national interest." Shortly after graduation, Cash took that route, going with a friend to Pontiac, Michigan, where he landed a job at the Fisher Body factory, "punching holes in pads for the hoods of '51 Pontiacs." But he hated the job and the living conditions in the big city; he lasted only a few weeks. When he returned to Arkansas, he tried working in the same Procter & Gamble margarine plant where his father had taken a job as foreman, but the filth, the heat, and the low wages drove him out quickly. Cash was adrift. In his second autobiography, he wrote that he decided to join the military as a way to get out of the cotton fields. "At the time, it was the thing to do," he wrote. "We boys wanted to serve our country." There may be some truth to that statement, but it is not the whole truth. More likely

Cash made the decision to enlist in the United States Air Force when the North Koreans launched a surprise attack over the 38th parallel into South Korea on June 25, 1950, one month and six days after Cash finished high school, just as he got thinking he had no future at the margarine plant.[21]

With all of the focus on containing the Soviets in Europe by protecting West Germany, the outbreak of war in Korea caught the United States off guard. At the time, American armed forces numbered 593,167, a level thought to be woefully insufficient to face the present crisis in Asia. Consequently, Congress and the president quickly agreed on an extension of the draft law, which Truman signed on the last day of June 1950. Over the next three months, the Selective Service would draft 180,000 young men into the Army. A working-class country boy with no other prospects, Cash practically walked out of central casting, ripe for a scene in a foxhole (alongside an Italian from Brooklyn and a bookworm from Boston, perhaps, if only for cliché's sake). Instead of waiting to be drafted, he looked back to Gene Autry for inspiration and enlisted. Cash signed up for the still-new (and newly integrated) US Air Force on July 7, 1950, twelve days after the North Korean invasion. He worried about seeing combat, but the Air Force seemed a safer bet than the Army. When he eventually landed in West Germany, it turned out he was right.[22]

As Cash went off to basic training at Lackland Air Force Base in Texas, few topics were of more interest in popular music than the draft, than who served and who did not. In the time between Cash's enlistment in July 1950 and when he shipped out overseas in September 1951, both country and R&B radio stations carried countless songs on this theme: Ray Anderson and the Tennessee Mountaineers' "Draft Board Blues"; Arkie Shibley and His Mountain Dew Boys' "Uncle Sam Has Called My Number"; Tani Allen and His Tennessee Pals' "I'm Back in the Army"; and Cactus Pryor and His Pricklypears' "(In Again, Out Again) Packing Up My Barracks Bags Blues"—all were in regular rotation on country stations. Meanwhile, the Vance Brothers' "Draftboard Blues"; Paul Mims' "My New Career Is in Korea"; Sonny Thompson's "Uncle Sam Blues"; Lloyd Price's "Mailman Blues"; and John Lee Hooker's (as Johnny Williams) "Questionnaire Blues" came out on the so-called race record labels in the same period. And at least three artists used the song title "Korea Blues," none more famously than Fats Domino in 1950. Many of the blues songs lament not so much a fear of military service or of dying for one's country as much as the heartbreaking prospect of losing one's girlfriend or wife while one is away.

Although gold record country singer Elton Britt returned to make wartime patriotic songs into a private cottage industry, and respected country artists like Roy Acuff and Gene Autry wrote tributes to General Douglas MacArthur after Truman sacked him for insubordination, the themes of lost love and heartache far outnumbered all others as the war stalemated. Autry, in fact, revived his World War II hit "At Mail Call Today," leading the field of Dear John songs about guys in Korea receiving breakup letters from their sweethearts. Both Red Foley and Tex Ritter—two of Cash's heroes—recorded "Dear Little Girls," a real weeper based on the true story of Pfc. John J. McCormick's letter to his daughters, which his wife received just after getting a telegram informing her of his death. And the Louvin Brothers' "From Mother's Arms to Korea" is a tearjerker, too.

While folk groups such as the Weavers recorded songs that were critical of the war, such tunes were harder to find among country music stars. Sonny Osborne's "A Brother in Korea" (written by his sister Louise about their brother Bobby, who had enlisted) is one exception, subtly criticizing a budding American militarism with a line about how "the people aren't happy unless they're fighting a battle somewhere." The song is also critical of a draft system that allows some young men to hang around with drunks at the local beer halls instead of answering the call to serve their country, while their brother risks his life.

On the other hand, country musicians were, by the time the Korean War started, also taking up the anticommunist cause. Ferlin Husky (as Terry Preston) recorded "Let's Keep the Communists Out" in 1950, while no less than Hank Williams recorded "No, No Joe," warning Uncle Joe Stalin not to mess with the United States. Roy Acuff's "Advice to Joe" fit the same genre in 1951. And within the next couple of years, several musicians recorded their own versions of "I'm No Communist," singing the praises of private property and being left alone by the government. Cash would have heard all of these songs before or during his time in the Air Force. As he began to explore his own musical inclinations, writing his first songs, it is clear that he gravitated not toward the ham-fisted polemical songs—he wrote nothing about the draft or Stalin, for example—but the tunes of heartache. He could relate to those.[23]

Cash took the train to Lackland Air Force Base in Texas not knowing if he would soon be traveling on to war in Asia. He put his trust in the Air Force and in his commander in chief. Although mobilization had gotten off to a rocky start, the vast majority of Americans came to agree with the editors of *Life*, who wrote that it is "the duty and power of the president to act for the United States in foreign affairs," not, say, the responsibility of Congress "to declare war" and "raise and support Armies," as it says in Article I of the Constitution. "His hands are America's hands," the editors wrote. "They must not be tied." Over much of the next twenty years, Cash essentially deferred to that view of the president's authority. After that, around the time he got his television show (in the middle of the next war), it got complicated.[24]

Because of the conflict in Korea, the Air Force condensed basic training from thirteen weeks to seven. When Cash took a battery of qualification tests, he showed an aptitude for distinguishing between competing sounds and an ability to type reasonably well. Maybe because he had long been obsessed with anything to do with "radio" or maybe because he sensed that working with radio meant being some

distance from combat, Cash applied to be a radio intercept operator. He left Lackland for six more months of training at Keesler Air
Force Base in Biloxi, Mississippi. There, his apparently natural ability to pick out actual transmissions from decoy transmissions caught
the attention of his supervisors. They offered him assignments on
either side of the Soviet Union—Alaska or West Germany. For a
country boy who had already grown up on the frontier, a chance
to see Europe was more enticing. He chose Landsberg, thirty miles
west of Munich, for his posting.[25]

Before Cash could join the Twelfth Radio Squadron Mobile
(RSM) in Landsberg, he had to return to San Antonio, this time to
Brooks Air Force Base, for additional specialized training. While off
duty one day, he and a buddy went to a nearby roller rink, where
he met a shy, seventeen-year-old beauty named Vivian Liberto. To
Cash, who grew up among lily-white Protestants in the fields of
Arkansas, Italian American Vivian, with olive skin and dark eyes,
seemed exotic. Mutually smitten, the two dated until Cash headed
back to Dyess for leave before shipping off to Landsberg, but promised to exchange letters while Cash was away.

Cash arrived in Germany the first week of October 1951. In
Landsberg, Cash found himself standing in the shadows of the
Third Reich and on the front lines of the Cold War. In the 1920s,
Adolf Hitler wrote *Mein Kampf* while imprisoned in Landsberg.
Since 1945, the former Wehrmacht compound served as a "displaced
persons" camp, home to thousands of Jews who had survived the
Holocaust (the last of them left Landsberg not long before Cash
arrived). Around the same time, the prison where Hitler had once
been held served as execution site for four Nazi concentration camp
officials found guilty of war crimes at Nuremberg. One could not
help but feel the weight—the gravity—of history in such a place.
More pressingly, by the time Cash made it to Bavaria, the Soviets
not only had enough armored units on the border that they could
have poured into West Germany virtually uncontested, but they had

the bomb, too. At home, congressional investigations put forward that the Soviets could not have developed the bomb on their own—they had to have spies in the United States passing along American atomic secrets. The unfolding Red Scare reached its frightening peak during Cash's time in the Air Force. A federal jury found the Rosenbergs guilty of conspiracy to commit espionage in March 1951, while Cash was still in Texas. Two years later, during his time in Europe, they went to the electric chair. Joseph McCarthy, meanwhile, captivated the public's attention in these years, until the televised hearings of his inquiry into communists in the Army turned public opinion against him. As Cash left the service in 1954, the Senate moved toward censuring McCarthy. Cash came home to a changed country, one in which anticommunism had become an article of faith—where young boys played with models of American Sabre jets and Soviet MiGs, sold widely at the time, alongside popular, war-themed comic books showing manly GIs killing "reds."[26]

As an Air Force radio intercept officer, Cash and the other forty men on his shift—known as a "trick"—listened to Soviet broadcasts, made in Morse code, and typed them up. In a room that resembled a large examination hall full of uniformed students in headphones—the only sound the tapping of typewriters—operators listened intently, straining to distinguish between an actual message and other signals meant as distraction or disguise. In eight-hour shifts, they typed messages that were still encoded and forwarded them to another team that specialized in cracking the Soviet codes. As Cash noted in letters to Vivian, "my job is very hard on the nerves." The classified nature of the work, and the knowledge that they were "only 16 minutes by air from that 'dangerous zone,'" he said, put him on edge. He cracked from the pressure at least once, throwing his typewriter out the window and earning himself a night off, but he otherwise impressed his supervisors. Promoted to staff sergeant and put in charge of a trick, he later received a commendation, which he could not actually keep because of its classified nature. "Because of

Airman Cash's untiring efforts, the squadron is one large step ahead in the completion of its mission," he paraphrased in a letter to Vivian. "He is to be commended for his outstanding efficiency." On one occasion, his supervisors chose him to be part of a select group doing undercover work in Foggia, Italy. For an Arkansas cotton picker, he seemed to rise from his humble origins to meet his historical moment. He did his "patriotic chore" well.[27]

Although Cash excelled at his work and acknowledged at times that he liked it, it sometimes made him miserable. At times, he spoke of the Air Force as a prison from which he could not escape. As early as March 1952, he wrote of his misery. "I feel like someone that's in a place that smells like rotten eggs and is trying to get a breath of fresh air, but can't." When he attended a mandatory orientation on the Marshall Plan, he quipped to Vivian, "I care about as much about the Marshall Plan as I do Roy Acuff's dog." In another letter he seemed like he had reached the limit of what he could take. "Just sitting here in this crummy lifeless hole, living for mail call, depending on drunken lazy punks to bring in the mail," he wrote. Given the immeasurable human misery suffered by Landsberg's only recently departed survivors of genocide, it is a little hard to take Cash's complaints about the boredom or tedium of life in his "lifeless hole" seriously. Still, it's clear, he plunged in and out of depression.[28]

Cash's letters to Vivian reveal, too, that he frequently seemed to inhabit all the worry, desperation, and loneliness he heard in those songs on the radio and on the records he bought at the PX. Although he admitted to occasional flings with German women, he constantly pledged his fidelity to Vivian and asked for the same in return. He worried endlessly about her betraying him or dumping him, imagining himself as the recipient of a Dear John letter. At one point, he proposed that they get married in Germany and live together in an apartment off base, but Vivian's father rejected the idea. And although Cash chastised her for drinking on occasion—saying that all his life he associated drinking only with "hungry kids and unhappy homes"—he himself fell off the wagon regularly. The letters show a constant struggle between teetotalling and getting completely plastered, and it is clear that he wrote some of these letters while drunk. Given his sorry state, it is no wonder that when he and some of his Air Force buddies formed a picking and singing group called the Landsberg Barbarians, and Cash started to think more seriously about a future in music, he leaned toward songs of loneliness and despair. As a Cold War serviceman and budding musician, Cash reflected not only a kind of conflicted citizenship, in which he served his country even if it sometimes irritated him as much as chopping and carrying hay back in Dyess, but also an impatient longing for love and commitment as a buffer against the prospects of nuclear annihilation. No one wanted to go home to an empty bomb shelter.[29]

Cash took his honorable discharge from the Air Force in July 1954, four years after he enlisted, and returned to Dyess a changed man. He had grown up and filled out, his parents noticed, and he had big plans, none of which involved staying in Arkansas. He aimed to marry Vivian Liberto as soon as possible and then settle with his new bride in Memphis, where he planned to pursue his dreams of making it onto the radio as a singer. "There was no question it was where I needed to be," Cash recalled years later. "Ever since that Sears and Roebuck radio came into our house, Memphis had been the center of the world in my head, the one place where people didn't have to spend their lives sweating bare survival out of a few acres of dirt." Cash thought of Memphis the way a lot of country boys and girls thought of the big city—fresh and exciting, offering endless possibilities and, most important, an escape from the lives they had known in the sticks.[30]

If Cash's main attraction to the city had come from the radio, in 1954 there could have been nowhere else in the world with a more exciting radio scene than Memphis. Four days after Cash got to town, Elvis Presley's first single, "That's Alright (Mama)," sent a charge through the city. Disc jockey Dewey Phillips debuted the song, recorded only three days earlier at upstart Sun Studio on Union Avenue, on his WHBQ *Red, Hot and Blue* show, but soon every station in the region picked it up. As Cash later recalled, Phillips mixed hillbilly, pop, blues, gospel, and pretty much anything else he felt like adding to his show. "He knew the big secret," Cash explained. "That there were a lot of white people listening to 'race music' behind closed doors. Of course, some of them (some of us) were quite open about it, most famously Elvis."[31]

To a returning veteran, Memphis also offered certain pathways that made success more likely than in, say, northeast Arkansas. For one thing, other veterans—like Cash's brother Roy—looked out for their own, and for another, the GI Bill provided funding for housing and education to veterans. Hoping perhaps to follow in Dewey Phillips's footsteps, Cash used his GI Bill money to sign up for a part-time course at Keegan's School of Broadcasting. At the time, only his $110 a month from the GI Bill kept food on the table in the first tiny apartment that he and Vivian rented on Eastmoreland Avenue. Just as the Resettlement Administration kept the Cash family afloat in Dyess, the GI Bill sustained Cash after he got out of the service—but he still needed to find steady work.

Through a series of referrals starting with Roy, Cash landed a position as an appliance salesman for Home Equipment Company. He did not have a lick of experience selling much of anything, but the company's president, George Bates, liked to look out for returning servicemen—his own way of giving back to his country. In theory, it should have been a great opportunity for Cash. By 1954, the United States had truly become a "consumers' republic," as the postwar economy grew by leaps and bounds thanks to the expanding middle class's hunger for new cars, new homes, and new appliances and television sets to fill those homes. Consumer choice, Americans were told, made the country great, certainly better than its ideological rival, the Soviet Union. When Vice President Richard Nixon famously debated Soviet Premier Nikita Khrushchev at the 1959 American

National Exhibition in Moscow, he claimed that while the Russians may have had more powerful rockets, American women benefited from a wide array of labor-freeing home appliances. "What we want to do, is make life more easy [sic] for our housewives," Nixon told Khrushchev, claiming that household appliances, and the model home on which the exhibition was based, were affordable—within reach of any steelworker or military veteran. Freedom of choice as consumers, Nixon implied, equaled political freedom as citizens. Unmoved, Khrushchev snorted. Unlike in the Soviet Union where the state provided housing for *every* citizen, "in America, if you don't have a dollar," you could wind up "sleeping . . . on the pavement." As Memphis appliance salesman Johnny Cash could have attested a few years earlier, Khrushchev had reason to be skeptical.[32]

If political freedom came from consumer choice, Cash, as a salesman, encountered a whole lot of unfree people. He could not sell an appliance to save his life—primarily because his client base, mostly Black Memphians, lived precariously and could not afford a new refrigerator or dishwasher whether they wanted one or not. The homes Cash visited as he went door-to-door were not the kind that Nixon would have wanted to profile later at the American expo in Moscow. Many were shacks, not so different from what he had seen in Dyess, homes to people who could barely afford food and clothing. He empathized with them, knowing from his own upbringing what one needed to survive and what one did not. "I hated trying to convince people they should have something they didn't really want," he later told one journalist. "I felt dishonest. I really didn't think all those gadgets would be a blessing." Cash made few commissions doing those rounds, but as it would become clearer later, he benefited from the experience in other ways.[33]

In the meantime, he had started messing around, playing music with three auto mechanics whom his brother Roy worked with at Automobile Sales on Union Avenue, Marshall Grant, Luther Perkins, and a guy with a funny last name, Red Kernodle. When Cash first met Grant, he said, "I hear you do a little pickin'?" "*Very* little,"

Grant replied, sardonically. "Me, too," said Cash, and the two men laughed, knowingly. Somehow, this group of low-talents would eventually make musical history and put Johnny Cash in a position to be a highly influential political artist. But no one could have predicted it at the time. They barely knew where to start.

Naturally, Cash took notice of the upstart label Sun Records, thanks entirely to Elvis Presley. During his first six months or so in Memphis, Cash heard Presley on every radio station in town, or so it seemed. Then he and Vivian saw him perform on a flatbed truck in front of Katz Drug Store in September 1954, during the opening of a new shopping center. Presley dazzled as a performer, and the audience swooned, but Cash came away from the experience impressed that just three instruments could make such a sound (years later, Cash often repeated that Presley did not get enough credit for being a great rhythm guitarist). Cash knew he wanted to record for Sun, too; he needed to meet Sam Phillips, the man who owned Sun Studio and recorded Presley.[34]

The story of Cash's Sun Records career is so much a part of the Cash mythology that it is hardly worth retelling here—except for one thing: Johnny Cash's rise to fame at Sun Records continued to owe a lot to his Cold War experience. In fact, the Sun years in Memphis might as well be seen as an extension of the Air Force years in Landsberg. It is not that he came up through Sun with a Memphis equivalent of the Landsberg Barbarians (a bunch of veterans who could not really play); neither Sam Phillips nor Cash's most notable label mates (Elvis, Carl Perkins, Jerry Lee Lewis, Roy Orbison) had served in the military, and they were all first-class talents.[35] But Cash, the sole veteran among them, approached his work with the same discipline he had applied to listening in on Soviet radio traffic. And the music he made grew almost directly out of those years in Germany.

Long after Cash became a superstar, it rankled him that Phillips so often got credit for discovering him when, in Cash's view, he had had to work so hard to prove himself—just as he, an Arkansas farm boy, had shown his mettle as a radio intercept operator. Cash practically stalked Phillips at Sun's unlikely location in a former radiator shop at 706 Union Avenue—the same street where all the car dealerships and mechanics' garages, including Automobile Sales, where his brother and bandmates worked, could be found. As he drove to Keegan's Broadcasting School nearly every day, he stopped in at Sun, trying to get an audition. Cash always referred to "Mr. Phillips" as if he were a superior officer, and although Phillips was no barking General Patton, he made clear who was boss. The two men had a lot in common—Phillips had grown up cotton farming in Florence, Alabama, and loved hillbilly music and "race music" equally. Cash admired Phillips's vision—that a music not yet called rock and roll would appeal to Black and white kids in a growing teen market, accessible on jukeboxes, transistor radios, and any car's AM dial. Sun Studio became the unassuming laboratory where Phillips became, in Peter Guralnick's memorable label, "the man who invented rock 'n' roll."

Cash's "unusual" voice may have impressed Phillips (and so, too, the raw boom-chick-a-boom sound driven mostly by Marshall Grant's bass and Luther Perkins's primitive guitar), but what set Cash apart was his songwriting. In fact, one could make the case that almost all of the early songs that Cash wrote and recorded for Sun Records—"Hey, Porter," "Folsom Prison Blues," "Cry! Cry! Cry!," "So Doggone Lonesome," and even "I Walk the Line"—sprang from the wellspring of heartache and loneliness Cash felt during his time in Landsberg. In "Hey, Porter," first published as a poem in *Stars and Stripes*, Cash translates every serviceman's homesickness into the joy of coming home, of surviving the war and getting back to the safety and comfort and love of familiar surroundings—as if he had just been released from prison. Cash wrote "Folsom Prison Blues" in Landsberg, too, after watching *Inside the Walls of Folsom Prison*, but later acknowledged that it came from his own experience of feeling locked up, at times, at the base. "I felt terrified sometimes because

I knew the door was locked for security reasons and I couldn't get out," he told his daughter, Kathy. "It was like being in prison," he concluded (in a way that any actual Folsom inmate would have laughed at).[36] "Cry! Cry! Cry!," although written after Cash returned to the States, could have been one of those Korean War–era songs directed at a cheating woman, out all night. Maybe his first inklings of the song came from his own resentment at Vivian occasionally going on dates with other men while Cash was in Germany. The explicit threat is that the unfaithful woman will be alone one day, thinking of "the fool you've been." On the flipside of "Folsom Prison Blues," Cash recorded "So Doggone Lonesome," which grew out of the same sentiment of worrying that his true love is abandoning him—just as he feared with Vivian. And although Cash famously wrote "I Walk the Line" while out on tour, as a pledge of fidelity to Vivian, who worried about the temptations of women on the road, his promises of faithfulness in the song sound exactly like those he expressed years earlier in his letters from Landsberg. Those four years in the service did a lot to shape him as a young artist and songwriter.[37]

In April 1955, Phillips signed Johnny Cash and the Tennessee Two to a Sun Records contract in the restaurant next door to the studio, sitting in the booths normally reserved for the mechanics and other wrench swingers in the neighborhood. Although Cash still introduced himself as "John," and had used "Johnny" only in his letters to Vivian, Phillips thought that the youth market would respond to a "Johnny" better than to a "John." Cash did not love the idea—he thought "Johnny" sounded like a little boy's name—but he trusted Phillips. It seemed like that trust was rewarded almost immediately when the group first heard "Hey, Porter" and "Cry! Cry! Cry!" on the radio. "To have that record played on WMPS that first day, that was it for me," Cash later said. "I was singin' on the radio, and that was as far as I ever wanted to go in life."[38]

Cash and his fellow Sun Records artists broke into mainstream culture in the mid-1950s and ran off with Middle America's children's hearts. At exactly the same historical moment that novels such as Sloan Wilson's *The Man in the Gray Flannel Suit* (1955) and nonfiction such as William H. Whyte's *The Organization Man* (1956) reflected American anxieties over the alienation of postwar middle-class success and commented on its stifling conformist culture, Elvis and Cash, as well as Carl Perkins, Jerry Lee Lewis, and Roy Orbison—all working-class boys—charted another path. They caught a wave of cultural rebellion represented as much by Marlon Brando in *The Wild One* (1953) and James Dean in *Rebel Without a Cause* (1955), in a time defined by the seemingly increasing likelihood of humanity being wiped out by the bomb. The madness of that moment, captured in Allen Ginsberg's poem, *Howl* (1956), and the rejection of that madness for a more jazzlike, spontaneous life as seen in Jack Kerouac's *On the Road* (1957), attracted millions of middle-class young people, all fascinated with "authentic" outsiders. Indeed, as one historian has argued, the United States became "a nation of outsiders"—or at least enchanted with the outsider figure—just as Cash signed with Sun Records. His own authentic story of growing up poor in Dyess, coming out of the cotton to sing songs about not only heartache but chain gangs and prisons, cowboys and Indians, captivated the middle class, who embraced him in the same way they would soon embrace folk song collectors. When Phillips got curious about Cash's "unusual voice," he meant the tone, but he could just as easily have been talking about Cash's ability to draw listeners into his own experience, to feel and relate to his lyrics and songs almost as if they had been there to witness whatever he sang about for themselves. Perry Como or Bing Crosby could never offer anything like that.[39]

Just as punks, the ultimate outsiders, would later glory in their lack of musical training, Cash and the Tennessee Two lacked the artifice to be anything other than what they were. "We didn't work to get that boom-chicka-boom sound," Marshall Grant later quipped. "That's all we could play." Phillips saw the value in spontaneity. "I told them not to be overly prepared," he later recalled, words no record producer ever said to Eddie Fisher, Vic Damone, or, heaven forbid, Frank Sinatra. Unlike those polished voices in sharkskin suits, Cash joined a roster of working-class misfits who completely upended American popular music in the space of a few years. "Everybody at Sun was white trash," rock critic Lester Bangs later said, but they sounded better than almost anyone else. Cash remembered the abuse he got from people who didn't like his sound or background—he recalled being sneered at as "rockabilly"—but a lot of it carried racial overtones, implying that he was a white guy who wanted to be Black. "I took it with pride because they were telling me, 'You're different,'" he recalled. Different felt special to Cash.[40]

Once their Sun records started getting airplay outside of Memphis, and the bands built their reputations playing any venue, no matter how small, invitations to appear on the *Louisiana Hayride* in Shreveport came in.[41] Broadcast on KWKH every Saturday night from Shreveport's hulking Municipal Auditorium, the *Hayride* guaranteed artists a chance to play in front of two thousand people and an enormous listening audience that extended throughout the "mid-South" of Tennessee, Louisiana, Arkansas, Texas, and even as far as New Mexico. A single appearance could raise an artist's profile and broaden his or her audience significantly. The first time Cash appeared, he and the Tennessee Two went on ahead of Elvis. Although some claimed that Cash and Elvis saw each other as rivals, Cash at times waxed lyrical about the camaraderie of the road and especially the *Hayride*. They watched each other perform, shared in each other's triumphs and disappointments. They were like "brothers and sisters" he later wrote, and Cash always stood in the wings when Elvis performed. (The feeling was apparently mutual. Long before June Carter met Johnny Cash, Elvis would talk to her about him and play his records on the jukebox at every opportunity. She said Elvis would tune his guitar to the first line of a Cash song every time.) That first night that Cash played the *Hayride*, the audience went so wild for "Hey, Porter" and "Cry! Cry! Cry!" he had to come out and play them both again. Soon the *Hayride* asked Cash to become a member, which meant making the seven-hundred-mile round trip from Memphis every Saturday, but he didn't hesitate to accept. In the space of six months, he seemed to have jumped from playing Little League to playing in Fenway Park. Cash's appeal and audience exploded. "It's everything good happening at once," he reflected. "Being wanted, being appreciated, doing what I love, basking in a great big family, playing music with my friends." Within a year of his first record's release—just over two years since he left the Air Force—he played the *Grand Ole Opry*.[42]

Thanks in large part to the success of "I Walk the Line," which Cash wrote in November 1955, the night after his first *Hayride* appearance, Cash sold six million records by the time he left Sun Records for Columbia in 1958. Six million records sold by a twenty-six-year-old Dyess farm boy and United States Air Force veteran, and on an upstart regional label, no less. No wonder Columbia wanted him. In 1959, his first year on Columbia and first year living in California, he made $250,000 (about $2.2 million in 2020). Cash could not sell kitchen appliances, but Richard Nixon could still have trotted him out in front of the Soviets as a rags-to-riches American tale of rewards coming to those who work hard.[43]

If Cash never became a Cold War poster boy, his wartime experiences continued to inform his new career. At the *Louisiana Hayride* one night in 1959, a young airman named Conrad Ward came from nearby Barksdale Air Force Base to see Cash perform. Ward had been feeling despondent in the days and weeks leading up to the show. "Nothing seemed to be going right," he remembered some years later. "The world seemed bleak and empty." He thought about suicide all the time. Cash's performance prompted Ward to seek him out after the show. He thought that maybe he could get the star's autograph, but when he started speaking to Cash, he said, "I felt a sudden compulsion to stop him and tell him my troubles." Cash put his arm around Ward and told him that he knew what it was like. "I've had those same feelings," Cash said of his Air Force years. He advised Ward that he found it helpful to remember that "life has corners, corners you'll find you have to turn even when you didn't know they were there." The circumstances in one's life might seem terrible at the time, he said, but "around every one of those corners is a new story and a new friend." Even when faced with the most difficult challenges, Cash counseled, one eventually finds something to look forward to. "Suicide is a dead-end street," he concluded. More than a decade later, in 1971, Ward wrote about his encounter with Cash, crediting the singer's empathy—that he understood the strains of Air Force life—with giving him enough strength to "get through those trying days."[44]

Even as Cash liked to joke to audiences that he spent "twenty years in the Air Force, from 1950 to 1954," and still thought of it in terms of "doing time," he nevertheless used the platform afforded to him by his growing stardom to support American Cold War policy. In 1959, he joined with other film, television, and music stars such as Boris Karloff, Tony Bennett, and Pat Boone, in recording a public service announcement for civil defense. Throughout most of the 1950s, the Federal Civil Defense Administration (FCDA) strived to convince Americans to prepare for the likelihood of a Soviet nuclear attack, given that the Soviets had developed increasingly more powerful hydrogen bombs and then, in 1957, beat the Americans into space. Bert the Turtle had been teaching American school kids to "duck and cover" under their school desks since 1951, as if that would save them from being vaporized like the children of Hiroshima. And dating to 1954, the FCDA had organized annual civil defense drills under the title "Operation Alert." Each year, the FCDA held a kind of national air-raid drill that required the participation of dozens of cities all on the same day because officials believed American urban centers were the most likely targets of an intercontinental ballistic missile. Just as President Dwight Eisenhower and his aides fled the White House for a tent city outside of Washington, Americans of all walks of life were expected to stop work and school and follow FCDA guidelines by taking shelter. "Listen and Learn through Civil Defense," Cash began his announcement, which could be heard on radio stations all over the country. "This is Johnny Cash. I'd like all of you to remember that America can withstand an enemy attack if we support the emergency plans of our community and learn to help ourselves. Make sure you're prepared. Contact your local Civil Defense Office today!" The "Be Prepared" message of these PSAs would have resonated with Cash, the former Boy Scout, and presenting the challenge of civil defense as a community-based project may have appealed to him, too, thanks to his experience living in a cooperative community like Dyess.[45]

Apparently, Cash did not question the absurdity of the PSA's central message that the United States could "withstand an enemy attack," nor did he blink at his willing participation in what critics called a dangerous government propaganda campaign. Although he became, in later years, more outspoken about the perils of the nuclear arms race, in 1959, he certainly did not see fit to join the dissenters who thought that by being better prepared to withstand a nuclear attack, Americans were practically inviting one. These protesters were comparatively few in number, but they received considerable press attention each year, especially in New York. There, police arrested growing numbers of resisters who, each year, refused to retreat to subway tunnels or other fallout shelters, who sat in silent protest, holding signs on city park benches. Led by Dorothy Day, founder of the Catholic Worker movement, A. J. Muste of the Fellowship of Reconciliation, and Bayard Rustin of the War Resisters League, the resisters argued that the Cold War obsession with civil defense constituted a kind of "psychological warfare" on the citizenry. Nuclear war, then or now, is unwinnable. Day and the others dared to say that by normalizing nuclear war—by accommodating the insanity of it, by claiming the country could "withstand" it—the

United States government required, by law, the suspension of one's critical faculties. Even at the time, mock news reports put out as part of the Operation Alert drills projected five million dead, five million injured, and another ten million homeless. Cash might have asked if those numbers qualified "withstanding" a Soviet attack, but his thinking had not yet moved in that direction.[46]

More likely is that Cash remained grateful for what the government had done for his family, and as a veteran he remained loyal and answerable to his commander in chief, not thinking twice about any requests from Eisenhower's FCDA. He also appeared more than once on *Guest Star*, a syndicated radio program sponsored by the United States Treasury Department. Cash urged listeners to use savings bonds as their basic savings plan because they were fully guaranteed by the government and would be replaced for free if lost. "I think savings bonds are a terrific investment," he declared. Similarly, in 1959, Cash and the Tennessee Three (which now included Carl Perkins's former drummer, W. S. Holland) played a ten-day tour of American military bases in Europe. At times, in West Germany, they played three or four shows a night, as a sign of gratitude to the troops. In 1962, Cash and the guys played at American bases in Japan and South Korea, both before and after the Cuban Missile Crisis brought the Americans and Soviets to the brink of nuclear war.[47]

BY THE TIME Cash had his own television show, his confidence as a public citizen led him to make numerous statements on the Vietnam War, but any misgivings he had about the war did not extend to those serving their country. In fact, Cash dedicated his December 16, 1970, show to a group of helicopter pilots who stopped by to speak to him at the Ryman Auditorium in Nashville as he prepared for the show's taping. They were on their way to Fort Polk, Louisiana and probably to Vietnam, Cash told the viewing audience. Using the same language he sometimes applied to prison inmates, he asked "all servicemen" to "remember that somebody cares and somebody loves you," and he began playing "Remember Me," a song not exactly about servicemen, but more about loyalty to one's friends. Later in the episode, he concluded a "Ride This Train" segment on the Civil War (a thinly veiled stand-in for the Vietnam War), by saluting toward the camera, as if he was still Airman John R. Cash based in Landsberg, West Germany. "Goodnight servicemen, wherever you are. I salute you."[48]

Cash often used his show's platform to celebrate servicemen. On a Veterans Day 1970 episode, Cash reminded viewers that November 11 is a holiday to celebrate the end of World War I, but it is also to honor the memory of the men who died, he said, believing they were fighting the "war to end all wars." "Well, unfortunately," Cash lamented, "it was not the war to end all wars. We've found ourselves in conflict many times since then," he said. Just since his discharge from the Air Force, the United States had mobilized to fight in Lebanon, Cuba, the Dominican Republic, Vietnam, and Cambodia—to say nothing of helping to overthrow governments in Iran and Guatemala. "But we must keep the faith," he said. "We must believe that peace will come and that this will be the war to end all wars." He then began singing the first verse of Bob Dylan's "Blowin' in the Wind" before returning to his monologue, which now seemed to take the form of a poem that he had written for the occasion. He spoke of how man had transformed him, the narrator, into a club, then a sword, and then a gun—all weapons of war. "What more could man devise?" he asked. The answer on Cash's mind, was the bomb. Man split an atom, he said, "and as the mushroom cloud did rise, I knew that soon there'd be an end to all other weaponry, and a final war would lay to waste what man had come to be." The Ryman Auditorium had fallen completely quiet. Not a sound could be heard, as though the people sitting in the seats were bowing their heads in silent prayer. One did not normally hear talk of a final war laying waste to humanity on prime-time television (on a Wednesday night, no less), but Cash finished even darker. When the smoke would clear after that final war, he said, "what was left of man, I'd see, once more is twitching his hand again in search of me." Perhaps sensing that he had gone too far in offering this frighteningly low estimation of humanity, Cash finished by saying "but maybe he'd learn not to pick me [a weapon] up ever again," even though everything else he had said suggested that he doubted it. As he returned to "Blowin' in the Wind," the television audience saw the live audience at the Ryman in a camera shot from the back of the balcony, applauding politely at first, followed by many—but not all—audience members standing to clap. The glimpse of some older folks remaining seated while the mostly younger audience cheered and whistled passed quickly, but it is hard not to imagine that both the standers and the sitters saw this soliloquy as a direct challenge to President Nixon and his supporters.[49]

From that first presentation of "The Big Battle" early in *The Johnny Cash Show*'s run in 1969, through the Veterans Day soliloquy on the instruments of war, Johnny Cash inhabited the kind of patriotism that both opposed war and honored the warriors. As a veteran from a family of veterans, Cash respected and related to those who fought, and also respected those who occupied the highest offices and were faced with making the terrible decisions about who should go to war. But his own experience taught him the cost—what it is like to lose someone so young, what it is like to be on the other side of the world, in a situation not of your own making, just worried that your sweetheart may not stay true. That had been his reality, and he imagined that it was the same for millions of other servicemen—why sugarcoat it?

At the same time, Cash seemed both accepting of official reasons for waging the Cold War and also skeptical there were not alternatives. He did not emerge from his Air Force service seeking or expecting validation for having served his country, for having sacrificed four years of his life. He showed no signs of having been indoctrinated as a fierce anticommunist, spouted no simplistic slo-gans about the evils of communism—not even in his letters to Vivian when he might have spoken without restraint. He was no ideologue. Although commentators often likened him, for his stature and patri-otism, to John Wayne, Cash had nothing in common with Wayne's *Big Jim McLain* (1951), the fictional House Un-American Activities Committee investigator who runs around Hawaii punching com-munists in the face, or Wayne's Col. Mike Kirby in the pro-war *The Green Berets* (1968). Even when he was fighting the Cold War, Cash never got caught up in McCarthyism, never seemed to say anything one way or the other on foreign or domestic policy (except for that crack about caring no more about the Marshall Plan than he cared about Roy Acuff's dog). "Everyone was against communism," one historian has written, "but there were limits to the exertions the av-erage citizen was willing to invest in that sentiment." For Cash, the limits were determined by his field of vision. He engaged Cold War politics of patriotism and service as he experienced them personally. Mostly he just wanted to put it behind him and look toward a new life as a singer on the radio. But as the politics around the Cold War showed him, it is as impossible to avoid the politics of one's country as it is to outrun history.[50]

3

Cash and Black Lives

To this day, *The Johnny Cash Show* is remembered as a showcase for younger artists that Americans rarely saw on television. The show presented plenty of mainstream country music artists, sure, but ask anyone old enough to have watched the show during its two-year run, and they will almost immediately begin rhapsodizing about seeing their favorite rock and pop acts on the show—from Bob Dylan and Joni Mitchell to Linda Ronstadt and Neil Young, to Creedence Clearwater Revival, the Guess Who, and Derek and the Dominos. The show rightfully won praise for upending country music variety show convention. It may have been filmed at the Ryman Auditorium in Nashville, home of the *Grand Ole Opry*, but in tone and form, it looked little like, say, *The Porter Wagoner Show* or *Hee Haw*—neither of those shows ever hosted Stevie Wonder or the Monkees.

You get the sense from a lot of *The Johnny Cash Show*'s admirers that they saw it as almost subversive, sneaking these countercultural artists into American living rooms, sandwiched between George Jones and Tammy Wynette. There are good arguments both for and against that claim, but if there is an Exhibit A in the evidence assembled to prove the show's radicalism, it is the appearance by the Black folk singer, Odetta. In an episode broadcast just after Woodstock dominated the nation's headlines, Cash introduced Odetta as his featured guest—the first to perform after Cash's own musical introduction. The camera panned to Odetta, standing alone with only a microphone before a moody, ominous set, and looking out at a mostly white, mostly Southern audience seated in a balcony bearing a sign that read "Confederate Gallery."[1]

Wearing a long, colorful dress and her hair in a natural Afro, Odetta could have been mistaken for a Black Power spokeswoman. But her power did not come from the barrel of a gun (as Black Panther leader Huey Newton, quoting Chairman Mao, liked to say). Rather, Odetta's power came from her majestic voice, singular in its range, from low levee wail to Metropolitan Opera soprano highs. She performed a mash-up of two songs, the most prominent of which is an obscure, smoldering blues called "Black Woman." That is, Johnny Cash brought Odetta, an artist widely known as a civil rights activist, to Nashville, a city still struggling with desegregation in 1969, to the Mother Church of Country Music, to sing a *blues* song called "Black Woman" to an almost entirely white, Southern audience.

Few could have imagined such a scene just a few years earlier. Odetta had never recorded "Black Woman" (and would not until the 1990s), but she had probably learned it from a Folkways LP, sung either by Rich Amerson or Vera Hall, in recordings made by the likes of folksong archivist Alan Lomax.[2] On stage that night, Odetta sang only certain lines, weaving in a line from her own 1962 song, "Stranger Here." "Oh, black woman . . . come and sit down on your daddy's knee," she quotes Hall or Amerson at the start, in a slow-building blues certainly unlike anything ever before heard on that stage. Midway through the performance, she introduces her own line, looking out at the audience and pausing before bringing the thunder: "Ain't it hard when you got no place to fall?" she wails, as if this place (the Ryman? Nashville? the South?) offers no welcome for her or her people, as if she and they are "strangers here," in their own land. The whole line is "Ain't it hard to stumble, when you got no place to fall?" but the original meaning is lost as she quickly comes back to the opening lines of "Black Woman." The audience is not seen at all. Everyone sits in dead silence until Odetta finishes, when they burst into enthusiastic applause.

When Cash came out to greet Odetta after the song, he took her hand as the lights came up. The whole tenor of the show shifted from serious, deep, dark blues to a giddy mutual appreciation party. "They call a lot of people soul singers, but I think they ought not throw that name around too much," Cash said, reflecting on Odetta's performance. "They ought to wait around until you come along to use that name, 'cause you really put your soul into it." The notoriously shy Odetta, possessor of a singing voice that was surely one of the Lord's most powerful instruments, could barely reply. "Oh, sweet darling," she said in a tiny voice, "thank you so much," at which point the two, sitting side by side, close together, on an artificial stone wall, started giggling.

Cash told Odetta that ever since he first heard her and bought her first album, "all those years ago" (in 1954), he had wanted to sing a duet with her. The orchestra began to play and the two of them—one a giant of American folk music and the other a giant of country music—sang "Shame and Scandal," a song from her second LP, *Odetta Sings Ballads and Blues* (1957). It's an old tune from the Caribbean about two Dutch brothers in love with the same woman, but to see it performed by Cash and Odetta on ABC, with lyrics that were difficult to follow, viewers might have thought the scandal of the song had something to do with interracial relationships. The two had so much fun singing together, it seemed almost flirtatious. Whereas moments earlier, Odetta appeared regal, now, as she sang with Cash, the two of them laughing through the song, she looked more like a teenage girl elbowing a boy she fancies on the bus ride to school. As they reached the end of the song, Odetta kissed Cash on the cheek. He seemed completely delighted, and slapped his leg as if he could not believe his luck. The audience cheered.[3]

The most obvious takeaway from these seven minutes is that Cash meant for Odetta's slot to be read as a rejection of racism and racial segregation. She had put out no new records in 1969, so she had not the usual reason to be hitting the television circuit. Cash had sought her out because he admired her, had been in love with her music since it first came out, and wanted to put that voice—both musical and political—before the American public on its biggest and almost inescapable stage: the television set. In the short time that the show had been on the air, it had featured other, safer Black artists, like the soul singers Joe Tex and O. C. Smith, and Cash could have continued with similar guests. But even in this probationary period, when the show was still just a summer replacement series, Cash made a statement about the show's—and his—identity. By telling the world he had been buying her records for years, he said, in effect, that he had been on the side of Black lives from the start.

How Cash came to be sitting next to Odetta, holding hands, that night in 1969 is a complicated story; it follows Cash out of the shadows of Arkansas racism, through the Air Force and Memphis, to writing an overlooked civil rights album, to promoting Black creative genius on his network television show. That story is essential to understanding how he would emerge as a spokesman for the underdog, whether African Americans, Native peoples, prisoners, or servicemen in Vietnam. He didn't come to this position overnight. As his commitment to public citizenship deepened, he followed no script. In the 1960s, he did his own thing—though he didn't do it perfectly, even on that stage with Odetta.

★

CONVENTIONAL WISDOM ON Cash says that he never really engaged with the Black experience at all—that, at most, he gestured at civil rights when he wrote "All of God's Children Ain't Free" (1965), a song more about poverty than slavery or segregation. Indeed, once he became widely known as an advocate for Native American rights and prisoners' rights, journalists sometimes criticized him for failing to stand up for African Americans, for almost ignoring their cause—which was, after all, contiguous with the causes for which he did fight. The charge always seemed to catch Cash flat-footed, though he should have expected it. He sometimes demurred that apart from singing about Native peoples, "social problems" were not often the subject of his songs. "My music is more of a personal thing than a vehicle to use to carry messages," he explained to a skeptical reporter in 1969. "It's mainly something to be enjoyed." To another, he responded lamely that he had never "said anything in print about black people because no one's ever asked me." Surely that could not have been true as late as 1970. "I can tell you that I think they're not getting a fair shake," he continued, trying to recover. "The only reason I haven't written a song about their problems is that the inspiration never came to me, and I have never been given any good material on the subject. But I am sympathetic to colored people and their problems. And there are a lot of things about the Southern whites that I'm ashamed of."[4]

Those comments are usually the entirety of what we talk about when we talk about Cash and civil rights, then and now: Cash took up the causes of Indians and prisoners, but mostly left the civil rights movement to others. Maybe "the down-South country folk who buy his platters," one journalist at the time speculated, "would rather not hear about these subjects," essentially implying that most country music fans were racists. But these kinds of assumptions, about both Cash and his audience, reveal how eager we are to assign easy political labels to our public figures and their followers; they serve only to distract us from the complex, subtle ways in which Cash, like many Americans, engaged political issues. As Cash's star rose, this supposed failure of his public citizenship came to look like an embarrassing footnote to his legend. In later years, he boasted of receiving hate mail from the Ku Klux Klan, perhaps in reaction to the 1965 National States' Rights Party's (NSRP) charge that, based on a grainy photo of Cash and Vivian, the singer had married a Black woman. Some writers have suggested Cash's fierce reaction, expressing his outrage at the NSRP for calling his children "mongrels," and threatening lawsuits, made it seem like Cash was saying that he would not be caught dead with a Black woman. But, he had said nothing of the sort. He didn't make a stand for interracial relationships the way Merle Haggard later did in "Irma Jackson" (the 1967 Supreme Court decision striking down bans on interracial marriages in *Loving v. Virginia* was still more than a year away), but Cash had, in fact, been serving up songs about race and racism on his "platters" for years. He just didn't make a big deal of it.[5]

The Johnny Cash Show episode featuring Odetta fits a longer pattern, one crucial to understanding Cash's intervention on questions of race and civil rights as part of his evolution in documenting the horrors of American history. If Bob Dylan and the Band went on a deep dive, exploring, in Greil Marcus's wonderful expression, an "old, weird America," Cash pursued what we might call the old, cruel America. Instead of singing about the likes of Tiny Montgomery, Mrs. Henry, and the Yazoo Street Scandal (as Dylan and the Band had), Cash filled his records with tales of chain gangs and lynchings, the betrayals and massacres of Native Americans, and the severity of American justice for the country's outlaws and prisoners. He went beyond the weird to the sinister. Cash's empathy was not so much rooted in solidarity as it was based on witnessing: documenting sorrows and struggle, making it possible for those normally kept out of view—the subjugated, the exploited, the marginalized—to be *seen*.

★

FOR A BOY growing up in Dyess, there could be almost no escape from the specter of racism. As an exclusively white outpost in a nearly majority Black county, Dyess was a pillar in the larger structure of Arkansas's systemic racism. No Black folk were allowed to apply for a home and farm in Dyess.[6] "Whites Only" and "Colored Only" signs, used to enforce local Jim Crow segregation laws, were unnecessary in Johnny Cash's hometown: "Whites Only" defined the whole community. "I would say that there was racism in Dyess," one of Cash's boyhood friends remembered. "No one wanted much to do with blacks." Just as it sometimes felt impossible to get the plow through the gluey, gumbo soil in a Dyess cotton patch, pulling oneself up out of the racist mire that in many ways defined life there proved to be no simple matter.[7]

Within Cash's family, one would have found no outspoken advocates for racial equality. On both of his parents' sides, he could trace his ancestry back just a couple of generations to men who fought for the Confederacy. Carrie Cash's grandfather, William Rivers, served in the 26th South Carolina Infantry, which fought one of the war's final battles at Petersburg, Virginia. Cash alleged in his second autobiography that his great-grandfather, Reuben Cash, owned a Georgia plantation destroyed during Sherman's March to the Sea, but Reuben owned neither a plantation nor enslaved peoples in Georgia (though census records show that in 1840, his father Moses enslaved five people). By the time of the Civil War, Reuben had already migrated to Arkansas where, "as a non-slaveholder too old for the draft," he may have, at most, participated in a skirmish or two as a reserve mustered to defend local interests. But, despite those facts, Cash self-identified throughout his life as a Southerner, and one with Confederate roots.[8]

There is real evidence of virulent racism running closer to Cash's branch on the family tree, too. His uncle, Dave, was likely a member of the Ku Klux Klan, and he reportedly coerced younger brother Ray (Cash's father) to go see the dead body of a Black man he had helped lynch. The scene shocked Ray, the story goes, but he said nothing. Long after Johnny became famous and wealthy, Ray maintained his own prejudices. As one biographer tells it, Cash once dropped by his father's house outside of Nashville with his daughters and a Jamaican boy who worked at their vacation home near Montego Bay. When they were leaving, and the kids said, "Goodbye, Grandpa," so did the Black boy, playfully. "No nigger's ever gonna call me Grandpa," Ray snapped. "In fact, I don't even like having niggers in my house!"* The episode embarrassed Cash, but he later reflected that it should not have surprised him. After all, he said, Ray "grew up in Arkansas," as if a patch of land on a map causes people to be racist.[9]

Long before Cash was born, of course, Arkansans had worked hard to build up and enforce racist policies in the state. One could point to numerous violent episodes carried out in the name of white supremacy, and still well remembered in the 1930s and 1940s, when J. R. Cash grew up there. None were more prominent than the Elaine Massacre, which started when Black veterans of the First World War dared to organize a tenant farmers' union there. Violence from the planters ensued, and soon mobs of white people from all over Arkansas and neighboring states descended on Phillips County, about one hundred miles south of Dyess, to kill hundreds of Black residents indiscriminately. Later, in the 1930s, when planters in Mississippi County and neighboring counties began mobilizing against the Southern Tenant Farmers Union, the memory of what happened in Elaine prompted organizers to move the union headquarters out of state, to Memphis.[10]

As the terrorizing of the STFU showed, frontier justice still reigned in Mississippi County. In a place where racial violence was common, it took little effort to raise a posse of night riders to intimidate union organizers with the threat of lynching. In fact, the most horrific lynching in the state's history had taken place in nearby

---

* Author's Note: I regret that some of the historical actors I write about in this book—including members of the Cash family—used racial epithets that are extremely offensive. But as a historian, I am obliged not to whitewash the racist language of the subjects I study and must provide a full accounting of the historical record.

Nodena in January 1921: a mob chained a Black man to a log, built a pile of gasoline-soaked leaves around him, and set him alight in front of his wife, children, and a crowd of more than five hundred. The sadistic scene brought national and international attention to Arkansas's culture of racial violence, but nothing came of it. The lynching was the first of seven in the state that year. Between 1883 and 1936, there were 284 lynchings in Arkansas. The state's last recorded one took place in Lepanto, the town just to the west of Dyess, where the Cashes were then in their second season of planting cotton along Road Three, also known as Lepanto Road.[11]

Even if young J. R. learned of such levels of violence only at a distance, he grew up witnessing other examples of state-sponsored coercion and abuse of Black Arkansans. Decades later, he sometimes mentioned onstage that he remembered seeing and hearing chain gangs coming in from working on the levees, talking and singing. Contrary to the Hollywood image of a chain gang—the *Cool Hand Luke* version—chain gangs throughout the South, and especially in Arkansas, were filled with Black men, often picked up on vagrancy charges in order to meet a labor need. This had been the Arkansas way since the period just after Reconstruction, when convict leasing—renting prisoners out to private enterprises—was a way of both filling the state's coffers and minimizing the state's costs of feeding and housing the imprisoned. Both the state and its lessees treated prisoners like they were disposable, like they could be worked to death and discarded. "One dies, get another," the prison overseers said. By the First World War, when convict leasing ended (it became too expensive), the state transitioned to chain gangs and prison farms. Chain gangs became so common that, in the middle of the Great Depression, approximately one hundred thousand prisoners worked on road gangs throughout the South. And chain gangs continued to be used on Arkansas roads into the 1950s. The visibility of men chained together at the ankles, doing manual labor under an unrelenting sun, served not so much to control the prisoners as it did to control the rest of the Black population. As Douglas

Blackmon pointed out in his Pulitzer Prize–winning study, the chain gang was "slavery by another name," and everyone who witnessed it knew it. Black people knew that if they got picked up on any minor charge, they could wind up on a chain gang the next day.[12]

The cruelties Johnny Cash saw in everyday life in Mississippi County were the same ones that John and Alan Lomax wrote so matter-of-factly about when contextualizing the origins of the prison work songs they recorded. Only on a chain gang or prison farm, they wrote in *Our Singing Country* (1949), could one find what they called the "sinful" (secular) music of African Americans "concentrated and preserved as nowhere else." The Lomaxes captured both the cruelty of inequality and the dignity of the unequal in equal measure—in ways that Cash himself would one day mimic.[13]

In his autobiographies, Cash barely touches on the question of race, and he certainly does not dwell for long on the racism he witnessed growing up. The most he has to say is that he saw his first race riot in Bremerhaven, Germany, while waiting for transport to Landsberg. "I had no problem sharing a barrack with blacks," he wrote, "and I couldn't imagine hating them so much that I was willing to wage a private war on them." His own views, born of the innocence of youth, he said, had not changed over the years. But that's a peculiar and rather feeble way of saying that one renounces racism. Maybe as late as the 1990s he still had not figured out how to discuss the subject in public; maybe it was easier, in a memoir, to smooth it over with platitudes; maybe his own past racism haunted him.[14]

Although Cash would become, in time, a very public advocate for Black equality, he carried some racist baggage of his own. His letters from Landsberg, written as a young man, provide the most damning evidence. "Honey, some Nigger got smart and I asked him to go outside and he was too yellow," Cash wrote to Vivian one night in April 1953, still wasted from the eleven beers he drank that evening. "He thought he could whup anybody in the club but he wouldn't even fight me. He's a yellow coon." The next day, presumably hungover, Cash wrote about the same incident in a separate letter. "I nearly had a fight with some smart Negro at the club, which wasn't my fault," he claimed, sober enough to remember to omit the slurs. "He came in the door pushing everybody, and walked down the aisle jigging when he walked, with his collar turned up," he wrote, drifting back toward racial caricature. The two got to pushing, but according to Cash, no fight resulted because the other guy would not step outside. "They're not so mean and tough when it comes to actually doing something." The drunken letter contains the most venomous expression of Cash's prejudice, but both letters traffic in harmful and racist stereotypes.

About a week later, Cash reported to Vivian of another near fight with a Black guy, this time amid too much drinking in Augsburg. The town was full of Army guys, so Cash and his friends took a bit of name-calling, all in good fun, until a "Negro" called Cash "a bus driver." Not so funny, apparently. "As soon as he saw I wasn't afraid of him, he started walking off, and I called him every name anyone has ever given a Negro," Cash reported to his sweetheart. "The further he walked away, the louder I yelled, calling him 'Coon,' 'Nigger,' 'Jig-a-boo,' and a few others. I yelled for a full 30 minutes that I could whip any Negro that walked on the face of the earth." Although he asked Vivian for forgiveness by the end of the letter, it seems more like he's asking absolution for his drinking again, rather than for his behavior toward his fellow American serviceman.[15]

Even taking into consideration the effect of his boozing on these two occasions, these letters offer clear proof of Cash's racism at twenty-one, and the unashamed manner in which he reported it to Vivian in the cold light of day suggests how just deeply engrained in him these racist attitudes were. But over the next ten years of his life, he worked, in fits and starts, to deprogram the Old South racism of his upbringing.

★

THE MEMPHIS TO which Cash moved following his discharge from the Air Force in 1954 was a lot like northeastern Arkansas. The city had built what wealth it had on the cotton trade and on the backs of slaves, and clung to its old ways by enforcing its racial hierarchy with violence. Memphis maintained a "plantation mentality" all the way through the Jim Crow era, not only in its worship of King Cotton, but also and especially in the way that the white power structure controlled the Black population. This permeated everything from seemingly inconsequential chamber of commerce boosterism to the franchise. For example, the only way African Americans could participate in the annual Cotton Carnival—a kind of cotton-themed Mardi Gras—was if they portrayed slaves or work animals; meanwhile, the Democratic Party, led by Edward Hull Crump, a cartoonish figure who looked like the charlatan behind the curtain in *The Wizard of Oz*, paid poll taxes for Black voters only so they could register and cast ballots for Democrats. In 1940, when those Black voters balked at this arrangement, Crump and Mayor Walter Chandler unleashed a three-month "Reign of Terror," sending police to occupy Beale Street and to stop, search, and arrest Black residents under the cover of supposedly "cleaning up Memphis."[16]

As it happens, Cash arrived in Memphis just after Crump died and in time to witness the emergence of new civil rights leaders in the city. Black voter registration increased dramatically in the next six years, and so did civil rights organizing. Notably, protests against the public library system—which kept Black Memphians out of the city's main library and limited them to smaller, less well stocked branches—began in 1957, the same year that mobs of white Arkansans and segregationists from all over the South tried to prevent nine Black students from entering Central High School in Little Rock. As Cash recorded hit songs at Sun Studio, Memphis built the largest NAACP branch in the South.[17]

Living and working in Memphis against this backdrop shifted something in Johnny Cash. For one thing, with nearly half of Memphis's population being Black, he encountered more Black culture than he ever had. Cash had never before lived or worked anyplace where, in the course of the day, he encountered only Black people, as he did in Memphis. He began to see shared cultural experiences: the radio was a lifeline for Black folks, just like it had been for Cash while growing up in Dyess. Neighborhoods like Orange Mound were abuzz with the sounds of WDIA, a pioneering Memphis station (where a young B. B. King worked as a DJ), and KWEM out of West Memphis, Arkansas, both of which played almost nothing but so-called race records.

One day, as he went house to house hawking appliances in Orange Mound, Cash came across an old man playing banjo on his front porch. The guy's virtuosic picking impressed Cash, who may have been under the mistaken impression, still common at the time, that the banjo originated as an Appalachian instrument, played primarily by white musicians like Earl Scruggs—when, in fact, it was brought to the Americas by enslaved people taken from Africa. The old man was Gus Cannon, who had been recorded by none other than Ralph Peer, the man who first recorded the Carter Family and Jimmie Rodgers, in 1927 in Bristol, Tennessee. Soon Cash was making a habit of ending his days on Cannon's porch, sometimes playing guitar and singing along with him, but mostly just basking in the wisdom and experience of a country blues legend.[18]

During this same time, Cash spent some of what little money he got from the government each month (and, later, his Sun royalty earnings) on records at a Beale Street shop called Home of the Blues. As he recounted in his Rock and Roll Hall of Fame induction speech more than forty years later, Cash not only bought Hank Williams, Carter Family, and Hank Snow records at Home of the Blues, but he also picked up gospel records by Mahalia Jackson and the Golden Gate Quartet, and blues records by Howlin' Wolf, Robert Johnson, Sister Rosetta Tharpe, Muddy Waters, Papa John Creach, Pink Anderson, and others. He no doubt bought those first Odetta records there and, most important, he claimed that Home of the Blues is where he found *Blues in the Mississippi Night*, an LP of "Authentic Field Recordings of Negro Folk Music" compiled by Alan Lomax. These were all his "earliest heroes," and they influenced his writing on songs like "Big River" and "Get Rhythm." He loved the place so much, he recorded "Home of the Blues" as one of his last singles on Sun.[19]

The story of Cash's fantastic success on Sun Records from 1955 to 1958 is so reified in the history of American music that it has obscured the way Memphis transformed Cash from a poor Arkansas farm boy and Air Force veteran into a sophisticated social observer interested primarily in, as he said, "documenting life in our country, in our time and in earlier times." By the time he departed from Memphis in 1958, heading out to California, he had moved a long way from "So Doggone Lonesome." This is not to diminish the importance of that familiar Sun Records story: in those four years, Cash put out the records that established him as a distinctive voice in country music and, given the millions of records he sold, as a crossover threat, embraced by rock and pop fans, too. But in between recording those singles, touring alongside Elvis, playing the *Hayride* and the *Opry*, and starting a family, Cash's worldview changed in ways that defined his work over the coming decade. As he matured as an artist, he gravitated to the music of others who were, like him, interested in social realities, who wanted to tell authentic stories of their land, past and present. Merle Travis's *Folk Songs of the Hills* relayed stories of the exploited working class, while Odetta's early records explored the experience of exploited Black labor. And Alan Lomax's *Blues in the Mississippi Night* captured, as almost no audio recording ever had, the horrors of the American racial caste system.

Cash made his break from Sun in 1958 not so much because Sam Phillips would not let him record a gospel record, nor because he did not give him enough attention (or skimmed on royalties), as is usually reported; Cash left because during his time in Memphis, he had outgrown Sun intellectually. Against the backdrop of an unfolding civil rights movement, Cash listened to WDIA and KWEM, he talked and played with Gus Cannon, and he breathed in all those records he bought at Home of the Blues. The convergence of these encounters with the Black experience not only changed the way he saw the world, it changed the way he saw himself as an artist in this world and what he saw as an artist's responsibilities to his times. Cash could not hope to equal the sociological power and authority of the music he loved by just recording one hit single after another for Sun. His work needed to add up to something more substantial. The historical moment demanded it. Thus, when Don Law—the man who had recorded not only country western stars Gene Autry and Bob Wills but also, incredibly, blues guitarist Robert Johnson—came calling from Columbia in 1957, promising him creative freedom, Cash did not hesitate to jump ship. Starting in the summer of 1958, he began recording for Columbia. Within a year, the label had put out three Cash records: *The Fabulous Johnny Cash*, *Hymns by Johnny Cash*, and *Songs of Our Soil*, the last of which constituted his first gesture toward a concept album.

Johnny Cash's shift toward making concept albums for Columbia in the early 1960s reflected a number of recent influences. The first came from Merle Travis's *Folk Songs of the Hills*, which had come out in a 78 rpm set in 1947, but which Capitol Records reissued as an LP in 1957. As it happened, Cash had been a longtime fan of Travis's and, in the same year that *Folk Songs* was reissued, he got to know the man himself when he played on the *Town Hall Party* television show in Los Angeles. A member of the show's regular cast, along with singing cowboy Tex Ritter, Travis hit it off with Cash, leading to a long association that culminated in Travis working for Cash on *The Johnny Cash Show*.

The influence of *Folk Songs of the Hills* on Cash is obvious: the record included versions of "John Henry," "Dark as a Dungeon," "Nine Pound Hammer," "Sixteen Tons," and "I Am a Pilgrim"— all songs that Cash himself later covered. More consequentially, the record featured Travis giving an avuncular spoken introduction to each track, highlighting its folk history before playing the song. Cash must have been inspired by this model because, before long, he started to think of ways to take listeners into the heart of the American past himself.

On *Songs of Our Soil*, Cash experimented, taking his first steps toward following Travis's example by recording a somewhat vaguely themed "folk ballads" album. It's a better LP than some give it credit for; Cash wrote some of the songs from his own personal experience growing up in Dyess. The one that has endured the longest, "Five Feet High and Rising," which recounts his family's experience in the 1937 flood, and "The Man on the Hill" reflect the precarity of farm life as Cash knew it. In contrast, in "Hank and Joe and Me" and "Old Apache Squaw," Cash imagined the hardships of others living at the margins. The latter is less about the elderly woman than about the difficulties her people have faced over many "lean years" marked by too many hungry children, and too many warriors going off to die. In his own song, "The Caretaker," about a cemetery worker who sees "hate and greed and jealousy" behind mourners' grief and vulnerability, and on the gospel tune "It Could Be You," Cash essentially pleads with listeners to think beyond themselves, to look out for those who—as in "The Man on the Hill" and "Old Apache Squaw"—are struggling.

Taken as a whole, *Songs of Our Soil* comes off as a noble effort, even if not all of the tracks are, in fact, songs of the soil. Unlike his Sun LPs, which were mostly collections of singles, and his first two Columbia records, *Songs of Our Soil* was multivalent; it braided the hard lives of workers and Native peoples, and in "It Could Be You," centered on a religious perspective based on empathy, tying the other songs together. Cash's ambitions may not have been immediately clear to the 1959 listener, but the album hinted at a new artistic direction. Whether he knew it or not, he was beginning to follow in the footsteps of no less than Walt Whitman. "Agonies are one of my changes of garments," Whitman famously wrote in "Song of Myself." "I do not ask the wounded person how he feels/I myself become the wounded person/My hurts turn livid upon me as I lean on a cane and observe." Over the coming years, Cash's empathy for his subjects found him, more often than not, observing closely the hardship of others and becoming "the wounded person" on his records.[20]

Cash's focus sharpened once he listened to *Blues in the Mississippi Night*. He received the LP, along with a number of other folk and blues records, as a gift from Columbia's president, Goddard Lieberson, and by all accounts could not stop listening to it.[21] Over the years, Cash repeatedly told interviewers it was his "all-time favorite album," that he still listened to it thirty, forty years after its 1959 release. Cash had already discovered other recordings made by John and Alan Lomax—like their historic recordings of Leadbelly (Huddie Ledbetter)—but *Blues in the Mississippi Night* and Lomax's seven LP *Southern Folk Heritage Series*, released the following year, changed him as an artist and citizen.[22]

Everything about *Blues in the Mississippi Night* bears witness to a deeply engrained culture of racial coercion and violence. The original cover image of a Mississippi riverboat cruising at dusk is somber, solitary, and almost ghostly. Alan Lomax positioned it as "authentic field recordings" of three blues musicians speaking freely and spontaneously about the origins of the blues and illustrating their points with snippets of song. At the outset, one of them dismisses the idea that the blues is something a man gets because of a woman; the blues grew out of deep pain—out of slavery—and has evolved to be about all manner of "troubles." But this is just the preamble. The balance of the album is a matter-of-fact indictment of a culture of white supremacy, a by-product of which is the blues. It's one of the most explosive American recordings ever produced—dangerous enough that the three bluesmen we hear, Memphis Slim, Big Bill Broonzy, and Sonny Boy Williamson, did not want Lomax to release it out of fear for their families' safety. Only when Lomax agreed to use the pseudonyms Leroy, Natchez, and Sib did the record get made.[23]

To Johnny Cash, *Blues in the Mississippi Night*'s appeal lay in the authenticity of the three men's voices and the delivery of their stories. As Leroy and Natchez trade first and secondhand stories of racial abuse, violence, and murder on Side One, it becomes clear that both have spent time working in levee camps and on prison farms (probably as the victims of racist vagrancy laws). They recount being ripped off by the levee camp bosses, being swindled at the company store, and being trapped in debt, just like sharecroppers who were routinely cheated out of earnings because planters did the weighing and the "figuring." If a worker died in the field, on the levee, or down at a barrelhouse at night, Leroy says, the general attitude was "if you kill a nigger, I'll hire another one." A Black man "didn't mean no more to a white man than a mule," Natchez says. When the discussion changes to chain gangs, Natchez recalls that although a prisoner might sometimes be chained to a big heavy ball, at other times, he might be chained to a stake in the ground. "They let him work till he get out to the length of that rope or that chain or whatsoever they have to him," he remembers, and "they then pull that stake up and put him to another stake." At Cummins prison farm in Arkansas, meanwhile, Leroy reports that "trusties," prisoners doing fifty- to one-hundred-year sentences, served as armed guards who whipped prisoners with cat-o'-nine-tails. To the world outside Delta prison camps, such horrors were virtually unknown—but it was a world Cash had glimpsed, too. Yet the album filled in gaps that he, as a white boy, could never have known.

In perhaps the record's most shocking tale—in an album full of stomach-churning atrocities—Natchez recounts the story of his uncle's lynching. It started when his sharecropper uncle beat up a planter who demanded that his uncle's pregnant wife work in the fields. When a posse came to get him, Natchez's uncle shot at least four of them, and he and his family got away. But not for long. Eventually, a mob, some fifty to sixty men, tracked him down and lynched him—"all because he didn't want his wife to work out on the plantation." At this point, the three begin playing the little-known "Another Man Done Gone."

Although the three men, at times, describe the blues as "a kind of revenge," because the singing of a song could be seen as "signifying," singing in code, so that the person singing could say things about the boss that they could not get away with otherwise, that analysis focuses on the form, not the origins, of the blues. As Leroy summarizes, the blues grows out of "your experience, and things you want to do, or want to know." It comes from "things that have really happened to you," Natchez agrees.

That insight meant a lot to Johnny Cash. His public citizenship over the next decade came as an extension of this understanding of the blues. His empathy originated, like the blues, with the promptings of his own personal experience, but where he did not bear witness directly, he researched his subjects so that he could more authentically capture their experience. He wanted to make albums that, like *Blues in the Mississippi Night*, could collapse the distances between lives, setting listeners in circumstances so distinct from their own that to be exposed to them—even if only for the forty-five minutes of a record—might change the way they saw the world. He wanted to privilege "voices that weren't commonly heard at the time—voices that were ignored or even suppressed in the entertainment media, not to mention the political and educational establishments."[24]

In short, he wanted to make what other people called "folk" records. Consequently, Cash began moving toward the social realism that he admired in Leadbelly, the Lomax recordings, and Odetta. He still loved Hank Williams, Jimmie Rodgers, and the Carter Family, but none of their recordings seized him in 1959 like *Blues in the Mississippi Night* did. On Cash's concept albums of the early 1960s, from *Ride This Train* to *Blood, Sweat and Tears* to *Bitter Tears*, he said that he simply aimed to document American life, past and present. "I was trying to write about history *so that people could understand what was going on* [italics added]." Like Odetta, who said that she got into folk music to learn "the history we were not being taught in school," Cash had devoted himself to that history. To teach history, in song, through the real experiences of ordinary Americans, to validate those experiences by elevating them to a large audience, served a political function.[25]

Around this same time, as Cash became more interested in this kind of songwriting, he also became increasingly dependent on drugs, especially amphetamines, ostensibly to sustain him through nearly three hundred concert appearances a year. But just as much, it's clear that he self-medicated to deal with the still inescapable depression he'd experienced since Jack's death. Either way, the effects on his work and life were profound. Between 1960 and 1966, Cash lost weight, destroyed his voice, and became increasingly erratic and unreliable, sometimes unable to perform or missing in action. At home, too, he turned into an absentee father and husband. And yet, in his frequently drug-addled state, he became an obsessive researcher, particularly on the subjects that formed the basis of his concept albums. "He had an unquenchable desire for knowledge," his manager, Saul Holiff, said of Cash in this period. The drugs didn't seem to affect Cash's "total recall," at least not when it came to realizing these recording projects.[26]

AMONG CRITICS AND fans, the albums that Cash recorded in the early to mid-1960s are not usually considered among his best, yet they were vitally important in the development of his artistic and political persona. Although the reputation of *Bitter Tears* has grown in recent years, at the time it was made, it sold no better than the others, and it was, for a long time, seen as just one chapter in a period of Cash's career associated with drug use and declining sales. But Cash simply could not have become the political artist we associate with the live prison records and the television show—a bold public citizen in a time of national polarization—had he not first immersed himself in the making of *Ride This Train, Blood, Sweat and Tears*, and *Bitter Tears*.

On *Ride This Train*, Cash married the influence of Merle Travis's *Folk Songs of the Hills* with *Blues in the Mississippi Night*. The album's subtitle is "A Stirring Travelogue of America in Song and Story," declaring it a tour charting American progress across the country. On the album jacket, Cash is dressed as a cowboy, or maybe an outlaw, sporting a couple of days' stubble, standing high on a western bluff, with a train rattling by in the background below. He looks ridiculous, staring into the camera, holding a six-shooter, as if posing in a frontier-adventure photo booth. The cheesy album cover contains none of the mystery of, say, the *Blues in the Mississippi Night* cover. Although it is a single LP record, with only two sides, it came in a gatefold cover featuring laudatory essays by Tex Ritter and Merle Travis (both of whom wrote songs for the album). The record itself begins with over three minutes of narration, as Cash name-checks more than a dozen places in the United States, most featuring Native names. As he summons the listener to "ride this train" across this "strange, wonderful land," we go back in time, to when European settlers first came to the Americas. He points out that there were millions of people already living here, in teepees, along rivers, hunting deer and buffalo. "And it's with a little regret that I think of how I pushed 'em back and crowded 'em out," to take their land, he says, but the sentiment is fleeting. Cash's thinking had not yet evolved to the point when, in 1965, he recorded an entire album about the plight of Native peoples. In this first effort, he moves on quickly, reciting the names of more than fifty Native tribes, as if to just get it on record.

The rest of the album is devoted to songs that take listeners to various parts of the country—to Kentucky coal-mining country, to Oregon timber-cutting country, to Cajun country on Lake Ponchartrain—exploring subjects, he said, "not taught in schools." In narration that sounds more authoritative than Merle Travis's conversational song introductions, Cash tried to bring listeners to these places, getting them to imagine certain scenes and characters. Most of these songs illustrate Cash's continued fascination with the experience of people who, like him, knew working-class struggle. But the most important political songs on the album are "Going to Memphis" and "Boss Jack," which provide clues to his fitful thinking about race.

The first song Cash brought into the studio for the *Ride This Train* album, "Going to Memphis," came from *Blues in the Mississippi Night*. Cash earned a writing credit by transforming key details from Leroy and Natchez's banter into lyrics. Leroy and Natchez described how prisoners sang about imagining where they would go when prisoners got parole, and Cash, in character, presents himself as narrating from a chain gang. Cash's narrator says that he had gotten into a bar fight in Natchez (a nod to one of his three guides on *Blues in the Mississippi Night*), and the next thing he knew, he is working a chain gang where prisoners were whipped like beasts of burden. In a line taken directly from the source album's dialogue, Cash's narrator says that if you complain at all, the guards would unchain you, hoping they would get to shoot you when you ran. As he begins singing, we hear the chain gang grunting and hammering, as if recreating some of Alan Lomax's field recordings of prisoners, with background talk meant to evoke Black prisoners. Cash sings how the captain broke his hand for drinking water from a "Mr. Prince Albert can," another reference to Leroy and Natchez, who joked that the racists in the South would not allow Black men to ask merely for "Prince Albert" tobacco (in order to show proper deference, they had to ask for "*Mr. Prince Albert*"). Cash weaves in more little tidbits from the original album's dialogue—mentioning Leroy, prisoners living off polk salad, card sharks taking money, and prisoners standing on a dead man's body to shoot craps—to transform the raw blues song heard on the Lomax recording into a vivid representation of a world unknown to the average Johnny Cash fan still listening to "Ballad of a Teenage Queen." "Going to Memphis" marked the emergence of Cash's fascination with chain gangs and other prison songs, and except for some faux prison dialogue that borders on caricature, it is remarkably successful at evoking the world described by Leroy, Natchez, and Sib. In taking an obscure prison holler, previously heard only on field recordings, and putting it out as a Columbia Records single, and then performing it on the *Grand Ole Opry*, Cash acted deliberately—not only to identify himself with a documentary form, as on the rest of the LP, but to say something about race for the first time.

But, then, two songs after "Going to Memphis," Cash scrambled any idea that he fully empathized with the Black experience with Tex Ritter's tune, "Boss Jack." The introduction to "Boss Jack" begins with Cash telling us that now we are riding this train to Dyess, Arkansas, where the cotton land is now so poor, the best one could hope for is "fair-to-middlin'"—which isn't good enough, he says. In the past, however, Cash's narrator says he once owned a plantation of six hundred acres where, in 1855, he had a bumper crop. "I had the best bunch of slaves you ever saw, and I treated 'em right," he claims without any trace of irony. Even after the Civil War and emancipation, he says, a lot of the freed slaves stayed with this apparently kind slave master. One day before the war, he found one of his slaves, Old Uncle Moses, sitting on a cotton sack memorizing a song that had come to him in the fields. It turns out that this gentle, elderly enslaved man had written "Swing Low, Sweet Chariot" in his mind, and now needed to commit it to memory.[27] Moses accepts that he needs to be punished for not being accounted for by sunset, but Jack, our narrator, takes Moses out of the fields and lets him fiddle around the house, where he not only sang "Swing Low" but another that made the slave master "awful proud," called "Boss Jack." Cash then sings a bizarrely upbeat song from the perspective of slaves who are so grateful for their compassionate master, Boss Jack.

There's no justification for releasing a song that argues in favor of the slaveholding class and its paternalism. But it's even more egregious considering the historical moment in which Cash recorded the song, on February 15, 1960, in Columbia's Nashville studios. Two days before, students in Nashville had led sit-ins at the lunch counters of three major department stores downtown. They had organized the protests as part of a wider civil rights initiative that started in Greensboro, North Carolina, to call attention to department store and drug store chains that were happy to take money from Black shoppers, but would not allow them to sit at a lunch counter for a hamburger or a cup of coffee. On that first day of protests, the students managed to shut down the lunch counters in each store for at least two hours, generating tremendous media attention. Cash and producer Don Law could not have been unaware of those sit-ins when they recorded "Boss Jack." One imagines that the same Johnny Cash who sought to document the cruelties of chain gangs and prison farms, who loved to listen to his Odetta records, who admired his blues mentor, Gus Cannon—*that* Johnny Cash—would have been sympathetic with any Black Nashvillian who wanted equal access to a cup of coffee.

In the following weeks, as the sit-ins grew, and as racists beat up the students at the lunch counters, the nation's attention turned to Nashville. The American public saw police arresting nonviolent protesters and racist thugs in seemingly equal number. By the end of March, CBS, the parent company of Columbia Records, produced a television documentary, "Anatomy of a Demonstration," about the Nashville sit-ins. In April, someone bombed the home of Black attorney, city councilman, and civil rights activist Z. Alexander Looby. The subsequent silent, peaceful march through the streets of Nashville to confront Mayor Ben West on the steps of city hall, made national news. Fisk University student Diane Nash got West to acknowledge that it was not right for a store to deny its customers equal service simply because of the color of their skin. All of this happened a stone's throw from Music Row, the *Opry*, and Ernest Tubb Record Shop—vital organs in the body of country music.

When Cash recorded "Boss Jack" in Nashville in February, he likely felt at home among so many in the city who considered themselves political "moderates," adherents to a long-standing culture of etiquette called "the Nashville Way." As one historian has argued, by declaring Nashville a "moderate city," the city's leaders emphasized "manners, decorum, and a hypersensitive avoidance of civic unrest." Mayor West famously had declared, "In Nashville, we don't have race relations, we have human relations!" but the sit-ins exposed such pronouncements as total fantasy. Moderate Nashvillians opposed what they saw as extremism—whether from the Klan or from Black Americans breaking the segregation laws—more than they were in favor of any solution. They wanted only that citizens behave with "civility," and in the case of Black folk, that meant upholding rules set down to enforce white supremacy. Johnny Cash probably did not think so hard about where, exactly, he stood on civil rights in 1960, but maybe this culture of so-called moderation accounts for Cash's recording of "Boss Jack"—or at least his failure to pull it from the album in a season of upheaval.[28]

Ride This Train came out in September 1960, some months after the violence in Nashville, when any segregationists among Cash's fans may have heard "Boss Jack" as a signal—a dog whistle, we would say today—that he shared their ideas about race. There were millions of Americans who still defended the Confederacy, and among them were country music fans and artists. As late as 1960, the country music star Jimmie Davis (who wrote "You Are My Sunshine") won reelection as governor of Louisiana on a crusading segregationist platform. Davis's resistance to the United States Supreme Court's school desegregation orders included trying to get Black parents to leave the state by striking 2,300 Black children off the state's Aid to Families with Dependent Children program. Davis is now in the Country Music Hall of Fame. Another Hall of Fame member, Roy Acuff, campaigned for Jack Owen, a segregationist candidate for governor of Alabama. Minnie Pearl, on the other hand, appeared at several George Wallace for Governor rallies in 1958, when voters in Alabama still considered the famously avowed segregationist Wallace too "soft" on race; they elected John Patterson, a more strident segregationist, instead. Most everyone else in country music came to the *Opry*, sang to the folks in the Confederate Gallery, and never said a word in public about civil rights.[29]

Sometime between 1960 and 1962, Cash's views on race sharpened; he devoted almost an entire album to documenting the cruelties of racism, a choice he never articulated or reflected on publicly. In retrospect, it seems clear that even he didn't fully appreciate how groundbreaking the work was, as he tried to wrestle with the nation's wretched legacy of white supremacy. He became a conduit for social realism, for documenting some of the most brutal structures of racism he saw around him and about which he learned so much from his Black idols, even if he never stepped to the front lines of the nearest civil rights march.

Any number of factors may have played a role in Cash's transformation into an overlooked civil rights artist. Since at least his time in Memphis, when he met Gus Cannon and began studying African American folk music, Cash had been, in a sense, preparing for this project. In 1960 and 1961, the civil rights movement rarely moved from the nation's headlines; Cash surely began to associate the movement's demands with the suffering he learned about in folk music—which dovetailed with the horrors of racism he had witnessed, heard about, and did not question while growing up in Arkansas.

It wouldn't have taken a lot of imagination to see how Black suffering and the struggle for Black freedom were intertwined. In the spring of 1961, the Congress of Racial Equality (CORE), organized the Freedom Rides on interstate buses throughout the South. John Lewis, one of the Nashville student sit-in leaders, was among the riders. When interracial groups of CORE activists rolled into Southern cities, Klan thugs reacted with spasms of violence in bus stations and on the highways. A mob of racists descended on Freedom Riders, firebombing one of the buses outside of Anniston, Alabama, while another mob beat them savagely in Birmingham, sending some to the hospital. When more attacks followed in Montgomery, President Kennedy finally intervened. The president negotiated with the governors of Alabama and Mississippi to provide safe passage of the Freedom Riders to Jackson, where he allowed local police to arrest them for disturbing the peace. Over the spring and summer of 1961, hundreds of Freedom Riders arrived in Jackson, were arrested, and were sentenced to up to two months in prison in places like Parchman Farm, a maximum security facility, where Alan Lomax had made some of the prison field recordings that fascinated Johnny Cash.

Caught in the wake of wave after wave of civil rights campaigns—and the shocking paroxysms of violent reaction that inevitably followed—Cash's interest in African American folk music only deepened. He bought the *Southern Folk Heritage Series* (1960), a seven-LP collection of field recordings made by Lomax that covered both white and Black spirituals, Appalachian bluegrass, and the blues (recorded mostly in Arkansas and Mississippi), including a few prison recordings from Lambert and Parchman Farms. As with *Blues in the Mississippi Night*, Cash played the set constantly on his portable record player—so much that he could name the titles of every song on each album, in order. Although Cash immersed himself in all kinds of folk music in the early 1960s—"both the authentic songs from various periods and areas of American life" (like the *Southern Folk Heritage Series*) and newer "folk revival" stuff—in 1962, he gravitated mostly toward what he called the "authentic." He became friends with Greenwich Village folkies like Ed McCurdy (who wrote "Last Night I Had the Strangest Dream") and Peter La Farge (with whom he would later collaborate on *Bitter Tears*) following his dreadful Carnegie Hall debut in May 1962 (his voice shot from taking too much speed), and Bob Dylan's debut album made an enormous impression on him. Over these two years he came to understand the link between folk music and the civil rights movement, as evident in the work of Guy Carawan, who did more than anyone to revise "We Shall Overcome" as a civil rights anthem and had produced albums on the Nashville sit-in movement and, with Alan Lomax, the Albany movement.[30]

But when Johnny Cash turned his artistic gaze toward race and civil rights, he did not follow the example of Carawan and others who sang "freedom songs." He kept to the models of Lomax and Odetta, Leadbelly, and even Harry Belafonte by recording songs that documented the distinctively American architecture of white supremacy. To examine the timing of this shift in Cash's work is to see a gradual but thorough engagement with the Black working class and Black prisoners, the men who, as Leroy and Natchez said, sang the blues as a kind of revenge. Cash recorded "I'm Free from the Chain Gang Now," a song mostly associated with Jimmie Rodgers, in July 1961. In some ways, it picks up from "Going to Memphis," but it is more upbeat, as the narrator muses about getting out of prison, returning home to his love. Similarly, Cash recorded Leadbelly's "In Them Old Cottonfields Back Home," though his version conveys little of the pathos put into the song by either Leadbelly or Odetta, on her first record. Both songs appeared on *The Sound of Johnny Cash* LP, released in August 1962, by which time Cash had already recorded another Leadbelly song, "Pick a Bale of Cotton," and released it as a single. In the case of both, it made sense that Cash, himself a former cotton picker, could relate to Leadbelly's songs. In fact, he might have considered recording either one for *Ride This Train* or *Songs of Our Soil*, but maybe it took the historical moment post–Freedom Rides to summon them to vinyl. With these songs, Cash is declaring a working-class solidarity and a vision of racial equality—everyone suffers equally in a cotton patch, in a railroad tunnel, or on a chain gang.

In July and August, Cash recorded a batch of songs that became the basis for *Blood, Sweat and Tears*, a record many regard as merely a concept album about working people. But *Blood, Sweat and Tears* is a concept album about race in America, about the violent enforcement of racial hierarchies in America. It is the one great record made in support of Black lives by a country music star, even if almost everyone missed its message when it was released. To be fair, when we think of a civil rights album, we think of those freedom songs. If Cash had just recorded his own interpretation of Odetta's "Freedom Trilogy" or, like Pete Seeger, brought news of the civil rights movement in song to a live audience, getting them to sing along on "If You Miss Me at the Back of the Bus," "Keep Your Eyes on the Prize," and "I Ain't Scared of Your Jail," it would have been much easier to label Cash as an activist artist, to *see* the work he was doing. But as John Lomax once argued, folk music could "provide ten thousand bridges across which men of all nations may stride to say 'You are my brother.'" To put down on record—both vinyl and historical— evidence of the shameful, despicable practices of white bosses against Black men and their families made for a bridge of understanding that better suited Cash's temperament than the freedom songs. On *Blood, Sweat and Tears*, he sings of racial bondage, of racial violence, of racist murder. He recorded these songs not to inspire activists so much as to confront his mostly white listeners with the shocking, documented brutality their silence made possible. His civil rights work, if we can call it that, is complementary; he stands as witness.[31]

Side One of *Blood, Sweat and Tears* possesses such cumulative power, rooted in violence, that it is hard to listen to it twice in a row. One really needs to flip the record to the other side to find some relief, even if it is in limited supply on Side Two. Cash most likely learned original versions of all three of the songs on Side One— "The Legend of John Henry's Hammer," "Tell Him I'm Gone," and "Another Man Done Gone"—from Lomax recordings (though, in the case of "John Henry," there were dozens of versions out there already). But, in each case, Cash arranged, adapted, and added his own lyrics.

Cash begins the album with an eight-minute version of "John Henry," following in a grand tradition of interpreting and rein- terpreting the song about the steel-drivin' man.[32] In Merle Travis's down-home introduction to the song on *Folk Songs of the Hills*, he says that people from different parts of the country—coal miners in Kentucky, ironworkers in Birmingham, railroad workers out West—have tried to claim John Henry. "I don't know myself where in the world John Henry came from," he says as he begins singing, and it is possible that, like a lot of white Southerners, he assumed that John Henry was white. By the time Cash considered recording "John Henry," his identity as a Black working man, if not a Black convict, was well known. In *Our Singing Country*, the Lomaxes described the "ballad of John Henry, the Negro steel-drivin' man" as "probably America's greatest single piece of folk lore." Later, in the liner notes to *Blue Ridge Mountain Music*, one of the seven LPs in the *Southern Folk Heritage Series* that Cash committed to memory, Alan Lomax repeats that the Mountain Ramblers' version of the song tells the story of "the Negro tunnel worker . . . who drove the steam drill down in a contest of the 'flesh against the steam.'" Years later, when Cash made a television program called *Ridin' the Rails* (1974), he devoted two segments of his history of the railroad to honoring the work of Black men—showing gandy dancers and section men laying track, and John Henry himself (played by a Black actor) swinging a hammer. There is no question that Cash understood in 1962, as he sang about John Henry, he was singing about a Black man. We know today that John Henry was a real man, pushed into convict labor on a thin charge, the way so many Black men were in the years after the Civil War, who died on the job (though not before driving more steel than the steam drill). But even by 1962 there had been plenty of representations of John Henry wearing a ball and chain—enough that Cash, poring over Library of Congress recordings, could not have missed it.[33]

Try listening to several versions of "John Henry" in a row—particularly Merle Travis's upbeat picking rendition, Odetta's more somber version, and Cash's treatment at the end—to get a sense of how varied the interpretations of the song can be. At the time that

Cash recorded the song, he was in the unyielding clutch of his drug addiction. Marshall Grant remembered him sitting on the floor banging pieces of rolled steel together to get the sound of the hammer hitting; he was so high he beat his hands bloody, apparently feeling no pain. In spite of his condition, his "John Henry" sounds like a continuation of the work he did on *Ride This Train*—not only because he again mimicked sounds from the field, as if to make it seem more authentic, but because in his delivery he is as much a narrator as a singer. But Cash doesn't sound squeaky clean, the way Merle Travis drifts into folk-crooner territory; instead, Cash builds momentum in the song, the way Odetta does, as the story reaches the part about the race between John Henry and the steam drill. Although Cash's rendition of "John Henry" on *Blood, Sweat and Tears* is undermined somewhat by the shape he was in when he recorded it (the editing together of two separately recorded parts is obvious), the song became a standard part of his show, so that by the time he recorded it again at Folsom prison, it had to be considered one of his best.[34]

Cash follows "The Legend of John Henry's Hammer" with "Tell Him I'm Gone," a retitled, rewritten version of Leadbelly's "Take This Hammer." Just as a chef who changes more than three things in a recipe can claim the recipe as his own, Cash must have figured that he altered enough of the lyrics to justify a new title. The Lomaxes' 1942 recording of Leadbelly singing "Take This Hammer" is pretty straightforward. It is the tale of a man fleeing from the chain gang, telling the new guy to whom he is giving his hammer to pass along a message to the boss, the captain: "Tell him I'm gone." He doesn't say much about why he is leaving except that he no longer wants "cornbread and molasses" because, he says, "it hurts my pride." In fact, the lyrics published by the Lomaxes in *Our Singing Country* included additional lines such as "Cap'n called me a nappy-headed devil" and "I don't want no cold iron shackles, around my legs, around my legs," giving a clearer sense of the singer's motives. When

Odetta recorded the song live, at the Gate of Horn club in Chicago in 1957, she basically used Leadbelly's version but reintroduced the "cold, iron shackles" line, too, which surely helped the audience better see the scene. Perhaps emboldened by Odetta's edits, Cash adds several lines to the song that make the captain more violent, more menacing. There is nothing about the lousy cornbread hurting his pride. He even dropped the "cold, iron shackles" from Odetta's rendition. Instead, Cash's prisoner escapes from the chain gang because he cannot take the "kicks and whipping." He says the captain called him "a hard-headed devil" (a revision of the "nappy-headed devil" line recorded by the Lomaxes), but since that is not his name, he is leaving. In all the previous interpretations of the song, it is pretty clear that the convict is confident that he is going to find freedom, but Cash introduces a degree of uncertainty, saying that if the captain ever catches him, "he gonna shoot me down" with his big gun, "about a .99 caliber." (This, too, is a modification of a line published by the Lomaxes—"Cap'n got a big gun, an' he try to play bad"—which made it into no other recorded versions.) When Cash sings "about a .99 caliber" the first time, he lets out a "whooooa," as if the character is both impressed with and deathly afraid of that gun. The howl sounds almost unhinged, desperate, and certainly not confident—like he knows he is risking his life. Taken together, the new lyrics describe an overseer who, as Cash said in "Going to Memphis," whips convicts like mules, taunts them with names, and has the capacity, thanks to his big gun, to snuff out a convict's life. As the saying went, "One dies, get another."[35]

"Another Man Done Gone," the third and final song on the first side of *Blood, Sweat and Tears*, effectively tells us what happened to the convict who fled the chain gang in the previous song. The Lomaxes first recorded the song in 1948, as sung by a Livingston, Alabama, dishwasher named Vera Hall. Unlike "Tell Him I'm Gone," which is narrated by the convict, "Another Man Done Gone" is told from the perspective of a witness to a crime involving the convict.

In Hall's version, it is the convict who committed the crime, but in Cash's version the convict is the victim. Hall sings that although she does not know the name of the man done gone, she could see that he came from the "county farm" and had a "long chain on." The most important line, in comparing Hall's original version to later renditions by other artists, including Cash, is that she says, "He killed another man." The man done gone is a killer who, though imprisoned and on a chain gang, has now killed again and is on the run. "I don't know where he's gone," she sings at the end. Odetta recorded "Another Man Done Gone" for her second, classic LP, *Odetta Sings Ballads and Blues* (1957), a collection of Lomaxian proportions, with some songs drawn from their book *Our Singing Country*. But instead of singing "He killed another man," Odetta changed it to "*They* killed another man," and she dropped the line about not knowing where he has gone; it's apparent that in this rendition our narrator knows that the man being "done gone" means he is dead, killed by those who chased him from the county farm or the levee or wherever else they may have worked him so hard that he fled. A year later, Leon Bibb, a less well-known Black folk singer who was a mentor to Odetta, added another line to the song—"They hunted him with hounds"—which dispels any doubt about what happened to our convict. Cash doubtless knew all of these interpretations and may have even been inspired by Bibb's introduction of a new line when he thought about recording his own.

Cash's version of "Another Man Done Gone" is simply the most harrowing on record. Except for a single opening strum of a guitar, Cash sings the song a cappella (like Odetta and Vera Hall), but his baritone sounds as though it is coming from the bottom of a well, resonant with a bit of echo; it contrasts, in call and response, with the crystal clear soprano of Anita Carter. Cash's and Carter's voices complement each other and lend a gothic feel to the original story. In Cash's telling, there is no mention of hounds; instead, he skips directly from "he had a long chain on" to "they hung him in a tree."

Worse than that, "they let his children see." These are Cash's lines, and he alone sings them. Carter repeats most of the lyrics sung by Cash, but not these about the lynching. It's as if the fragile purity of her voice cannot bear the weight of what our narrator has witnessed. But even here, Cash is not satisfied that his listeners will fully understand what he seems to have grasped—maybe from his Arkansas boyhood, maybe from family stories—about the repulsive evils of lynching. "When he was hanging dead," he sings in his lowest register, "the captain turned his head, the captain turned his head." The scene of a man's lynching in front of his family is so distressing that even the captain, the man who led the lynch mob, cannot bear to look. Cash isn't aiming for a hit single: he is aiming to turn our stomachs, and not gratuitously, either, because he recorded it in the summer of 1962, when violence lurked everywhere. (Just months after the album came out, Klansman Byron De La Beckwith shot down NAACP organizer Medgar Evers in his driveway, in front of his wife and children.) The song punctuates Side One like an exclamation point, insisting that the lives of these exploited Black men, all in chains, mattered.[36]

The second side of *Blood, Sweat and Tears* lacks the gathering sense of terror of the first, but its tone is still somber. Cash leads off with Harlan Howard's song "Busted," which Columbia released as the album's only single. Howard set the song of a guy who is so poor that "a man can go wrong" in coal mining country, but Cash moves it to the cotton fields. As such, his slow lamentation is more consistent with the songs on the first side; it sounds more like an Odetta song than a Burl Ives (who had previously recorded it) or Ray Charles (who turned it into a hit at nearly the same time Cash released it) song. Cash followed with "Casey Jones," the well-known folk song about the daring railroad engineer who died in a wreck around the turn of the century. The origins of the song are murky; it is probably a composite of several old folk blues tunes sung by railroad workers, but at the time Cash recorded it, the Lomaxes and others agreed that a Black engine wiper named Wallace Saunders wrote the song. Saunders worked in the Canton, Mississippi, roundhouse and apparently knew Casey Jones. In Cash's presentation, alongside these other songs of the Black experience, then, "Casey Jones" functions as an example of interracial harmony, a song by a Black engine wiper honoring the memory of a brave, white engineer.[37] "Nine Pound Hammer," the Merle Travis song from *Folk Songs of the Hills*, is more sober than the original, even as it relies on banjo picking as its signature sound. Cash's narrator sounds exhausted as he sings. If *Blood, Sweat and Tears* was merely an album about workingmen, Cash could have chosen "Dark as a Dungeon" by Travis, but in selecting a song about another hammer swinger, he seems, again, to be singing about a Black man's nine pound hammer. The next song, "Chain Gang," another by Harlan Howard, confirms the theme by describing a guy getting picked up on vagrancy charges and winding up on a chain gang—likely a Black character, given that the overwhelming majority of men railroaded into being convict laborers were African American. "There ain't no hope on a chain gang," Cash sings. Unlike the first side of the LP, these songs are more ambiguous about the race of each one's subject, so listeners could have assumed that the subjects were white. But given Cash's experience, it's hard to believe that's what he thought.[38]

Blood, Sweat and Tears is a landmark achievement in the contemplation of race by a country music artist, even if Columbia did not market it that way. It's possible that Don Law didn't fully appreciate what Cash had done with this album, and Cash himself remained strangely quiet. Perhaps he felt compelled to comment on Jim Crow segregation by drawing from the wellspring of African American folk blues, but also felt that, as a white Southerner, he couldn't directly address it. "I was trying to write about history so that people could understand what was going on," he said. Cash brought his own experience, his own witness, as an Arkansas white boy, as well as his research to the material. Years later, when he described his fascination with *Blues in the Mississippi Night* and the Lomaxes' prison recordings, Cash acknowledged that although he felt comfortable recording some songs from that canon, he couldn't play them all. One gets the sense that he felt like an interloper, not knowing if it was his place to give voice to some of these songs born of Black pain. And still, he showed no eagerness to speak out beyond his music. At least, not yet.

It would be easy to look from our own vantage point at *Blood, Sweat and Tears* today and accuse Cash of cultural appropriation, particularly for lifting those three songs on Side One from Black singers. No one used the term "cultural appropriation" at the time, but in more recent years it has been applied to stars like Elvis Presley for ripping off Big Mama Thornton and Arthur "Big Boy" Crudup, as well as against the Beatles and the Rolling Stones for stealing songs and riffs from Chuck Berry and other Black stars. Unlike the Beatles and Elvis, Cash took old songs—songs whose authorship often could not be determined—that had been handed down by many others and reinterpreted them. No less than Blind Willie McTell acknowledged that he "jumped" songs from other writers, "but I arrange 'em my own way." Odetta said something similar: "There are those people who are at their best when they are inventing," she once said. "And there are people who are idea people, interpretive . . . I am not inventive. My category, I would think, would be embellishing invention. The interpreter." On *Blood, Sweat and Tears* Cash similarly jumped, embellished, and interpreted. The album honors the African American folk tradition without bastardizing or commodifying it. It is worth comparing Cash's interpretations on this album to, say, Patti Page singing Leadbelly's "Boll Weevil" on *The Ed Sullivan Show* that same year, 1962. It is simply cringe inducing. Leadbelly sang from experience, knowing the damage a boll weevil could do to a sharecropper's family, and that feeling of desperation comes across when he sings the song; but it is also clearly about Black migration, which Leadbelly had also experienced. Patti Page, who seems never to have gotten her fingernails dirty, turned it into a children's song, a theme to a suburban sitcom for a mass audience. That is a kind of embellishing and interpreting, too, but it is not the kind that interested Cash. The folk music that Cash liked had a sharp edge. His interpretation of most of the songs on *Blood, Sweat and Tears* tells the story of America's history with racial violence. It is not for children. It is not even for Ed Sullivan.[39]

The significance of *Blood, Sweat and Tears* escaped the attention of segregationists and others who may have thought that Cash, after "Boss Jack," was one of them. The album peaked at number eighty on the pop charts, and although Cash performed "John Henry," "Busted," and "Casey Jones" frequently in his shows, he said nothing publicly as the clashes between civil rights activists and racists in the South intensified in 1963, 1964, and 1965. In these years of the March on Washington, Freedom Summer, and the Selma to Montgomery March, Cash did nothing more to provoke the segregationists. Under pressure from Columbia, he at least managed to produce "Ring of Fire," his first hit in years, and after that, he began devoting himself almost exclusively to making *Bitter Tears* (1964), his next concept album. He did record "All God's Children Ain't Free" as the B side to his single "Orange Blossom Special" at the end of 1964, the year that President Lyndon Johnson signed the Civil Rights Act. The song, Cash said, is mostly about poor people not being equally free, but it also gestured toward prisoners and, with phrases about "opening doors" and "walking any street," it hinted at support for civil rights. But when he fought back against the National States' Rights Party for alleging that he was married to a Black woman, it seemed less like a principled stand than an isolated personal feud.

BY 1969, WHEN Cash started appearing on television every week, anyone who saw him in action would have concluded that he supported civil rights—even though he still, at times, sounded like a guy who defended the Confederacy. Even within the space of a single show, Cash could be found both endorsing Black equality and expressing sympathy for the Southern rebels of the previous century. On the very same episode on which he sang side by side with Odetta, Cash took viewers to several Civil War battlefields during his "Ride This Train" segment. At Vicksburg, Sharpsburg, Gettysburg, and elsewhere, Cash reported, even the victors were losers because they fought "a war that both sides had to lose no matter which side won." Wars, Cash said, generalizing, "can only leave bitter feelings, broken bodies, a wounded nation that only time will heal." One did not have to read into his comments to know that he was signaling his skepticism over the Vietnam War as much as he seemed to be commenting on the Civil War. But as he wrapped up this portion of the show, he directed himself to the camera and said, "You know what, folks? I always was for the underdog, and in the case of the Civil War, you just gotta know whose side I'd be on." He then sang "Johnny Reb," a tribute to the Confederate soldiers. "You fought all the way, Johnny Reb, Johnny Reb," he sang, in a tone one might use to cheer up a child whose Little League team just got beat despite playing a good game. One has to wonder what Odetta, offstage, thought of this performance.[40]

What might have seemed incongruous to the alert viewer or to Odetta herself clearly did not seem strange to Cash. He rarely took "stands" on political issues in conventional ways; instead, he approached each issue based on feeling. Given his depth of feeling for African Americans, as expressed on *Blood, Sweat and Tears*, and his obvious admiration for Black artists, it's hard to read his sympathy for "the underdog" as a simple defense of slavery. But as he derived empathy for Black Americans through his own experience and through immersion in the documentary evidence he found in so many folk archive recordings, he could not give up completely his own sense of himself as an underdog from the South. To Cash, playing "Johnny Reb" was a way of asserting his white Southern identity even as he championed Black equality.

As if to prove this point, Cash devoted one "Ride This Train" segment in April 1970 to reenacting the levee camp stories of *Blues in the Mississippi Night*. As he speaks to the camera, in character, he describes a levee built in Pine Ridge, Mississippi, claiming he was once coerced into a chain gang after being picked up amidst a bar fight in Natchez. Just as he describes it on the *Ride This Train* LP, Cash tells stories of the boss whipping convicts. He says the prison warden promised the "walkin' boss"—a trusty—that if he shot two escapees, he would be granted his own parole. As Cash starts to sing "Going to Memphis," the audience might have assumed that his chain gang character is white, but his real identity as a Black man is revealed when he sings, lamenting that he can't make it to Chicago, "I couldn't get past Tennessee with Mississippi all over my face." He goes on to mention dogs chasing a guy down, returning with blood on their mouths, and convicts being whipped "under a blisterin' one-hundred-degree sun," leading some to lose their minds. But then he comes to the whole point of this dramatization: confronting the public's indifference. "You think things like this don't happen in this country now, well it does," he says to the audience. Still in character, he describes six prisoners who had simply reached the limit of what they could tolerate, using a ten-pound hammer to break each other's legs. The silence in the Ryman is overwhelming. "They got out of work, alright," Cash's convict character reports sarcastically. "Now they're in the hole, on bread and water, and God, at night, you can hear them moan." He practically spits the last line: "It's almost enough to make a man give a damn." As if Cash's gruesome description of these desperate men maiming each other was not enough, he seemed to hold the audience responsible for turning a blind eye. As he began singing "Another Man Done Gone" (with Anita Carter offstage doing call and response), he may as well have played prosecutor and brought up everyone who tuned in that night on charges of First-Degree Apathy and Accessory to Murder After the Fact. Even then, he sang only the "he had a long chain on" and

"I didn't know his name" verses; he made his point without singing the two lines about the lynching. Although Cash did not explicitly refer to race, the Ryman audience knew the score; they would never have imagined white prisoners—even on a chain gang—being treated so brutally.[41]

In a variety of ways, *The Johnny Cash Show* became a rare vehicle for interracial harmony on American television. Although African American magazines such as *Ebony* and *Jet* had predicted in the 1950s that television, this new technology, would play a leveling role in the struggle for civil rights, it hadn't turned out that way. Until the 1970s, one struggled to find proportionate representation of African Americans on TV. But Cash's show was an exception. No other variety shows featured, over the course of two years, three artists who sang at the 1963 March on Washington (Bob Dylan, Odetta, and Mahalia Jackson). Cash invited Black artists from country, blues, rhythm and blues, and gospel traditions, from the Staple Singers, Joe Tex, and O. C. Smith to Charley Pride, Stevie Wonder, Louis Armstrong, and Ray Charles, with several making multiple appearances. And when they did arrive on his stage, Cash praised them lavishly. He called Charley Pride "brother" when he shook his hand, and when the two men sat down to sing a duet, Cash told him that he thought no one in country music sang as much like Hank Williams as Pride did, perhaps the highest praise anyone in country music could offer a peer. "You know, if I were asked to say something great about country music in just a couple of words," Cash remarked on another episode, "I think I'd say, 'Charley Pride.'" When he welcomed Ray Charles to his stage for the first time, Cash said, "everybody loves you here, man . . . well, of course the whole world loves Ray—this [the thunderous applause] is nothing new for you." They compared notes on growing up poor and sat together on Charles's piano bench trading verses of "Busted." In Nashville in 1970, in the midst of ongoing struggles over school busing plans, Cash's hearty embrace of a man who just a few years earlier would have been kept out of the city's best hotels and restaurants meant something.

As a further measure of just how far Johnny Cash had come from his all-white upbringing in Dyess, his interactions with both the oldest and youngest Black artists to perform on his show are telling. "This country has given the world three original art forms," he told the audience in October 1970, "country music, jazz, and Louis Armstrong." Cash's thrill at having jazz's greatest ambassador on the show was contagious when he urged Armstrong to tell the story of recording "Blue Yodel No. 9" with Jimmie Rodgers in 1930. When Cash asked if they could reenact that historic event, with Cash singing and yodeling in place of Rodgers, Armstrong joked, "We'll give it to 'em in black and white," and the audience ate it up, giving the performance a standing ovation. Similarly, when Cash introduced Stevie Wonder two weeks later, he recast the lyrics from his own "Get Rhythm" to showcase Wonder switching between instruments—from piano to organ to harmonica to drums—with each exchange. Wonder, only twenty at the time, dazzled. He then went on to sing the socially conscious "Heaven Help Us All" with lines like "Heaven help the black man if he struggles one more day/Heaven help the white man if he turns his back away." As one journalist pointed out at the time, "political activists may grouse" that Cash did not do more for civil rights, but "it should be noted that he presents black performers with obviously warm mutual respect." It is not clear that any political activists did, in fact, grouse over Cash's supposed lack of engagement on civil rights, but as these interactions on his television show demonstrated, his feeling for Black America, for the hardships African Americans had endured, ran deep. For a white man who grew up in some of the most dangerous parts of the country for Black Americans, he had come a long way. Cash had sincere love and respect for Black contributions to the nation's musical heritage. And his understanding of the old, cruel America that provided the seedbed from which Black artistic genius grew informed his public citizenship long after his popularity peaked in the early 1970s.[42]

4

Cowboys and Indians

I n that first summer that *The Johnny Cash Show* aired on a trial basis, as the program's host and writers tried to find a winning formula, they made a habit of inviting at least one young, attractive female singer-songwriter to appear each week. Joni Mitchell sang with Cash in the first episode, and in the two following weeks, Evie Sands and Linda Ronstadt performed. Invariably, Cash introduced them by complimenting both their musical talents and their looks.

On the fourth show, which aired July 5, 1969, Cash followed roughly the same script, welcoming to the stage Native folk singer Buffy Sainte-Marie by telling the viewing audience that her voice "is as sweet as a rippling stream in the mountains"—as if she sounded like Dolly Parton. Whoever wrote that line had never heard Sainte-Marie sing. Her voice has never been "sweet." Especially live, her vocal style is so forceful and insistent it trembles with vibrato. The Ryman audience sat transfixed as Sainte-Marie, in white go-go boots and a fringed mini dress, launched into "Quiet Places" in a distinctly unquiet, unsweet way. A song notable for its countercultural edge, with lines about a "world that's all gone mad" and is "less than kind," carried by Sainte-Marie's plaintive wail, it sounded more like a roaring waterfall than a rippling stream. She sang in a full-throated tremor, whirling with her guitar the way the Nashville audience might have seen gyrating hippies doing on the news during San Francisco's Summer of Love. More than Joni Mitchell or Linda Ronstadt, who were more mainstream, Sainte-Marie brought to Cash's show—to the stage of the *Grand Ole Opry*, no less—a sense of the real counterculture, of unpredictability.

Sainte-Marie's reputation preceded her. Unlike Mitchell and Ronstadt, who were known in the summer of 1969 for popular songs like "Both Sides, Now" (Mitchell) or "Baby You've Been on My Mind" (a Dylan song recorded by Ronstadt), Sainte-Marie had entered the public's consciousness thanks to "The Universal Soldier," her 1965 single still in heavy rotation in the countercultural GI coffeehouses found outside military bases throughout the South, and popular, too, at peace marches. Save, perhaps, for Dylan's "Masters of War," Sainte-Marie's indictment of those responsible for making war—including the voters who put the masters of war in power—ranks as one of the most powerful antiwar compositions in an era filled with peace anthems and songs of resistance. To be aware of Sainte-Marie's stand and then to see her, probably for the first time, wailing as she did on "Quiet Places" must have been unsettling. Here is a real radical, some in the audience must have thought, perhaps a little bewildered. You come to the home of the *Opry* to see Johnny Cash and June Carter, maybe a guest star like Loretta Lynn—not this howling, angry hippie. But like Odetta some weeks afterward, Buffy Sainte-Marie did not come to make nice with the national audience. If she blew back some Nashville hair, fine. Cash, for his part, doubtless knew that this performance would test the limits of ABC's tolerance for him choosing his own guests. But given the network's insistence on putting a Hollywood hack like Doug McClure on the same episode (he sang a fantastically off-key duet of "Cowboy Buckaroo" with Cash), perhaps Cash sought to balance the show with more provocation.

When Sainte-Marie finished singing "Quiet Places," Cash strode across stage, sat next to her, and told her (and the audience) that he had "just a little bit of Cherokee" in his blood. "That's what I hear," Sainte-Marie replied with a smile, "and I'm sure you're very proud of it, and we're very proud of you, John." The moment passed quickly, but by saying "we're very proud of you," Sainte-Marie spoke as if she represented all Native peoples, happy to have Cash on their side at a moment in history when Native peoples, like Black Americans, struggled for equal treatment and equal attention. "For some reason," Cash replied, "I feel 100 percent [Cherokee] tonight." At this point, Sainte-Marie and Cash began singing Peter La Farge's tune "Custer," which Cash had recorded on his 1964 concept album, *Bitter Tears: Ballads of the American Indian.* Out of Cash's vast repertoire, "Custer" is not a song he often played in concert; and except for this occasion with Sainte-Marie, he never played it again on any of the other episodes of his television show. But one can easily imagine his sense of caution. The song is, after all, an irreverent commentary on the slaughter of George Armstrong Custer and his Seventh Cavalry at the Battle of the Little Bighorn. To mock the killing of an American serviceman—even a guy as reviled as Custer—in the middle of the Vietnam War ran the risk of offending more than a few people. As most American schoolkids knew at the time, Custer, a self-aggrandizing showboat of an Army officer, foolishly divided his men as they went to scout the Little Bighorn River in 1876, looking for a large Indian encampment. Before they knew it, they were overwhelmed by thousands of Lakota Sioux, led by Crazy Horse, and quickly wiped out. With American and Vietnamese war dead numbers reported on the nightly news, it is a wonder that Cash and Sainte-Marie dared to perform the song on national television that Saturday night at all.

But it wasn't just that this was a song about an Army officer responsible for killing women and children in earlier battles, who ends up "barbered violent" (scalped) for his sins. It was the way the two performed it, laughing through the lyrics, as if this annihilation of

American forces was a shared joke. Sainte-Marie kicks off the song, playing a traditional mouth bow while Cash strums guitar, but when he sings the first line about not being "a fan of Custer," she has to pause because she is smiling so broadly that she cannot play the bow; it is as if she can't believe that he said something so radical on American television. The two trade verses, lines, and laughs throughout the song. "It's not called an Indian victory but a bloody massacre," sings Sainte-Marie, pausing for comedic effect, "there might have been more enthusing if us Indians had been losing." Cash guffaws knowingly. In a United States still enthralled with cowboys and Westerns, in which popular culture so favored the cowboys, laughing through a song about a "massacre" of white Americans could only be regarded as subversive. Only Odetta's appearance six weeks later matched Sainte-Marie's for its political potency.

Johnny Cash's warm welcome of Buffy Sainte-Marie, and his enthusiastic participation in the "Custer" duet, tells us a lot about his empathy for Native peoples and their plight. Among many fans, Cash's well-established advocacy on behalf of American Indians has been touted, along with his obvious concern for prisoners, as clear evidence of his standing up for the downtrodden. But Cash seemed to stand up, or stand in, for cowboys as much as Indians in an era when it was almost impossible to find any Native characters in popular culture that were not based on caricature. Readers still devoured Zane Grey's mass-market paperback idealization of the West in huge numbers while a book like *Black Elk Speaks* found an audience mostly through university course reading lists. In a time when millions of white suburban kids were playing "cowboys and Indians" in their backyards, Cash celebrated the Old West as if he was the cultural son of John Wayne. But he also brought attention to the social realities of the Native experience, in part, through a kind of role-playing, of inhabiting the personas of those he studied and sang about. He had done this to a lesser degree when he pretended to work on a levee gang on "Going to Memphis," and on "John Henry," but on *Bitter*

Tears (1964) and *Johnny Cash Sings the Ballads of the True West* (1965), he more fully embodied the personas of historical characters. The more he bore witness, the further he walked in their shoes, the more he could relate their experiences to his own. Out of that relating and witnessing came an understanding and sense of identification that helped to define his public citizenship.

RAY CASH LOVED to tell stories of the Old West, both folklore and stories of his own life, which fascinated young J. R. and his siblings. Ray claimed that, at fifteen, he had seen Buffalo Bill Cody's Wild West show in San Antonio (if true, it would have been 1913, when the show's long run came to an end with Cody's bankruptcy) and regaled his sons with tales of what he had witnessed. His pre-World War I service in the Army, too, had taken him to Deming, New Mexico, in pursuit of Pancho Villa on the actual frontier of the United States. "I heard my father tell some really historical things over the years," Cash later recalled. "And he really didn't embellish them too much because they were real, and he didn't need to."[1]

Cash's fascination with outlaws may have stemmed, too, from the occasional visits to Dyess of Old Jim George. In multiple interviews Cash recalled how just about every year at harvest time, George would come up to Dyess from southeast Texas. He always wore a bandana around his neck, even in the hottest weather. When Ray asked him about it, George, then about eighty years old, said he wore it to cover the rope burns on his neck. He said he had been hanged as a member of the James Gang in 1882, but his executioners let him go, as was the custom, because the hanging did not kill him. "We didn't know whether to believe him or not, but we didn't have any reason not to," Cash later said. "He was convincing." No one in the James Gang ever went to the gallows, in fact (Robert Ford, who assassinated Jesse James, had been sentenced to die by hanging, but the governor of Missouri granted him clemency), though that does not mean that Jim George had not been hanged. J. R.'s older brother Roy became so enthralled with all of these tales of outlaws that he wrote a poem, "Wild Western Outlaw," published in the *Dyess Colony Herald* in 1936. The poem told of an outlaw who ran with "Banty Bill" and "Kansas Jake," robbing banks and trains, "slinging lots of lead" along the way. Quite a few people die, including Bill and Jake, in Roy's poem, perhaps reflecting a typical frontier boyhood imagination.[2]

Gene Autry similarly fueled Cash's imagination about the frontier, but updated to the present day. Cash said that he saw his first Autry film in 1937, which means it could have been one of eight made by the Singing Cowboy that year, the most popular of which, *Public Cowboy No. 1*, featured Autry helping to snare some modern-day cattle rustlers using old-fashioned, straight-shootin' cowboy skill. Autry "appealed to the taste culture of many lower-income people" as one of his biographers has written. Americans whose educations "typically ended in grade school" and "who were working in blue-collar" jobs saw in Autry a romantic picture of the West as a place of New Deal progress, a place where dreams could be realized. For a kid like Cash, then, growing up in Arkansas, where "taming the frontier" was central to the state's identity, boyhood frontier imaginaries included both outlaws preying on the innocent and singing cowboys working for the collective good.[3]

But "taming the frontier" almost always got conflated with "fighting Indians," even though the Natives who lived in what is now Arkansas over the last three hundred years were primarily hunters, not warriors. We know that Hernando de Soto encountered Natives when he made it to the western banks of the Mississippi in what is now Arkansas in 1541, and that the French did, as well, when they settled the Mississippi River valley in the 1680s. Over the next century, driven by encroachments of settlers to the east, and attracted by abundant game in the Delta, the Quapaw, Choctaw, Cherokee, and Osage migrated to the area, more as visitors than permanent residents. The establishment of Arkansas's territorial government in 1819, however, eventually led to the eviction of its Native populations to "Indian Territory" in what is now Oklahoma. When President Andrew Jackson removed the Cherokee from the southeast to Indian Territory, the "Trail of Tears" traversed Arkansas, too. Still, the relative absence of Native peoples in Arkansas after the 1820s did not prevent the *idea* of Indians becoming central to state mythology well into the twenty-first century. Although none of these Native peoples remained in Arkansas by the 1930s, when the Cashes moved to Dyess, white Arkansans remained captivated by the idea of Indians in the state's fabled past. To take just one example, in 1931, Arkansas State University (ASU), in nearby Jonesboro, adopted "Indians" for the name of its sports teams (previously called the "Aggies" or the "Farmers"), with a mascot named "Jumpin' Joe," a cartoon Indian with exaggerated features carrying a tomahawk in one hand and a scalp in the other. Pretty standard ethnocentric nonsense for the period, uncorrected until ASU changed their teams' names to the Red Wolves in 2008. Even so, according to one scholar, "most" Arkansans claimed an Indian princess somewhere in their ancestry as late as the turn of the twenty-first century.[4]

Johnny Cash grew up in this milieu, down the road from Jonesboro, surrounded by communities that, to this day, give their sports teams Indian names, and believing that he, too, had Cherokee ancestry. "I've known I've had Indian blood since I was a kid," he told biographer Christopher Wren in 1970. "I saw the picture of my mother's mother; because of the part of the country, it would have to be Cherokee." Others reported, as late as the 1990s, that Cash's great-great-grandmother had been a "full-blooded Cherokee." Ray Cash told one reporter that both he and his wife were about one-eighth to one-quarter Cherokee. "We men in the family have all the Indian features," he said, including high cheekbones and "generally hairless complexions." (The only thing missing from these myths are the tales of an Indian princess.) At some point, following some genealogical work, Johnny Cash learned that, in fact, no Cherokee blood ran through his veins (and no Irish blood, either, apparently, because late in life he described himself as entirely descended from Scots, at least on the Cash side). But in the 1960s, he very much believed the Cash family lore about their Cherokee heritage.

Cash grew up an avid reader of books about Native peoples. "I read all the time when I was a kid," he told one writer, and thanks to that big library in Dyess, he devoured Walter D. Edmonds's *Drums Along the Mohawk*, James Fenimore Cooper's *The Last of the Mohicans*, and according to the folks who now curate his boyhood home, he repeatedly read James Willard Schultz's *Lone Bull's Mistake*, among others. "I read all the Indian books I could get," Cash remembered, even though he claimed to know no other kids reading these kinds of titles.[5]

Of course, there is a long tradition of non-Native people immersing themselves in Native life, of "playing Indian," in American history. From the Boston Tea Party in 1773 to modern day Mardi Gras in New Orleans, non-Native Americans have adopted Indian identity for the day, like so many adults going out for trick-or-treating. It is all about staking a claim to a certain imagined freedom. As one scholar has argued, even as European settlers and their descendants systematically pushed Natives from their land and, in time, hunted them down on the western plains, the idea of Indians seemed to summon the "spirit of the continent." Whites "desperately desired that spirit" for themselves. In some cases, participants have drawn on medieval carnival traditions to perform "Indianness," as they envision it, "signify[ing] freedom, inversion, rebellion, and aboriginality." If the idea of American freedom meant an opportunity to be totally and ultimately free, ideas about Native freedom represented almost the purest ideal—an absolute freedom outside any "system." The irony of taking away all of that freedom, imprisoning Indigenous peoples on reservations at the tip of a bayonet, was lost on white America.[6]

Johnny Cash's sincere adoption of his supposed Cherokee heritage manifested itself similarly, almost as a costume, a disguise, but not as a symbol of freedom. For the cover of *Bitter Tears*, Cash did not go full regalia, as he had on *Ride This Train*, but his headband and eye makeup, along with the dramatic shielding of his face from the sun, do suggest that he is "performing Indian." By self-consciously (or not) adopting an Indian disguise, Cash made his own identity more fluid. By this time, just judging him by his album covers, fans knew him as a poor Arkansas farm boy, a devoutly faithful gospel singer, a would-be train robber and narrator of Americana, and now an Indian (and later, a convict). This tendency toward embracing disguise might seem odd, given Cash's obsession with authenticity. How could one be *real* while in disguise? But, in fact, he seemed to don these identities less out of aspiration to *be* the person he impersonated so much as to understand and empathize with the reality of his situation. As Philip Deloria points out, "wearing a mask also makes one self-conscious of a *real* 'me' underneath." In the case of Cash's Indigenous disguise, he did not play an idealized version of Indians—the way he sometimes did with cowboys. With the latter, Cash often tried to show how brutal life on the frontier could be, but still as a kind of masculine, rugged individualism fantasy. In contrast, as a Native, Cash disguised himself to document the oppression of Indigenous peoples. But his expression of empathy for Indigenous peoples derived as much from his shared experience of poverty as his affinity for Indians. Whether Cherokee blood pumped from his heart or not did not really matter. In the marginalized lives of Native peoples, Cash saw something of his own experience as a poor kid.[7]

IF CASH HAD picked one word for a song lyric that best heralded his empathy for his subject, it would have to be "tears." Before he even recorded the albums *Blood, Sweat and Tears* and *Bitter Tears: Ballads*

of the American Indian (which includes his song, "Apache Tears"),
he wrote "Old Apache Squaw" in the late 1950s, a song which first
made ample use of the word "tears." It is a good rhyming word, but
more than that, it signals pain, a pain to which Cash, as songwriter
or singer, clearly relates. Cash often spoke of "Old Apache Squaw"
as his first attempt to write something meaningful about Indigenous
peoples, but he said that in those days, no one—including Columbia—seemed very interested. It's a simple, but powerful, song. It
describes an Apache woman who had seen the great chief Cochise
make his "last stand" (whatever that means—Cochise did not die
in battle, but of a stomach ailment or maybe cancer in 1874), so she
must have been very old, indeed, by the late 1950s. Cash focused,
however, on the woman's poverty, painting images of her "shiver-
ing in a cold teepee," witness to countless hungry children and too
many "bloody" warriors "running" or "fleeing" to the sea (which also
makes little sense, since the Apache wars with the US Army took
place in Arizona, not on the coast). The song painted a much different picture of Indian life compared to the essentially racist portrayals
of Indians-as-savages in the movies of the time. The emphasis on the
cold and hungry in this song is the beginning of a long thread that
runs through Cash's empathetic songs—including "The Man on the
Hill," from the same *Songs of Our Soil* LP—whether they described
the experiences of whites, Blacks, workers, prisoners, soldiers, or
Native peoples. It's as though he distilled the suffering from his own
experience, growing up poor, witness to the even greater deprivation
of others—like the sharecroppers across the road—and extrapolated
from that suffering to make legible the suffering of others. Through
this, he made a kind of backdoor appeal for equality among all peoples. Among the poor and destitute, after all, no one is better or
better-off; everyone is just poor. They shed tears equally.

And yet, Cash saw that the government treated different groups
of poor people differently. The New Deal gave his own family the
chance to own their own farm, a stroke of luck and the privilege that

changed their lives. In contrast, Cash had learned from Leroy, Natchez, and Sib on *Blues in the Mississippi Night* that Southern sheriffs picked up poor African Americans for any little infraction and put them to work on the chain gang. White folks could get their own farm while Black folks got the chain gang. He had only to listen to those Alan Lomax recordings to see the difference. Meanwhile, the federal government continued to break treaties and steal land from destitute Indigenous peoples. By the 1960s, the civil rights movement made the cause of racial equality for Black Americans the most important public issue of the day, but to Cash, it seemed like no one cared about Native peoples. Johnny Western, who toured with Cash a lot in the late 1950s and early 1960s remembered that "because of his poor background," Cash "had this underlying feeling for the underdog, and there was nobody more an underdog than the American Indian."[8]

Just as Cash got an education on the realities of Black Southerners' lives from Gus Cannon and the field recordings of Alan Lomax, he learned about the plight of Indigenous peoples from folk singer Peter La Farge. Much has been made of Cash's friendship with La Farge, not only of the way that *Bitter Tears* is indebted to La Farge, but some argue that Cash more cynically adopted a folk persona through his association with La Farge and thus expanded his audience beyond country music. Drug-induced screwups notwithstanding, he was still Johnny Cash, the Columbia Records star, singing to sold out shows all over North America and beyond in the early 1960s. He did not need to "court" the comparatively tiny folk music audience. Just as he did serious research in Library of Congress field and folk recordings, he immersed himself in the American folk scene, especially in New York. That is where he met La Farge, where they hit it off, and where they shared their love of Indigenous culture. Like Cannon and Lomax, La Farge acted as a guide who, armed with a key to a gateway of new knowledge, energized Cash in his obsession with Indigenous peoples and cultures.

Cash and La Farge did not come from similar backgrounds, but they shared certain experiences, not least of which included false claims of having descended from Indigenous peoples. Although all of La Farge's 1960s recordings for Folkways Records claimed that the singer with the long, dark hair was from a wiped out tribe of "Nargaset" Indians, and was adopted at an early age by the renowned anthropologist, Oliver La Farge, none of it was true. For starters, "Nargaset" is either a made-up name or a bastardization of Narragansett, the name of a peoples who lived near the saltwater bay now named for them in modern day Rhode Island (there is some evidence that family legend held that the La Farges were 1/128th Narragansett, but it has never been confirmed or disproved). More important is that Peter La Farge was born into privilege, the biological son of Oliver and Wanden Mathews La Farge. His father's work focused on Indigenous peoples, the Olmec and the Navajo, and he also authored *Laughing Boy: A Navajo Love Story* (1929), winner of the Pulitzer Prize for fiction and widely regarded as a classic of American literature. Following his parents' divorce, Peter grew up mostly in Colorado, on a four-thousand-acre ranch, with his sister and mother, a highly educated and devoted philanthropist. Wanden Mathews La Farge established a health clinic on the Jicarilla Apache Reservation and maintained longtime friendships in the Santa Clara Pueblo of the Pueblo people. Peter La Farge grew up with Indian culture all around him, and at sixteen, he left home and took to the rodeo circuit, learning to play guitar along the way, mentored by Big Bill Broonzy and Woody Guthrie's sidekick, Cisco Houston. Not unlike Cash, when faced with the prospect of being drafted during the Korean War, he joined the Navy.

When Cash met La Farge after his disastrous Carnegie Hall show in 1962, La Farge had already established himself as a fixture on New York's folk scene. He and Ed McCurdy took Cash to some of the folk clubs downtown, including the Gaslight, where Cash felt right at home. Already deep into his obsession with the various folk recordings of songs he would soon make his own on *Blood, Sweat and Tears*, Cash made an eager student. According to La Farge, Cash wanted to get out from under "the heavy legend that binds him to hillbilly heaven," but there is no evidence to suggest that is true. More likely, Columbia gave Cash the latitude to pursue his artistic interests, which, at the time, included the history and present plight of the unsung, overlooked, and ignored.[9]

By the time they met, La Farge had already released one LP for Columbia which included "The Ballad of Ira Hayes," the gateway drug that plunged Cash into his Indian addiction. La Farge's lyrics artfully tell the story of Ira Hayes, of the Pima people (in present-day Arizona), who fought with the Marines on Iwo Jima and participated in the flag raising so gloriously depicted in the famous photo and at the Marine Corps War Memorial in Arlington, Virginia. The iconic triumph at Iwo Jima comes in the middle of the song, only after La Farge describes the "proud and peaceful" Pima who, as masters of irrigation, farmed the Phoenix valley for thousands of years, until the US government effectively deprived them of their life-sustaining water and tried to coerce them into assimilation in the 1920s. Hunger and deprivation followed, as it did for so many during the Great Depression, and in that context, Ira Hayes sought a better life in the military. The upshot of the song is that although Hayes returned from the war a hero, often trotted out for various victory celebrations, his standing as "just a Pima Indian," meant that he got no material benefit from his service and citizenship. Like the rest of his people, he remained poor, trapped with no future. He started to put a regular hurting on the bottle, landing himself in jail dozens of times, until he finally died of exposure, alone in an abandoned adobe hut, following a drunken binge. In its own way, "Ira Hayes" portrays the structures of exploitation and the devaluing of human life as well as, say, "The Legend of John Henry." Both depict actual men, genuine heroes, who died penniless and discarded by society. It is no wonder that the song resonated so much with Cash that, in the spring of 1964, he felt compelled to record it himself.

In "Ira Hayes," Cash saw that La Farge shared his obsession with realistic presentations of American cruelties, and more than that, he could see that the guy could really write. Which was good, because La Farge could not sing to save his life. His limited vocal range undermined the poetry and power of his lyrics and certainly limited the size of his audience. Although his 1963 LP, *As Long as the Grass Shall Grow*, is not made up of field recordings, if not for the vocals, it could have come close to equaling *Blues in the Mississippi Night* for its documentary power. Instead of following the true-life experiences of Leroy, Natchez, and Sib, we follow La Farge's collection of songs based on his own extraordinarily deep research. The whole package, from album cover to songs and liner notes, conveys a sense of Lomax-like realism. On the album sleeve is a photo of Vincent Myers, a Comanche Indian from Oklahoma, recipient of the Distinguished Flying Cross during the Second World War, driving a tractor on his 160-acre farm—a model American citizen. Over the course of the record, La Farge recounts a long series of injustices done to Indigenous peoples by European settlers, starting with the Spanish in the sixteenth century and through various white betrayals of natives: breaking treaties with the Seneca, killing off the buffalo on the Great Plains, the forced removal of the Cherokee via the Trail of Tears, stealing Alaska and subjugating Indigenous peoples there (turning it into "the Mississippi of the North"), and poisoning the natural environment in white efforts to control the land. The ten pages of liner notes culled from scholarly sources detailed descriptions of the crimes against humanity committed by whites against Indigenous peoples, giving special attention to the Trail of Tears.

The album's best songs, such as "Custer" and "Hey, Mr. President," are well crafted and witty, ideal for coffeehouse performances among folkies hip to all of the jokes. They're as good as anything Phil Ochs, perhaps the most successful political folk singer of the age, did. In "Hey, Mr. President," La Farge riffs off an old Almanac Singers tune to imagine a world in which the president is charged rent for breaking treaties, whites are put on reservations, and Indians are the tourists who come to watch them dance. La Farge's "Custer" is slower, flatter than the lyrics demand, and ultimately disappointing, especially after one listens to Cash's version a year later and the duet with Buffy Sainte-Marie, which tops all other performances of the song.

Even so, La Farge's *As Long As the Grass Shall Grow* rivals those Alan Lomax field recordings and Odetta's early records for their impact on Cash. He clearly accepted La Farge as an authentic source and knowledgeable guide in Indian territory. As his daughter Rosanne said many years later, Cash would sometimes "attach" himself to people who really inspired him, and these kinds of issues resonated with him because they were "part of his own woundedness." It is less clear if he consciously thought to himself that he could bring La Farge's songs, which described intolerable injustice, to a wider public that might, in the context of the civil rights revolution, actually act on them, but that is, in effect, what he did. Following a big year in 1963, in which he more than made up for disappointing sales on records like *Blood, Sweat and Tears* by scoring his first big hit in years with "Ring of Fire," Cash decided to record his own version of "Ira Hayes" and then an entire album of "ballads of the American Indian" in 1964. It turned out that La Farge's songs needed an authoritative voice like Cash's—as well as the pacing of the Tennessee Three and the polished production available in Nashville—to bring them to a mass audience. "I had such a feeling for Ira Hayes," Cash later said. He had been through Apache country, at least, and witnessed the conditions. "I had seen the poverty and had a feeling for it." And, of course, some of his own experiences mirrored Hayes's: the impoverished upbringing, the military service, the substance abuse. He could relate.[10]

At the same time, Cash could not understand how the marginalization of Indians continued to happen at the hands of the United States government. One might expect to look back and find, in the age of slavery, the dispossession and mistreatment of Indigenous peoples, but now? In the America of abundance and affluence? Cash learned from La Farge and his own research that, in fact, the US government had made life harder on Native peoples, not easier, in the years since World War II. As early as 1950, Dillon S. Myer, the head of the Bureau of Indian Affairs (and the same guy who had rounded up 120,000 Japanese Americans as director of the War Relocation Authority), promoted a policy ominously called "termination." In effect, termination meant a forced assimilation of Indigenous peoples into the rest of the American population—an end to treaties, to reservations, to any and all federal aid and services. A companion relocation policy (Myer's favorite solution, apparently) promised to move Indians off the reservations and into American cities, where they would find good jobs and nice homes. Arthur Watkins, the senator from Utah, hailed termination as the "final solution" to the Indian problem as if he didn't understand the significance of the term (or maybe understood it perfectly). As Antonino D'Ambrosio has argued, in fact, termination just meant another old-fashioned "land grab." When the House of Representatives approved termination in House Resolution 108 in 1953, Congressman John F. Kennedy of Massachusetts voted to support it. Over the next fifteen years, the federal government removed more than two million acres of Indigenous land from protected status and deprived more than thirteen thousand Natives of their tribal affiliation, putting them under the legal jurisdiction of the states wherein they now resided. The promised jobs and homes almost never materialized.

In the midst of the Cold War and the civil rights movement, most Americans did not follow these events closely, which made it easier for the federal government to continue pushing Indians around. In New York State, the United States seized Seneca land and water rights to build the Kinzua Dam, a betrayal at the center of Peter La Farge's song "As Long As the Grass Shall Grow." Although President Kennedy had reconsidered his support for termination and said during the 1960 campaign that "there will be no change in treaty and contractual relationships without consent of the tribes concerned," he still gave final approval to the controversial plan that ultimately flooded one-third of the Allegany Reservation of the Seneca Nation, including burial grounds, and leaving untouched, in the words of one observer, "only wooded hillsides and towns occupied by whites under leases executed by Congress in the late nineteenth century." The House, meanwhile, voted 398 to 18 in favor of funding the dam. The Seneca had no friends in power; officials pulled up outside Seneca houses, piled everything into trucks, and torched their homes. They relocated some six hundred families, bulldozed their ancestors' remains, and the Army Corps of Engineers built the dam. It was enough to make Andrew Jackson, the architect of the Trail of Tears, proud.[11]

Peter La Farge wrote "As Long As the Grass Shall Grow" to expose the historical context of the betrayal of the Seneca, which fueled Cash's sense of outrage. The song begins as a talking blues, with La Farge recounting how the Seneca chief, Cornplanter, had come to an agreement with George Washington's administration in 1794 that the land occupied by his nation along the New York–Pennsylvania border would remain Seneca forevermore—for "as long as the grass shall grow." As a rhetorical device in song, invoking the good word of the nation's first president established the standard by which subsequent presidents, especially Kennedy, should be judged. No president, La Farge made clear, could be trusted to honor the government's treaties with the Indians. It seemed a treaty could just be torn up and replaced by a cascade of human rights violations: the forced displacement of hundreds of families, the flooding of their richest farming and hunting land, the desecration of their burial sites. Cash, who immersed himself in the long history of this saga, couldn't understand why his fellow citizens weren't outraged. La Farge's brilliant songwriting might not reach the masses, but Cash's could. He decided to bring this message to them himself.

Not for nothing is "As Long As the Grass Shall Grow" the first song on *Bitter Tears*.[12]

Cash recorded the songs for *Bitter Tears* in the last heady days of June 1964, amid high drama over civil rights in Washington and the South. Ten days before Cash entered the studio, the United States Senate finally passed the landmark bill that would become the Civil Rights Act of 1964 when President Johnson signed it on July 2 (two days after Cash's recording session ended). Moreover, three civil rights workers—Andrew Goodman, James Chaney, and Michael Schwerner—went missing on June 21, somewhere near Philadelphia, Mississippi, about five and a half hours southwest of Nashville. Six weeks later, the worst was confirmed: a lynch mob had murdered the three men and buried their bodies in an earthen dam. More directly, Fisk University's annual Race Relations Institute meeting, in Nashville, brought civil rights activists, including La Farge, to the city the very same week of the recording sessions. One activist at the meeting got headlines by saying that American Indians also were "not receiving justice."

La Farge did not play on *Bitter Tears*, but he joined Cash, the Tennessee Three, the Carter Family, bluegrass musician Norman Blake, and others in the studio as they recorded songs for the album at exactly this moment, when the entire nation seemed focused on civil rights. Unlike four years earlier, when Cash recorded "Boss Jack," or 1962, when he quietly recorded an album about race, the *Bitter Tears* sessions brought Cash—still hooked on drugs but focused—to the point of asserting his politics of empathy more publicly. "By the time I actually recorded the album I carried a heavy load of sadness and outrage," he later remembered. "I felt every word of those songs. . . . I meant every word, too. I was long past the point of pulling my punches."[13]

It might seem surprising that a guy done pulling punches would tolerate some of the circumspect liner notes by his friend, the legendary country music disc jockey, Hugh Cherry. Compared to the blunt force of the music on the record, the back-of-the-sleeve essay seems overly gentle, as if Cherry wanted to carefully broach a touchy subject with the potential record buyers. "We, as Americans, have many things of which we can be proud," he wrote. But there are some things in the nation's history "that we must wear as millstones of shame." The rest of the liner notes carry on in this fashion, skirting a direct accusation of the systematic erasure of whole cultures in favor of a tragedy narrative. White explorers and settlers became so "blinded" by their "greed for land and fur and gold" they did not see "the indignities [they] were forcing on another of the human kind." (Cash, at least, surely understood that white settlers were not in any way blind to what they were doing to Indigenous peoples.) According to Cherry, Americans had spent three hundred years "misunderstanding the Indian," which hardly excused leaving them with "fewer lands, less game, broken promises and more broken promises." At last, Cherry acknowledges that Americans "fail to remember that we, the white men, were the invaders," and that whites are "still displacing the American Indian" to make way for the Kinzua Dam. In the end, the point of the album is presented so reasonably, it is not hard to imagine most folks standing in the aisle thinking, in the middle of the civil rights revolution, "I need to listen to this."

When they got the record home, listeners heard Cash's second civil rights album as more of a direct appeal to action than the first. Whereas *Blood, Sweat and Tears* served more as an accompaniment to the struggle for Black equality, *Bitter Tears* called for an equivalent movement on behalf of Indigenous peoples. Cash, who identified with Indians dating to his youth, could not tolerate, in a historical moment marked by a great national awakening to the wrongs of racism, the absence of national outrage over Kinzua, not to mention "termination." *Blood, Sweat and Tears* was certainly not for the faint of heart, but it made its points perhaps too subtly for most listeners to understand. *Bitter Tears* is anything but subtle. With the help of La Farge, Cash set out to school white America.

Taken together, the eight songs on *Bitter Tears*, five of which were penned by La Farge, mix historical tales with contemporary commentary to paint a broad picture of Indigenous life and experience. Cash could have kicked off the album with "Ira Hayes," the song that moved him so much, and the one single from the LP, but instead he left it for Side Two. Side One's first song is the most politically potent, the most accusatory, and the most appropriate for 1964: "As Long As the Grass Shall Grow." For listeners unfamiliar with the Kennedy administration's dismissal of Seneca concerns, the song is an education, meant to drive home the point that the historic dispossession of Indigenous peoples carries on to this day. With the Carter Family's backing harmonies and Cash's resonant and authoritative voice, it is also a more beautiful rendition than La Farge's. Cash follows with his own song, "Apache Tears," lyrics to which came to him after meeting Ira Hayes's mother on the Pima Reservation in Arizona. An "Apache tear" is what the Pima call a smooth, black, glassy stone found only in that part of the world, where the US Cavalry had killed scores of Apache warriors as they tried to coerce Cochise's people onto reservations. Hayes's mother told Cash that they represented the tears of Apache women who were forced to leave the bodies of the dead on the ground. Cash, of course, had already recorded "Old Apache Squaw," and knew Apache history, but nothing prepared him for Ira Hayes's mother giving him an "Apache tear." The song tells the story of thousands of "smooth black nuggets," the petrified tears shed by Apache women in the aftermath of the Army's final subduing of their people. There is more than a hint of menace in the portrayal of a young squaw tortured to death, perhaps raped. Not pulling punches, indeed.

The last two songs on Side One are, alternately, also by La Farge and Cash. Cash performs "Custer" more animatedly than La Farge did on the original—more up-tempo and with greater vocal inflection—but not quite as cheekily as he would later sing it with Buffy Sainte-Marie. Still, he chuckles at Custer's misfortune and downfall, saving a laugh for the line about him getting "barbered violent," as if to say, "that's what you get for being an asshole!" In the following track,

"The Talking Leaves," Cash moves to the sophisticated Sequoyah, the Indigenous intellectual who invented the Cherokee syllabary—essentially an alphabet based on syllables—of eighty-five characters. Sequoyah, Cash tells us, took inspiration from the "talking leaves," the white man's pages of written word, and transliterated Cherokee into its own system of talking leaves. By the end of Side One, we have had two stories of violent dispossession of natives, followed by two stories of achievement—whipping the US Army at the Little Bighorn and documenting a language more complex than English. It's a mix of tragedy and triumph.

As the lead track on Side Two, Cash's version of "Ira Hayes" (which he retitled as "The Ballad of Ira Hayes") carries much more force than La Farge's original. Whereas La Farge came off sounding like a mildly drunk, pompous graduate student on his own recording, Cash sings with enough pathos that he could have been mistaken for Ira Hayes's father or older brother. His voice is deep, resounding, and authoritative, but also just a bit shaky—in the way that, say, a father's voice quavers when speaking to the press about an injustice suffered by his family. When Cash sings the part about where Hayes died, his voice gives way—not quite cracking as much as deflating at the thought of the young man's life ending the way it did. Other songs on the album—maybe "Custer" or "Drums"—would have made better singles, but Cash and Columbia released "Ira Hayes" as the single; it was the right decision.

Two more songs by La Farge, "Drums" and "White Girl," follow in succession, with the former taking listeners back to the late nineteenth and early twentieth century, and the latter bringing us up to today. In many ways, "Drums" is the most defiant track on the *Bitter Tears* album, practically an "I Ain't Scared of Your Jail" freedom song for Native peoples. La Farge wrote it from the perspective of an Indian forced to attend a "governmental school" such as the Carlisle Indian Industrial School in Pennsylvania (1879–1918), at which Indigenous teenagers taken from reservations essentially went through a forced assimilation program, the goal of which was to make them like whites. The school tried, in the words of its founder, US Army Captain Richard Henry Pratt, to "kill the Indian" but "save the man." Eventually, the government established another two dozen of these indoctrination schools. When an adolescent arrived, headmasters changed their Indian names to Anglo names—in La Farge's song, the narrator is called "Billy"—traded their traditional clothes for European styles, and cut off their long hair. In five hundred years, Billy cracks, "not one Indian turned white." As Cash moves through the song, with backing vocals from the Carter Family, the tempo picks up with each verse, the chorus warning that there are drums "beyond the mountain," as though Native warriors are closing in, "getting mighty near." Our narrator doesn't buy any of the school's lessons, reeling off his own list of famous Indian leaders almost as an Indigenous people's counter-history to the school's official lessons. We taught history to you first, "Billy" argues, while you white people have only shamed yourselves by cheating the Indian rather than learning from him. The drums beyond the mountain, he seems to imply, herald the end.

The last two songs on the album, "White Girl" and "The Vanishing Race," are a kind of one-two combination, leaving us laid out with no doubt about who is crying the bitter tears of the record's title. The two songs together provide a natural bookend to the album, opposite the first two songs, "As Long As the Grass Shall Grow" and "Apache Tears," both of which covered the dispossession and torment of Indigenous peoples. In "White Girl," La Farge wrote about an Indian who, despite the warnings of his elders, falls in love with a blonde girl, only to be dumped. Cash sings the narration in a way that recalls his Sun recordings: spare, with only the Tennessee Three thumping gently in the background. Although the white girl tells our man she loves him, she cannot marry him simply because he is an Indian. He is left sad and alone, and clearly still in love with her, but he feels used, too, as though she treated him like a "white girl's pet . . . showed off and discarded." Compared to the album's tales of Crazy Horse, Sequoyah, or even Ira Hayes, his woeful story shows just how precipitously far he has fallen: he has not been betrayed by the full force of the United States government, his life has just been undone and discarded by a white girl. By contrast, "The Vanishing Race," a previously unrecorded song by Johnny Horton, Cash's dearly departed friend (who died in a 1960 head-on collision), is a slow lament, marking the displacement of the Navajo by the wagon trains from the east. It puts us back in mind of the Seneca and Apache at the start of the album, a reminder, as if the listener needed it at this point, of the totality of white theft from Indigenous peoples.

The album mixes snapshots of white settler villainy with moments of Indian resistance, but the knockout we know is coming arrives in the eighth round. Along the way, *Bitter Tears* are shed by the Seneca, Apache, Pima, and Navajo, not to mention the hapless ex-boyfriend of a white girl. The Sioux get in their licks against Custer, Sequoyah dazzles with his talking leaves, and the school boy promises a comeback in "Drums," but the comeback never comes. The listener emerges from the experience with a clearer understanding of the structures of racism erected by whites to justify their dispossession and continued subjugation of Indigenous peoples. But what now? Cash's identification with, and empathy for, subjugated and struggling Native peoples is obvious; but the question is, what will you, the listener, do now that you are armed with all of the same knowledge of these crimes against humanity? The upshot is that people need to demand justice in the same way that civil rights activists demanded equality and justice in that very same summer.

It is hard to find another album made by a major artist on a major label of such political force in the middle of the archetypal turbulent decade of the sixties. Certainly, Cash stood alone among country artists, as he had with *Blood, Sweat and Tears*, in producing a concept album about nonwhite peoples. The LP maybe did not sell at the same clip as some of Cash's earlier (or later) records, but with more than one hundred thousand copies sold in the first months after its release, and millions more since then, it was still a commercial success. When the record came out in October, *New York Times* music critic Robert Shelton listed *Bitter Tears* alongside albums by Bob Dylan, Joan Baez, Pete Seeger, and Woody Guthrie, among others, as representing the best in folk music. But the achievement often gets overshadowed in the recounting of a famous dustup over radio airplay, largely prompted by Cash himself.

The controversy arrived suddenly, like a summer thunderstorm, following a gushing reception at the Newport Folk Festival. Cash and company performed eight songs at Newport less than a month after the Nashville studio sessions, including a powerful rendition of "Ira Hayes" that won a standing ovation. The rave response raised his expectations for the album. But Cash soon learned from Columbia that DJs were balking at playing the four-minute song, keeping it out of rotation. He and his manager, Saul Holiff, also suspected that Columbia lacked sufficient enthusiasm for the whole project and did not put their muscle into promoting it. In a summer when "Ira Hayes" would have to go up against the Beatles, the Supremes, and the Beach Boys, the DJs and the folks at Columbia needed to do their jobs.

Cash took matters into his own hands by writing an ad in *Billboard* that attacked country music DJs and station owners, but, in effect, blasted the whole country music establishment. The full-page advertisement reads like the nearly incoherent rant of a guy who is obviously high, alternating between defiance ("classify me, categorize me—STIFLE me, but it won't work"), disgust ("You're right! Teenage girls and Beatle record buyers don't want to hear the sad story of Ira Hayes"), and a challenge, wrapped in an insult ("Would you, or those pulling the strings for you, go to the mike with a new approach? That is, listen again to the record?"). As proof of the song's value, he pointed out that he played it to twenty thousand people at Newport to thunderous applause. He doubled down on his supposed Native heritage, claiming that as "almost a half-breed Cherokee-Mohawk (and who knows what else?)," he was obliged to stand up to an industry "afraid" to play "Ira Hayes."[14]

Among some fans, the *Billboard* ad is just one more example—along with claiming to shoot "a man in Reno just to watch him die," flipping off the camera man at San Quentin, and spending some time behind bars—of Johnny Cash's badassery. But there is nothing badass about publishing a drug-fueled harangue. Looking back, it's easier to see the ad as a kind of theater performance more than anything else, and not political theater, either. Sure, he threw in references to the racial uprising in Rochester, New York, the previous month, and to the gathering storm in Vietnam (Congress had just approved the Gulf of Tonkin Resolution), but they were non sequiturs, unrelated, really, to his complaint about his single's lack of airplay. Some in the country music field essentially told him to get lost. "I'm disgusted by you," wrote one country music magazine editor, offended by Cash's arrogance, as if Cash thought he was smarter than everyone else in the industry. He urged Cash to resign from the Country Music Association. In the end, thanks or no thanks to the ad, "Ira Hayes" eventually climbed to number three on the country charts. But the *Billboard* letter heralded the start of a slide.[15]

CASH'S DEEPENING DRUG addiction and related troubles took over more and more of his life in late 1964 and 1965, and his political engagement, consequently, suffered. His obsession with documentary realism—which helped him to produce some of his most politically interesting work—took him to the Old West where he continued to try to relate to people from other walks of life, but these projects mostly took him away from politics. He seemed scattered. Obviously, he had never lost interest in the stories that his father and Old Jim George, allegedly of the James Gang, told about the outlaws and cowboys of the West. And artists he admired in the folk scene—notably Peter La Farge and Ed McCurdy—had recorded cowboy and outlaw records, too. Unlike La Farge, however, Cash had no real-world cowboy or rodeo experience, so he took to doing his own private reenactments of life on the Western frontier. He would drive his 1946 Jeep out from where he lived (but spent little time) in Casitas Springs, California, to the desert, where he would sleep under mesquite bushes and otherwise fumble around.

Out of these experiences came *Johnny Cash Sings the Ballads of the True West*, usually considered to be the first country music double LP, which, in spite of having twice the vinyl to work with, is also the weakest of Cash's concept albums. One only has to read the liner notes to see that this project suffered from a lack of focus. Cash wrote the notes so that they read like a middle school primer, complete with a glossary of "Western Lingo," but more than that, he also told tall tales of his Jeep outings, claiming, for example, to have taught himself to "kill a jack rabbit with a Bowie knife from forty yards away." (It is a pretty unlucky jackrabbit that dies from a drug addict's amateur toss of a bowie knife from such a distance.) The liner notes are meant to convey authenticity—to show that Cash had done his research not only by reading books, but by trying to live as these historical figures had lived. "Even though the people I sing about are gone, I saw something of what their life was like," Cash wrote. "Most of it I enjoyed. Some of it was mean as hell." Whether he realized it or not, he put on a kind of tough guy act; even in the album cover photo, he is dressed like a mustachioed villain, six-shooter in hand. It is hard to square the strained efforts at realism with the obvious evidence of fakery. Judging the album just by its external packaging, it comes across almost as child's play, less serious than Cash's earlier concept albums. If only the songs were better than the packaging.

Compared to the tidy execution of *Blood, Sweat and Tears* and especially *Bitter Tears*, *Ballads of the True West* is a real dog's breakfast, a scattered mess. For starters, it seems strange that on an album about the West, Indigenous peoples are practically absent, especially after Cash went to such lengths to bring their plight to his audience only twelve months earlier. He begins the album with "Hiawatha's Vision," a piece based on Longfellow's epic poem *The Song of Hiawatha*, but it meanders, unsure of its destination. For Longfellow, the portion of his poem called "The White Man's Foot" (which Cash takes as his primary inspiration) is a tale of the coming assault on Native peoples, but for Cash, it functions mostly as an introduction to two records that focus almost entirely on white experiences in the West. He doesn't shy from the menace whites represented to Indians, but he hurries through it, as though he doesn't know the history. But of course, he *did* know; every single song on *Bitter Tears* offered evidence of the entanglements of whites and Indigenous peoples. Although Vivian Clark Gilbert and Mary Margaret Hadler wrote "The Shifting Whispering Sands, Part 1," Cash begins by reciting again his experience in the desert, implying that he authored the song—or tried to—while sitting under a manzanita bush in what turned out to be "an old Indian burial ground." (In fact, it is a lazy interpretation of Billy Vaughn's 1962 recording, which begins with a similar narration spoken by Ken Nordine.) Other than that, there is virtually no further mention of Native peoples on the record.

Instead, the rest of the double LP is devoted mostly to outlaws, killers, and cowpokes—some not even in the West. "Mr. Garfield" describes the assassination of President James Garfield in 1881—a long-drawn-out event (it took Garfield more than two months to die from infections caused by his medical treatment) set entirely on the East Coast. If anything, it's a Ballad of the True East. The same is true of "Johnny Reb," the Merle Kilgore song previously recorded by Johnny Horton that honors the soldiers of the Confederacy. Cash strains in the liner notes to say that the Civil War drove "thousands upon thousands" of Americans to migrate west, but this migration is not the subject of the song. Instead, it makes heroes of the rebels ("even though you lost, they speak highly of your name") in archetypal Lost Cause fashion. If anything, it's a Ballad of the Untrue South.

Blood, Sweat and Tears gave a clearer picture of the True South, but Cash's admiration for the rough and tough fighters on this album—and his efforts to walk in their shoes, to experience what they experienced—blinded him to the role "Johnny Reb" played in defending slavery and maintaining the worldview that made chain gangs and lynchings possible for decades after the Civil War. The Klan, whom Cash rightly hated, undoubtedly loved "Johnny Reb." Odetta, whom Cash adored, undoubtedly did not. This is the problem with inhabiting a role: it can go too far. "We are what we pretend to be," Kurt Vonnegut famously wrote, "so we must be careful about what we pretend to be." On *Ballads of the True West*, Cash had ceased being careful. The unintentional result is a segregated album almost entirely about white people. If he had not already recorded LPs devoted to the experiences of Black and Native peoples, it would be hard not to conclude that Cash's brand of social realism extended only to his own kind.

And yet, in spite of Cash's interest in cowboys and outlaws, and even as Cash became more publicly associated with the cause of prisoners after the recording of the *At Folsom Prison* LP in 1968, he remained committed to Indigenous issues. In December 1968, he passed up a $10,000 show in London to do a free benefit concert for the Saint Francis Mission on the Rosebud Reservation in South Dakota. "It surprised me that they needed somebody like me to come in and help them raise money to build a school," he told journalists. He puzzled over the lack of government attention for the reservations. "I wonder where in the hell's the federal aid, the state aid, where's the funds the people's supposed to have for things like this?" When his own family faced crippling poverty, the government's intervention had saved them. The Cashes did not have to worry about raising money to build a school in Dyess; the New

Deal built it. Cash's experience as a man who had known poverty mattered more than his supposed Cherokee heritage. At Rosebud, a Lakota leader asked the Great Spirit to watch over Cash, so that he would grow to a ripe old age. When Cash appeared on stage that night, the audience, including Lakota elders in full headdresses, could see that he was visibly moved. "I got very little Indian blood in me, myself," he said softly into the microphone. "Except in my heart: I got 100 percent for you tonight" (a practice run for virtually the same line he used on his show with Buffy Sainte-Marie).

When a Lakota "medicine man" learned that Cash would travel to Wounded Knee the next day, to see the site of the US Army massacre of some three hundred defenseless men, women, and children—payback by the Seventh Cavalry for Little Bighorn—he told Cash that Cash would write a song called "Big Foot," after the Lakota chief. Sure enough, Cash took a tour of Wounded Knee, where he saw the massacre grounds, and he wrote the song. At the site, it's easy to see how these unarmed people were trapped in a shallow canyon and wiped out by the Hotchkiss repeating rifles—the earliest machine guns—and left dead in the bitter cold. One of Cash's guides knew exactly where his grandmother's body had been found. "There was a mystical air that hung over the place," Cash soon recounted. Just as the medicine man predicted, Cash quickly scribbled out the lyrics to the new song.[16]

After *Bitter Tears*, "Big Foot" is Cash's most important musical-political act on behalf of Indigenous peoples. This is not merely because it tells the story of the state-sanctioned mass murder in song more than a year before Dee Brown's exposé, *Bury My Heart at Wounded Knee*, was published to great fanfare, though there is that. More important is that "Big Foot" is Cash's own song—not Peter La Farge's or anyone else's—and more than any of the songs on *Bitter Tears*, it combines a critique of American policy toward Native peoples with a critique of American militarism. The lyrics to "Big Foot" read like a long poem, relating most of the details Cash learned that day. They summarize the historical context—the revenge of the Seventh Cavalry fifteen years after Custer's death—and the entire ordeal of the massacre, from Big Foot's own murder to that of hundreds of women and children. "Death showed no favorites," Cash wrote, noting that babies died while other infants cried for their murdered mothers.

Cash didn't release "Big Foot" immediately. He could have put the song on one of the four LPs he released between 1969 and 1971, but instead, he held onto it, releasing it to much more dramatic effect in 1972 on the double LP, *America: A 200 Year Salute in Story and Song*. It is significant that Cash put "Big Foot" on a record like this at all—it had begun as a compilation of songs about American history intended for the Apollo astronauts—but choosing to release it a year after the million-selling "The Battle Hymn of Lt. Calley" tried to gloss over a similar American mass murder at My Lai, in Vietnam, meant something. In 1972, "Big Foot" served as a blunt assessment of the kind of American military policy that somehow fostered twin massacres nearly eighty years apart in two different parts of the world.

By the time Cash started recording episodes for his new television show, just a few months after his Wounded Knee trip, Indigenous peoples were still on his mind. He included something about Native peoples in three of the first six episodes. Indeed, two weeks after he sang "Custer" with Buffy Sainte-Marie, Cash devoted the "Ride This Train" portion of the show to the Kinzua Dam controversy. He described the dam as creating a man-made lake for watersports, built by white men over the objections of the Seneca. According to Cash, the white man said, "This is progress; don't you understand?" but he said that, in fact, whites were guilty of not understanding Native peoples. "Fear comes with misunderstanding," he told the audience, and that fear left Indians "with fewer lands, less game, broken promises, and more broken promises." At this point, he sang "As Long As the Grass Shall Grow" about the Seneca, followed by a speech about the Pima in Arizona, as an introduction to "Ira Hayes." After the song, he lamented that after three centuries of misunderstanding "it's a little too late now to make up—we can only say we hope we don't make the same mistake again." Following such an impassioned dissection of American mistreatment of Indigenous peoples, it is a strangely passive note on which to end. By saying "we can only hope," he left the power with whomever occupied the White House, even though he knew how well that had turned out for Native peoples. By that fall, he acknowledged to one reporter that despite his concern for "the Indian problem," on a "national scale, I can't see as yet how my voice has really helped them."[17]

In the context of the times, it would not have been so outrageous to expect Cash to go a little further. By the late 1960s, despite what the government did to the Seneca, talk of "termination" had largely receded. In 1968, Congress passed the Indian Civil Rights Act, which aimed "to ensure that the American Indian is afforded the broad constitutional rights secured to other Americans," though it did so less to protect Natives from the United States government than from what it characterized as "arbitrary and unjust actions of tribal governments." To outsiders, a civil rights act for Indigenous peoples sounded good, but for a lot of Natives, it constituted further federal encroachment—without consultation (Natives did not elect representatives to Congress)—on Native governance. They were right to worry. Although the American Indian Movement (AIM) had begun the previous summer in Minneapolis, in the summer of 1969, most Americans still had not heard of the organization, though they would before the end of that first season of *The Johnny Cash Show*.

On November 20, 1969, a group of eighty-nine Native peoples landed on Alcatraz Island in the middle of San Francisco Bay, beginning an occupation that lasted until June 1971. Calling themselves Indians of All Tribes, they said that they were reclaiming Alcatraz as a cultural center where "the old Indian ways" could be preserved for future generations. In time the occupation grew to more than six hundred Natives, and Buffy Sainte-Marie headlined a benefit concert for the occupation at Stanford University. Among other songs, she performed "Now That the Buffalo's Gone" and "My Country 'Tis of Thy People You're Dying," both condemnations of white America not only for breaking promises but for lying to themselves about it—of writing lies into American history to conceal the systematic crimes against humanity committed against Indigenous peoples. The occupation attracted widespread media attention, nationally and internationally, and helped introduce the world to the American Indian Movement. For the rest of *The Johnny Cash Show*'s run, Natives occupied Alcatraz, and their movement seemed to be winning more popular support among white Americans than ever before. During this time, Cash grew again more assertive, using his weekly public platform.[18]

Starting in his show's second season, Cash began to change the language he used when he discussed Native peoples. On the show that aired February 4, 1970, Cash asked viewers to "Ride This Train" with him to Cherokee country, to Tennessee, Georgia, and the Carolinas, land and waters where, for ten thousand years, the Cherokee hunted and fished. He introduced his song "The Talking Leaves" by telling the story of Sequoyah and his syllabary—which he said was "one of the greatest accomplishments by Western man in the last three hundred years." By characterizing Sequoyah in this way, he did something that no Hollywood Western had yet done—he included Indigenous peoples as part of "Western man" or Western civilization, instead of as a people vanquished by it. When Cash held up an old scroll containing, apparently, the Cherokee syllabary, the audience applauded enthusiastically. But he wasn't finished. He told how, despite the Cherokee's sophistication, the southeastern states began passing laws to remove the Cherokee; "the good president Andrew Jackson," he said, would not use the power of the presidency to overrule states' rights—he would not start a civil war, Cash said, over states' rights. So the Cherokee found themselves on the forced march to Indian Territory in present day Oklahoma, walking the Trail of Tears that cost more than eight thousand Cherokee and Creek their lives. At best, this is a gross misreading of American history. At worst, it's a shameful effort to hide Jackson's and the federal government's true role in the persecution and dispossession of the Cherokee. In Cash's rendering, the states were somehow to blame, even though the instrument came from Congress, which, at Jackson's urging, passed the 1830 Indian Removal Act.

But leaving aside this misrepresentation, Cash's insistence on going into this level of detail on the Trail of Tears, against the backdrop of the Alcatraz occupation, could be read as signaling support for the American Indian Movement. In fact, there is no record of his thoughts on Alcatraz—he seems never to have been asked about it by reporters—but the language he used to conclude that chapter of "Ride This Train" provides clues. "Well, have we failed our Indian brothers?" he asked the audience. "We broke the treaties that said the land would be theirs for as long as the moon shall rise, as long as the grass shall grow." Unlike the previous July, when he said "let us hope" not to repeat these crimes, on this occasion, he placed more responsibility on himself and his audience: "Let us be careful not to make the same mistake again, for, as men, we're all brothers under the sun." Cash's shared understanding of poverty certainly fueled his empathy for Native peoples, but as his comments made clear, so, too, did his Christian sense of brotherhood.[19]

A few months later, Cash returned to the Natives-as-brothers theme in an eleven-minute-long chapter of "Ride This Train." Once again, he told the stories of the US government breaking the treaty with the Seneca to build Kinzua Dam, of Wounded Knee and Big Foot, and of the Pima Ira Hayes, singing each of the respective songs that he and La Farge had written to draw attention to these conditions. "Of all the great tragedies of North America, perhaps the greatest of all has been the white man's treatment of his red brother,"

Cash said to his audience, sounding much like a schoolteacher summing up a lesson for his students. "For, with the coming of our ancestors to these shores, the great, proud people who had lived here for thousands of years were pushed back and reduced little by little to a state of poverty, grief, and hopelessness. Pushed back even to the very brink of extinction." The result, Cash said, is that today, Native peoples are so marginalized—"cast out of the mainstream of our society"—they have become strangers in their own land. "Now is it not time to think of these strangers here among us as our own brothers? Is it not time that we turned back to the message of Gitche Manitou, the Great Spirit of the red man, and do unto them as they were ready to do unto us?" As Cash, the Southern Baptist who sang hymns at the end of nearly every show, put it, the lesson suddenly sounded like a variation on the Golden Rule taught in Sunday school—to treat people the way you want to be treated. It's a lesson so simple, it is taught to children. For Cash, the simple lesson needed to be taught to white America and its leaders.[20]

There is no evidence that Cash's appeals on behalf of Indigenous peoples reached the halls of power in Washington, but we know that Richard Nixon paid attention to Cash in this period—enough that he invited Cash to perform at the White House in April. That summer, Nixon outlined in broad terms a change in US government policy toward Indigenous peoples, putting an end to "termination" and forced assimilation, while calling for an easing of federal "paternalism." For the first time, an American president acknowledged "centuries of injustice" at the root of Native peoples' present isolation and inequal status. Dating to European arrival in the hemisphere, Nixon said, "American Indians have been oppressed and brutalized, deprived of their ancestral lands and denied the opportunity to control their own destiny." He sounded as though he had heard Cash's statements on behalf of Indigenous peoples. "We must assure the Indian that he can assume control of his own life without being separated involuntarily from his tribal group," the president declared. "And we must make it clear that Indians can become independent of Federal control without being cut off from Federal concern and Federal support." Nixon stopped short of referring to Natives as his brothers, but as a break from prior policy, what he proposed certainly sounded good. Too bad the proposal remained largely unrealized.[21]

By the time Nixon announced this new policy direction, Cash's advocacy on behalf of Indigenous peoples led producers at National Educational Television (the forerunner of PBS) to cast him as Cherokee Chief John Ross in the full-length TV episode "The Trail of Tears." Narrated by Joseph Cotton and starring Jack Palance as President Andrew Jackson, the film goes into great historical detail, providing a ninety-minute lesson on this ugly episode in American history. To its credit, it portrays Jackson as more deliberate in pushing for the removal of the Cherokee and Creek from the southeastern states than Cash had on his own show. Once the Cherokee try to set up their own government within the state of Georgia, Palance's Jackson says they have to be moved; it was a dangerous precedent for a foreign power to establish a state within a state, he argues. He promises that in the territory set aside for them west of the Mississippi River, Indians can do what they want, unperturbed by whites. Cash, as John Ross, speaks to the camera as if it were another "Ride This Train" portion of his own show. He defends the Cherokee as the last "small forest . . . the only embodied people now remaining of the first natives of their native land." Speaking to viewers, he says, "Look—here are our treaties with the United States. These promise us protection." Pleading, he exclaims, "Brothers, you cannot break that promise!"

In the end, of course, the government did break its promises, and much of the film is devoted to showing the Cherokee being rounded up and herded into what look like concentration camps before being forced to march more than one thousand miles to Indian Territory. For Cash, the role is his best acting part to date. He played Ross seriously, forcefully, and seemed comfortable, as if he had produced the role for his own show. But for Johnny Cash, the public citizen, the role functioned as an extended public service announcement on an issue with which he had been associated for a long time. It is a culmination of Cash's commitment—taking the private work he did at the Saint Francis Mission, as well as the *Bitter Tears* record, and bringing it to a much larger, national audience.[22]

By the 1970s, Native peoples certainly regarded Cash as an ally, if not one of their own. In fact, the Seneca so appreciated his outspoken condemnation of the United States government's betrayal over the Kinzua Dam that they had already adopted him as a member of the Turtle Clan, naming him "Ha-gao-ta" for "Story Teller." When he struggled to find funding for his film, *A Gunfight*, the Jicarilla Apache invested $2 million to get the film made. In 1977, when Sammi Smith, the country singer best known for singing Kris Kristofferson's "Help Me Make It Through the Night," and a descendant of Apache chief Cochise, asked at the last minute for Cash to perform at a benefit concert for an Apache high school on the San Carlos Reservation in place of an ailing Waylon Jennings, Cash hopped on a plane to make the show.

None of this continued identification with Indigenous peoples diminished Cash's love of cowboys, though. He simply did not see cowboys and Indians in opposition. At times, his show featured guest spots by big names in television Westerns: both Lorne Greene and Dan Blocker from *Bonanza*, Doug McLure of *The Virginian*, and *Death Valley Days* host Dale Robertson appeared, as well as film star Kirk Douglas, with whom Cash made *A Gunfight* in 1971. Toward the end of the show's run in February 1971, he produced an episode dedicated entirely to *Ballads of the True West*. Cash understood that for Native peoples, the problem had always been politicians, the ones who break promises and make settler colonialism possible. Cowboys were settlers, too, and some were gunslingers and killers, the kind of folks who wound up swinging from the gallows. But Cash saw the problems as structural, as failures of the government.

And he related to the cowboys—to the ones on the wrong side of the law or trapped in a harsh system of American criminal justice, caught up in structural problems of their own. But it took recording a couple of live albums that made him a superstar before he got those messages to the masses.

An Arkansas sharecropper family evicted for being members of the Southern Tenant Farmers Union, nearly a year after the Cashes moved to Dyess, 1936.

The first known photo of Cash's boyhood home at 266 Road Three, Dyess, Arkansas, 1936. Either young J. R. or brother Jack stands out front.

(Above) Cash's identification with his hometown was well known to his fans by the time he became a superstar. Here he returns to his boyhood home for a LOOK magazine photo shoot, 1968.

Photo by Joel Baldwin, LOOK magazine collection, Library of Congress, Prints & Photographs Division, LC-L9-68-3986-KK, no. 6 [P&P] LOOK - Job 68-3986.

Cash (center) follows the example of his father, brother, and singing cowboy idol, Gene Autry, by joining the United States Air Force just as the Korean War broke out.

Photo courtesy Cash Family Estate.

Once Cash became a star, he returned to Germany on tour, stopping in at the American Forces Network radio station in Frankfurt to serve as guest DJ on AFN's "Hillbilly Reveille," his favorite show when he was stationed at Landsberg.

Growing up in rural Arkansas, Cash saw Black prisoners working on roads and levees in chain gangs—a painfully common sight. Decades later, he sometimes mentioned onstage that he remembered seeing chain gangs coming in from working on the levees, of hearing them talking and singing.

Photo taken sometime between 1934 and 1950, Lomax Collection, Library of Congress, Prints & Photographs Division, LC-DIG-ppmsc-00420.

At the height of the civil rights movement, and against the backdrop of white supremacist violence, Cash recorded an underappreciated concept album on Black lives, *Blood, Sweat, and Tears*, 1962.

Courtesy of Sony Music Entertainment.

On *The Johnny Cash Show* (1969–71), the host used his weekly platform as a showcase for interracial harmony and the celebration of African-American artistry. Here, Odetta and Cash prepare a duet in a show that aired just after Woodstock, in August 1969.

Photo by Walt Disney Television / © ABC/Getty Images.

Cash's support of Native peoples and Indigenous rights went beyond his 1965 LP, *Bitter Tears*. Here, Cash joins an unidentified Lakota elder at historical marker for the 1890 Wounded Knee Massacre site, the day after playing a benefit concert for the St. Francis Mission on the Rosebud Reservation.

Photo courtesy Red Cloud Indian School and Marquette University. Holy Rosary Mission – Red Cloud Indian School Records, ID 0061.

On his show's fourth episode, Cash performed Peter La Farge's irreverent "Custer," with Buffy Sainte-Marie.

Photo by Walt Disney Television / © ABC/Getty Images.

Following the fantastic success of *Johnny Cash At Folsom Prison*, Cash accepted the invitation to perform at several reelection campaign rallies for Arkansas governor Winthrop Rockefeller, who had demonstrated a commitment to prison reform.

Republican Party State Headquarters Collection, University of Arkansas-Little Rock Center for Arkansas History and Culture.

Rockefeller brought the Johnny Cash Show to Cummins Prison to perform for the inmates and a handful of state legislators, with television cameras recording the whole event.

©1969 Arkansas Democrat-Gazette.

After the show, Cash mingles with the Cummins convicts.

© 1969 Arkansas Democrat-Gazette

Thanks to the success of the *At Folsom Prison* and *At San Quentin* LPs, Cash was invited by Senator Bill Brock to testify before a Senate subcommittee on penitentiaries in 1973. Following his testimony, Cash and Brock stopped by the White House to discuss the issue with President Richard Nixon.

Photo by Oliver Atkins, courtesy Richard Nixon Presidential Library, National Archives, WHPO-9649-27-33.

January 1969, GIs react to Cash performing at Long Binh Army Base in Saigon, South Vietnam.

Overseas Weekly photographs, Contact Sheet 14936, Hoover Institution Library & Archives, Stanford University.

After Cash expressed his support for Nixon's handling of the Vietnam War on his television show, the White House invited Cash to perform. Cash's performance of "What Is Truth?"—a new song sympathetic to youthful protesters—surprised the president.

Photo by Jack Kightlinger, courtesy Richard Nixon Presidential Library, National Archives, WHPO-3366.

In February 1971, Cash produced an "On Campus" episode of his television show, parts of which included segments of Cash speaking to students at Vanderbilt University. On the same episode, he debuted the song "Man in Black," in response to a student's question.

Photo by Herb Peck, Jr. Courtesy of Vanderbilt University Special Collections and University Archives.

In May, 1970, in the wake of nationwide protests over the Cambodia invasion and the Kent State and Jackson State shootings, Cash appeared at the Rev. Billy Graham's "Crusade" at Neyland Stadium in Knoxville, Tennesee.

Copyright Jack Kirkland—USA Today Network.

Patriot or protester? Cash and the flag from the photo shoot for his 1972 LP, *America*.
Courtesy of Sony Music Entertainment.

Fellow Highwayman Kris Kristofferson liked to call Cash "the Father of our country."
Cash, the Grand Marshal of the Grand Bicentennial Parade, rides down Constitution
Avenue in Washington, DC, July 3, 1976.

Photo by Pictorial Parade / Getty Images.

5

Going to Prison

When Johnny Cash recorded the very first episode of his television show in the spring of 1969, he made sure to acknowledge his debt to the men incarcerated at California's Folsom State Prison. Without them, he would have had no television show—he would not then have been on the cusp of superstardom. "I've always thought it ironic that it was a prison concert," he wrote years later, "with me and the convicts getting along just as fellow rebels, outsiders, and miscreants should, that pumped up my marketability to the point where ABC thought I was respectable enough to have a weekly network TV show."[1]

Thus, in tribute to all of those men heard on his *At Folsom Prison* LP (1968), Cash dedicated the very first "Ride This Train" segment to the prisoners at Folsom. He sang Harlan Howard's "The Wall," a song Cash had recorded on his *Orange Blossom Special* album (1965), and just about one of the saddest tales of prison loneliness ever written. The song's main character contemplates an escape because his "gal" has written to tell him she is marrying another man. Our inmate hero pledges to be the first to get over the wall of the prison, but when he makes a break for it, he is killed. The song's narrator tells us, in the end, that having witnessed the grim scene, he knows it was no escape attempt; so certain was his failure, it could only have been a suicide. On his television show, however, Cash withheld the song's ghastliest details, perhaps not wanting to spoil the launch of what was, after all, a family TV show, broadcast to Middle America.

Cash went on to paint a sympathetic portrait of the prisoners during the segment, describing how he met an inmate named Glen Sherley at Folsom, surprising him by performing Sherley's song "Greystone Chapel" for the Folsom audience. Following the sorrow and misery of "The Wall," then, Cash here comes back with a kind of feel-good story from the *At Folsom Prison* album. He concluded the segment with "Folsom Prison Blues," famous for its line about shooting a man in Reno "just to watch him die," but, really, darker still for putting us in the shoes of this prisoner who knows he "can't be free." As in his approach to civil rights and Indigenous rights, Cash's approach to carceral politics demanded imagining himself in the position of the marginalized. His show brought to the public not the old, cruel America, but the state of the nation in 1969—*today's* cruel America.[2]

Some weeks later, Cash again used "Ride This Train" to take viewers to California's San Quentin State Prison, site of his recently released live prison album. By the time the episode aired on August 23, that LP had climbed to the top of not only the country charts but the pop charts, mostly on the strength of Cash's novelty hit song "A Boy Named Sue." But on "Ride This Train," Cash avoided the easy cross-platform marketing that Columbia Records executives no doubt hoped he would exploit. Instead, he focused on the men in the prison, imagining them dreaming of their eventual release, searching for a job, and returning to freedom. He mused about the little things that might "brighten their faces—a song, a letter, or a kind thought," and then began singing "Send a Picture of Mother," a song from the *At Folsom Prison* LP. He also performed his new song, "San Quentin," which he debuted during the recording at the namesake prison earlier that year, but as he sang, viewers at home saw footage taken from the prison—intended, it seemed, to give his audience a sense of what prison life is like. "San Quentin, may you rot and burn in Hell," Cash sang, mocking the prison itself, as well as law-and-order congressmen for failing to see that it "does no good." The song won prolonged applause from the Ryman audience. Cash finished by telling the oft-told story of being approached years before by a San Quentin ex-con who, try as he might, had not been able to fund his trip back to his home state of Louisiana. Desperate, the man asked that if Cash got to Shreveport before he did, would he "give my love to Rose." As Cash sang the song of the same name—one of his best prison songs—he impressed upon his audience a degree of sympathy for the men imprisoned.[3]

More than half a century has passed since Cash made those prison albums, but his identification with prisoners occupies a privileged place in the way we remember him. Not only did he make those recordings at Folsom and San Quentin (with the latter concert the subject of a Granada Television documentary broadcast in England but now widely available on DVD), but he later released another live prison album, *på Österåker* (1973), recorded in Sweden, and did a live concert at the Tennessee State Penitentiary for television (also widely available on DVD as *A Concert Behind Prison Walls*). Cash's public association with prison issues was so well known that the United States Senate welcomed his testimony before a subcommittee on penitentiaries regarding prison reform.

But *why* Cash became so publicly invested in prison issues has received comparatively little attention. The easy answer is that, as with Native peoples, Cash always spoke up for and on behalf of the downtrodden. Yet that, while true, does not fully answer the question. Plenty of country artists—going back at least as far as Vernon Dalhart's "The Prisoner's Song" (1924) and Jimmie Rodgers's "In the Jailhouse Now" (1928), to name just two obvious examples—have interpreted songs from the perspective of convicts. But Cash, more than anyone else, related to the lot of prisoners. His own experiences, as ever, fed a politics not of party platforms, but one that grafted a sense of solidarity from his own short stints in jail with a sense of witness from having seen the inside of so many penitentiaries as a performer. Cash showed this in the best way he knew how, by documenting prison life on vinyl the way the Lomaxes had once recorded prison chain gangs on their Presto disc audio recorders. Remarkably, Cash brought the voices of prisoners to the American public during the same years when politicians like Richard Nixon and Ronald Reagan framed their candidacies around a return to law and order, when the nation embarked on its now decades-long spending spree of building and expanding prisons. At that historical moment, Johnny Cash, practically alone among political artists, called for prison reform, demanding that we *care* about prisoners and their rehabilitation.

IN ADDITION TO bearing witness to actual prisoners—whether German POWs or chain gangs in northeast Arkansas—Cash's imagination extended prison metaphors to include those bound by circumstance. Of course, he complained of being locked up in a "lifeless hole" in Landsberg, as if it were Alcatraz, even though no one from Alcatraz could pop over to San Francisco for a night on the town the way Cash and his fellow airmen could in Munich. Still, he more convincingly described the poor who could not break the grip of poverty, who seemed trapped in shotgun shacks where hunger and despair festered. Later in life, when he reflected on the appeal of his prison albums, Cash said, "whether we know it or not the words of a song about someone who is actually in prison speak for a lot of us who might not appear to be, but really are." It may be naive for Cash himself to equate being trapped in a dead-end job in the military, stuck in a loveless marriage, or unable to escape one's drug addiction to incarceration in a penitentiary, but he was sincere when he suggested that "most of us are living in one little kind of prison or another."[4]

Cash's viewing of the B movie *Inside the Walls of Folsom Prison*, while still an airman in Landsberg, is usually cited as his inspiration for writing "Folsom Prison Blues," but its real importance lay in getting him to think seriously about prison reform. The film, some of which was shot at Folsom and included a handful of inmates in acting roles, depicts Folsom as a medieval institution, led by an old-school warden with a taste for using brute force to enforce discipline and punish violators. Following a prison riot against this regime, the prison board sends a university-trained reformer, Mark Benson, to be captain of the guards and introduce a number of changes. Benson treats the inmates like human beings, improves their diet, lets them speak to each other during meals, restores the discipline of the guards, and even offers to help a soon-to-be-paroled convict get a job. This do-gooder is eventually run off by the warden, who cracks down on the prisoners, bringing convulsions of violence. In a final segment, viewers were told that the film had depicted just one story from the prison's past. In 1951, the narrator reports, Folsom is a reformed institution, led by an "enlightened penologist" and guards chosen by exam. The prisoners now, the narrator says, are treated as individuals, and they do things to occupy their minds, getting paid for making license plates before most of them get paroled. "You can't lock them up and forget them," the film concludes. "Sooner or later one of them may be your neighbor." It's a message Cash never forgot.

Within a few years of his arrival in Memphis and the start of his Sun recording career, Cash not only recorded "Folsom Prison Blues" but took his touring show to prisons. Inspired perhaps by the Lomax recordings of prisoners at places like Angola Prison or Parchman Farm, or by Sam Phillips (who had bussed actual convicts from the Tennessee State Penitentiary in Nashville to Memphis to record as the Prisonaires as early as 1953), Cash and the Tennessee

Two accepted their first invitation to play at a prison when they performed, in 1957, at Huntsville State Prison in Texas. Although a thunderstorm nearly electrocuted Luther Perkins on a jerry-rigged stage in the middle of the Huntsville prison yard, the show went so well that Cash asked his manager, Stu Carnall, to look out for other opportunities to play prisons. But he did so not to grandstand. He played prisons, he later wrote, because as the *Inside the Walls of Folsom Prison* narrator warned, "you can't lock them up and forget about them." Cash wanted the inmates to know "that somewhere out there in the free world was somebody who cared for them as human beings."[5]

We do not have eyewitness testimony from that Hunstville Prison date, no reports from inmates in the crowd, but we do have at least one authoritative account on Cash's first free concert at San Quentin. In fact, over the years, a small-time petty criminal and escape artist from Bakersfield named Merle Haggard described the scene of Cash's New Year's Day 1958 (or 1959 or 1960—accounts vary) show in numerous interviews. "Cash wasn't nearly as famous as he is today, but it was easy to see the raw talent in that tall, hungry-looking dude from Arkansas," Haggard wrote in his first autobiography. Haggard, who had already performed on a few small Bakersfield stages himself—before landing in the joint—only got serious about a future in country music after seeing Cash at San Quentin. "I remember he just looked *terrible*," Haggard recalled of Cash that day. "He was hungover from the night before and his voice was almost gone—but hell, he came out on that stage and just blew everybody away." Although prison officials presented a real variety show to bring in the New Year—it had also featured Larry and Lorrie Collins, "The Collins Kids," from Los Angeles, as well as a blues band, some opera singers, and a host of San Francisco strippers—somehow Cash alone impressed the prisoners. Unlike the other performers, Cash made it clear that he identified with his audience. When he looked to the side during his set and saw a guard who, not really paying attention to the show, chewed mightily on his gum, Cash mocked him, miming exaggerated chewing. "He didn't have to sing," Haggard recalled. "He had 5,000 prisoners who loved him immediately because he'd made fun of the damned screw." The prisoners seemed startled that a performer—an entertainer—so readily related to them. "This was somebody singing a song about your personal life," Haggard later said. "Even the people who weren't fans of Johnny Cash—it was a mixture of people, all races were fans by the end of the show." Cash had "made us *forget* where we were," Haggard marveled. "Anybody who can actually make a group of men forget they're in San Quentin is some kind of magician." The next day, in the yard, anyone with a guitar—and some without—tried to teach themselves "Folsom Prison Blues."[6]

Although few free-world fans had any idea that Cash performed occasionally at prisons, it would have been easy to get the idea, by the mid-1960s, that the Arkansan had developed some kind of prison obsession. Most albums he put out in this period featured at least one song with a criminal, outlaw, or convict theme.[7] Plenty of country and blues artists recorded prison songs over the years, but no single artist threaded these themes throughout so much of his recorded output as Cash. Even Merle Haggard himself, an actual ex-con, had recorded only five prison songs by the late 1960s.[8] More than that, Cash's carceral songs tended to be darker laments, mixing intimations of violence with self-loathing, whereas Haggard's self-disgust in, for example, "Mama Tried," is delivered still in that shiny Bakersfield sound.

Although Cash later acknowledged that he had been arrested a number of times—most famously in the liner notes to the *At Folsom Prison* LP—all but his widely reported 1965 trip to the El Paso pokey would have escaped most fans' attention. Police had arrested Cash as he came back from Juarez with more than a thousand pills stuffed in socks inside his guitar and suitcase. The Associated Press photo of Cash in handcuffs, wearing dark sunglasses, being escorted by marshals from the El Paso County Jail appeared in papers all over the country. Still, judging by his fan club publications, in fact, most in his audience were either unaware of, or willing to forgive, much of Cash's drug-induced bad behavior. Missed dates, a damaged voice (a product of too much speed and cigarette smoking), and an absence of hit singles did not dim fans' enthusiasm for his shows. June Vosburg, the vice president of the Johnny Cash Society (JCS), reported in November 1966 that she had seen Cash perform in Albuquerque with a case of "the flu," and against doctor's orders. Another JCS stalwart, Mable Somland, told of seeing Cash perform with "a bad cold" in Flint, Michigan. "Johnny kept singing in spite of the fact that he was losing his voice," she wrote admiringly. Even the legendary San Francisco music critic, Ralph Gleason, reported on a November 1966 Cash show in Oakland, noting that the singer could not "stand still," prowling the stage with a "burning intensity" that almost certainly came from the pharmaceuticals running through his veins, but which Gleason chalked up to his innate "magnetism." Although Cash's run-ins with the law may have made local headlines here and there (mostly in California), and he may have been regarded in Nashville, by 1967, as a bit of a joke—a washed-up has-been in self-destruct mode—the only hints of Cash's desperado past appeared on his record sleeves, when he posed as an outlaw, and in the great many prison songs he recorded.[9]

Viewed in this light, the claims of some biographers that Cash cynically manipulated his outlaw image and allowed the public to think that maybe he had done prison time in order to "trade on the myth"—to profit financially from fans' fascination with his dark side—are a little overwrought. Not until Cash released the first *American Recordings* album in 1994 did he and his label peddle a version of his persona that deliberately played on his long association with convicted criminals. Had he wanted to make a bigger deal of it to his fans in the 1960s, he certainly had enough opportunities to tell them about his numerous prison concerts, and his own run-ins with the law, but he didn't. Cash performed at one prison after another with little fanfare—except among the inmates, whom he won over easily. As one Folsom convict wrote following a 1966 show, Cash "made himself one of us" when he came off the stage to meet some of the inmates and shake hands. Even the most jaded felt like Cash really related to them. "I've been here 11 years," one prisoner said, "and thought I had learned to hate everything connected with the prison, but . . . this show is the first thing I've enjoyed in those 11 years." No one could say that Cash benefited in any way from interactions like these, except maybe spiritually, by witnessing to the forgotten and the shunned. He certainly did not cash in financially, since he did most prison concerts for free, and few in the music business would consider associating with inmates a profitable career strategy.[10]

Rather, as Cash headed into the epochal year of 1968, nearly free from drugs, and prepared to record a live prison album, he pursued the same goal as when he went into the studio to record *Ride This Train, Blood, Sweat and Tears, Bitter Tears,* and *Ballads of the True West.* Johnny Cash wanted to capture the reality of a particular human condition—in this case, of prison life—on vinyl, the way that a kid catches a lightning bug in a jar. Cash had long dreamed of recording a prison concert because he wanted listeners to imagine themselves in the prison, among the inmates, seeing the show—to hear and feel the energy for themselves.[11]

In this way, Cash upped the authenticity ante on other country music prison albums like Porter Wagoner's *Soul of a Convict.* Wagoner, one of country music's biggest stars, hit number seven on the country charts with his prison concept album (which included his own version of Cash's "Folsom Prison Blues") in 1967, so Cash could hardly come back and do his own prison concept album in the way of *Ballads of the True West.* It would have been seen as copying Wagoner. Instead, he aimed to give a sense of real life in a real prison, not by again recording himself singing chain gang songs in a studio, but by recording actual inmates reacting to his prison songs inside the walls of a penitentiary. As such, *At Folsom Prison* would be the capstone concept album project, the one that brought up to date how the cruelties of America's past lived on to the present day, in 1968.[12]

And yet, in his approach to the mercilessness of prison life, Cash chose not to focus on the violence that characterized so much of *Blood, Sweat and Tears*, but instead foregrounded what he saw as another kind of violence, a foundational cruelty: that prisoners were being left to rot by their fellow Americans. By its attitude toward crime and punishment—built on prisoner erasure—the American public made possible the inhumanity of the country's prisons. As he played penal institutions around the country, he saw a common theme: incarceration was so pointlessly alienating that it crushed men's souls. "A lot of them just had that living-dead look on their faces," Cash told one writer. He performed increasing numbers of prison concerts to show the convicts that someone *did* pay attention to them, but that was not enough. By recording a prison performance, by putting the prisoners themselves on the historical record, and by showing how he, Johnny Cash, related to them, he called the public's attention to their basic humanity. He was walking a line between empathy and advocacy.[13]

Fortunately for Cash, he found a producer who saw the vision of realism in his concept albums as true art. Bob Johnston, a Texan the same age as Cash who had recorded Bob Dylan, Leonard Cohen, and Simon & Garfunkel, came to Nashville to replace Don Law upon his retirement from Columbia Records, in 1967.[14] Johnston saw something special in Cash and equated him with Dylan. "You're fuckin' artists," Johnston told Cash. "You don't just make records. You make records that mean something to you and the people who hear them." Cash saw something where others did not and tailored his art so his listeners could see it, too. In Johnston, he found more than a producer; he found a co-conspirator.[15]

The historical context for the making of this legendary album is important. Folsom State Prison is located about twenty miles outside Sacramento, the capital of California, home to a government led, at the time, by Ronald Reagan. In the 1966 gubernatorial election, Reagan had defeated the incumbent, Edmund G. "Pat" Brown, by running primarily on a law-and-order platform and hammering Brown for being soft on crime, for opposing the death penalty (even though he had signed thirty-six death warrants as governor), and especially for coddling campus radicals. No state university militants would be tolerated on Reagan's watch: in the spring of 1969, a year after *At Folsom Prison* came out, faced with further Berkeley protests in defense of "People's Park," Reagan would say to his police and National Guard chiefs, "If it takes a bloodbath, let's get it over with—no more appeasement." Johnny Cash arrived in Reagan's California to record an album that essentially asked listeners to identify with—sympathize with—convicted killers, rapists, and thieves. As Cash and his group rehearsed at the El Rancho Hotel in Sacramento the night before, Reagan himself held a fundraiser in an adjacent banquet room and stopped in to say hello. The two men exchanged pleasantries, but one wonders what the former actor— who thought that locking people up and throwing away the key were movie lines to live by—thought of a fellow entertainer giving voice to prisoners.

No one could have known what the spring of 1968 would be like, but by the time *At Folsom Prison* came out in May, the United States showed signs of imploding. Following the Tet Offensive that began in Vietnam in late January, public opinion turned sharply against the war and led Senator Robert F. Kennedy to join Senator Eugene McCarthy in challenging President Lyndon Johnson for the Democratic Party's nomination for president. Sensing his political vulnerability, Johnson withdrew from the race—"abdicated" the presidency, some said. Four days later, an assassin killed Martin Luther King Jr. and the nation erupted in grief and outrage, prompting scores of uprisings in cities all over the country. Students soon took over parts of Columbia University in New York, only to be beaten savagely by police. And in May, just when the album came out, the world's most famous baby doctor, Benjamin Spock, went on trial with four others in Boston on federal conspiracy charges stemming from their participation in the draft resistance movement against the Vietnam War. During the trial, news came from Los Angeles that Kennedy had been assassinated. When protest led to a "police riot" in Chicago during the Democratic National Convention in August, it seemed like the final act. The country, unable to keep its balance through the violent, buffeting winds of 1968, just tipped to one side and plunged.

Against that backdrop, the release of *At Folsom Prison* seemed less like the folk-intellectual preservation work or documentary archival efforts of Lomax as much as it seemed like a reflection of certain American pathological realities. Columbia Records promoted the album as if it were a field recording, stressing that "some people may buy it just to hear the audience" of convicts shouting and whistling. Those inmate responses are different from you, the free-world record buyer, "because they're not walking around like you are." The ad suggested that this album is the closest listeners will get to knowing what prison is like. The same could have been said of the field recordings from Parchman or Angola, too, and certainly *Blues in the Mississippi Night*, but none of those recordings had an industry giant like Columbia Records pushing them, and none of them had Johnny Cash. Unlike most Americans, Cash *did* know what it was like to be inside prisons, and "not always on a visit" (which was not strictly true, of course, because he had never done prison time; he had only done jail time, though he had performed in many prisons). That last fib gave away that, on some level, the whole album project was a contrivance, put together by a savvy artist, his producer, and his record label, except that very few caught it. In fact, despite a few deft production interventions and the marketing frame, everything about the album seemed real, authentic, and in the spring of 1968, in the midst of so much disorder, just as valid a reflection of the health of the nation as anything. The proof was in the listening.

So much time has passed since the release of *At Folsom Prison*, and so much of the music and between-song banter on the record have become iconic, it is harder to listen to it now and appreciate just how otherworldly it seemed when it was released. Thanks to reissues and box sets, we can now listen to the two complete shows that Cash played in Dining Hall 2 of Folsom Prison in the morning and early afternoon of January 13, 1968. Neither of the performances trotted out Cash's hit songs, recent or otherwise. He offered up no big numbers—no "I Walk the Line," no "Ring of Fire." Instead, he tailored the show around prison songs and other laments that were not, in fact, songs about being locked up, but may as well have been. On the original 1968 release, Cash effectively transported record buyers to another world the way *Blues in the Mississippi Night* had transported Cash to a different world.

The power of the record comes not only from songs that were bound to resonate with the inmates (like the show opener, "Folsom Prison Blues"), but also from the reactions that Cash's offhand remarks get. After he sings Merle Travis's "Dark as the Dungeon"—the characterization of a coal mine as a dungeon doing double duty in the home of an actual dungeon—Cash reminds the prisoners that the show is being recorded for an album on the Columbia Records label, so "you can't say 'hell' or 'shit' or anything like that," he says. (As he predicted, Columbia bleeped out "shit" on the original pressings.) Listeners hear the prisoners laugh at the transgression, and then hear them laugh even harder as Cash turns to Johnston and asks, mischievously, "How's that grab you, Bob?" It feels like a moment of solidarity, in which Cash, by a simple gesture throws in his lot with the hundreds of other transgressors in the room.

But with "Cocaine Blues," singing the tale of a life gone off the rails, his voice cracking slightly, Cash makes clear his intent to collapse the distance between him and his audience, as if he just awoke to tell his new cellmates how he got there. The song starts with Cash singing in first person of how, high on cocaine, he shot his unfaithful girlfriend, but then went home and tucked his "loving .44" under his pillow and went to sleep, a stone-cool killer. The inmates respond with the most enthusiastic applause of the concert so far, reacting to practically every line. Verse after verse, Cash winds them up with his story of running for the border, being picked up in Juarez, and getting brought back to stand trial. Despite all the bravado up front, when the guilty verdict comes in, he growls out, "I hollered 'Lordy, Lordy, have mercy on me!'" again eliciting a knowing rumble and whistles from his captive audience, each of whom had heard himself declared guilty by a judge or jury foreman. But the most raucous applause comes at the end when, like all convicts, our narrator is compelled to reflect on where he went wrong. Sentenced to ninety-nine years "in the Folsom pen," he says he will never forget the day he "shot that bad bitch down." Cash's fellow "miscreants," as he later called them, roar—undoubtedly in part because he called his girlfriend a "bitch," but just as much because his tone is not really one of remorse. He regrets shooting her less, it seems, than he regrets letting the cocaine and whisky determine his fate. The thunderous applause, the hoots, and the whistling crackle and quake with danger, but somehow also convey the warmth of acceptance toward the singer. (When a *Rolling Stone* writer asked, "Where must Cash be *at* to relate so well to those we have put into our dungeons?" he had to have this performance of "Cocaine Blues" in mind.)[16]

At this point in the show—we are only four songs into Side One—the listener could be forgiven for thinking that things were getting out of hand, confirmation of which comes in the sudden announcement by a voice of authority, presumably the warden (but actually famed country music DJ Hugh Cherry, who came along to act as emcee), that certain prisoners were wanted "in reception," identifying them by their last name and prison number. Listening at home, it sounded like the warden intervened. Such an intrusion into the show could easily have been left off the recording, but Bob Johnston cleverly spliced it in from the recording of the second concert. Not unlike the conjured hooting at the "shot a man in Reno" line on "Folsom Prison Blues" at the start of the album, Johnston manipulated the recording for dramatic effect. For the listener, the quick succession of the inmates' reaction to "Cocaine Blues" followed by the reimposition of some order by an authoritative voice could only make the recording seem that much more authentic.

Cash took pains to make clear his feelings of solidarity with the prisoners regardless of what they had done to land themselves in Folsom. As soon as the man we listeners think is the warden finishes his announcements, Cash starts in on "25 Minutes to Go," the Shel Silverstein tune, which he acts out lightheartedly—or as lightheartedly as anyone can act out a hanging—conveying a sense of bemused fatalism about the enduring prospect of the death penalty.[17] Across the rest of Side One, Cash acts as if he's among friends. At one point before "Orange Blossom Special" he says, "How ya doin', Sherley?" as though he already knows inmate Glen Sherley from having previously done time with him (he did not). Minutes later, after Cash sings Lefty Frizzell's "Long Black Veil," he asks for a glass of water. He has to ask three times, and the inmates start jeering at the staff for taking so long, for disrespecting the star. Cash jokes about the water tasting like something that ran off of guitarist Luther Perkins's boots, and then asks, deadpan, "You serve everything in tin cups?" Cash then throws the cup from the stage, perhaps toward the side, near the guards (one of whom apparently catches it). The prisoners cheer this indiscretion as if Cash had been trying to bean a guard with the cup, the way a pitcher misses when he brushes a hitter back off the plate. "He caught it, didn't he?" Cash chuckles from the stage, as the inmates hoot and whistle. On Side Two, as he sings "The Wall," he says of prison wardens,

"They're mean bastards, ain't they?" as if he spoke from experience. Cash's performance of two Jack Clement–penned novelty songs, "Dirty Old Egg-Sucking Dog" and "Flushed from the Bathroom of Your Heart," shows how, by this stage of the show, he has the convicts eating out of his hand. These goofy, sad-sack songs were hardly worthy of the rest of his repertoire, but he passes them off as the kind of bad jokes we, the listeners, might imagine prisoners tell each other in the yard. The inmates reward him with raucous shouting and applause at every punch line.

Thanks to Bob Johnston, presumably, the album ends with a brilliantly composed set of prison-themed songs. Although almost all the songs on the original album came from the 9:40 a.m. show, Johnston spliced in two songs from the later performance to create a downbeat/upbeat/downbeat/upbeat pattern and a seesaw of emotion. First, starting softly, Cash sings "Give My Love to Rose," the song he wrote about the dejected ex-con who, knowing he would probably never get his life together enough to get home to Shreveport, asked Cash to look out for his wife and son the next time he performed there. The song is touching and affecting, bringing appreciative applause from the inmate audience, but the mood is subdued throughout. Johnston comes back by splicing in "I Got Stripes" from the second show, a dazzling rendition of a song Cash had released as a single in 1959 and which was a clear rip-off of Leadbelly's "On a Monday." At Folsom, June Carter and the Statler Brothers provide spirited backing vocals as Cash winds up his audience, taking them higher before dropping them back on death row with "Green, Green Grass of Home." Porter Wagoner had recorded the Curly Putnam tune for his *Soul of a Convict* album, but the Welsh crooner Tom Jones's subsequent version guaranteed that "Green, Green Grass of Home" enjoyed a level of pop familiarity greater than any other song Cash performed that day. But unlike Wagoner and Jones, Cash sings the song to men who have surely had similar dreams—of leaving prison, coming home, and being greeted by family amid the familiar green, green grass of home. The climactic twist comes in the last verse, as the narrator awakens and realizes that at dawn, he will go to the death chamber, accompanied by a guard and a "sad old padre," that he will soon be buried beneath the old oak tree he played on as a child, under the green, green grass of home. We might hear the soulful Tom Jones version on the car radio and imagine little of the character's final walk to the gas chamber, but when we hear Cash singing it to convicted criminals, it's hard not to think about every one of those real men's yearning for home.

But the album's pièce de résistance is the final song on Side Two, "Greystone Chapel," written by Folsom inmate Glen Sherley and introduced by Cash to enthusiastic applause. "Hope we do your song justice, Glen," Cash says earnestly. "We're going to do our best." With backing vocals from Carter and the Statlers and Carl Perkins's sparkling lead guitar licks, the performance possesses a gathering gospel power. The subject of the song is Folsom's actual chapel—"a flower of light in a field of darkness," as Sherley wrote—but the troupe's soaring vocals make it seem as though one could have found the tune in a Baptist hymnal dating from 1900. It turned out to be the perfect match of a skillfully written song with musicians of exactly the right temperament and background, a piece of art that briefly transforms a room of men just recently cheering a killer on the run to Juarez into a prison cafeteria congregation of sinners seeking redemption. In terms of sheer pathos, the performance of "Greystone Chapel" equaled (and maybe surpassed) "Cocaine Blues." Millions of fans all over the world wore out the grooves in their vinyl listening to those songs, bookends on a historic performance. To cap it off, before the turntable arm lifted, listeners heard the real assistant warden, a perfectly named "Mr. Faustman," presenting Cash with some kind of unspecified prison gifts (easily imagined, correctly, to include a prison uniform), and Hugh Cherry—again sounding like he must be the warden—announcing that all prisoners must hold their seats until released by the guards to exit via the side door. The din of post-show inmate chatter closes out the record while we, at home, are free to go about our lives.

★

ALTHOUGH MANY BIOGRAPHERS have described *At Folsom Prison* as a project Cash knew would revive his professional prospects, risking the appearance of being pro-criminal in 1968 hardly seemed careerist. In retrospect, it's easier to see how the album changed Cash's life and put him on the path to superstardom, tapping as it did into the middle-class fascination with outlaws, but at the time, there was enormous risk in challenging the status quo. Besides, taking into consideration the earlier social-realist records, *At Folsom Prison* was no comeback project. It was a culmination. Whether he knew it or not, Cash had been working toward it for a decade.[18]

Cash made his most cohesive and coherent statements about prisoners and their treatment in his Grammy Award–winning liner notes for the album. Printed on the back of the cover as a facsimile of Cash's own handwritten notes, they are all about relating to, and empathizing with, the nation's incarcerated. "The culture of a thousand years is shattered with the clanging of the cell door behind you," Cash famously began. "Life outside, behind you immediately becomes unreal. You begin not to care that it exists." Having never been sentenced to time in prison, Cash could not actually know any of this from experience, but as he alluded slightly disingenuously, he had "been behind bars a few times." Sometimes, he said, he had been there "of his own volition," but other times it had been "involuntarily." And each time, he said, "I felt the same feeling of kinship with my fellow prisoners." This kind of seemingly earnest and true tale, we know, is overstated, though the person reading the notes in the record store aisle could not have been blamed for accepting it as truth. Just as he had extended his shared sense of poverty with Native peoples to a fuller understanding of their plight, here Cash imagines beyond his shared experiences of being arrested and going before a judge; as an artist, he imagines beyond what he has witnessed, and he tries to bring his audience with him.

More important is that Cash, in this season of law and disorder, dared to muse openly on the effectiveness of prison, philosophizing on its utility in modern society. He invited the album's listeners to put themselves in the inmates' place: "Behind the bars, locked out from 'society' you're being re-habilitated, corrected, re-briefed, re-educated on life itself," he wrote. Subjected to a program that combines "isolation, punishment, training, briefing, etc.," all with the aim of making "you sorry for your mistakes" and "re-enlighten[ing] you" on lawful behavior outside in the event of parole, you, the prisoner, are "supposed" to be welcomed and forgiven by society. Here, Cash's own skepticism is obvious. "Can it work???" he asks. "'Hell no,' you say." "How could this torment do anybody any good?" Cash asks. "But then, why else are you locked in?" Ultimately, that is the question that lingers, for Cash seems to take it as a given that the primary purpose of prison should be to rehabilitate, but if we agree that prisons do not, in fact, perform this rehabilitative function, why lock anyone up?

Cash shows that the sole purpose of American prisons is purely punitive. Of course, the Nixons and Reagans of American politics would hardly even deny such a charge, which only makes it that much more remarkable that Cash would say so. When he suggests that prisoners have had all the things "that make a man a man" snuffed out of their lives in prison, and lists them ("women, money, a family, a job, the open road, the city, the country, ambition, power, success, failure—a million things"), he does not say that they brought it on themselves; he makes it clear that this is what prisons do to inmates, and he bids the readers of these liner notes to listen, to "hear the sounds of the men, the convicts—all brothers of mine—with the Folsom Prison Blues" on the record, and come to their own conclusions.

And plenty of people did listen. Although Cash had produced crossover hit songs like "Ring of Fire" in the past, no previous album hit the *Billboard* charts as hard as *At Folsom Prison*. Over the summer of 1968, it reached number one on the magazine's country charts and number thirteen on the pop charts. For 92 weeks, it remained on the country charts, and for an astonishing 124 weeks (almost two and a half years), it remained in the *Billboard* Top 200. Some listeners found the performance so convincing they believed Cash was actually imprisoned at Folsom. Lloyd Kelley, the prison recreation director who had, with the Rev. Floyd Gressett, organized Cash's concerts at Folsom over the years, reported that he received many calls "wanting to know when Johnny would be out, how he was, if they came, could they talk to him, [and] did he need anything?" The reviewer for *Time* titled his column "Empathy in the Dungeon," remarking that Cash's "empathy with jailbirds is a natural extension of the attitudes expressed in his songs, that life both in and out of prison is a kind of sentence to be served."[19] And even though he offered no new material—even the single, "Folsom Prison Blues," was a rerelease—the badass persona seen in the song selection, in quips from the stage, and in the liner notes led Cash to be embraced by the counterculture. Once Tom Donahue, the legendary underground DJ, began playing the record on San Francisco's KMPX, other FM stations all over the country did the same, and soon Cash found himself the object of young people's fascination. In New York, jazz critic Nat Hentoff wrote that although Cash "started as a country-and-western storyteller," he had "gone on to make so strong an impact on the folk and pop fields that now there's no hemming Johnny Cash into any one category." Hentoff did not write this explicitly about Cash's politics, but he may as well have. After *At Folsom Prison*, Cash's political persona could not be so easily categorized, either.[20]

IT TOOK THE governor of Arkansas, Winthrop Rockefeller, noticing Cash's public stand on prison reform to draw Cash into mainstream politics. At a moment when controversy over the state's prisons had drawn as much negative national attention as former governor and white supremacist Orval Faubus's desperate efforts to prevent de-segregation of Little Rock's Central High School a decade earlier, Rockefeller needed Cash, an Arkansan now widely seen, thanks to *At Folsom Prison*, as an authority on penitentiaries.

In 1966, Rockefeller became the first Republican elected gover-nor of Arkansas since Reconstruction, winning the election to replace Faubus on promises of reform. Rockefeller represented a breath of fresh air in the state. Although he grew up a child of privilege in New York, the grandson of Standard Oil tycoon John D. Rocke-feller, Winthrop had decamped to Arkansas in 1953 with the aim of showcasing state-of-the-art cattle farming. He found the everyday racism of his adopted state appalling, and for much of his two terms as governor, Rockefeller directed his energies at burying the state's racist past.

Even before his swearing-in, Rockefeller learned that the need for prison reform was greater than he had imagined. Most every-one in Arkansas knew that little had changed since the nineteenth century at the state's two prison farms, Cummins and Tucker, but the conditions were more medieval. Faubus knew as much, having commissioned a report from the Arkansas State Police's Criminal Investigation Division (CID) on the Tucker farm—a report he left for his successor to release. Rockefeller warned journalists before he took office that the report would "shock you beyond anything you could imagine," but maybe not everyone shocks so easily.

The CID investigation found certain practices—especially re-garding nutrition and punishment—to be barbaric. Most prisoners were so malnourished that they were, on average, forty to sixty pounds below their regular weight; inmates were lucky if they re-ceived meat once a month. "Flies were very thick" in the kitchen, investigators reported, tainting the food served in the swelter-ing Arkansas heat. Most horrifying, the CID report described the smaller prison's routine use of a torture device called the "Tucker

Telephone." It consisted of "an electric generator taken from a ring type telephone, placed in sequence with two dry cell batteries, and attached to an undressed inmate strapped to a treatment table at the Tucker hospital, by means of one electrode to a big toe and the second electrode to the penis, at which time, a crank was turned sending an electric charge into the body of the inmate."[21]

Although similar devices later showed up in Hollywood films, the routine torture of inmates should have prompted outrage. But in most quarters, it barely registered. An "alarming number" of the state's citizens, according to the governor's public relations officer, thought that "criminals should be confined and forgotten, that whatever happened to them, no matter how brutal, was what they deserved." Johnny Cash had to confront the possibility, therefore, that even as he came out in favor of rehabilitation, of not making convicts into hardened career criminals, many of his fellow Arkansans could not be bothered to care. When the State Penitentiary Board called the CID report a bunch of "lies" and refused to accept it, the lack of public indignation made it easy for them to get away with it. But Rockefeller, to his credit, would not let it go.[22]

The new governor used the CID investigation to justify the hiring of a new assistant superintendent of the Arkansas State Penitentiary named Tom Murton. A committed reformer with a zealot's sense of righteous indignation, Murton came in hot, spouting off to the media, and finally claiming the state superintendent's job. He ended use of "the strap" (leaving Mississippi as the only state to still whip prisoners as late as 1968), took steps toward ending the notorious "trusty system" (which made some prisoners into de facto guards, armed with shotguns), and campaigned to replace cotton picking with "an education or vocational training program" for prisoners. But when Murton started digging up the fields around Cummins looking for the bodies of murdered inmates and uncovered three corpses, he brought unwelcome attention to Arkansas. Rockefeller ordered an investigation, but police found no evidence of foul play.

The governor would not act without more concrete evidence, and Murton, though he was sure that prison officials had once killed inmates with some regularity, if not routinely, could not provide it. He took it up with the press, implicitly criticizing Rockefeller for not doing more, which got him sacked by the prison board in March 1968, two months before Johnny Cash released *At Folsom Prison*.[23]

Rockefeller probably did not anticipate the risks to his political reputation when he threw himself into prison reform; it didn't help that the Arkansas public had not reacted well to Murton's bullish style. Rockefeller tried to introduce legislation that would have implemented most of the reforms Murton had called for—an end to the trusty system, an end to corporal punishment, the start of education and vocational training, separation of young first-time offenders from hardened repeat offenders—but the General Assembly rebuffed him. Going into the 1968 election, this is where things stood: Rockefeller's best efforts at reform had produced controversy but few concrete results. Perhaps taking note of the fantastic success of the *At Folsom Prison* LP—which had been certified a gold record by the fall—Rockefeller looked for an ally in Arkansas native son Johnny Cash.[24]

In some ways, Johnny Cash lending political muscle to a Rockefeller campaign did not make sense. In no way did Cash, who had grown up so poor, relate to Rockefeller, a poster boy of wealth and privilege. In fact, when Cash served in the Air Force, he once wrote in a letter to Vivian that he had always been proud of being "a country boy," that given the choice, he would rather be poor than rich. "My life's ambition," he recalled to Vivian, "was to walk up to John D. Rockefeller and tell him rich people don't go to heaven." But by 1968, it seems, Cash's views of the Rockefellers had softened. He agreed to perform at a series of Winthrop Rockefeller campaign rallies that fall—the first time he staked his name and reputation to a mainstream political candidate. There is no correspondence between Rockefeller and Cash in the governor's archives, but we know from journalists that Cash agreed to bend his policy of not endorsing political candidates because the governor seemed committed to prison reform. Rockefeller had also publicly supported civil rights. Following the slaying of Martin Luther King Jr., Rockefeller, alone among all Southern governors, eulogized King in a public memorial. Likewise, he added thirty-five African Americans to the state's previously all-white draft boards, making them more closely resemble the "little groups of neighbors" the Selective Service System claimed them to be.[25]

In late August, just two days before the nation would watch the Democratic National Convention dissolve into protest inside the Chicago convention hall while, out in the streets, a "police riot" (as a later investigation labeled it) on protesters raged, Johnny Cash played a down-home campaign rally in Winthrop, Arkansas. Governor Rockefeller chose the rural southwest Arkansas community for the event simply because it coincidentally bore his first name. Much of the day's program focused on the campaign to thwart the return of the old, corrupt Faubus crowd of Democrats before Rockefeller could implement his reforms, but it was also a day of fun. Thanks to audio recordings held at the Center for Arkansas History and Culture, we can hear Cash's performance, mixed in with local entertainment and appeals on the hot summer evening, for the folks who had already bellied up to the barbecue and those still arriving by train. This is watermelon country, someone says, and there's plenty to go around.

The Rockefeller campaign paid Cash to play six campaign rallies between August and October. Such arrangements were not unusual. If a candidate wanted Minnie Pearl or Roy Acuff, they had to pay up, too, though most observers understood that these stars did not perform just for the money—they supported the candidates, too. In Cash's case, the audio recordings show that he did very little politicking on Rockefeller's behalf. In the three extant recordings, he mostly just plays an abbreviated version of his regular show.[26] But at the Harrison, Arkansas, rally on September 19, as Cash introduced "Suppertime," a song made popular by segregationist Governor Jimmie Davis of Louisiana, he paused to say, "and, incidentally, be sure and vote for Rockefeller—I'd like to put in a word for our governor." To hear it now, it hardly sounds like an enthusiastic endorsement, but given that Cash had never before spoken on behalf of any candidate, it was a big deal. Cash saw his loyalty to Rockefeller tested a few weeks later when guards fired bird shot into a crowd of eighty prisoners waging a sit-down strike in protest of conditions at the Cummins prison farm, wounding twenty-four. Shooting into a crowd of peaceful, unarmed inmates: it seemed like little had changed, at least at Cummins. Perhaps Rockefeller reassured Cash that he would soon replace the prison superintendent who defended the violence, because Cash showed up for the governor's last two rallies anyway.[27]

IN THE FINAL months of 1968, as Arkansans reelected Winthrop Rockefeller, and as the nation voted to send Richard Nixon to the White House, Johnny Cash's popularity soared. He not only won the Country Music Association's award for best album (for *At Folsom Prison*), played a triumphant show at Carnegie Hall, and toured the United Kingdom and Canada, but he also went out of his way to play the benefit for the Saint Francis Mission at the Rosebud Reservation in South Dakota, before heading to Vietnam to play for GIs in January 1969. It would have been hard for him to be more identified with the public issues of the day, associating himself as he did with prison inmates, Native peoples, and servicemen fighting an unpopular war. That he had grown more comfortable speaking to political issues became clear when he played two of his most famous prison shows, at San Quentin in California and Cummins in Arkansas. In 1969, Cash, who, by his own estimation, had pulled his punches on *Blood, Sweat and Tears* and become more outspoken with *Bitter Tears* and *At Folsom Prison*, had plainly found his public voice.

Although Cash's friend Tom T. Hall would later say that it is never a good idea to "try to write something twice," that is exactly what Cash did when he recorded another prison album just thirteen months after he taped the show at Folsom. The *At San Quentin* album would prove to be an exception to that rule, selling even more copies than the *At Folsom Prison* record and cementing his status as one of the music industry's biggest stars, and one of America's most prominent artists. Its release in June 1969, timed to coincide with the start of his network television show, guaranteed maximum exposure, and by the end of the year, the album reached number one on both the country and pop charts; its hit single, "A Boy Named Sue," made number one on the country charts and number two on the pop charts. By December, record stores were selling each of Cash's prison records at a clip of sixty thousand per week. Not even the Beatles could compete.

Cash's sudden success was no accident. It came from a carefully choreographed rollout, coordinated between his manager, Saul Holiff, and Columbia Records, with Cash himself involved in each critical decision. But Cash's main role continued to be putting himself before the public, acting as a public commentator, a citizen with a platform. He had not, after all, recorded any big hit songs between 1963, when he released "Ring of Fire," and 1969, when "A Boy Named Sue" debuted on the second prison album. His popularity skyrocketed more because of his persona—the public persona that Americans suddenly felt like they knew because of the prison albums and the television show. He said and did things that Americans admired. He seemed real.

Which is why the place of the *At San Quentin* LP in Cash's oeuvre is so interesting, precisely because it is simply not as "real" as *At Folsom Prison*. If you want to start an argument among Cash fans, just ask them to debate which prison record is the best one:

At Folsom Prison or *At San Quentin*. Whereas the Folsom recording's power derived from the way Cash empathized with the inmates more subtly and more consistently, in song and stage banter, on the San Quentin album (especially on the original release), he is more intentional about identifying with the prisoners in his statements from the stage and in presenting one song written expressly for them. Although the San Quentin album seems, in many ways, more contrived than the apparently more spontaneous Folsom record, the song selection is not as neatly tailored to the convict experience as it could have been. "Wreck of the Old 97," "I Walk the Line," and "Darlin' Companion," are great songs that Cash performed regularly as part of his usual show, but which spoke not at all to the prison experience. What sets the San Quentin record apart is a story about one of Cash's own arrests at the end of Side One, followed by his best effort to put himself, in song, in the shoes of a San Quentin prisoner at the start of Side Two.

Since we now have access to the complete concert at San Quentin, it is easy to see how the album, as originally released, is the product of clever editing, but of course, in 1969, none of this would have been obvious. Instead, listeners heard Cash reporting, at the start of Side One, that June had said "there'd be some people from the South here tonight because some of you guys get out here in California and the damned place is so crazy, you just gotta get something to eat some way, don't ya?" The prisoners laugh and cheer as Cash and his Southern troupe begin to play the song he had written recently with Bob Dylan, "Wanted Man." That brief example of relating to the assembled inmates sets the tone for what is to come, and for listeners, it's another example of Cash feeling at home in a home that would terrify the rest of us.

Much more deliberately than on *At Folsom Prison*, Cash proceeds to show the ways that he, like the convicts, resents authority. He alludes to being run a little ragged, touring a lot, before arriving in San Quentin, as if under some pressure from his label. "Put the screws on me, and I'm gonna screw right out from under ya, is what I'm gonna do," he says defiantly. "I'm tired of all that shit," he concludes to the cheers of the inmates (though the label bleeped "shit" out on the original release). When he reminds the prisoners that the show is being recorded as well as filmed for a British television network, he claims that producers had told him (implausibly) which songs he had to perform, where he had to stand, which marks he had to hit. "They just don't get it, man," he sneers to his audience. "I'm here to do what *you* want me to and what *I* want to do." Again, wild applause follows and, as if to demonstrate the last point, he invites them to shout out requests. Even at the time, such repartee sounded a little manufactured, as though Cash understood that his camaraderie with the inmates was the crucial chemical compound in the winning formula of *At Folsom Prison*, and that he could reliably use it again at San Quentin.

Following "Darlin' Companion," Cash again signals to the prisoners that he is just one of them, a guy who cusses and maybe is not honest all the time. When he cannot seem to tune his guitar, he turns to someone and says, "will you tune this sum'bitch?" (though, again, Columbia wielded the bleep), prompting howls of laughter. In a mostly unscripted moment, Cash asks if someone will fetch his briefcase from backstage—"my kit back there, where I got all my dope, er, all my things . . . all the songs I stole"—so that he can unveil a new song. At this point, it is clear, he is just playing with his audience, both in the joint and at home. Even as he continues to talk about a song he wrote about San Quentin, he tells the story of being arrested in Starkville, Mississippi, at two in the morning, just for picking flowers: a night in jail and a thirty-six dollar fine for breaking a curfew. "You can't hardly win, can you?" he asks a group of men who could surely relate to run-ins with the law. "No tellin' what they'd do if you pull an apple or something." As he plays "Starkville City Jail," elaborating on that arrest, we hear that, for this album, the song, sung in the first person, performs the same function as "Cocaine Blues" did on *At Folsom Prison*. By recounting his experience at the mercy of the justice system, Cash conveys his empathy for the men sitting before him, regardless of what they did to wind up there. There is enough shared experience in catching a bad break, in being treated unfairly, that the sense of solidarity is audible.

Flipping the record, listeners found the most powerful song on the album, performed not once, but twice in a row. Cash introduces it by saying that he has played San Quentin several times before, and he got to thinking about the inmates the day before as he wrote this song. "I think I understand a little bit how you feel about some things, it's none of my business about how you feel about some other things, and I don't give a damn how you feel about some other things," he declares. It is a funny line, and we hear the inmates fall about themselves, laughing, but Cash's emphasis on how they "feel" is once again telling. He could not be more explicit about trying to empathize with them. "I tried to put myself in your place, and I believe this is the way that I would feel about San Quentin." Unlike "Folsom Prison Blues," which does well to convey the sense of loneliness and regret any convict might feel, "San Quentin" is defiant, accusatory, and political. It is a far more brazen performance than any of the songs he had performed at Folsom, with the inmates hollering through nearly every line. The big applause lines come when Cash sings, "San Quentin, I hate every inch of you" and "San Quentin, may you rot and burn in hell"—in each case, the inmates erupt, almost in glorious disbelief that an entertainer would come and sing those words directly to an audience that included all those armed guards manning the perimeter. But the song's real potency comes from questioning the value of an institution that the only purpose of which is to beat men down. Cash sings to the prison by name as if it could answer for itself. Sure, he admits, he will leave prison weakened, but no one will be able to claim that he emerged from San Quentin a better man. Of course, Cash seems to suggest, even if the rest of the world comes to see San Quentin's failings, the people in power—he specifically cites members of Congress—do not get it. They have no feeling, no empathy, no understanding of how badly their carceral policies have failed.

As Cash must have intended, however, the listeners who hear this performance *do* get it. In the camaraderie between singer and audience, between Cash and the inmates at one of California's most notorious prisons, we hear that, at least from the perspective of those who have experienced it, San Quentin is most successful at breeding hatred for the place. We are so thoroughly on the side of murderers, rapists, and armed robbers, we do not even mind that Cash grants their request to play the song again. By the end of the second rendition—for which the inmates were more muted in their cheering, almost reflective—it is obvious that Cash is making a statement about prisons and the need for prison reform. Everything he says in the song—about the ignorance of congressmen, about the futility of rehabilitation under present conditions, about prisons existing only to punish—will be central to his public calls for reform in the coming months and years. And it bore repeating.

That essential point has been obscured by the hard-to-resist fascination over Cash's power, had he chosen to use it, to call for a prison uprising right there, in the middle of the song, and the subsequent apparent release of pressure with the debut of "A Boy Named Sue." Both of those stories are significant moments in the Johnny Cash mythology—not least because the guards seemed truly nervous, and because "A Boy Named Sue" became Cash's biggest crossover hit—but they're side stories compared to what Cash did, in a matter of minutes, to bring the public along to "see" the prisoners again, when the vast majority of Americans were accustomed to them being so totally out of view, and out of mind. When Cash asked for a glass of water, "if any of the guards are still speaking to me," he acknowledged that he had chosen sides.

Across those two prison records, Cash did as much as any politician, lawyer, or advocate to put prisoners before the American public, and he did it just as a law-and-order president began his term in office. As one historian has shown, Cash inverted Nixon's "forgotten Americans" message. Where the president claimed to represent the law-abiding, hardworking voters left behind by the

Democrats—the people who "drive the trucks, plow the farms, man the fields, and police the streets," in strategist Kevin Phillips's famous line—Cash's forgotten Americans were the inmates populating the nation's prisons, put away for, in fact, *not* abiding the law.[28] *At San Quentin* may have been a live recording, with plenty of evidence of spontaneity sprinkled throughout, but no one could deny its carefully crafted political message.[29]

Cash's sudden superstar status, built on his engagement with public issues, guaranteed that interviewers would ask about those subjects, and prisons most of all. For the most part, Cash offered two messages: "I just don't think prisons do any good," he said repeatedly. "They put 'em in there and just make 'em worse, if they were ever bad in the first place, and then when they let 'em out, they're just better at whatever put 'em in there in the first place," he told one journalist. At the same time, he seemed to recall the message of *Inside the Walls of Folsom Prison* that "prisoners are people" still. "You just can't cut them off from society and say 'the hell with them.' They're alive. And they can change." Cash knew from experience—from overcoming seven years of drug addiction and from all of his run-ins with the law—that a man could turn the corner.[30]

Cash's growing comfort with speaking out on prison issues became evident, in fact, when he joined Governor Winthrop Rockefeller for a benefit concert at the Cummins prison farm in Arkansas in April, about six weeks after the San Quentin appearance. Rockefeller, stymied for the most part in his prison reform efforts during the previous legislative session, brought Cash to Cummins to perform not only for nearly a thousand prisoners, but for a handful of legislators, too, in a show that would be taped to air later on KATV, the ABC affiliate in Little Rock. "Governor Rockefeller swore that he was trying to clean up that scandal, that mess down there," Cash recounted to one reporter, so he agreed to help him out.[31]

The governor used his own jet to fly Cash to Pine Bluff, and on the way to the prison, and later at lunch, the star gathered intelligence on life at the prison. He learned from staff members and inmates that, among other things, Cummins "made a quarter of a million dollars in profit" each year, but not a dollar had come back to be invested in the prison, and that the inmates had taken it upon themselves to launch a fundraising campaign to build a chapel because it seemed hopeless to expect prison officials to pay for one. "I didn't know too much about Cummins and Tucker before today," Cash explained to the inmates from the makeshift outdoor stage, but over the course of the day, he said, he heard "about what's been going on here and I learned quite a bit about Cummins farm. I know the governor is trying to help you." Just as he had written a song about San Quentin, Cash revealed that at lunch that day, he wrote a song about Cummins.[32]

But if Cash's song "San Quentin" introduced a measure of political passion into his prison song repertoire, the hastily written "When I Get Out of Cummins" added no small hint of political intimidation. Cash insisted that prisoners—including Curley Henson, who had once played guitar behind him at the *Grand Ole Opry* in 1961 and 1962—sit in the front rows on the field, while the legislators sat toward the back where they could see the inmates react to Cash's lyrics:

> *When I get out of Cummins, I'm going up to*
> *   Little Rock*
> *I'm gonna walk right up those Capitol steps,*
> *   and I'm not even going to knock*
> *If the legislature's in session, there are some things*
> *   I'm going to say:*
> *Did you say you've seen the figures on the profits*
> *   we made all those years?*
> *I'd say look here, don't you think you could give us*
> *   back a little of it?*

At this point, Cash paused to look over the heads of the inmates and addressed the ten squirming politicians who had come down to Cummins from the capitol. "A lot of things need changing, Mr. Legislator Man," Cash said, sounding a bit like the muscle sent by the governor to persuade the representatives to quit stalling. "You *say* you're trying to rehabilitate us. Then show us you are," Cash demanded, with the television cameras whirring away in the bright sun. When he finished the song, reporters saw only one of the ten legislators clap his hands. "The others were silent," wrote one.[33]

Cash also pulled no punches in appealing for support of the inmates' chapel fund. In addition to announcing that he planned to donate $5,000 of his own money (about $35,000 today), and that Rockefeller would give $10,000, Cash looked directly into the cameras and challenged the state's wealthy—"You, rich man, sitting on your Arkansas farm, Mr. Viewer with money jingling in your pocket"—to match his $5,000 gift. No doubt Cash had the heirs of the big plantations in mind as he tried to shame them into action.[34]

It is hard to imagine Cash having had the nerve to confront the rich and powerful so directly before the success of *At Folsom Prison*. But the attention that album had brought to him and his interest in prison reform, combined with his growing sense of outrage and a willingness to talk about that outrage, made this political moment on the Cummins stage possible. When the new corrections commissioner, Robert Sarver, presented Cash with "an honorary life sentence" after the show, he admitted to the crowd that Cash had said "some things that I've been afraid to say," presumably to the legislators. "That's alright," Cash demurred. "I had nothing to lose."[35]

Cash's concert left his Cummins audience full of hope. The next issue of the prison newsletter, *The Pea Pickers Picayune*, featured a prisoner's portrait of Cash wearing a "King of Cummins" crown. "He came, he sang, he mingled with the inmates and fired morale to a tempered, glittering high seldom, if ever, seen" at the prison, the editor wrote. "Johnny Cash became a bona-fide hero to the Cummins Crew." The paper predicted excitedly that Cash's "daring" appeal for the Inmate Chapel Drive would bear fruit when the show aired later that summer. In fact, Cash served as honorary chairman of the chapel drive and ultimately gave $10,000 toward the build-ing of two chapels, one each at Tucker and Cummins. The Tucker Chapel opened in the fall of 1969, though it was another eight years before the Cummins chapel did. In the meantime, just weeks after the Cash concert, the Arkansas legislature approved the first prison reform appropriations in the state's history.[36]

SELLING MILLIONS OF records would boost anyone's confidence, and following the success of the *At Folsom Prison* and *At San Quentin* LPs, Cash spoke increasingly about prison reform on his new tele-vision show. On the first season, he encouraged his old pal, Merle Haggard, to finally come clean about his San Quentin past (though producers ended up editing it out, so only the Ryman audience heard the confession). It was a tentative first step, but Cash's renewed com-mitment to his faith, his interest in bearing witness to the poor and disadvantaged, played an important role in his increasingly blunt but earnest statements on behalf of the nation's convicts.[37]

In an episode that aired at the start of *The Johnny Cash Show*'s second season, on January 28, 1970, with Cash now at the peak of his popularity, the star showed signs of honing his prison reform message for maximum appeal. At the start of a "Ride This Train" segment that brought viewers behind prison walls, Cash describes the inmates as "the ones of us who are guilty that got caught," sug-gesting that the guilty who did not get caught might be tuning in from home. The price convicts pay, Cash tells the audience, comes in the form of "longing for things lost and for things always loved" in the free world, and most of all in loneliness. All of this is a set up for a performance of "Green, Green Grass of Home," a senti-mental appeal to make us more receptive to what comes next. "We hear a lot about prison reform these days," Cash says to the cam-era, "and in my travels, I've visited a lot of institutions where some conditions were so barbaric that they make a mockery of the word 'rehabilitation.'" He describes prisons where "two- and three-time losers" shared a dormitory with a fifteen-year-old boy, "a boy that was in there for stealing a car because his daddy wouldn't let him have the family car that night." He holds his hands up about six inches apart to show the distance between the boy's bed and the hardened criminals, and lets viewers draw their own conclusions. "With conditions like these, there's little or no chance of reform," he concludes. Cash tried to end on a more positive note, recounting how California prison officials, following Cash's recording of Glen Sherley's "Greystone Chapel," transferred Sherley to a medium security facility in Vacaville, California—showing perhaps that one person caring can make a difference. But it was the fifteen-year-old boy that stayed with viewers. While Cash had played prisons many times before he made the Folsom and San Quentin albums, at no point in the recordings on those days—nor in the media rollouts that followed each record's release—did he distinguish between prisoners as predators and prey as he did here.[38]

Cash had seen, after all, how the earnest efforts of prison reformers did not move the electorate in Arkansas and elsewhere. Although a federal judge had ruled the entire Arkansas prison system unconstitutional, citing the filth, the corrupt trusty system, and the high incidence of rape all as violations of the Eighth Amendment's prohibition of "cruel and unusual punishment," by the time Winthrop Rockefeller ran for reelection in 1970, he had instituted measurable reforms: repairing existing facilities and beginning construction on a new, modern maximum security unit, and planning a new center for education and vocational training, too. It didn't matter. Democrat Dale Bumpers won nearly 62 percent of the vote, beating Rockefeller handily on Election Day.[39]

Aside from voter apathy, Cash also had to be aware that he spoke out for reform at a moment of tremendous upheaval, conflict, and violence in American prisons. Starting in 1968, the number of riots began to climb—from fifteen in 1968 to at least forty-eight in

1972—accompanied by a sharp rise in clashes between guards and inmates. Between January 1970, when Cash made his appeal for prison reform on television, and August 1971, more than forty people were killed in California prisons alone. Compared to the alluring but basically benign rowdiness heard on the *At Folsom Prison* and *At San Quentin* albums, news reports made prisons out to be either sites of violent revolution or violent repression. At the same time, so many popular books had been published by Black prisoners or ex-cons in recent years—*The Autobiography of Malcolm X, Soul on Ice* by Eldridge Cleaver, and *Soledad Brother* by George Jackson—that the muckraking writer Jessica Mitford wisecracked that "literary agents are scouting prisons for convict talent." The revolutionary writings of Malcolm, Cleaver, and Jackson caused many outsiders to see the prisoners' rights movement as an arm of Black Power, one tool radicals hoped to use to gain power. In reality, prisoners all over the country, from Folsom to Cummins to Attica, were simply, as one scholar writes, "fighting for control of their lives." In that same twenty-month period starting in January 1970, prisoners waged strikes or takeovers or made their escape at institutions in California, Minnesota, Kentucky, Nevada, Pennsylvania, Kansas, Florida, Maryland, Idaho, Louisiana, and New York. All over the United States, prisons had become sites of "low-intensity warfare." Despite all of the available evidence showing how badly the country needed prison reform, against the backdrop of so much violence, it got harder for someone like Cash to call for it.[40]

Cash might have used events at Folsom Prison, with which the public associated him so closely, to advance the cause of prison reform in late 1970, but he seemed oddly silent. In November 1970, prisoners at Folsom went on a work strike that lasted nearly three weeks. Some 2,400 inmates—practically the whole prison population—stayed in their cells rather than contribute to the daily running of what they called "the fascist concentration camps of modern America." In a manifesto that originated at San Quentin, the Folsom strikers called for wide-ranging, reasonable reforms, the kinds of things with which Johnny Cash would probably have agreed: access to books, access to better medical care, a fairer parole board system, adequate legal assistance, a labor union for prison workers, equality of treatment of white and Black prisoners. But by framing it in revolutionary terms—using labels like "fascist" and calling for the freeing of political prisoners—it attracted a taint of radicalism in the mainstream media. Maybe that put Cash off. Perhaps he saw talk of revolution, talk of freeing political prisoners, going beyond what originally concerned him: the replacement of drudgery and horror with rehabilitation through education and training.[41]

Still, it is hard to imagine that Cash, the man who so movingly recorded chain gang songs derived from the Black experience on *Blood, Sweat and Tears*, would not have been as horrified by the structural racism of American prisons as anyone else. The prisoners for whom he advocated were disproportionately Black, after all—by one estimate, 30 percent of the prisoners in the audience for Cash's San Quentin performance were African American (at a time when Black people made up approximately 12 percent of the population), and when he played "San Quentin" the first time, a Black inmate stood and gave the Black Power salute, holding his fist high in the air. Even if he had not read George Jackson's *Soledad Brother* when it came out in 1970 (which seems hard to believe of a man widely described as a voracious reader in this period, particularly while touring, and so interested in prison affairs), Cash would certainly have been aware from press reports that its central premise focused on the institutional racism of California's penal system.[42]

Cash's reaction to the massacre at Attica Correctional Facility in upstate New York is a useful barometer. Tensions had been running high at Attica throughout the summer of 1971, as inmates pushed prison administrators for many of the same reforms called for at Folsom. When George Jackson was killed in the middle of an attempted escape from San Quentin on August 21, 1971, inmates at

Attica staged a one-day silent memorial and fast. The sense of unity and solidarity arising out of the day's dignified protest set the stage for a violent confrontation. After guards beat an inmate senseless (rumors spread that they had killed him) on September 8, an uprising began the next day. For four days, the prisoners held dozens of hostages and the nation's attention as they negotiated with prison officials, under the lens of the media. When they reached an impasse, Governor Nelson Rockefeller (brother of Winthrop) called for use of force. Helicopters dropped tear gas on the prisoners and the hostages as police and guards waged a tactical assault on the prison yard, discharging thousands of rounds of ammunition. In the end, they killed thirty-nine people (including ten hostages) and wounded eighty-nine in the worst prison massacre in American history.[43]

When reporters asked Cash to comment on the the news out of Attica, he gave a characteristically nuanced reply. He said that he had spoken with Glen Sherley, who had been paroled from Vacaville earlier that year, and they both agreed that "violence is not the solution" regardless of what had happened there. Cash said he thought Attica "probably . . . was understaffed with guard personnel," suggesting that, as in Arkansas, prisons suffered from chronic underfunding, which only made them more dangerous. He sounded a little forlorn as he asserted that the inmates raised legitimate concerns. "Certainly, the men had some grievances that were worth hearing," he said. "I'm not sure that they gave proper hearing to those grievances." Still, he did his best to convince the reporters (and maybe himself) that, despite the obstacles, prison reform was coming. "I'm sure that the authorities, the people in government, don't know much more about how to go about reform than the average layman does," Cash acknowledged. "Because it's something that's brand new, that's never been tried." In a lot of cases, he said, rehabilitation had not worked because it had not been properly implemented. "But I think better and more attempts are being made to correct the things that are wrong with the prison system," Cash concluded, perhaps too optimistically.[44]

Cash's faith in—or hope for—prison reform brought him to the attention of Bill Brock, the Republican senator from Tennessee. In July 1972, Brock invited Cash, Sherley, and Harlan Sanders (another convict-musician befriended by Cash) to Washington to testify before the Senate Subcommittee on National Penitentiaries. Brock introduced Cash as not only a man who had performed at many prisons but one who had been behind bars himself. Cash, for his part, began by reading a newspaper description of an unnamed prison as an "incubator for crime" where, instead of being rehabilitated, inmates go to "crime school." The excerpt, it turned out, came from a newspaper dated December 1865, and Cash's point was simple enough for the senators to understand: not much had changed in 107 years. Cash said that over the last 17 years, he had performed in a lot of prisons, and he came away thinking that maybe one-fourth of the inmates really needed to be there; the other 75 percent were being put through harrowing conditions for no reason.

Cash went on to demonstrate how two stories that he had heard firsthand from prison eyewitnesses helped him to refine his arguments for prison reform. He did not empathize, strictly speaking, because he had not experienced these horrible stories that he now entered in the public record firsthand, but he could sympathize because they were conveyed to him by prisoners to whom he could relate. He started with the story he told on his television show, about the fifteen-year-old boy sent to prison for the first time for car theft, but he filled in the picture with details unfit for the Ryman and ABC audience. He said that the boy had been sent to a Southern prison (almost certainly Cummins), and that officials there told Cash that in this prison, where "all of the bunks are all jammed up together," with no separation of youth from "three-time losers and sadistic killers," the other inmates raped the boy "continually all night long," until "he died the next morning." In another incident in Virginia, Cash reported, prison officials took the clothes away from a new teenage inmate, "to shame him for his crime," and the teenager, fully humiliated, hanged himself. Cash later wrote a song, "Jacob

Green," about this latter incident, released on his 1973 prison album, *på Österåker*, which essentially retells the story but holds the public accountable. In Cash's estimation, the American public, by looking the other way, made it possible for this inhumanity to continue. He warns the indifferent listener that "someone that you love" might be the next one who "gets done like Jacob Green got done." In both his Senate testimony and in "Jacob Green," Cash basically told all who would listen that the old, cruel America remained very much alive in the nation's penal institutions.

Now that Cash had essentially grabbed the senators by their lapels and had their attention, he moved to the second part of his argument. The purpose of prison reform, Cash asserted, is not merely to improve conditions for inmates, but also, ultimately, to minimize crime—"that our streets, that our cities should be a safe place for a wife and children to walk down." In order to make that happen, Cash said, "the men in prison have to be treated as human beings." If they are not treated as human beings in prison, he reasoned, we cannot expect them to act like human beings when they get out. Sherley and Sanders backed him up, speaking with the authority of those who had seen guys come to prison on short sentences, only to be sucked into the subculture and turned into a "repeater."

Over the next hour or so, Cash and his friends urged passage of Brock's bill because they believed it would bring some consistency to the sentencing of first offenders. In particular, he singled out marijuana laws for destroying "many young, innocent, inquiring lives." He acknowledged that the reforms he sought—to build appropriate facilities to separate young from old, first offenders from hard timers—would cost a lot of money, but the safety of citizens inside and outside the prison required it. In fact, as he responded to questions about the parole process—widely regarded as outdated and unfair—Cash suggested that prisoners coming up for parole "need a lot of help from the citizenry." It might be necessary to "draft" citizens the way jurors get selected, he said, but parole boards need the help of lawyers, clergy, "philosophers and humanitarians," so that each inmate would know that he would "get a fair shake" when it was his turn. In effect, on matters of prison reform, Cash called not only on the Senate to pass the right laws, but also on his fellow Americans to think of their citizenship more expansively. Only if Americans stopped turning away, as he would later write in "Jacob Green," and committed themselves to bringing "a caring spirit" to questions of incarceration, would prison reform actually work, and would American communities be safer.[45]

But he was pleading into the advancing swirl of a hurricane. Today, "mass incarceration" has entered the national lexicon, shorthand for Americans locking up more of their population, per capita, than any other country in the world, and also interchangeable with "the new Jim Crow," the vastly disproportionate incarceration of Black men in post–civil rights movement America. Through the 1990s, at least, the vast majority of the population showed little interest in bringing "a caring spirit" to the imprisoned. Increased use of the death penalty, lowering the age at which a child could be prosecuted as an adult, mandatory sentencing for drug offenses, "three strikes and you're out" laws: almost no public policy seemed to stand for rehabilitation in the face of the expanding prison industrial complex. More recent polling shows a softening of the hard-hearted attitude behind that policy regime, but Cash did not live long enough to see it.[46]

Indeed, by the late 1970s, Cash himself had grown disillusioned about his foray into prison politics. He did his best, as an individual, to bring the caring spirit to prisons and individual prisoners. When he played Leavenworth, he told the inmates, "We came here because we care. We care. We really do. If there's ever anything I can do for you all, let me know somehow, and I'll do it." He appeared before the Tennessee Board of Pardons and Paroles to ask that twenty-four-year-old Larry Hilton, convicted for selling $900 worth of drugs to an undercover agent, have his eleven-year sentence commuted to five, making him eligible for parole in July 1976. Cash told the board about his own struggles with drugs, and said that he met Hilton when he played a show at the Tennessee State Prison and Hilton convinced him that he had reformed his ways. In the end, he had to know that although he could make a difference in the lives of a handful of prisoners, it made no structural difference.[47]

And sometimes he couldn't help even those individual cases. Most famously, he went through the personal pain of observing, as he said on his television show, the in-prison blossoming of Glen Sherley only to have to witness his free-world demise. Following the success of "Greystone Chapel," and Sherley's transfer to Vacaville, Cash had helped him to record an album—a very good live prison album of his own, very much in the Bob Johnston–modified Lomax tradition—and appealed on his behalf for early release. When he got out, Cash took him on tour, and brought him to Washington. But Sherley drank too much, probably suffered from depression, and ultimately threatened Marshall Grant with violence, just for the hell of it. Cash let him go, and Sherley descended into isolation and drug abuse until he killed himself in 1978. In this instance, at least, Cash's empathy for a man who, like him, possessed both talent to spare as a songwriter and a dark side that landed him behind bars did not lead to a happy ending.

But it did not stop Cash from speaking out on issues that moved him—and that moved him, usually, from some sense of shared experience. In those same years that Cash became so closely identified with prison reform, he also came to his politics on the Vietnam War from the perspective of his own experience, with particular sensitivity for those locked into military service. He managed to baffle fellow citizens who both supported and opposed the war, again by identifying primarily with those who now walked a line similar to the one he had once walked.

6

A Dove with Claws

At the end of the same episode of *The Johnny Cash Show* featuring the story of the fifteen-year-old and the "three-time losers," Cash offered a surprising monologue on the most pressing political issue of the day: the Vietnam War. In contrast to his often-subtle television engagement with hot-button politics, Cash made his intervention more directly, and more daringly, in the form of an announcement—like a declaration of faith or a pledge of allegiance. "In times like these, when our country's in trouble, peace is uppermost in all of our minds," he began uncontroversially enough. But then he said, "My family here, and I, stand behind the President of the United States in his quest for a just and lasting peace." One might have expected enthusiastic applause from the supposedly conservative country music audience, but there was only silence. Except for his campaign appearances for Winthrop Rockefeller, which took place outside of the national limelight, Cash had never so openly associated himself with a political figure as he just had in endorsing Richard Nixon's handling of the Vietnam War.[1]

Nixon, who had campaigned on a promise to achieve "peace with honor" in Vietnam, had been in office for one year; for most of that time, the antiwar movement had given him space to make good on his promise, but over the few months before this episode aired, the public's patience had worn thin. October and November had seen some of the largest antiwar demonstrations in the nation's history. Nixon responded by trying to marginalize the dissenters, casting them as a "vocal minority" unrepresentative of the vast majority of Americans—the "silent majority"—who supported the president's peacemaking efforts. Cash, by endorsing Nixon's position on his own initiative, without solicitation, seemed to make vocal his alignment with the silent majority. The president, for his part, could not have been happier to have one of the most recognizable figures in American popular culture seemingly on his side.[2]

There can be little doubt that Nixon, whose taste in music ran more to Broadway show tunes, heard about Cash's support only after the show's broadcast. He also probably missed the only clue Cash provided as to why he decided to voice his support for the president. "Although the fighting is many thousands of miles from our shores," Cash had continued to say, "ask any mother who has a son in Vietnam, and she'll tell you that the war is right at her front doorsteps because it's that close in her heart." In effect, Cash asked his audience and, by extension, the president, to put themselves in that mother's place and think about how it must feel to worry about a child fighting in a war that had, by then, lasted longer than the Second World War, with no end in sight. "Here's hoping there will soon be peace," Cash added as a gentle nudge to the White House before performing the hymn "Peace in the Valley." Cash clearly aimed to remind Nixon not so much of his promise to achieve peace with honor, but of what was at stake for American families.[3]

Although you would not have known it from *The Johnny Cash Show*'s initial run as a summer replacement series in 1969, no political issue dominated the host's years as America's most prominent public citizen more than the Vietnam War. As it happened, his rise to superstardom, fueled by the success of the prison albums and his network television show, coincided with the most contentious years of the war. Pundits routinely (and too casually) lamented the "unprecedented" levels of political polarization, of dissent, division, and disunion in America—as if the country had never gone through a civil war. And yet they were not completely wrong: this winter of America's discontent stretched beyond seasons, into years, leaving the public dazed—especially after the events of 1968—and overcome with a kind of cataclysm fatigue. All anyone wanted was for the endless fighting, in Vietnam and at home, to end.

In that historical era, as Cash took his position on the public platform of network television in June 1969, he seemed at first curiously quiet on the Vietnam War. In retrospect, for a guy who so boldly signaled his political engagement on questions of race, Indigenous rights, and prison reform, the near silence on the war seemed out of character. Where did Cash stand—not only on the war, but on the antiwar protests that, in 1968, accompanied the supposed mortal wounding of the Democratic Party, the sudden decline of the "liberal consensus," and maybe the end of the "age of great dreams?" It was hard to say. That first summer on television, Cash appeared to stand off to the side, hesitant, perhaps, to weigh in too fully.

Cash made very few references to war, let alone the Vietnam War or protest against it, in the show's short first season. On the September 22nd episode, he acknowledged, between "America the Beautiful" and Woody Guthrie's "This Land Is Your Land," the political divisions in the country. "America, it is time to be refreshed," he said, as though he could wish some level of comity into the body politic based on a romantic appeal, that maybe he could smooth the jagged edges of American political discourse with the sandpaper grit of these old songs, with their universal appeals to the beauty of the land. But if he did truly think this, he greatly misjudged his fellow citizens; by the end of summer, anyone—even Cash—could see the political storm clouds on the horizon. The war was, by that time, so all-consuming that it required contemplation and commitment—for or against—from every American.

The war itself kindled this sense of national division, but the emergence of the "generation gap" won a privileged place in the national discourse, too. For the generations that survived the Depression and the Second World War, and then built the postwar "Affluent Society," the relentless challenges coming from their children—over civil rights, the bomb, poverty, and the war—amid so much abundance smacked of ungratefulness. But for the baby boomers coming of age at the end of the 1960s, sold on American greatness since grammar school, the complacency of their elders in the face of the nation falling so far short of its own stated ideals reeked of hypocrisy.

Of course, these are overgeneralizations. Most Americans, young and old, tried to stay out of trouble and find a comfortable place in the job market, a home in the real estate market, and TV dinners in the supermarket. But one would not have known that from watching the news. Tuning in, one got the impression that the country had gone to war not only with the Viet Cong but with itself.

Even so, when *The Johnny Cash Show* began airing, its host almost certainly did not think that he would spend the next two years working in the lengthening shadow of Richard Nixon. If Cash's engagements with civil rights, Indigenous rights, and prison reform were surprising interventions to appear on a weekly variety show, his standing as a prominent public citizen almost demanded intervention on questions about the war and dissent. Of all the political issues of the day, war and protest were the ones reporters asked him about the most, and they are probably the ones about which Cash's audience most wanted to know where he stood. Depending on how one looked at it, Cash either fit in like everyone else or not at all.

In examining Cash's politics at the height of his fame, it is the Vietnam War that has always confounded journalists, biographers, and scholars. Because Cash expressed support, at times, for President Nixon's handling of the war while also calling for peace, as well as tolerance of protest, journalists at the time (and scholars since) largely accepted Kris Kristofferson's supposed label of Cash as a "walking contradiction." How could he support the president *and* his critics? How could he hold opposing views on the same subject? On the war, pundits who were used to dividing Americans into camps could think only in terms of hawks and doves, and they could not make sense of a guy who defied their categories. But it made sense to Cash. Like so many Americans, Cash experienced politics viscerally. As ever, once he decided to address a political topic, he explored it through his own experiences: Cash's treatment of war in his songwriting and from the stage in the Ryman consistently identified with the soldiers and working-class families that sent their sons in disproportionate numbers to Vietnam. As a working-class Southerner, a veteran, and a man who had experienced the tragic wartime loss of his older brother as a child, Cash repeatedly returned to themes of pain and suffering during wartime in his art.[4]

Cash's defiance of ideological categories only added to his appeal for a rapidly growing audience. For the millions of Americans buying his records and tuning into his weekly television show, Cash's apparently conflicted stand on the war resonated with their own internal conversations about the war and what it was doing to the country. Working-class families also viewed the war through the keyholes of family, home, and community and were more (not less) likely to oppose the war even as they thought of themselves as patriotic. As in country music more broadly, "feeling and relating" mattered more to those affected by the war than anything else.[5]

CASH'S ATTITUDE TOWARD issues of American Cold War policy had changed little since his stint in the Air Force and his rise to prominence, in the late 1950s and early 1960s, as a popular fixture on the country music scene. He still valued patriotism and citizenship—the idea that a man should serve his country—but those feelings were entangled with memories of isolation, anxiety, and grief. As a veteran, he remained loyal to his commander in chief, but without denying the way that military had felt to him like an after-school detention that lasted four years. Although his struggles with drug addiction limited his opportunities to perform for troops, he played for American soldiers overseas when he could; he first performed for a sitting president, Lyndon Johnson, at a convention in 1965, and he held presidents in high esteem.[6]

By the time Cash commented publicly on the Vietnam War, he had suffered repeated reminders of his brother Jack's early death. In the space of three months, from August to October 1968, Cash bore witness to the untimely passing of four people close to him. Luther Perkins, the Tennessee Three guitarist who did so much to define Cash's sound, died in a fire when he fell asleep smoking. The following month, Cash's former Sun Records labelmate Roy Orbison lost two young sons, ages eleven and six, when their home burned down, next door to Cash's home, while Orbison was on tour in Europe. And in October, during Cash's own tour of England, news reached him that Jimmy Howard, the son of songwriter Harlan Howard and singer Jan Howard (who sometimes performed with Cash's troupe), had been killed by a landmine while on patrol in South Vietnam. June Carter left the tour to go home to comfort the family, who were dear friends.

Each of these premature deaths shook Cash deeply. In later years, he wrote movingly of each tragedy, with the kind of empathy that only someone who has himself lost a loved one far too young can convey. Cash bought the property where Orbison's home had burned to the ground and planted an orchard where the home had been so that "strangers wouldn't live where his children had died." And he never got over Jimmy Howard's combat death. "I'll never forget standing with our friend Jan Howard at the funeral of her son and the terrible feeling that came over me as they folded up the flag that had been draped over the coffin and handed it to her," he wrote in one of his memoirs. "I loved that boy; I'd seen him grow from a baby. It just tore me to pieces to see him and other boys all around us, just eighteen, going off to fight those other boys in Southeast Asia." Just weeks before Jimmy died in battle, his mother had released a single, "My Son," that both lamented how quickly he had been called to duty and prayed for his safe return.[7]

Just as Cash stressed the grief of family during wartime in his 1962 song "The Big Battle," his own grief, and especially that of his friends, fueled his instinctive response to the Vietnam War. Moreover, two of his nephews, Reba's son Donny and Roy's son Roy Jr., were in the Army and Navy, respectively, and Cash had to worry that they might suffer the same fate as Jimmy Howard. Around this time, fan club members noted the attention Cash gave to young men who were serving in Vietnam, even recording messages of encouragement for them.[8]

Although he produced no concept album documenting the lives and deaths of American servicemen, Cash did address the subject in song long before he made his public pronouncements on the Vietnam War. In addition to "The Big Battle" and various songs that referred to the Civil War, Cash recorded two other war-themed songs after Lyndon Johnson escalated the Vietnam War that hinted at the direction his public citizenship on the war would eventually take.

On his 1965 album *Orange Blossom Special*, Cash recorded the classic Irish folk song "Danny Boy" but changed the original with his own interpretation. He started with an extended introduction, describing his father, a serviceman, coming home from France to Arkansas, where he met an Irish immigrant working the Cotton Belt railroad line who first told him the story of Danny Boy. The whole tale could have been apocryphal, but it linked his family's military service to that of the song's subject, supposedly a Daniel McKinney, who had a sweetheart named Rosalie, who sees him off to war but bids him to come home and find her. In the traditional version of the song, Danny leaves his dearest love but returns to find her dead. Cash's version, however, inverts the original. Instead of Rosalie dying, Cash has her pledging her everlasting love even if Danny falls in battle. "I'll come and find the place where you are lying," Cash sings in the voice of Rosalie, "and kneel and sing an Avé for thee." Anyone who has been to a good Irish wake knows that the traditional rendition of "Danny Boy" is a guaranteed tearjerker, designed, it seems, for a good end-of-night cathartic bawl. It suits the departed perfectly, no matter who he is or what he has done with his life, because all any of his loved ones want is for him to "come ye back when summer's in the meadow." But Cash, who recorded the song in December 1964, just four months after Congress passed the Tonkin Gulf Resolution, felt compelled, as he had in "The Big Battle," to make the song's expression of grief specific to the wartime death of a young man. It's not a great version of the classic tune; Cash sounds a little out of it, rambling even—no doubt owing to his drug intake—and the recording lacks the attention to polish that came through on *Bitter Tears* months earlier. But it is an earnest rendition sung by a man who has also known deep grief.

TWO YEARS LATER, in October 1967, Cash tightened his field of vision on dead American boys in Vietnam. By the time Cash recorded "Roll Call," a song written by a fellow Landsberg Barbarian, nearly twenty thousand Americans had perished in Vietnam. "To Annabel in Memphis, it was just another day," Cash begins. "But her sweetheart and his buddies died ten thousand miles away." Given the context, it's a clear reference to the increasingly familiar home front experience of losing loved ones in Vietnam. Cash goes on to sing about a company captain calling roll in the aftermath of a bloody battle. Name after name, he gets no reply until he calls it again to the heavens. All the GIs echo, as though shouting from a tomb in the sky. It's a little corny. But the state of the war and American opinion on the war—then nearly evenly divided between those for and against the war—gave it an air of gravity it would have otherwise lacked. Even with that emotional heft, it wasn't a prominent song in his oeuvre. Cash released it as a B side to the single "Rosanna's Going Wild" and never put it out on an album of its own.[9]

In January 1969, in the aftermath of Jimmy Howard's death and amid the planning for the recording at San Quentin the following month, Cash took his show to Vietnam. He did not go as part of one of those Bob Hope USO tours, complete with Hollywood pinups like Ann-Margret and Joey Heatherton. Cash went on his own, with the Tennessee Three, Carl Perkins, and Cash's new wife, June Carter. The war had clearly been weighing on him, and in the wake of the Tet Offensive a year earlier, public opinion had turned sharply against the conflict. So in the same way that he researched his concept albums by visiting historic sites and putting himself in others' shoes, he took the first opportunity to see what was happening on the ground in Vietnam. While the rest of the nation watched Richard Milhous Nixon take the oath of office on the steps of the Capitol on January 20th, Cash played to American servicemen outside Saigon.[10]

It's too bad that Cash and Columbia did not think to make a live concept album of him playing to GIs in Vietnam. He could have brought his documentary style to it, capturing the mix of pride and patriotism, despair and loss that, as he knew himself from experience, accompanied any soldier's tour of duty. And unlike earlier trips to the Far East, when Cash played to servicemen in South Korea and Japan in times of relative peace, this time, in Tokyo, Okinawa, Manila, and Saigon, he would perform for men at war, even in the middle of a combat zone. Like the prisoners at Folsom and San Quentin and Cummins, these servicemen got to see Cash during a brief break from their everyday hell. He had to know that their response would be powerful.

Thanks to the archival recordings released on *Bootleg Vol. III: Live Around the World* (2011) we have a sense of what a Vietnam War concert album might have sounded like. *Bootleg III* includes just nine songs performed at the Annex 14 NCO Club at Long Binh Army Base, about twenty miles northeast of Saigon (a small sample given that the troupe played as many as ten shows a day), but it captures beautifully the sense of total release experienced by the GIs. Cash later claimed to have been suffering from pneumonia when he got to Vietnam, and on the recording, in fact, we hear him tell his audience that a base doctor told him earlier that day that he could not perform, not with a fever of 102 degrees ("I said, hell, my normal temperature is 110"). But he also later acknowledged that he relapsed into drug abuse while in-country. Either way, he does not sound well on the recording. Not that any of this mattered to the NCOs, every one of whom seems smashed—hooting, hollering, whistling, and cheering throughout the set. Anytime Cash speaks from the stage, he has to talk over GI interruptions, shouts of song requests, and various unintelligible outbursts capped with a "yahoo!" or "yee-haw!" Instead of "Wreck of the Old 97" or "Cocaine Blues," it would have been interesting to hear them react to a song like "The Big Battle," which spoke directly to their condition, but if Cash played it, we have no record of it. Instead, we hear him introduce the only war-themed song among the nine, "Remember the Alamo," saying "There was another time in this country's history when we had to stand and watch somebody else's shore." When Cash begins singing the first line, about Lt. Col. William Travis challenging the Texas volunteers to be willing to give their lives for the cause, the loudest drunken trills of the evening come up. Maybe none of them had ever seen combat. Maybe they were just a bunch of hammered REMFs (Rear Echelon Motherfuckers), raising hell only because, somehow, Johnny Cash had traveled halfway around the world to play for them in a war zone. But it's hard to listen to soldiers' reactions and not imagine that these are guys who have seen and survived the horrors of war, with no guarantee that they might live another day. "They let off more steam than a prison audience," Cash later recounted, and it sounds like it.[11]

Missing from the recording is how Cash also expressed his solidarity with his audience by bashing the antiwar movement. Onstage at the main enlisted men's club, playing to eight hundred rowdy servicemen, Cash said, "I want you to know that I don't hold with those shitheads back home who are marching and demonstrating." He told a reporter from *Overseas Weekly*, a GI newspaper, that he wanted the troops to know "that not everybody is carrying signs, and marching and raising Cain against our government." Plenty of Americans were, like Cash, "pulling for them."[12]

The Vietnam trip had a powerful effect on Cash. Although the group sometimes played to large audiences, on other occasions, he and Carl Perkins moved through the Quonset huts of wounded GIs, bed by bed, singing themselves into exhaustion. He later recalled a young man badly burned and "hidden" in bandages. "When I walked through, he busted out in tears and asked if I'd sing 'Folsom Prison Blues.'" Johnny Cash, a man accustomed to singing to thousands at a time, performed for an audience of one.[13]

In his later comments to journalists and in his own writing, Cash described his experience in Vietnam in a way that showed he related to the GIs not only as a former serviceman but as someone who had been close to too many who had died too young. As he described seeing the wounded come in on helicopters, "torn and bloody and filthy, often reeking of napalm, sometimes burned beyond recognition as human beings," memories of his brother, the Orbison boys, Luther Perkins, and Jimmy Howard no doubt came to mind. "I almost couldn't stand it." He and Carter made a point of writing down names and addresses of some of the wounded, and when they made it to Okinawa, she called their families. "The hardest thing for me in Vietnam wasn't seeing the wounded and dead," Cash remembered. "It was watching the big transport jets come in, bringing loads of fresh new boys for the war." Later, for *The Legend* box set, he wrote, "I got sick of what was happening to our boys." As he moved through 1969, the inevitability of his public engagement with the Vietnam War took shape on record, on stage, and on television.[14]

The thing is, Cash returned from Vietnam angry—at both the war and those protesting against it. When one writer asked him if he supported the war, Cash responded, "I support our government's foreign policy. . . . I don't know that much about the war." He then described the experience of seeing the wounded come in on helicopters, and, he said, that "makes you a little mad about some of these folks back home." Although he sometimes joked that he spent twenty years in the Air Force from 1950 to 1954, he still made the point in 1969 and 1970 that he thought "everybody should serve their time" in the military. "It's not up to every man to decide when it's time to go defend our country. We elect men to decide that for us." He spoke here as a member of a military family who held draft resisters and draft dodgers in low regard. Not only had Cash done his "patriotic chore," but his father, two brothers, and two nephews had all served in the military, too—and his nephews were still in the service. Regardless of the politics, they supported the troops.[15]

Like most Americans, Cash gave the new president time to make good on his vow to achieve peace with honor in Vietnam. Cash had a new prison album to record, after all, and he spent much of the spring of 1969 preparing to launch his television show. Even during the trial run of the show's summer replacement series, Cash managed to weigh in on political issues like race relations, wealth inequality, Indigenous rights, and prison reform without getting any grief from ABC. It's possible that both he and the network learned from the example of the Smothers Brothers, who had run a similarly formatted variety show from 1967 to 1969, complete with comedy and rising stars in pop and rock. But the folk-comedy duo repeatedly ran afoul of CBS censors for broaching supposedly controversial topics that, in retrospect, seemed controversial only because the network had made an issue of them. Cash had negotiated certain creative control terms with ABC (though he also had to concede to having certain mainstream guests he would never have chosen himself), and it may be that producers let slide certain subjects and guests—Buffy Sainte-Marie, Odetta—rather than make a big deal out of them as CBS had done. This was the only way the show could avoid being just another country music–themed goofball variety show like *Glen Campbell Goodtime Hour* or *Hee Haw*. And yet, despite that freedom, Cash barely alluded to the Vietnam War in the show's first season. Perhaps he believed Nixon to be the man of peace he claimed to be.[16]

Nixon fooled a lot of Americans in the first half of 1969. He announced plans to reform the Selective Service System by introducing a more equitable draft lottery and doing away with most of the deferments that legally shielded university students and others from conscription. The president also introduced his plan to "Vietnamize" the war. By giving the South Vietnamese more responsibility to fight their own war, the president could start bringing Americans home; he announced the first troop withdrawals in June. To many Americans, it seemed like Nixon was keeping his word in seeking an honorable end to the war.[17]

Of course, by the spring of 1970, Americans learned that Nixon had used the combination of draft reform, Vietnamization, and troop withdrawals as a carefully orchestrated ruse designed to create the impression that he was scaling back on the American commitment in Vietnam when, in fact, at the very same time, he expanded the air war dramatically and, in secret (and illegally), started bombing targets in Cambodia. It turned out that Nixon's secret plan to end the war was just another plan to *win* the war.

By the time the first episodes of *The Johnny Cash Show* aired in June 1969, neither Cash nor the rest of the American public knew of Nixon's deception. Even so, in that summer of debating the draft and how to end the war in Vietnam—the same summer in which *At San Quentin* reached number one on the pop charts—it's clear that Cash remained haunted by Jimmy Howard's death and by what he had seen in Vietnam. In August, he quietly recorded a Vietnam War–themed song for his next release, *Hello, I'm Johnny Cash* (1970), an album that would go to number one on the country charts and number six on the pop charts.

"Route #1, Box 144" gets practically no attention from scholars or Cash biographers, but it is the most accurate barometer of Cash's feelings on Vietnam. Cash sets the tone by commenting on how the death of a serviceman—someone's husband and father—had become so common it is hardly news. In a spoken word segment, Cash describes how the serviceman, a "good boy," had grown up on a farm outside of town, married his high school sweetheart, and settled on their own farm out on Route 1. He is just an ordinary American boy, but by the time Cash sings, "He never did great things to be remembered," we know it's not true: not only married but soon to be a father, he could have legally avoided military service—instead, he joined the army. Not much later, news came that he had been killed and his body returned to the farm on Route 1. Maybe he had not previously made much of an impression, but in making the ultimate sacrifice for his country, the good boy who grew up to be a good citizen is memorialized as if he was President Kennedy. The lyrics do not mention the Vietnam War explicitly, but the song's subject is almost certainly inspired by Jimmy Howard, whom Cash similarly described in his first autobiography as a "popular boy in school, a quiet boy at home, a 'good boy.'" An earlier, handwritten draft of the lyrics implied a critique of American indifference or ignorance of the costs of the war while simultaneously speaking to the universality of wartime loss and pain. While the family out on Route 1 mourned, everyday life continued downtown, with people eating dinner, going about their business, most of them unaware of the family's—the community's—terrible loss.[18]

Although "Route #1, Box 144" honors the sacrifice of an American soldier, without romanticizing or valorizing him à la Barry Sadler's hit song "The Ballad of the Green Berets" (1966), its social realism highlights the pain of a decent American family and urges the listener to recognize each American's death—an impossible task, given the number of men killed and missing in action by the end of 1969. Many country artists plumbed similar themes during the war years.[19] As early as 1966, Loretta Lynn sang "Dear Uncle Sam" about needing her man more than the military did. The tension of patriotism (she loves her country, she says) and heartache (first of him "answering the call" and then of getting the "I'm sorry to inform you . . ." telegram) gets close to the pain that Cash described in "Route #1, Box 144." Similarly, rockabilly queen Wanda Jackson, in "Little Boy Soldier" (1968), describes bringing her young son to the train station to meet his father's flag-draped casket, while Dolly Parton's "Daddy Won't Be Home Anymore" (1969) is sung from the perspective of a mother struggling to find the courage to tell her children that their father has died "fighting in that far-off land." Likewise, the Wilburn Brothers' "Little Johnny from Down the Street" (1970) describes a more mischievous boy than Cash's "good boy" who is missed nevertheless when he gets killed in action.

Most of these songs of wives losing their husbands, mothers losing their sons, and children losing their fathers in a distant war have been overshadowed in our memory by the which-side-are-you-on patriotic country songs recorded early in the war years, but it makes more sense to think of country music artists' prolific war-themed songs as an extended conversation. Early on, some of country music's biggest stars—Ernest Tubb, Hank Snow, Marty Robbins, Stonewall Jackson, Autry Inman, Dave Dudley, and others—once again rallied to record songs celebrating the valor of America's fighting men and the rightness of the cause as if it were 1942. Tubb's "It's America (Love It or Leave It)" became both a patriotic anthem and a popular bumper sticker all over the country. Dudley did an entire album of patriotic songs, including one each from Tom T. Hall and Kris Kristofferson before both songwriters turned against the war. Autry Inman's "Ballad of Two Brothers" told the story of a bearded, impertinent state university protester who is moved by the combat death of his own brother to see the error of his antiwar ways and join the service. In similar fashion, Snow and Robbins recorded singles about (fictional) young men dying in combat, though not to call attention to family suffering so much as to celebrate their heroism.[20]

In "Route #1, Box 144," Cash exemplified those country artists interested not in arguments for or against the war but in reckoning with the cost, in lives, of the war. In this way, Cash and the others—Loretta Lynn, Dolly Parton, the Wilburn Brothers—continued to acknowledge the sacrifice of American servicemen, but rather than stand on all of those flag-draped coffins to wave their "America: Love It or Leave It" bumper stickers, they pointed a spotlight into the homes of servicemen's loved ones. If the public, by 1969, showed signs of hating both the war and the antiwar movement—and public polling demonstrated this, clearly—Cash and the others found a way to engage with the politics of the war from a widely shared, relatable position of grieving. They refused to point fingers at this villain or that villain. "I had no really firm conviction about the rightness or wrongness of the war," Cash wrote in his 1997 autobiography. "My mind just wouldn't approach it at that level when my heart hurt so badly." For Cash, and for many of his fellow citizens, dead and wounded American boys overshadowed everything else.[21]

In fact, by the time Cash recorded "Route #1, Box 144" in August, the biggest Vietnam-themed country song of the year had been Glen Campbell's "Galveston." Written by Jimmy Webb—riding a wave of success after writing massive pop chart hits "MacArthur Park" and "Up, Up and Away"—the song is neither antiwar nor antiprotest. It's more like Cash's version of "Danny Boy": the narrator has gone off to war, leaving his sweetheart waiting, with both fearing that he will never return alive. By the summer of 1969, it seemed like the country music community had room enough for voices that at least asked if this war was worth the price. But a single song from Cash's old pal, Merle Haggard, changed all that.

When the sun set on the summer of 1969, the nation's political climate followed the early frost, and Haggard unwittingly found himself cast in a walk-on role in an autumn spectacle largely directed by Richard Nixon. Armchair historians like to prattle on about how the sixties dream exemplified by that summer's Woodstock Music and Art Fair died while the Rolling Stones played Altamont in December, but really, Nixon kneecapped it in November—in a deliberate effort to fracture and polarize the American population. Haggard could not have seen it coming when he recorded "Okie from Muskogee," but two months after the song came out, many were hailing him as the voice of the "silent majority." Whole books have been written about "Okie from Muskogee," trying to divine just what the hell Haggard meant by writing a song that, although it made fun of hippies and protesters, seemed just as popular with Grateful Dead fans as with Marty Robbins's audience. The song positions the good, decent, law-abiding folks of Muskogee, Oklahoma, against the "hippies out in San Francisco," listing all the things that good folks do compared to these naughty youngsters. "Okie" does not explicitly mention the Vietnam War, but its narrator does say that "we don't burn our draft cards down on Main Street," and that "we" still wave "Old Glory" over at the courthouse, both of which were heard by most listeners as patriotic stands distinguishing the good people of Muskogee from the draft card burners.[22]

The song came out just a few weeks before the first major confrontation between the antiwar movement and Richard Nixon. In fact, the two largest peace demonstrations in American history to date took place in mid-October and mid-November, marking a dramatic end to the president's Vietnam War honeymoon. It seemed like the new war boss was the same as the old boss. Consequently, on October 15, millions of Americans answered the call of the national

Vietnam Moratorium Committee to take the day off from work and school to participate in a wide array of antiwar demonstrations all over the country. More than one hundred thousand people turned out on Boston Common to hear antiwar Senator George McGovern (D-SD) speak, but Americans gathered everywhere—in cities, small towns, and college campuses—to show their support for ending the war. Hundreds of Wall Street businessmen, dressed in suits and ties, read the names of American war dead in a ceremony at Trinity Church. "Surely this is a unique day in our nation's history," NBC News reported. "Never had so many of our people publicly and collectively manifested opposition to this country's involvement in a war." In the weeks leading up to the Moratorium, President Nixon tried to preempt the protest by speaking dismissively of this first challenge to his wartime authority. "As far as this kind of activity is concerned, we expect it," he told the press. "However, under no circumstances will I be affected whatever by it."[23]

But in the weeks following, and in anticipation of the November 15 sequel, Nixon obsessed over how to torpedo the peace movement. Privately, he fumed that the scale of the protests undermined his negotiating position with Hanoi; he could not convince the North Vietnamese that he could escalate the bombing if he wanted to when anyone with a television could see millions of Americans demanding an end to the war. Consequently, the president decided that he would stop dismissing the power of the peace movement and, instead, overpower it from the bully pulpit of the Oval Office before the next Moratorium.

When Nixon appeared on national television on November 3rd, rather than report on new developments or make proposals, he simply defended his handling of the war. He argued that a "precipitate withdrawal"—he used the term frequently in the speech, to emphasize how reckless it would be to seek a quick end—would only cause more violence, more war for the United States down the line. It would only encourage Soviet aggression, which would force the United

States to try to contain its enemies' ambitions in the Middle East, Europe, and "eventually in the Western Hemisphere." None of this was particularly remarkable, but Nixon was lying through his teeth. When he said he sought a "negotiated settlement," he meant that he intended to bomb North Vietnam into submission, to win the war sufficiently enough that an independent South Vietnam could be maintained in perpetuity. By this time, he had been bombing targets in Cambodia for eight months, illegally and in secrecy—without the knowledge of Congress or the public—because he knew that if he did it openly, the country would explode.

The genius of the speech came at the end, when Nixon smacked the antiwar movement with his rhetorical yardstick. He acknowledged that "honest and patriotic" Americans did not agree with his "plan for peace." But he wrote off those who disagreed with him—those whom he had seen in the Moratorium footage—as a "vocal minority" who must not be allowed to prevail over "the will of the majority." Nevertheless, he wanted "the young people of this Nation" to know that he respected their idealism and their desire for peace. "I want peace as much as you do," said the man secretly bombing Cambodia. In a final flourish, he lamented that he had to write, just that week, eighty-three letters to the loved ones of men killed in Vietnam. "There is nothing I want more than to see the day come when I do not have to write any of those letters," he said. It would have been hard to question his sincerity, at least on that point.

But Nixon didn't expect to persuade the young people of the "vocal minority." Instead, as he wrapped up, he looked into the camera and asked "the great silent majority of my fellow Americans" for their support. "The more support I have from the American people," he claimed, the sooner peace could be achieved. "Let us be united for peace. Let us also be united against defeat. Because let us understand: North Vietnam cannot defeat or humiliate the United States. Only Americans can do that." At last, the president had revealed his true objective that evening—to marginalize the antiwar movement and to call forth enough of Middle America to support him that he could pursue his policies in Vietnam the way he saw fit. By saying that only a "vocal minority" could "defeat or humiliate" the "strongest and richest nation" on Earth, he all but called on Americans to listen to "Okie from Muskogee," to choose sides, to be for or against the United States.[24]

It is hard to know how Johnny Cash reacted to the silent majority speech—he never commented on it directly—but over the next couple of months, he said enough about Vietnam that we can draw some conclusions. It seems possible—even likely—that Cash thought that Nixon made a reasonable, practical, and even sensitive presentation of the options facing the nation in Vietnam. And although Cash worried about the war and the men sent to fight it, we know from his televised endorsement of the president's "plan for peace" (which aired on January 28, 1970, though it was recorded on January 7) that he thought the country should give the president a chance to execute that plan. Like many Americans, he no doubt saw Nixon's policies as clear signs of disengagement.

At the same time, it also seems likely that the November 15 Moratorium showed Cash the patriotism and sensitivity among those not cowed by Nixon's efforts to shame the peace movement. In the "March Against Death," the centerpiece of the demonstrations, ordinary citizens carried out the seemingly endless task of conveying signs with the names of American GIs killed, and Vietnamese villages destroyed, and depositing them in caskets in front of the US Capitol building. News reports showed the solemnity of the march, which began at Arlington National Cemetery. As participants walked silently, in a sea of candlelight, past the White House (where each broke his or her silence to read the name of the serviceman or village on their small placard), news cameras showed not the caricature of protesters but a representative group of Americans grappling with the horror of the nation's longest war to date. With more than forty thousand names to be placed in the caskets, the march, which began at 6:00 p.m. on Thursday, November 13, did not conclude until 7:30 a.m. on Saturday the 15th. For Cash, who plainly experienced the war through the prism of his own experience, the March Against Death put the emphasis where he would have agreed it belonged. Regardless of what Cash thought of Nixon and his speech, he would have found it difficult to object to the purpose and tone of that protest.

JOHNNY CASH FINALLY started speaking publicly about the Vietnam War in the weeks following the Moratorium protests and Nixon's silent majority speech. The last episode of his television show's trial season had aired on September 27, the same week that Haggard released "Okie from Muskogee," and more than two weeks before the first Moratorium events; he would have to wait until taping for the second season began in January to comment on the war from his platform on ABC. But when he broke all previous attendance records at Toronto's Maple Leaf Gardens on November 10—a week after Nixon's speech, and three days before the start of the March Against Death—Cash told the audience about his trip to Vietnam earlier in the year. "You know, nobody hates war more than I do," he declared. "It scares the hell out of you when you lie in your bunk at night and hear the shells five miles away." But after surviving that terror, he said, you come home and "you don't have the energy to throw rocks and yell" (in an apparent reference to protesters). According to one journalist, despite presenting "a queer, slightly ambivalent discussion of the Viet Nam war," Cash had "a presence that seems to quiet any criticism." Over the coming weeks, Cash refined his statements in light of Nixon's speech and the recent protests. He was finding his footing.[25]

When Cash brought his show to New York to play Madison Square Garden a few weeks later, he went on record regarding the Vietnam War—this time with the American press paying attention.

The concert took place on December 5, 1969, a month after Nixon made his "silent majority" appeal, four days after the first draft lottery, and in the same week that *Life* published the shocking photographs from My Lai, the South Vietnamese hamlet where American soldiers massacred more than five hundred unarmed Vietnamese civilians. The political tension in the country felt reminiscent of the summer of 1968. Even at Altamont, where the youth of the Bay Area gathered for another peaceful music festival the next day, on December 6, people were on edge.

It is unlikely that the Madison Square Garden crowd expected Cash to speak from the stage about the war, but he made it a centerpiece of his show that night. Cash and his whole troupe—the Tennessee Three, Carl Perkins, the Carter Family, and the Statler Brothers—performed in the round, on a stage that rotated, which made a show in front of more than nineteen thousand people seem more intimate. Five songs into Cash's set, he introduced "Remember the Alamo" in much the same way he had at Long Binh earlier in the year, describing the 1835 scene at the San Antonio mission.[26] "180 Americans against 5,000," he said, and paused for effect before repeating the line. Then, as if Nixon himself sat in the audience, Cash said, "Mr. President, that's the kind of odds we['ve] got today," making clear that, even as he launched into a tune that honors fighting men for their collective sacrifice, he saw no prospect for victory in Vietnam. We may pay tribute to the Texans who fought with such bravery at the Alamo, he suggested, but remember the battle primarily because they all perished.

The reference to Vietnam might have slipped by practically unnoticed except that when Cash finished singing, he addressed the war directly. He said that lately, wherever he went, people asked him questions they "didn't use to ask." He noted that "everybody's concerned about our national problems, about the war in Vietnam," and that people repeatedly asked him how he felt about the war. "I'll tell you exactly how I feel about it," he went on, sounding like a man who, having given a lot of thought to a subject, felt obliged and confident enough to offer his point of view when asked for it. When he began by describing the trip to Long Binh in January, the crowd immediately interrupted with an immense ovation, but Cash seemed less interested in the audience's approval than in making his point. He recounted that a reporter friend of his, remarking on the trip to Vietnam, asked "that makes you a hawk, doesn't it?" Cash replied, "No, that don't make me a hawk," to more applause. "But if you watch the helicopters bring in the wounded boys and then you go into the wards and sing for them and try to do your best to cheer 'em up, so that they can get back home—it might make you a dove with claws." This time the crowd absolutely erupted in claps and cheers—by far the loudest and longest of the night—as if hawks and doves alike had heard in Cash's cryptic line a bluntly poetic echo of their own conflicted feelings.

Perhaps most surprisingly, Cash then began singing a familiar (if uncommon for his repertoire) refrain: "Last night I had the strangest dream I've ever known before," he sang as some in the crowd responded in recognition. "I dreamed that all the world agreed to put an end to war." At some point during the song, the Ed McCurdy-penned peace anthem associated more with folk singer Pete Seeger than anyone else (and which Cash had performed when he described the troop trains on his show that summer), he flashed the two-fingered peace sign to the crowd.[27]

Somehow, in the space of six minutes, Johnny Cash criticized the Vietnam War, called for an end to all war, and paid tribute to America's fighting men for their honor and sacrifice. Reviews of the show also said that he "endorsed Richard M. Nixon's conduct of the war," though that is not heard on the recording. But in expressing all of these supposedly contradictory positions, Cash rejected Nixon's simplistic dichotomy of a vocal, disloyal minority and a silent, patriotic majority, and instead spoke for a truer majority of Americans represented by the audience—for people who analyzed the war less as a question of geopolitics but more from the heart, for people who by the end of 1969 seemed to both hate the war and support the troops.

The evidence of this lies not merely in the thunderous response of the Madison Square Garden crowd, but also in its composition. A reviewer for the *New York Post* emphasized the startling mix among the record crowd that night: truck drivers, "law-and-order ladies," "graying, gray-suited men," "foot stamping . . . Wallacites," other "lesser conservatives," and "longhairs." From the looks of license plates on cars "overburdening the parking garages in the Garden area," he concluded that most came from the "country music strongholds" in Pennsylvania, New Jersey, and Connecticut. Still, he noted, some seemed from Avenue C "where the Underground is breeding big Johnny Cash fans who are no less devoted." Another writer overheard a Columbia University student say, "Oh man, is he cool. The president of our school should have hired him to bring peace on the campus when we had those riots." Somehow, then, on the question of the war, only a month after Nixon's speech, and four days after the first draft lottery, Johnny Cash spoke for this cross section of Americans.[28]

That "dove with claws" line, which Cash later came to regret, is often pointed to as proof that Cash cared more than anything about not alienating any part of his growing audience. The implication is that he tried to have it both ways: supporting the president would have been appreciated by Cash's traditional country music audience, long assumed to be politically conservative, while his critique of the war would have won praise from his newer, countercultural audience turned on to his prison albums and his television show. But there is no evidence to suggest that Cash somehow made a calculated stand aimed at holding together his diverse audience, nor is there any evidence that the country music audience was any less conflicted about the war than the rest of the country. If that had truly been his primary concern, it would have been easy enough for him to go to

Vietnam quietly, play for the troops, and simply not comment on the subject from the stage or on television.[29] For Cash himself, nothing that came out of his mouth that night sounded contradictory. But it is so hard to extract ourselves from the political parlor game of categorizing everyone who lived through the Vietnam War as either a hawk or a dove that it makes it difficult to see that, for Cash, his stances on the war were completely consistent. He experienced the war, like so many Americans, on a more deeply emotional level.[30]

When *The Johnny Cash Show* returned to prime time for a second season the following month, he referred to the Vietnam War in both of the first two episodes. The endorsement of Nixon's handling of the war came in the second episode, but often overlooked is the way Cash broached the subject at the end of the first broadcast in a monologue about, of all things, love. "You know, love is all that really matters," he advised, sounding as though he had been spending a lot of time lately listening to the Beatles' "All You Need Is Love" (1967). Most of the problems of the world, Cash said, "could be made smaller or even solved by love and understanding." He went on to say that love and charity could overcome misunderstanding and resentment, which sounded fine enough, if maybe a little trite coming from the man famous for singing about shooting a man just to watch him die. But he finished with a line aimed at Nixon, or at least at the American and Vietnamese diplomats then at an impasse in Paris: "And where there is strife and war, how about a little love for your fellow man being included in the negotiations?" Anyone among the millions tuning in that night, unaware of any statements Cash may have made in support of Nixon during a recent concert, would have heard that line as a plea for peace, as a call to speed up the negotiations and bring this war to an end.[31]

When you start your new season saying, one week, that all we need is love and, the next week, all we need is Nixon, there is bound to be some confusion. In a *Newsweek* profile, music critic Hubert Saal mocked Cash a little, writing, on the one hand, that trying to understand him was like "looking for him in a maze of mirrors," and, on the other hand, suggesting that he had joined the ranks of the "famous" who suddenly think of themselves as "instant seers and wise men," making pronouncements on important issues. Even as other commentators, such as the humorist Cleveland Amory, applauded Cash for taking any stand, even if it was in support of Nixon, Saal pushed Cash to defend his support of Nixon. "I said on TV that I felt safe in following President Nixon," Cash responded. But he also said that he made that statement while seeking to "remind our leaders that we must bring the boys back home." All he cared about, he told Saal, was bringing the boys home "faster than they said they can—if that's at all possible."[32]

Richard Nixon saw nothing confusing or contradictory about Cash's political assertions because, like a lot of the singer's fans, he heard only what he wanted to hear. That "Route #1, Box 144" finally came out on Cash's new album, *Hello, I'm Johnny Cash*, the same week that Cash endorsed the president's plan to achieve "a just and lasting peace" surely escaped him. A few days later, on February 2nd, Nixon wrote appreciatively to Cash, thanking him for his "confidence and understanding." The president appreciated "the good will and patriotic spirit" that prompted the televised announcement. Before long, Nixon's secretary called to invite Cash to perform at the White House.[33]

Other performers might have hesitated to be too closely associated with a president still prosecuting an unpopular war, but Cash jumped at the chance. Maybe he did so, as one journalist wrote at the time, because he "shared the workingman's awe of elected authority." Cash himself later said, "I think the dignity of the office of the President of the United States should be maintained no matter who is our President." Nixon "is our President," he went on, "and we the people have elected him whether you or I voted for him or not." In any case, the entire Cash show prepared for a performance on the nation's best-known political stage, but a funny thing happened on the way to the White House. Cash made clear from his own platform on ABC that his views on Vietnam were more sophisticated than his apparently unquestioning support for the president.[34]

Cash made no more mention of the president on television that spring, but he instead began to weave into his show more attention to dissenting views on the war, including from some of his guests. On the episode that aired on February 18, 1970, Cash welcomed crooner Jimmie Rodgers (no relation to the namesake father of country music), who had just released an album called *Troubled Times*, to sing "What Will We Do When They're Gone?," a song, Rodgers said, "about some of the things that are happening today." The lyrics paint a pretty dark picture of America, where parents are out of touch with their children, who are off getting into trouble doing a variety of things they should not be doing. Among the ways that parents, shirking their duties, might lose their children is "the fight in distant lands that take our boys away from home." The lyrics mention a character named Danny who is now "gone," lost, it seems, to the war. It is as though someone tried to think up a song to go opposite "Daddy Sang Bass," the popular Cash song (written by Carl Perkins) about a family singing and living in perfect harmony. Even more striking is that Cash came back out and joined Rodgers in a duet on "Danny Boy." When the two paused to talk about the meaning of the song, Cash interjected that "the pipes are still calling, still calling for battle, but let's hope it won't be too long until those pipes will be playing for all the boys to come back home." The episode aired only three weeks after Cash said he backed Nixon on Vietnam, yet here he was pressing for a withdrawal of American troops.[35]

The following month, Merle Haggard showed up at *The Johnny Cash Show* and performed like it was his own audition for a Nixon White House concert. He kicked off the episode with not one but two songs associated with the "silent majority." He started by playing the first couple of verses from his big hit "Okie from Muskogee," and then transitioned into his new single, "The Fightin' Side of Me," which might as well have been called "The Fightin' Side of Nixon." Maybe the meaning of "Okie" had been ambiguous enough that Haggard could say it was all tongue-in-cheek, but "The Fightin' Side of Me" basically updated Ernest Tubb's "It's America (Love It or Leave It)" mantra to say that anyone "runnin' down our country" or "runnin' down our way of life" was cruising for a bruising. Among those walking on the singer's fightin' side are those "harpin' on the wars we fight" and "squirrely" war objectors. Someone on Nixon's staff must have noticed, too, because about a year later Haggard performed both songs for the president and his guests at the White House.

It could have been no coincidence, however, that Cash, at the end of the very same episode of his show, answered Haggard's ode to the silent majority by debuting a new, as yet unreleased song, "What Is Truth." He introduced it by recalling how he and June had been in Los Angeles recently, and as they came down the Sunset Strip, they could not get over how many young people they saw. "Some people call these young people 'hippies,'" he explained, sounding like a tour bus guide. He acknowledged that "they may look strange to us, the way they dress," but as far as he could tell, they were peaceful. "If that many young people had been out on the streets back in my part of the country, say, thirty years ago, damned if there wouldn't have been a fight every twenty feet," he claimed. Out on Sunset, though, they "seem to be the nonviolent variety." He did not approve of the "few bad apples" who got all of the attention from the press, of course, but he believed "that most of our young people are good, and all they desire is to be listened to. They're only exercising their freedom of speech, and God help you if that's ever taken away from them, America." If it had been twenty years later, he could have dropped the mic with a thud and walked off stage, but he had a song to play.

"What Is Truth" essentially decries the role played by older Americans in widening the generation gap—for not even listening to the "lonely voice of youth." In one verse, Cash sang (in an obvious reference to the Vietnam War) of a father having to explain what war is to his three-year-old son. In the next verse, Cash described a seventeen-year-old in Sunday school, facing the prospect of going to war in another year and maybe, like Jimmy Howard and the good working-class boy of "Route #1, Box 144," losing his life. Given such stakes, Cash asks, who could blame young people for asking questions, even for asking "what is truth?"

There is no other way to read Cash's introduction of this just-recorded song as anything other than a friendly rebuke to Haggard's opening medley. Where Haggard basically warned anyone "running down" the country—that is, exercising their free speech rights—that they risked a fistfight, Cash's "What Is Truth" is an appeal to drop the fighting posture and listen to young people, even if they are critical of America. Cash may have been a veteran who had unambiguously aligned himself with Richard Nixon, but here he was defending the "lonely" voice of youth. To any Nixon supporter, this choice of adjective must have seemed puzzling—how could they be lonely when so many of them turned out for demonstrations on television? Youthful protesters could only be seen as lonely because, as Cash understood, they were being shouted down by the president and his supporters in the public square. But the song shows Cash's mind focused on the prospect of the Sunday school boy having to risk his life when he turned eighteen, the cascade of agony that he knew from experience would befall the young man's family. With the stakes so high, Cash argued, it is reasonable to ask questions, to demand answers, to dissent. One may not agree with the protesters (the people he had only a year ago referred to as "shitheads"), but in Johnny Cash's world, protest is not inherently wrong. It is as American as the Fourth of July.[36]

ON APRIL 17, 1970, the day that astronauts from the imperiled Apollo 13 mission landed safely in the Pacific Ocean, Cash performed for President Nixon and some three hundred guests at the White

House. "On this historic day," the president said in his introductory remarks, it was appropriate that Cash should play in the nation's capital. Just like the astronauts, Nixon declared, Johnny Cash "belongs to the whole country." Cash's music, the president contended, was like the daring missions to the moon in that it "speaks to *all* Americans . . . in a way that touches the *hearts* of all Americans."

Given that ample controversy preceded the event, the president gave a gracious introduction. Indeed, both at the White House and in the press, tension defined the preparations. For one thing, a mad scramble to get a seat in the East Room followed the concert's announcement. Everyone associated with the administration, it seemed, lobbied for invitations not only for themselves but for other Nixon supporters. Nixon's secretary, Rosemary Woods (later a household name during the Watergate investigations), had to find space for another seventy-five chairs somewhere in the room.[37] Meanwhile, someone from the White House made the mistake of requesting that Cash perform Haggard's "Okie from Muskogee" and Guy Drake's "Welfare Cadilac [*sic*]"—two conservative favorites. Cash refused, saying they were not part of his repertoire.[38] Some journalists gloried in making it appear that Cash had taken a principled stand against Nixon.[39] Following a rehearsal at the White House, a reporter asked Cash if he really supported the president on Vietnam; Nixon's public approval ratings on Vietnam were already dropping steadily. Cash responded by saying, "I consider myself a dove. I don't believe in war," but again asked, "who's gonna get us out of Vietnam faster" than the president?[40]

The White House performance began uneventfully enough, with Cash giving no hint that he planned to address the Vietnam War. He told his audience that the program he had put together—and would perform with the Tennessee Three, Carl Perkins, the Carter Family, and the Statler Brothers—would tell them something about "who we are" and "give you a little taste of the soul of the South." They proceeded to play songs about picking cotton, cutting down timber, surviving floods, the train wreck of the Old 97, and a gospel song about Christ the carpenter. Twenty minutes into the show, however, Cash began talking about young people in contemporary America. It wasn't clear that this had anything to do with the soul of the South, but he said that he had written a poem for the youth of America. "In order to say something to somebody that might be meaningful, you gotta kinda get 'em on your side," Cash said, as if passing along a songwriting tip. This song, he said, is on the side of young people. He then began singing his new single, "What Is Truth," to the President of the United States. Instead of singing "*you* better help that voice of youth find what is truth," as it is heard on the recording, at the White House, Cash sang "*we* better help that voice of youth find what is truth [italics added]." The song's message "seemed to surprise the president a bit," Dan Rather of CBS News reported dryly. Beyond Rather's observation, we have no record of how Nixon reacted to this song (it was just a few weeks before Nixon would, himself, describe the protesters who shut down college campuses all over the country in response to the Cambodian incursion as "bums"), but the audience applauded vigorously.

Several songs later, Cash again brought up the war, recounting the outpouring of support he had received for saying on the television show that he supported the president's plans for peace in Vietnam. "I've pledged to stand behind our president on his policies on Vietnam . . . and to those who wouldn't pledge support, they better stay out of my way so I can stand behind him." Now, in a segue to the old hymn "Peace in the Valley," Cash looked directly at the president, sitting ten feet away, and said, "Soon, we hope that all the boys will be back and, Mr. President, I hope it can even be sooner than you hope (or than you think) it might be." Anyone in the audience could have been forgiven for concluding that Cash came to the White House to make a point about the war. There sat the commander in chief, at the end of a long day, basking in the reflective glow of the Apollo 13 crew, riding a national outpouring of emotion, relief, and gratitude, and here comes his country music star guest—a man he thought of as an ally—wanting to talk about the president's most persistent and vexing problem. That godawful war.[41]

Richard Nixon, the professional political polarizer, had just received a lesson in the ways that politics does not follow a script. Cash said he stood behind the president, but he also urged him both to bring the troops home sooner than even he planned and to stop demonizing the young as a "vocal minority." Of course, Nixon ignored the lesson. At the end of the month, he went on national television and announced that he had ordered American combat troops into Cambodia, and thus seemed to prove the antiwar movement's worst fear—that rather than end the war, Nixon was now expanding it. The country churned in a frenzy of outrage. Students on hundreds of college and university campuses went on strike, shuttering most of their institutions for the rest of the school year. At Kent State University in Ohio, National Guard units unleashed a barrage of gunfire that killed four and wounded nine. Nixon responded to the upheaval on the campuses by contrasting "bums" protesting on campuses with American soldiers, whom he called "the greatest." The students were "the luckiest people in the world, going to the greatest universities," but, he suggested, they protested for protest's sake. That they might have legitimate grievances didn't factor. In the final inversion of Cash's lesson, Nixon recast the singer's line describing his support of Nixon when he said of American soldiers, "they stand tall and they are proud . . . and we have to stand in back of them." The president had missed the larger point.[42]

Following the fruitless Cambodia invasion and the violence of Kent State, Johnny Cash never again made the mistake of saying he stood behind Richard Nixon on Vietnam, at least not publicly.[43] And while other country music stars went full hawk in 1970—see Bill Anderson's "Where Have All the Heroes Gone" and Bobby Bare's "God Bless America Again" for some ham-fisted patriotism—Cash steadily aligned himself more clearly with the lonely voice of youth. In a coincidence of timing, the May 6, 1970, episode of *The Johnny Cash Show*—which was taped before Nixon's Cambodia announcement—ended with a Cash monologue on the generation gap. He started by mocking a public service announcement he had heard on the radio urging listeners to lock their cars and take their keys. "It might help save a teenager from a life of crime," it said. Cash asked his audience to think of how a teenager might hear that supposed public service announcement. "I think a *dis*service is done by saying such things," he observed. He then recalled a headline from a national magazine—"How to Tell If Your Child Is On Drugs"— and wondered why it did not publish headlines like "How to Tell If Your Child Is Confused" or "How to Tell If Your Child Needs Help or Understanding." Why not try "love and understanding with the young people," he asked, "instead of judging them without trial?" Although it said nothing about the war, the monologue captured Cash empathizing with young people in this era of protracted crisis.[44]

The third season of *The Johnny Cash Show* began in late September 1970, and from the start it was clear Cash planned to continue to give space to young artists questioning the wisdom of their elders. Considering that Cash had come back from Vietnam somewhat angry about protesters, offering his network television show as a platform for critics of the war distinguished him not only in country music, but on American television. To be sure, none of these artists came on stage throwing verbal Molotov cocktails, but they got their message across. On that first episode of the season, Arlo Guthrie, the son of Woody and famous for the countercultural song and film "Alice's Restaurant," performed his new release, "I Could Be Singing." The song is bluntly antiwar and anti-Nixon even as it ends on the hopeful note that "the new world is coming together." It ridicules Spiro Agnew, who famously criticized the press corps as "nattering nabobs of negativity," for not wanting to hear anything, but it also argues that "they"—Johnson, Nixon, the Establishment—like beating on protesters in Chicago, and killed them in Ohio, and "they like sending you to war the most." This new world Guthrie called for would not be presided over by the likes of Nixon and Agnew, but by a majority of citizens of goodwill.[45]

At the same time, in his and his young guests' commentaries on "some of the things that might be wrong in this country," Cash privileged positive messages and calls for unity. His own monologue at the end of that first episode could be seen as a response to Guthrie's sharp critique at the start of the show (not unlike how he had countered Haggard's seeming intolerance for dissent with "What Is Truth" in the spring). In spite of the nation's problems, Cash said, when he and his show toured over the summer they saw "a lot of good, free, happy people holding onto ideals and principles that this country is founded upon." He could have been talking about anyone—no matter where you stood in Cash's broad audience, you could imagine him describing you as one of those good, free, happy people hoping, in this season of division, for "peace in the valley."

Other early third season guests used Cash's stage to talk about the war, too. In October, the Canadian psychedelic band The Guess Who appeared on the show. Rather than play their big recent hit, "American Woman," they played "Share the Land," a song that deftly folds commentary on the personal costs of going to war into an anthem of togetherness triumphing over the turmoil and sadness plaguing the land. A couple of weeks later, Cash and June made a point of introducing Melanie (Safka) as a "positive young lady," as if his audience might be skeptical of this hippie who had played Woodstock, famous for the soaring hit "Lay Down." "She believes peace will come, and so do we," Cash said, by way of introducing her to sing the song by that name, "Peace Will Come." Older viewers were getting an education in the thinking of the younger generation whether they liked it or not.[46]

In no episode did Cash make more obvious his identification with the nation's youth than in the "On Campus" episode filmed partly at Vanderbilt University in early 1971. Not only did he leave the Ryman Auditorium to visit a university campus (for many viewers, synonymous with protest) to speak with students, but he presented a slate of rising young stars: James Taylor, Linda Ronstadt, Tony Joe White, and Neil Young. At first glance, the Vanderbilt students appeared to hold little in common with Cash's working-class farm boy character in "Route #1, Box 144." By 1971, though, student deferments from the draft had been eliminated, and the Selective Service had already held two lotteries that included students. Despite reductions in troop levels, there remained no end in sight in Vietnam. The Vanderbilt students, therefore, continued to face the existential threat that Cash himself had known in 1950: of being called to serve and possibly die. In this way, Cash's Vanderbilt broadcast provided a vivid picture, in living color, of those he thought were entitled to question and even protest policies that affected their lives.[47]

In the "On Campus" episode, Cash revealed that he wrote a new song, "Man in Black," in response to a Vanderbilt student's question the week before. Soon to be one of his signature compositions, Cash debuted the song during the episode—even reading the lyrics from cue cards because he had finished writing them only earlier that day. For some fans, all the evidence anyone needs to prove that Cash was an outspoken advocate for the underdog and the downtrodden can be found in "Man in Black." Cash wore black, after all, for "the poor and beaten down," and offers a long list of those left behind, from prison inmates to drug addicts to the elderly and infirm, atheists, and zealots. But it's important not to lose track of the song's origins. When Cash went to Vanderbilt, nearly a year after his White House performance and the national turmoil over the Cambodian invasion, Kent State, and the "Hard Hat Riot" in New York (where construction workers whaled on antiwar demonstrators protesting the escalation), he used the climactic verse of "Man in Black" to repeat his primary message about the war and remind the nation of the rising price of a war seemingly without end. When he sang, for the very first time, "I wear the black in mourning for the lives that could have been"—and calculated the cost of losing so many men week after week—the students erupted in applause for the largest ovation of the night, and left viewers with the sense that the students, as much as anyone, claimed Cash as their own.[48]

Less than a month later, during an end-of-episode monologue, he played "Man in Black" again, dedicating it to a group of servicemen from Fort Campbell, Kentucky, who came to see the show at the Ryman. After writing it for the youth protesting the war, Cash was purposefully associating the song with American servicemen. The camera panned to show the men in uniform, and Cash said, "This is my uniform. For four years I wore the uniform of the United States Air Force; now they call me 'the man in black.'" This time, Cash played a more austere version of the song—with him alone playing guitar, the rhythm section down in the mix and not visible. As he sang and got closer to the line about wearing black in mourning, he got more animated, projecting his voice to the point of almost shouting, displaying a sense of anger at the thought of losing a hundred fine young men each week. In response, the Ryman audience gave him a massive, supportive ovation.[49]

One week later, Cash again debuted another brand-new song, as yet unreleased, called "Singin' in Vietnam Talkin' Blues." "I wrote a song yesterday for all the men in the military, especially for those who are overseas and want to go home," he announced. "I know how it feels." The song is a folk coffeehouse–sounding narration, an actual talking blues, of his January 1969 trip to Long Binh. He recounts performing for the GIs, seeing the dead and wounded, and his and June Carter's "scary" experience of living with enemy shelling the base "night after night." In the last part of the song, Cash again asserts that "whether we belong there or not" is less his concern than honoring the troops and being aware of the human costs of the war. As he reached the last line about hoping they all come home to stay, he again practically shouted "in Peace!" Within a matter of months, the "Singin' in Vietnam Talkin' Blues" came out on Cash's new LP, *Man in Black*, which reached number one on the country charts.[50]

In total, from "The Big Battle" to "Roll Call" to "Route #1, Box 144" to "What is Truth" to "Man in Black" and to "Singin' in Vietnam Talkin' Blues," Cash recorded nearly an album's worth of songs that addressed American boys dying at war and their families' suffering, and made some deliberate statements in favor of peace. Cash acted, intentionally or not, as the self-styled national conscience, reminding the nation that families continued to pay the cost of the Vietnam War. In this way, he differed from certain subsets of the antiwar movement that mobilized at least as much out of concern for the suffering of Vietnamese civilians as for the loss of American GIs.[51] When Cash discussed the war and his hopes for peace coming sooner than later, he never mentioned the Vietnamese. Since so much of his political engagement sprang from the promptings of his own personal experience, and he had no direct connection to the suffering of the Vietnamese (the way he did to, say, Jimmy Howard), he stuck to what he knew.[52]

When ABC did not renew Cash's television show for a fourth season, the Man in Black lost his primary platform for addressing the issues facing the nation, but he did not stop talking about the Vietnam War. In 1972, he released *America: A 200 Year Salute in Story and Song*, an album widely misunderstood as merely a patriotic project, a love letter, like Harlan Howard's recent LP, *To the Silent Majority, with Love* (1971), pitched to the flag wavers of Middle America. In reality, the album originated with a request from the Apollo 14 crew to take a tape of Johnny Cash music with them to the moon. Cash obliged, but when word leaked, Columbia decided to give it a proper recording and release. Although the record primarily includes songs that walk the listener through American history, from "The Road to Kaintuck" to "Come Take a Trip in My Airship," there are a couple of clues that Vietnam still nagged at Cash. For one thing, he appears on the album cover, standing on the porch of a wood cabin, wearing olive drab Army fatigues, next to an American flag draped around a tree. But he does not look like a serviceman so much as a veteran returned home—just like all of the Vietnam veterans who descended on Washington the year before to protest Nixon's continuation of the war. On the album cover, with his longer, tousled hair, Cash could be mistaken for the older brother of John Kerry of Vietnam Veterans Against the War, who won widespread praise for his testimony before the Senate Committee on Foreign Relations. In addition to the album cover, Cash squeezed "The Big Battle," his oldest antiwar song, into his survey of American history. He used it in reference to World War I, a subject he could have skipped entirely. But more than any of the other songs on the album, it speaks to the theme established on the front cover—and it reminded listeners once more that, with the Vietnam War still raging, American families were still losing their husbands, fathers, and sons in battle.[53]

When the American war in Vietnam finally ended in January 1973, Johnny Cash showed up at a film premiere at the Fox Theater in San Diego, dressed not as the Man in Black, but wearing a white suit and tie over a blue and white speckled shirt. Observers might have guessed that the new getup had something to do with Cash's film, a story of Christ's life called *The Gospel Road*, but they would have been wrong. Cash told the crowd of perhaps three thousand people that although he did not feel particularly comfortable wearing white, he wanted to celebrate "the fact that the fighting, dying and killing of Americans in Vietnam had stopped." With the war over, he only got more strident. "That war just made me sick," he told two journalists. "I'm not supporting that war or any other war." He hoped Vietnam had taught Americans "a hard lesson to not be involved in foreign wars," even as he must have known there would be others.[54]

Two decades later, in 1993, when Cash first started playing songs for Rick Rubin, the wunderkind who would produce all his *American Recordings* albums, he played a song called "Drive On" that showed how deeply the Vietnam War had wormed its way into his soul. Cash said he had written it four years earlier—around the time when a lot of Hollywood films about the war and the period garnered considerable attention. As he later described the song's origins, Cash and June had read nearly every book and article they could find on the war over a six or seven year period, and as Alan Lomax would have, they became fascinated with the language of the troops. From John Del Vecchio's novel *The 13th Valley*, Cash picked up on this expression, "drive on," that the troops would use in the face of any hardship—to drive themselves forward, to stay alive regardless of the horrors they experienced. "I wrote this song," he said, "as if I was there." It would be hard to do a better job of conveying the trauma of battle in a song that is as listenable *and* believable. It's like a slice of *Blues in the Mississippi Night* came from the Mekong Delta, with hints of the violence of battle, and of the nightmares from seeing so many good men die, and the cruelty of an indifferent welcome home. Although Cash tried to separate "Drive On" from politics, saying the song "wasn't pro-war or antiwar or anything else—it was just pro-people," it serves as a capstone to all of his earlier Vietnam War songs, only this time from the perspective of a veteran—maybe the man we see on the cover of *America*—who has lost buddies and who now, in old age, walks with a limp and talks with a tremble in his voice. Americans, including his own family, may not understand, but Vietnam was not like it looks in the movies, the song seems to say. "Nobody tried to be John Wayne." For a man whom Americans had once associated so closely with God and country, especially in the years after *The Johnny Cash Show*'s run, the deliberate distancing of himself from the image of John Wayne, signaled a degree of self-awareness not accounted for in the mythology growing around the Man in Black.[55]

God and Country

By the middle of the second season of *The Johnny Cash Show*, viewers had grown accustomed to joining Cash on his "Ride This Train" adventures, trundling through different eras of American life, absorbing lessons on the virtues of hard work and perseverance. No one used the term at the time, but Cash's travelogue through time and space was quintessential "Americana." But then the train that Cash had been conducting all over the continental United States unexpectedly rounded a bend and caught an invisible trestle, spanning the vast Atlantic, that brought him and his audience to Israel, to the land he described as "sacred to the Jew, the Christian, the Muslim." Viewers were likely bewildered by this sudden train leap—and a leap of Faith, no less—to another country. In no prior episode had Cash stretched his imaginary railroad network beyond American borders, not even to Canada. What would be next? A high-speed train to Paris or Tokyo?

Yet, sitting on the stage of the Ryman Auditorium, Cash recounted that he and June had made a pilgrimage to Israel at Eastertime two years earlier. He didn't mention it, but the trip became the subject of *The Holy Land* LP, which came out after *At Folsom Prison*. That is, the man who sang "Cocaine Blues" with such gusto at Folsom had, just weeks later, sought out the most famous sites of the New Testament. And if Cash intended the "Ride This Train" portion of each show to explore American roots, his own roots, it was not much of a stretch. He said he felt drawn to the places he had heard so much about in story and song as a child. For Cash, Israel represented the place where the mythology of all of those gospel hymns connected. After singing "Land of Israel," he described visiting Cana and touring the church built where Christ performed his first miracle. The experience moved him to write "He Turned the Water into Wine" the same day. As he sang the song on his live show, viewers saw images of the Cana church's stained glass, spliced with footage of Cash and Carter visiting these holy sites, looking like awestruck tourists. After the song, he spoke of visiting Calvary, where Christ had been crucified. "With the battle lines drawn," he said a little cryptically, "we look to that living God at this coming Eastertime, for peace on Earth—not only in the hills and valleys of Judea, but let's hope and pray it's the world over." He then sang "God Is Not Dead," the final song from *The Holy Land* album, meant as a reply to the controversial 1966 *Time* magazine cover story entitled "Is God Dead?"[1]

Aside from the vague reference to "battle lines" and the prayer for peace, the segment seemed to bear little connection to previous shows. A few weeks later, though, in an episode that aired just before the White House concert, Cash offered a monologue on the Ten Commandments as available to the counterculture, to "some of us who are again wandering aimlessly, confused, and troubled." Much like his references to the Vietnam War and to the generation gap, these gentle invocations of biblical lessons seemed aimed at healing the nation's wounds.[2]

Devoted Johnny Cash fans know where the story usually goes from here: Cash kept talking about religion on television, dooming his show and hurting his career. And there is some truth to it. As ABC executives and Screen Gems producers fretted over Cash introducing a Sunday school element to his variety show, Cash doubled down. In November 1970, he confronted the issue directly in a monologue at the end of an episode. "All my life I have believed that there are two powerful forces," he began. "The force of good and the force of evil, the force of right and the force of wrong, or, if you will, the force of God and the force of the devil." Obviously, the "Number One most powerful force" is God, but he knew from experience that the devil, the "Number Two most powerful force," can "take over" once in a while. He said that over the years he had had to fight, claw, and kick the devil, giving the sense that it was a constant struggle, including on the show, because it seemed like the frequent talk of God on air had made the devil mad. "He may be coming after me again," Cash mused about the devil, but "while he's coming, I'd like to get in more licks for Number One." Producer Stan Jacobson said that the show's tipping point came with that monologue. "You could see it in the ratings," he said. "John had gone too far."[3]

It's hard to resist this narrative turn in the life of Cash, a man whose livelihood seemed defined, on some level, by peaks and valleys, by success, failure, and redemption. But making a villain of Cash's faith, with Jesus in the role of Yoko Ono, breaking up his career at its peak popularity—that narrative has problems. It risks not taking Cash's faith seriously, obscuring the vital place of spiritual belief in Cash's political persona. It is important to remember that Cash came into those television years having just become reacquainted with his faith (though he had never lost the depth of feeling he had for gospel music, even when he was strung out on pills). At first, he did not explicitly attach his faith to his intervention on various political issues. But during the years that Americans watched him on television, when he felt an increasing responsibility to speak up on political questions, his faith and politics became entangled. He attracted the attention not only of President Nixon but of the nation's best-known evangelist, the Reverend Billy Graham, who had long stood for a muscular, flag-waving patriotism then under assault, allegedly, by the swirling, dissident energies of the 1960s. Some critics and some in Cash's audience started to see Cash, Graham, and Nixon as a kind of Holy Trinity, guardians of traditional values and all that made America great.

But they misread Cash. As his music, his television show, and his life after television demonstrated, Cash's faith had informed his politics of empathy for years, and it continued to drive his public citizenship in the 1970s and beyond. It's easier to see this now than it would have been at the time, because Cash's spiritual journey had many twists and turns and, in the way that it included contending with the political issues of the day, it defied the usual categories. It's a complicated story. Even if religion hurt Cash's career, it both broadened and sharpened his focus as a citizen.

GROWING UP IN Dyess, Cash lived in an old, fundamentalist, revival tent world. Preachers told congregants that, faced with the prospect of the sudden Rapture, promised in the Book of Revelation, they needed to get right with God or get left behind. Accept Jesus as your savior or be cast into a lake of fire. Cash went to church three times a week, twice on Sunday, and when the various heirs to Billy Sunday set up their tents for a week of revival meetings in town or nearby, one could not very well ignore it. Religious fervor ran through the community like cracks of lightning. It left children in awe and fear in equal measure. Cash later wrote that, at just four years old, "I'd peep out the window of our farmhouse at night, and if, in the distance, I saw a grass fire or a forest fire, I knew hell was almost here." When the time came, twelve-year-old J. R. Cash, inspired by his brother Jack's devotion, stepped forward at church one Sunday and accepted Jesus Christ as his savior. He emerged from Arkansas with the narrow understanding that religious experience centered on one thing and one thing only—being saved from hell and damnation.[4]

Many of Cash's letters to Vivian during his time in the Air Force showed just how deeply his distrust of all other faiths had been ingrained in him. He worried about her family's Catholicism and confessed that his family did not like Catholics, owing to their acceptance of "moderate drinking." And even though he had a habit of getting hammered with his Air Force buddies, he told Vivian that he could not "stand before God" if he had a wife that drank alcohol. "You're not pure when you're drinking, Vivian," he wrote. "You're filthy and unsure and unclean when you've got a drop of that in your naturally pure body," he wrote (ironic, given that he would one day be a legendary drug addict). When Cash came across a Catholic pamphlet discouraging marriage to Protestants, he asked Vivian if she planned to try to convert him, as the pamphlet advised in worst-case scenarios. "I'll die a Baptist," he swore. In later missives, he softened his hardline positions, allowing that the two had "differences in belief," and asked that she explain Catholic belief in detail "so I can understand, and not criticize." Once the two were married, Cash took a Catholic instruction course with a priest in Memphis. As he subsequently reported, it gave him a new "understanding and tolerance for other faiths."[5]

Cash would never have claimed to be a good Christian in the years after he and Vivian married. During his rise to stardom and then toward superstardom, he showed few signs of being deeply engaged with his faith. Oh, he still loved the music. That love came through most prominently on two albums of gospel music, *Hymns by Johnny Cash* (1959) and *Hymns from the Heart* (1962). And when he adapted Black spirituals like "Were You There (When They Crucified My Lord)," Cash could bring his live audiences to sustained silence of reverence, as the troupe sang of crucifixion causing them "to tremble." And yet, it is not like he spent much time in church. Rather, the devil seemed to have him by the ankle—just as he had recalled in that televised monologue—dragging him down the alley of drug addiction, infidelity, and selfishness. By all accounts, including his own, he made a lousy husband, father, and colleague in those years, hardly a worthy example of someone who feared God's wrath. Which is why the story of his redemption—his redemption song— is so compelling. Nothing beats seeing a sinner sunk so damned low that even a modest comeback is cause for celebration. And Cash's comeback was better than modest.

Once he shook himself (mostly) free from his pill habit, Cash steadily recommitted himself to his faith. He always claimed that he could not have beaten his addiction if not for the help of June Carter and God. And even as he dipped back into the well of stimulants now and then—at Folsom, at Long Binh—he did not let it take hold of his life again until a series of relapses in the late 1970s and 1980s. By then, however, he had become one of the most recognizable people in America, a man defined in large part by his love of God and country.

Well before Cash got clean, he harbored hopes of making a trip to Israel to do an album. As early as January 1966, a month after pleading guilty in El Paso, Cash told Dixie Deen that he planned to make an album called "The Holy Land," based on research into "the very earliest religious songs known to man." By "religious" he meant "Judeo-Christian," and even hoped to include a song "written during the time of Christ, if we can find one." By the time Cash and his new bride made it to Israel, the Six-Day War, which took place the previous June, had rearranged the map: Israel had claimed the Sinai Peninsula from Egypt, the Golan Heights from Syria, and the West Bank and East Jerusalem from Jordan. It may have seemed peaceful enough to the tourists, but Israel remained on high alert. Cash knew that Jerusalem was holy within three major faiths. But what enthralled him most, like countless other pilgrims to the ancient city, was its centrality within Christianity. Focused on religion, he and June steered clear of the vexing politics of the city, and the Middle East more broadly; they roamed the holy sites with the help of a guide, recording their impressions in photographs and on audio tape.[6]

Those recordings form the basis for *The Holy Land* album, a record that should be mentioned in the same breath as all of Cash's other concept albums. In fact, it is the second of three concept albums released in succession in 1968 and 1969; coming as it did between *At Folsom Prison* and *At San Quentin*, it may as well have been called *At the Holy Land*. Unlike the prison albums, though, it is not a concert recording; it's more reminiscent of *Ride This Train* and *Ballads of the True West* in the way that it alternates narration with songs. Unlike those albums, for which Cash recorded narration in the studio, the *Holy Land* narration comes from what are essentially his field recordings of his travels through Israel. Cash guides us in our audio travels to Bethlehem, Nazareth, Cana, the Sea of Galilee, Mount Tabor, the Wailing Wall in Jerusalem, the Garden of Gethsemane, the Via Dolorosa, Calvary, and the Church of the Holy Sepulchre. Cash's album picks up the authentic sounds of Israelis going about their daily business near these ancient sites, much like Alan Lomax recorded Southern blues in situ. We hear a man hammering out a pan in Nazareth, a radio tuned to an Arab station along the Via Dolorosa, as well as Jews praying in Hebrew at the Wailing Wall. At one point, on Mount Tabor, with the wind buffeting the microphone, Cash turns over the narration to his guide, Jacob, who tells the story of Christ's transfiguration. The effect goes beyond a mere catechism lesson, transporting the listener to the holy sites at a time when few country music fans—few Americans—could make the trip themselves.

Although Cash came out of an evangelical tradition, *The Holy Land* is not an act of evangelism. If he had simply been interested in convincing listeners to accept Christ as their savior, he could have done so easily enough without going to Israel. But by using the field recording approach, he added depth to the experience. Cash's own reverence for the places he visits is evident—he speaks in hushed tones at times—but he does not proselytize so much as report. His only gesture toward evangelizing comes at the very end when he recounts Christ saying that he is going "to prepare a place for you" in his Father's house and promising to return, but Cash does not follow with the usual admonishments to commit one's life to Jesus, to get right with the Lord before it's too late. Sitting at home, playing the record on the hi-fi, listeners had to make sense of Cash's account for themselves. Following the fantastic success of *At Folsom Prison*, the album reached number six on the country charts, and number fifty-four of the pop charts.

By the time *The Johnny Cash Show* debuted in 1969, Cash had gone no further in his public Christianity than making this documentary tour of holy sites, releasing the album between his two smash hit prison records. He may have been engaged right from the start with certain political issues on the show, but he did not, in the early going, bring his Christian beliefs to bear on those political questions, at least not publicly, even if most shows ended with a gospel tune. But over the next couple of years, all of that would change. In the same way that he gradually found his voice and stopped "pulling punches" on political questions between *Blood, Sweat and Tears*, *Bitter Tears*, and *At Folsom Prison*, Cash grew more and more bold in his pronouncements of his religious beliefs on television. Over time, those beliefs influenced and became intertwined with his political stands, reshaping his persona as a public citizen in ways that he did not plan and would eventually try to correct. The frustration came because he shifted away from social realism, where he had been most comfortable. As Johnny Cash the Country Singer became Johnny Cash the All-American, the public's understanding of his politics and religious beliefs got corrupted, oversimplified. His association with Richard Nixon and Billy Graham and the assumptions that those relationships prompted among the public were factors, but the irony is that it was not his public professions of faith that sank his television show so much as working on the television show led him to speak about his faith differently.

The trouble started with the Reverend Billy Graham. Cash, like any decent evangelical Christian, held Graham in high esteem. The former Fuller Brush salesman had become, over the course of the 1950s and 1960s, America's foremost evangelical preacher. Tall, blonde, and handsome, the charismatic minister with the startling blue eyes had been filling sports arenas and stadiums with the faithful, saving souls by the thousands, doing the Lord's work on a scale that past celebrated evangelists like Aimee Semple McPherson or Charles Grandison Finney could not have dreamed. While Cash was still in Vietnam, playing to GIs at Long Binh Army Base, Graham led the prayers at Richard Nixon's presidential inauguration, Nixon's first White House worship service, and the first National Prayer Breakfast. Members of the press started referring to him as "the chaplain to the White House."

When Graham first approached Cash toward the end of 1969, he came not as an ambassador of Nixon's though, thanks to Cash's admiration for Graham, combined with his suddenly outspoken support of the president in January 1970, some observers may have construed it that way. Cash had mentioned Graham in his remarks between songs at the White House concert that spring, calling him "this great man" and describing him as concerned, like Cash, with the nation's problems. But, in truth, Graham came to Cash because he thought Cash could do the Lord's work through his music. As Cash said at the White House, Graham wanted to talk about songs—religious songs that would speak to the country, "that said something for the people of today," and especially younger people. That conversation prompted Cash to write "What Is Truth."[7]

Graham must have talked to Cash, too, about using his television show to spread religious messages more deliberately than just by playing a spiritual at the end of each episode. Cash remarked casually to the White House audience that since he met with Graham that first time, he had had a lot of conversations about what "we, as individuals" need to do about the problems facing the nation. With his platform on network television, he had come to realize that he had an obligation to spread the Word.

Consequently, starting in *The Johnny Cash Show*'s second season, and with greater frequency in its third season, Cash gradually shifted away from the documentary approach at the heart of *The Holy Land* LP toward a more obviously evangelical model. The same spring that Cash rode this train to Israel, he also produced segments that celebrated small country churches as the "faithful symbol of strength and hope to the hard-working people" and spoke of going to church with his mother, a "little, bitty boy" dressed in his Sunday best, making "the rafters ring" with gospel songs. In one episode, he brought his sixty-six-year-old mother to the Ryman stage to play piano, accompanying him on "The Unclouded Day," just as she had the first time he ever sang in church at the age of twelve. Rather than proselytize to the audience, urging them to find Jesus, he rhapsodized about the uplifting music and the comfort offered by a small, country church. He came closest to evangelizing when he remarked that the doors of the church are always open, "so be there, will you?" A later "Ride This Train" celebrated circuit riders, the itinerant preachers who traveled on horseback, as his grandfather had once done, bringing the Word to remote parts of the country, predecessors to modern-day evangelists. In Cash's rendering, circuit riders and modern evangelists like Oral Roberts and Billy Graham were like the subjects of so many "Ride This Train" meditations: simple working men who "tell it like it is."[8]

There can be no doubt that songs such as "What Is Truth" and "Man in Black," as well as Cash's frequent monologues on behalf of young people, were inspired by his discussions with Billy Graham. The preacher clearly saw in Cash a kindred spirit, a man concerned about the generation gap and the problems facing American youth in a time of national division, and a vehicle for spreading his own message. He invited Cash to participate in one of his revivals, held in the football stadium at the University of Tennessee in Knoxville in May 1970, just a few weeks after the Cambodian invasion and Kent State killings. Graham may have been able to fill a stadium with believers day after day, but Cash could reach a television audience numbering in the millions. By 1971, Cash and Graham became collaborators, working together and separately, reinforcing each other's messages to young people. For his part, Graham wrote *The Jesus Generation*, a book "*to* the young, *about* the young, and *for* the young," but also "for the older generation to help them in bridging the generation gap." The cover of the book featured a psychedelic design, with images of young people and a hand extended upward, looking, at first glance, like the two fingered peace sign, but actually an index finger pointing to the cross inside Christ's silhouette. Cash, meanwhile, went out to Vanderbilt, where he filmed his earnest conversations with students on campus. When he debuted "Man in Black," he not only sang about the poor and beaten down and of losing a hundred men a week in Vietnam, but he also sang that he wore black for young people who had never encountered Christ's teachings.[9]

That performance for the Vanderbilt students turned out to be the table setter for the following week's episode, which Cash devoted entirely to gospel music, and on which Billy Graham made a special guest appearance. No less than Mahalia Jackson, Stuart Hamblen, the Staple Singers, and the Oak Ridge Boys, among others, sang spirituals, and Cash introduced Graham to perform an as yet unrecorded song with him, "The Preacher Said, 'Jesus Said.'" The song starts off sounding like an old Sun single, as Cash warbles about looking for answers in times of trouble, but cuts to four separate interludes in which Graham, standing dramatically at the back of the stage, backlit within the shadow of a huge cross, preaches several lines of the gospel by quoting Christ. It was a remarkable sight for a prime-time network television show. Each time, Graham began by saying, "And Jesus said . . ." followed by relatively familiar lines from the gospel, including the ones used by Cash at the end of *The Holy Land* about Christ preparing a place for each person and planning to return— a hint at the coming Rapture. When they finished the song, Graham came forward, looking almost hip in his black suit, white shirt, and polka dot tie, to be introduced by Cash for some straight-up preaching. "Young people today are searching for purpose and meaning in their lives," he said, tritely. "They want to know where did I come from, why am I here, where am I going, what is life all about?" To quiet this confusion, he claimed, thousands of American young people had turned to Jesus Christ for answers. "They're listening to the words of Christ as perhaps no other generation in the history of this country." He explained that no matter who they were, listening to him at home or in the seats in front of him, Jesus loved and forgave them. But like any storefront evangelist, he could not help but press for his viewers to commit, "right now," to Jesus. "You could do it, right now, tonight, if you made your commitment to Him." By the end, Graham had preached for five straight minutes and been on stage, including the performance with Cash, for nearly ten—unprecedented exposure in the days before televangelists could be seen on cable television every day. Cash doubled the gift by making "The Preacher Said 'Jesus Said'" the first song on his *Man in Black* album, released two months later, which went to number one on the country charts and number fifty-six on the pop charts.

Cash's close association with Graham risked alienating portions of his audience. For one, Christian evangelism as practiced in the United States often undermines its offer of universal love and salvation by demanding worship of "the one true God" in ways others find didactic or obnoxious. Cash avoided taking that approach as much as possible, but by letting Graham evangelize from his television show and his latest album, he chanced turning off some segment of his millions of non-Christian fans. It is very hard to be an everyman, after all, when you seem to ask every man and every woman to accept Jesus as their savior. And even though Cash had said little about Nixon since the Cambodia invasion and the protests it set off, his clear association with the "chaplain of the White House" would have been enough for most people to assume that Cash still aligned himself with the so-called silent majority. Anyone who had heard "What Is Truth," "Man in Black," or "Singin' in the Vietnam War Talkin' Blues," would have wondered how he could be on Nixon's side, but many thought that Cash had turned into another John Wayne, a brawny, broad-shouldered defender of God and America.

Indeed, if one didn't look or listen closely, one could get the idea that just as Cash started performing regularly at Billy Graham revivals—or "crusades," as he called them—he had also started to wrap himself in the American flag. It would make sense: a veteran who came from a family of veterans, Cash later acknowledged that he came from "a long line of flag wavers."[10] The year after he released *Man in Black*, he recorded the album that started out as a project for the Apollo astronauts, *America: A 200 Year Salute in Story and Song*. Although he looked like a member of Vietnam Veterans Against the War on the album sleeve, it is the American flag in the foreground, leaving Cash partly in shadow, that we notice first. And the combination of narration and song on the album plainly celebrates the nation that landed the first men on the moon. Two years later, he recorded another album, *Ragged Old Flag*, that begins with a talking song of the same name, describing how the American flag has survived through all sorts of difficulties over the years. On the album sleeve, Cash looks toward the camera as he points behind him at an enormous flag, riddled with holes, as if it is a fifty-star version of the Fort McHenry banner that inspired Francis Scott Key to compose the national anthem. Cash's identification with God and country so permeated the American mind that it must have surprised no one when organizers chose him as grand marshal of the nation's Bicentennial parade in Washington on July 4, 1976. The following year, on the bicentennial of the American flag, Cash recited "Ragged Old Flag" from the rostrum of the United States House of Representatives.

Upon closer examination, though, it is easier to see now that Cash's evangelicalism and patriotism were as complicated as his support of Richard Nixon's supposed plan for peace in Vietnam. Cash represented competing trends in evangelical Christianity in the

1970s, and although he saw eye to eye with Billy Graham on many subjects, they did not agree on everything. Similarly, Cash's love of country required more than mere flag waving, which any knucklehead could do. Celebrating the flag and expressing love for one's country had its place, certainly, but Cash's love for his country was not blind, and at times, even after the Vietnam War, he continued to take one side or another on various issues. As a public citizen, he had high expectations for his country and his fellow Americans— expectations that, alas, they did not often meet.

IN POPULAR MEMORY, we associate the 1970s with both born-again Christianity and with Christian conservatism, the forerunner of the new Christian Right in American politics. The surge in evangelicalism that, in 1976, gave the nation its first born-again president, Jimmy Carter, also sowed the seeds of the Moral Majority and the Christian Coalition in the 1980s. At least, that's the simplified version; the story is thornier than that. In fact, American Protestantism had experienced sharp divisions dating at least to the beginning of the twentieth century, when those leaders of the faithful who put saving souls above all else disagreed with others who thought that the churches should prioritize saving the social order. This disagreement arose not only from the context of the times—defined by rapid urbanization, industrialization, and immigration—but also from competing interpretations of the Book of Revelation. The soul-saving folks, later labeled as "fundamentalists," believed in something called "premillennialism," while the social order savers believed in "postmillennialism." Premillennialists expect that Jesus will return suddenly, judge the living and the dead, cast the unworthy into the lake of fire, and then usher in a thousand-year reign of peace before ascending, with his flock, into heaven. The only way to prepare for Judgment Day, then, is to accept Christ as your savior. You need to be ready, like, *today*. Postmillennialists, which included

theologians and ministers associated with the Social Gospel movement, believed it was their responsibility to save the whole of society,
to bring about the one-thousand-year reign of peace *before* Christ
would return. Or something like that. These are crude summaries
of byzantine theological disputes, but the general idea is that Protestants living through an age of terrible inequality, discrimination, and
violence—the 1910s—either saw it as evidence of the coming end-
times (in which case, they needed to fill the revival tents to the brim
and save as many souls as possible) or as a call to intervene in the
machinery of society, to work toward building a beloved community
that would honor Christ's designs.

Johnny Cash came out of an enduring premillennialist tradition, but by the time he got to Memphis in the mid-1950s, heirs
to the Social Gospel like Martin Luther King Jr. and the Southern Christian Leadership Conference were kicking down these
definitional barriers. The struggle for Black equality, in particular, not only energized the postmillennialists of the Social Gospel
tradition, but it created enough stress among the fundamentalists
that some, including Graham, argued that evangelicals needed to
concern themselves with societal problems, too—not merely the
saving of souls. These mid-century "neo-evangelicals" remained
in theological agreement with mainline fundamentalists, but they
thought that paying attention to social issues not only won more
converts but modeled a "politics of decency." To his credit, Graham led racially integrated revival meetings in the South as early as
1953 and repeatedly said that everyone, regardless of race, is equal
in the eyes of God. He did not agree with the disruptive tactics
of the civil rights movement, even when led by godly ministers,
nor did he think that government had any special role to play in
breaking down the structures of racism on which Jim Crow segregation had been built. Instead, Graham believed that Christians could
change the hearts and minds of American racists, bring them to the
light, and get them to treat their Black fellow citizens as equals. He

was not alone, but not much such talk came from the pulpits of the mainstream churches. Mostly, parachurch organizations such as Youth for Christ (which supported Graham) promoted these ideas, and successfully enough that they were central to the evangelical conversation by the early 1970s. When Graham met Cash, the poor and the marginalized were considered by the mainstream fundamentalists who published and read the influential magazine *Christianity Today* (co-founded by Graham in the 1950s) as worthy of special attention. A few years later, Graham brought thousands of evangelicals from all over the world to Lausanne, Switzerland, for the International Conference on World Evangelism. The resulting "Lausanne Covenant" affirmed "that evangelism and socio-political involvement are both part of our Christian duty."[11]

Graham and his allies at *Christianity Today* did not reorient evangelicals toward social issues on their own. They were also increasingly pushed in that direction by an insurgency of more radical evangelicals who published their own magazine, *The Post-American* and later, *Sojourners*. The radicals, mostly younger evangelicals coming out of divinity school in the late 1960s, alienated by what they saw in Vietnam, began to formulate a critique of the United States as fundamentally in opposition to the message of the gospel. They interpreted the New Testament, particularly the language of Saint Paul and Christ himself, as a "gospel of liberation." In the first issue of the *Post-American*, editors pledged to articulate "the ethical implications of that gospel, by working for peace, justice, and freedom." Eventually, talk of "liberation" led to the formation of Evangelicals for Social Action and an emphasis on building "community." By the time *Sojourners* launched in 1975, the evangelical community behind the publication had moved to southern Columbia Heights, a poor, Black neighborhood in the nation's capital, modeling its opposition to mainstream fundamentalism's embrace of individualism, capitalism, and patriotism—all obstacles to saving the social order.[12]

In the meantime, a growing number of Christian conservatives saw this drift toward trying to intervene in the nation's social problems as a mistake. Rather, they saw evidence of national decline in the behavior of young people—their embrace of radical politics, their disrespect for authority, their use of drugs, their sexual revolution, and the devil's music—all sins for which they must be made to repent. What the world needed, they thought, was a firm, masculine hand to reclaim control of the American family and the nation—a patriotic patriarchy. Ronald Reagan won their support in 1980 by promising to arrest the sense of national decline by standing up to the godless communists of the "evil empire" Soviet Union, by being tough on crime, and by mobilizing a "moral majority" opposed to abortion, the Equal Rights Amendment, and gay rights. It is here that Christianity was implicated in the origins of what we now call "the culture wars," pitting a robust, Christian flag-waving patriotism against a radical secular humanist counterculture.

Johnny Cash, as both public citizen and public Christian, did not fit neatly into any of these camps, even as he, too, worried about his nation in decline and sometimes acted in ways that signaled his alignment with one group or another. As ever, he spoke on the issues based on his own experience, his own ability to relate to those most deeply affected by the question at hand. And just as he did not fly his flag up any particular ideological flagpole, neither did he hang it from the roof of one or another theological school of religious doctrine. Even as the close friend of the most prominent evangelical in the country, Cash did not always follow Billy Graham's example.

Cash self-identified as an evangelical Christian, but he concluded pretty early on that he would not be an evangelist. Instead, he made himself available to evangelists when he thought he could be helpful. As in the case of "The Preacher Said, 'Jesus Said,'" performed with Graham on his television show and on *Man in Black*, Cash and Graham made an impressive team. Not that they necessarily shared the same concerns. Whereas Graham worried most about sexual permissiveness—about premarital sex, abortion, divorce—among young people as the nation emerged from the free love sixties and entered the swinging seventies, Cash spoke more about the danger of drug abuse.

No matter how much the good Reverend Graham tried to reach America's youth, he spoke mostly *at* them, not *to* them, and he could not connect with them as well as the superstar Johnny Cash. For one thing, although Graham believed sincerely that evangelicals needed to be concerned with contemporary societal problems, at the end of the day, he still thought primarily in terms of sin—of saving the souls of sinners by bringing them to Christ. Cash, on the other hand, rarely spoke of sin. In interviews, he explained the attraction of drugs, he empathized with the hunger for drugs and the addiction that followed, but he never judged. He tried to teach from his own experience. "Kids say that drugs turn them on to love," he said to one reporter. "But I'll tell you, there's no such thing as love when you're on drugs" because "drugs are the whole center of your life. You'll do anything to get them, betray anyone who's precious to you," the way he had betrayed everyone around him when he was hooked. The evil of drugs came from their power to deceive, to make young people think that they were finding truth, love, or even Jesus in the experience, when, really, they would only find what he had found: loneliness, pain, and the prospect of an early grave. In this approach, Cash came across as he had on his television show, as if delivering a public service announcement, not a sermon from the pulpit. He didn't tell anyone to find God; he related to their pain.[13]

Still, Cash's PSA approach complemented Graham's preaching and only brought them more collaborators and bigger audiences. As it happened, Cash's alliance with Graham coincided with the rise of the Jesus Movement, a fusing of the counterculture and evangelicalism that started on the West Coast but which, by 1971, had spread nationwide and made the cover of *Time* magazine. The Jesus people made Christ out to be cool, edgy, even an outlaw. They made up wanted posters with Christ's image looking remarkably similar to the face of the guy on Zig-Zag brand rolling papers. Graham and *Christianity Today* were excited about this new movement, and Cash, too, told one journalist he thought it was "the greatest thing that has ever happened to this country." More mainstream evangelical organizations like Youth for Christ and Campus Crusade for Christ soon got in on the Jesus Movement action, with the latter organizing "Explo '72," a weeklong revival in Dallas that culminated with an eight-hour concert headlined by Cash. Graham, the event's honorary chairman, described it as a "religious Woodstock." Dallas police estimated that more than 150,000 young people, all of whom were supposed to commit themselves to the unfortunately named "Operation Penetration" (their mission was to go home and recruit five more people for Jesus), were present for the final concert. Although Cash did not proselytize from the stage, he did testify that he had been freed from a life of drug taking "by the grace of God." He later introduced Graham, who preached to the massive crowd that Jesus would come back as the King of Kings and save "a world headed toward Armageddon," but he urged the attendees to go home, study their scripture, and "go out and change the world." In the end, it seemed like an old-school revival meeting dressed up in paisley and love beads, consciousness expanding maybe, but only within the confines of the New Testament.[14]

BEYOND CASH'S PUBLIC alliance with Billy Graham, he exhibited few signs of being a mainstream evangelical, except, perhaps, in the way he inhabited the role of old-fashioned patriarch. At the same historical moment that the women's movement split the world open, demanding equality not only under the law but in Americans' personal lives, too, Cash seemed, like most evangelicals, to stand for traditional gender roles. For his part, Graham believed in equal pay for equal work, but he saw women's liberation as dangerous to the institution of the family. "God has appointed you husbands to be the head of the home," he said to the men. "When a woman opposes that order, she rebels against the will of God." Treating women equally within the family amounted to a form of permissiveness akin to all the other signs of moral decay Graham saw afflicting American society at the time.[15]

Certainly, *The Johnny Cash Show* presented a traditional man's world on television every week. In all of those "Ride This Train" segments, not once did Cash focus on women. Despite coming from a working-class family in which women and girls—his mother and sisters—always worked, Cash's Americana train ride through the annals of honest toil made no stops to admire the grit, determination, and perseverance of, say, a woman like his mother. No mothers, no teachers, no nurses, not even Rosie the Riveter, the celebrated heroic symbol of the World War II home front, got the "Ride This Train" treatment.

Moreover, like most male television hosts, Cash had a bad habit of introducing his young, female guests by complimenting both their talent and their good looks. In this way, country music television differed not at all from the rest of the American entertainment universe, the working-class feminism of Loretta Lynn and Dolly Parton notwithstanding. On the show's very first episode, Cash reacted to the twenty-five-year-old Joni Mitchell's performance by asking the audience, "Isn't she pretty?" Evie Sands, Jeannie C. Riley, Anne Murray, Lulu, Merrilee Rush, Lynn Kellogg, and Melanie got similar treatment. When Linda Ronstadt appeared on the show in a minidress, his paternalistic flirtations veered toward leering. Fortunately, the only women he kissed on the lips were his wife and his mother. Although his admiration for Mother Maybelle Carter always shone through—he later said that no one influenced him more musically (not even Dylan or Lennon) than Maybelle—one did not get the impression that Cash treated his wife, June, as an equal. Together, they presented themselves as a pious ideal of a married couple (amusing, given the less-than-pious origins of their relationship), but it seemed somewhat beyond old-fashioned when he came out with an album called *Johnny Cash and His Woman* (1973).[16] Perhaps only *Johnny Cash and His Dog* or *Johnny Cash and His Boat* would have made worse titles.[17]

Although the *Sojourners* and *Christianity Today* crowds debated Christ's views on feminism, Cash did his best to stay out of these kinds of doctrinal debates. When a reporter asked him, in 1970, what he thought about women's liberation, he blurted out, "Aw, hell," as if he knew he could not answer the question without making someone angry. Instead, he hailed June as the "ideal" woman because she did not hide her love or appreciation for her husband. "She's a perfect woman because she knows how to treat her man like a *man*," he declared somewhat vaguely. He also stood against "free love" and swinging, saying that he enjoyed his love life with his wife as much as any man could. Another pretty woman might turn his head, he admitted, but he valued the "spiritual bond" he had with June, and said "it would be a sin for anyone to come between us." For her part, Carter later wrote that she blamed her previous failed marriages on her career ambitions. Now, she affirmed, "the greatest thing in my life is being a wife and mother and a helpmate to my husband. A woman is truly liberated when she gets these things into perspective." Carter agreed with Billy Graham that women's liberation followed the Bible's call for men to be heads of households and for women to submit.[18]

Unlike Graham, Cash often made the point that he felt uncomfortable telling people what to do or what to believe—that he preferred simply to say what he believed. But as a prominent public evangelical—"a C+ Christian," he said—he had the power to put Christ's name up in lights, as he did in the film he produced called *The Gospel Road*. Similar to his concept albums, Cash conceived of the project as a film that walks viewers through Christ's life in story and in song. Over thirty days shooting in Israel, Cash essentially took the same approach as on *The Holy Land* but running cameras instead of tape recorders almost the whole time. Cash said he wanted to make the film for young people, to "show how, for two thousand years, people have killed and lied in His name, and that wasn't what He wanted." Violence in the name of faith drove him crazy. "We only need to look at Northern Ireland," he explained. "Everyone over there claims that Christ is on his side, and they go on slaughtering each other." Ultimately, he wanted young people to understand that "they don't have to relate to the bad things that have been done in the name of Christianity."[19]

The Gospel Road tells the story of Christ's life, primarily in his adult years, through his crucifixion and resurrection, but viewers learned as much about Cash's thinking as an evangelical as they did about Jesus. Although Cash would later get help from Graham in distributing the film as widely as possible, the choices of what to highlight from the New Testament reveal a Social Gospel leaning, a sense that maybe Cash had been influenced more by the evangelical radicals at the *Post-American* than previously noted. In a film with little dialogue beyond Cash's narration, we see Jesus accused of being a false prophet, a fool. The scribes and Pharisees, "the keepers of the law," he narrates, labeled Christ "as a radical, as a revolutionist, as a man to be feared, for his words represented change." So far, Cash's Christ fits the wanted poster distributed by the Jesus people, but it's all pretty imprecise. The picture of Cash's Jesus slowly comes into view in his song "Gospel Road," written with journalist Christopher Wren: "Time has come to help the poor and those in need, who wait upon that Gospel Road," Cash sings. The film recounts the mockery and criticism Jesus suffered for reading the gospel of Isaiah, describing all the things that he was meant to do. His calls for "repentance and reform," Cash intones, draws attacks from the powerful even as "the mass of the people, especially the poor and underprivileged, followed him in such numbers that they walked on top of each other just to touch the hem of his garment." At this point, it has become clear that Jesus may as well wear black for the "poor and the beaten down," for the hopeless and hungry of his own time and ours. Cash takes pains to dwell on the Beatitudes, from Christ's Sermon on the Mount, in which he lists all those who are "blessed," famously counting the "poor in spirit," "they that mourn," "the meek (for they shall inherit the earth)," "the pure of heart," and "the peacemakers," among others. Of course, such passages, as recounted by, say, Matthew, have been contested for centuries, but taken in the context of evangelicalism in the early 1970s, it is hard to imagine that Cash would direct the audience's attention to these lines thoughtlessly. By singling out the meek, the merciful, the humble, the peacemakers, Cash's Christ is calling on his followers to not merely commit themselves to Him, but to commit themselves to each other—to build a beloved community. When the film comes to Christ's last moments, he is shown on the cross at Calvary, just as Cash described in *The Holy Land*. But across the next several shots, we see him on the cross in several American locations: in Brooklyn Heights, overlooking the East River with Lower Manhattan in the background; on the Las Vegas strip; by the Hollywood sign; in Death Valley. Director Robert Elfstrom claimed that Cash came up with the idea of doing the crucifixion in all these places "to show that Christ died for people all over the world," but it is telling that, in 1973, all of these locations, except for Death Valley, were urban dens of sin and deprivation. Jesus may have died for people all over the world, but in *The Gospel Road*, his cross is like a pushpin on a map, hinting to viewers where the saving of the social order may begin. It is a wonder that as the Watergate scandal consumed the nation's capital, Cash did not also stage Christ's crucifixion on the National Mall, but then, maybe that is what he was going for with Death Valley.[20]

Cash put *The Gospel Road* out into the world and let viewers come to their own conclusions. "This is my expression of faith," he said, without offering an extensive interpretation of what he meant. But Elfstrom credited Cash with teaching him that religion is not just the church. From Cash, the director learned that Jesus was "a social reformer and revolutionary," and that "His life was similar to our time. If you substitute senators and congressmen for the Pharisees," he reasoned, "you can see the parallel." There is no reason to doubt Elfstrom, but Cash drew no such explicit parallels in public, saying only that "as Christians, we're called on to witness" and a film "is just another way that you can witness." To a layperson, the call "to witness" sounds, perhaps, like it is merely a call to observe. But heirs to the Social Gospel usually said it in reference to the down and out—to witness to the poor, to witness to the imprisoned, to witness to the marginalized—to empathize with the problems that cause inequality and deprivation, bring attention to them, and fix them. Cash believed that Jesus wanted him "to show love for his fellow human beings." There are many kinds of love, he acknowledged, but "I'm talking about the type of love man has for the plight of others," he said. "It is my obligation as a Christian to show Christ's love by loving all men." In *The Gospel Road*, Cash subtly signaled that he went beyond the vague commitment to "engagement" with social issues called for by his friend Billy Graham. He indicated that he would do more.[21]

In fact, in retrospect, it seems clearer that Cash remained more rooted in the 1960s—especially in the way he emphasized witnessing to the downtrodden and seeing love as the ultimate answer to all of society's problems—than representative of the Christian Right we associate with the 1980s. While conservative Christians condemned feminists, homosexuals, and abortion rights activists in increasingly virulent terms, and while even Graham continued to say that he saw in rising instances of permissiveness the coming Armageddon, Cash stuck to witnessing and spreading a message of love. Above all, Cash emphasized not only the importance of finding a way to empathize with, and love, all people as brothers and sisters, but to *act* on that empathy. Cash encapsulated this vision of his faith in "What on Earth (Will You Do for Heaven's Sake)," the last song on the

Ragged Old Flag album. He challenges his fellow Christians, asking if they are "patient with the weak," if they would clothe the poor, if they can "overlook a beggar's dirt." He is very specific, but he is not trying to save souls. Instead, Cash asks believers to contemplate just how deep their commitment to Christ goes by making them answer the question posed in the song's title. Will you, in this hour, in these times, merely talk the Christian talk, or will you walk the Christian walk? These were not mere idle questions in 1974, when the great postwar economic boom finally came to a sputtering end, with unemployment and inflation in the double-digit percentages, seemingly crashing the nation into a second depression. Unemployment lines, gas lines, homelessness—these images began to define the American landscape when Cash released *Ragged Old Flag*. "I mean, to go into church is great," Cash summed up, "but to go out and put it all into action, that's where it's all at." Among evangelicals, he lamented, "I haven't seen a lot of action."[22]

Unfortunately, Cash's challenge to the faithful in "What on Earth," laid down at the end of *Ragged Old Flag* the way he would finish his concerts with a medley of spirituals, could not compete with the album's title track. Thanks to that song, and the image on the sleeve, the American flag got more attention than Jesus. More than anything else, the imagery associated with that album solidified Cash's public standing as a patriot and statesman. But nearly everyone misread it. Here was a guy, they thought, standing up for the flag, standing up for America. But with Cash, nothing is ever that simple.

In the same way that Cash came to his understanding of his faith via his own path, he also came to a more nuanced kind of patriotism on his own. Just as so many Americans misunderstood Bruce Springsteen's "Born in the USA" ten years later, a great many heard only what they wanted to hear in "Ragged Old Flag." But with both songs, nothing is more important than the historical context in which they were written. Cash wrote "Ragged Old Flag" in the middle of a constitutional crisis. By the time the song and album came out in May 1974, the country had been living with the Watergate scandal for nearly two years. Richard Nixon, the man who had twice welcomed Cash to the White House, was losing his grip on the presidency (and, in fact, would resign in disgrace a few months later). "Ragged Old Flag" takes listeners through a series of military clashes dating to the Revolution; anyone could have written a song like that at practically any time in the nation's past. Cash wrote it in 1974 to take measure of the present. Toward the end, he narrates how, as a symbol, the flag has become a source of shame. "She's been burned, dishonored, denied, and refused," he says flatly, just a statement of the sad reality of the polarization of the Vietnam War years. But it is the present government, not the flag, Cash emphasizes, that is "scandalized throughout the land." If the flag, as a symbol, had suffered disrepute in recent years, Nixon and his cronies were to blame. Rather than end on such a downer, though, he finishes by saying that in spite of the beating the country has taken in recent years, both the flag and the republic will endure. It is a patriotic stand of sorts, but not of the "my country, right or wrong," variety. The album is the most political album he put out after the television show, with several songs that refer slyly to Watergate, the environment, unemployment, and poverty—even the country's growing turn against the New Deal order and welfare state. For Cash, it's clear, patriots are those willing to see their country's strengths and weaknesses for what they are, not to try to puff up the one and diminish the other. Listen closely to the album, and it's easy to see that although Cash did not want anyone to lose sight of what he thought made America great, his God commanded him to intervene on behalf of those his country left behind. Perhaps ironically, just when Cash seemed to be everywhere, a still commanding presence on the American cultural landscape, it seemed like no one listened closely to his albums.

Indeed, the most vexing challenge Cash faced in the mid-1970s was reckoning with his overexposure. Even before he wrote "Ragged

Old Flag," it seemed like you could not get away from him. The unceremonious cancelation of his television show by ABC in 1971 did not at first dim the brightness of his star. He kept putting out records, touring, and hosting television specials, making guest appearances and making television commercials. He was everywhere, but he looked a lot less like the outlaw of old and more like an *entertainer*, singing duets with Carter with just a microphone in hand, no guitar, as if they were Sonny and Cher or, worse, Donny and Marie Osmond. By 1975, many country music fans had decided, as music journalist Peter McCabe reported, that Cash, like Billy Graham, had become "hopelessly middle class." He still had an enormous following, McCabe noted, but "his charisma seems to have acquired a tarnish." His reputation had suffered enough in some circles that by the mid-1970s, Big Mack McGowan spoke for many Americans in Jim Szalapski's film *Heartworn Highways* when he remarked, casually, "I believe that Johnny Cash has done already shot his wad."[23]

The cynicism about Cash ran so deep that some questioned his public Christianity, wondering aloud if he was using religion to sell records and books (he published his first autobiography with the Christian press Zondervan in 1975). Music writer Nick Tosches said that he found "Cash and his God" to be a "particularly tedious act." He especially hated the song "Sold Out of Flagpoles," calling it "an absurd mess of godly patriotism" representative of the state of Cash's "monomaniacal" mind. Cash was baffled. He pointed out that mentioning God on his television show had caused ratings to drop, and the same had happened with his record sales; if he wanted to make money, there were better ways to do it than by invoking the Lord.[24]

By the time Cash served as grand marshal in the nation's Grand Bicentennial Parade, rolling down Constitution Avenue in the back of a classic car, he looked less like Public Citizen Number One than a former hero of the baseball diamond, trotted out to throw the first pitch on Opening Day. Snap a few photos and "see you next year." Years later, he said he never liked being held up as a statesman or role model, but it's clear that he was speaking specifically about these years when he was one of America's most recognizable citizens, yet unable to control his own narrative. Without the weekly television show, it got harder for him to articulate for himself, to so many Americans at once, exactly what he thought about their lives and times. He did not stop practicing a public politics outside the usual definitions of "patriot" and "evangelical," but most observers missed Cash reaching back to draw upon his roots among the down-and-out and put his faith into action. While critics focused on his declining record sales and absence from the charts, Cash embodied a "godly patriotism" that stood up for the Americans left behind—not merely for the "downtrodden" and the "underdog" as so often mythologized, but for the countless citizens who felt like they had done everything right, followed all the rules, and still got the short end of the stick. Johnny Cash was the right man for the grand marshal job at the Bicentennial parade alright, but not because he wrapped himself in the flag; it was because he stood up for all those poor bastards.

This is not to say that the myth does not have some basis in fact. Cash did, of course, continue to look out for the downtrodden, the needy, the neglected, and ignored. He still played prisons to let the convicts know that "someone out there cares," but also, as he reported to the inmates at Soledad Prison in California during a concert, because his faith commanded him to. When Cash learned that he had a fan in convicted killer Gary Gilmore, soon to be executed, at his own request, by firing squad in Utah, and the first to die since the Supreme Court had again allowed capital punishment, Cash didn't get drawn into the media frenzy or morbid fascination with the death watch. He simply sent a copy of his memoir, *Man in Black*, to Gilmore, and called him on death row the night before his execution. At a historical moment when most Christian conservatives favored the use of the death penalty, Cash acted only to comfort the condemned man by sharing the story of his own faith journey.[25]

Beyond prisons, Cash continued to put his money and muscle where his Christian mouth was through charitable donations, benefit concerts, and the seeking out of specific acting roles. In a period of economic downturn, when social service budgets were being cut, and charitable organizations were forced to compete with each other to raise limited funds, Cash performed more benefit concerts and gave more donations than he could count.[26] As with his prison concerts, Cash did this work with little fanfare, and not for anyone's approval but because he felt obligated to go beyond Christian witness, to act on his beliefs. In fact, it is hard not to see Cash's selection of socially conscious roles in television movies—in *The Pride of Jesse Hallam* (1981), *Murder in Coweta County* (1983), *North and South* (1985)—as additional evidence of Cash's particular brand of Christian patriotism. His characters in these three films did not deny the nation's failings, but instead provided models for confronting and overcoming those failings. He said he related to the middle-aged everyman Jesse Hallam's struggle to overcome illiteracy because he had known people "exactly like him." And as Lamar Potts, Cash played the Coweta County, Georgia, sheriff who brought to justice a powerful landowner named John Wallace—the first white man convicted and sentenced to death on the testimony of Black citizens. The year 1985 saw his turn as abolitionist John Brown in *North and South*, the celebrated Civil War miniseries; Cash had come a long way since recording "Boss Jack" in 1960 and aligning himself with the underdog Confederacy on his television show.[27]

Still, with all of the attention that has been given to chronicling Cash's post-1960s decline, to showing his 1970s and 1980s musical career as a slow-motion train wreck (culminating in Columbia Records finally dropping him in 1986), it is easy to miss not only a lot of great music but also very astute observations on the nation's political culture. Sure, for a variety of reasons, none of those records made in the decades after *At San Quentin* really rivaled the two prison albums, or even the concept albums of the early to mid-sixties. For one, Cash simply spread himself too thin and put out too many LPs for which he, himself, had written too few songs. The results were predictably uneven. Relying on other songwriters and constantly shifting production approaches at a time when country music sounded either like the polished "countrypolitan" crossover sound of Nashville or the "outlaw country" of Willie Nelson and Waylon Jennings didn't help—Cash seemed to lack a distinct musical perspective. And yet Cash continued to bring his sense of Christian obligation, his sense of witness, to the economic plight of Americans as well as to questions of war and peace. You just have to pick your way through the vinyl bargain bin to find the gems.

Throughout the 1970s, Cash wrote a string of songs from the perspective of the ordinary guy who cannot catch a break. If he had put all of these songs together in a single album, it might have rivaled Bobby Bare's *Hard Time Hungrys*, an underappreciated album of mostly Shel Silverstein–penned songs that reflected the dire circumstances of so many Americans living through "stagflation" years of high unemployment and high prices in the mid-1970s. But as it was, almost every LP Cash made in these years included song lyrics that few self-described patriots or statesmen would dare to utter. In "The Little Man" (1971), "Country Trash" (1973), and "King of the Hill" (1974), Cash described hardworking folks, doing their honest best, only to be knocked down by chance or circumstance. On "I'm a Worried Man," co-written and co-performed with June Carter on *Ragged Old Flag*, the narrator is out of work and cannot feed his family, just as the nation began its plunge into a crisis of hunger and homelessness. For a man who had become fantastically wealthy, Cash apparently never lost the feeling for the Arkansas dirt on his bare feet.

BETTER SONGS ABOUT class stratification in America would be hard to find, particularly at the tail end of the great redistribution of wealth that built the mid-century American middle class, when parents and teachers still told every elementary school kid in the country that she could grow up to be anything she wanted, even as the vast number of good union jobs that had been central to that mid-century middle-class achievement dried up. The coming service economy, based on finance, real estate, and retail, would guarantee that the numbers of Americans falling behind would grow exponentially. Those were the folks for whom Cash now made much of his music.

At times, he related to the average hardworking, under-rewarded American by imagining those folks finally getting their due, and sometimes at the expense of those higher on the economic ladder. He not only recorded Jerry Chesnut's "Oney"—a song in which the narrator, retiring after twenty-nine years of toil under an unscrupulous, petty supervisor named Oney, plots to kick his ass on his last day of work—but he also wrote songs like "Strawberry Cake," in which a former strawberry picker, now homeless in Central Park during America's Bicentennial year, steals a cake from an absurdly decadent dessert tray in the Plaza Hotel. Cash wrote the song after seeing a homeless man in Central Park and thinking that if not for the grace of God, Cash could have found himself in the same sorry situation. It's a silly song, really, but in the context of the Bicentennial and the grim state of New York City at the time, Cash sang not about the nation's two-hundredth birthday cake but about a decadent confection looted from a recognizable site of fantastic wealth and consumed by another American everyman in the bushes. Among mainstream evangelicals, it would have been hard to find similar expressions of witnessing to the poor.

Cash's empathy for ordinary Americans struggling to pay their bills came through, too, in his rendition of Billy Edd Wheeler's song "After Taxes." When Cash performed it on his "Spring Fever" CBS television special in 1978, he sang it as a novelty song, joking about how, after he pays his taxes, there is nothing left to put toward a new Pontiac or fence for his farm. But to millions of Americans drowning in the inflationary 1970s, taxes were no laughing matter and, indeed, the anger led to the passage of numerous tax limitation measures in some states (Proposition 13 in California and Proposition 2½ in Massachusetts being the most famous). It is not that Cash saw himself as part of the not-really-grassroots "tax revolt" of the late 1970s.[28] Rather, the appeal of Wheeler's song for Cash came from its expression of the average man's modest desires—to be able to take his family on vacation, to buy his wife a bracelet—instead of giving all his money to the tax man. It is a wink of understanding to all of us who groan when it is tax time, even if it is perhaps not as convincing as some of his earlier songs of solidarity with the down-and-out.[29]

Not surprisingly, of all working people, Cash related best to farmers, millions of whom were, in the late 1970s and 1980s, fighting for their survival. American farmers did comparatively well, thriving into the mid-1970s thanks to global grain shortages, which drove the price of American wheat to historic highs. When the Nixon administration encouraged farmers to plant "fencepost to fencepost" in order to "feed the world," many expanded their operations by taking out bank loans. Given the inflationary climate, the value of farmland grew rapidly, too—enough that banks were happy to keep loaning money to farmers who put their land up as collateral. But like any economic bubble that bursts, prices started to fall and then plummeted; farm income decreased by a whopping 83 percent by the mid-1980s. Farmers took out more and more loans to stay afloat until the banks finally said no and started demanding repayments. Given that the federal government, under multiple administrations, had effectively encouraged expansion and deficit spending, when the end came so swiftly, farmers—"the most valuable citizens" of the republic, according to Thomas Jefferson—were stunned and angry.[30]

Cash first signaled his concern for farmers during the long economic crisis of the 1970s by recording "Muddy Waters," on his 1979 album, *Silver*. He could have chosen any number of songs to mark his twenty-five years in the music business, but he deliberately included this song by Phil Rosenthal, which chronicles the flood-borne destruction of family farms but may as well be a metaphor for the entire farm crisis—for the merciless devastation wrought by virtually unseen forces washing away the work of generations all at once. As the farm crisis deepened in the early 1980s, with the nation's newspapers filled with headlines of farm foreclosures and farmer suicides, Cash recorded two Bruce Springsteen songs, "Highway Patrolman" and "Johnny 99," that possessed a particular urgency. "Highway Patrolman" is a song about two brothers: Joe, who became a cop when the plunging prices of wheat made him feel like his farm family was "getting robbed," and Frankie, a veteran who, seeing no future for himself, does something stupid and winds up on the run. Similarly, "Johnny 99" is a character whose life is thrown into turmoil when a factory shutdown strips him of his livelihood, leaving him with "debts no honest man could pay." Farm or factory: in the 1970s and 1980s, both were precarious places to work. Cash could relate to the characters teetering on the edge of survival, reminiscent of his own family's struggles in the 1930s and 1940s; he could have covered any Springsteen song he wanted, but what would have been the point of recording "Hungry Heart" in this season of actual hunger?

When Willie Nelson organized the first Farm Aid concert in 1985, Cash not only appeared as one of the Highwaymen—the country music supergroup he formed with Nelson, Waylon Jennings, and Kris Kristofferson—but he performed with his own band and June Carter, too. By all accounts, Cash brought down the house as night fell when he led the crowd of 78,000 people at the University of Illinois's Memorial Stadium in a parody of "Old MacDonald Had a Farm." "Old MacDonald's up a tree, and the government's got no sympathy," Cash sang, reflecting his expectation that the government ought to act as it had when it helped his family in the 1930s. Instead, Cash continued, a banker winds up with the farm, "but he can't plant and he can't sow, 'cause he don't know his butt from a row." The stadium roared because Johnny Cash, the statesman, the patriot, the Christian, had just indicted both the United States government and its financial system with a nursery rhyme.[31]

When Cash said that the Lord expected him to witness to the poor, to take action, this is what it looked like. Cash's gospel-inspired politics of empathy put him out ahead of most evangelical Christians on economic questions and certainly on the farm crisis. No one saw Billy Graham on that stadium stage that day, after all, and although both *Sojourners* and *Christianity Today* eventually ran cover stories on the farm crisis, they lagged years behind Cash.[32]

Cash first initiated the Highwaymen project mostly because he thought it would be fun to play with his friends, but when it came to making a record, he led the group in speaking to the plight of the marginalized in 1980s America. Given the popularity of television shows like *Dallas* and *Dynasty* or *Lifestyles of the Rich and Famous* at the time—not to mention the mockery of welfare recipients in Reagan's presidential campaign—the Highwaymen cut against the grain by recording the Paul Kennerley song "Welfare Line." Cash, Nelson, and Jennings trade verses, singing about poor people—a steelworker in Bethlehem, Pennsylvania, a veteran, a Georgia convict on a road gang, and a man who buries his wife in a pauper's grave—throwing ice water on Reagan's "morning in America" smoke and mirrors game. Maybe more amazing, Cash and Nelson, along with singer Johnny Rodriguez, recorded "Deportee (Plane Wreck at Los Gatos)," Woody Guthrie's famous song about the 1948 plane crash that killed twenty-eight "braceros," or Mexican citizens brought to California to do farm work. Cash sings the lines, "some of us are illegal, others not wanted," relating to a kind of farm work not so different from what he had seen on neighboring plantations when he was a kid. As Congress debated the bill that would become the Immigration Reform and Control Act of 1986, Nelson sings Guthrie's words, describing Mexican farm workers not as "deportees" but as dear friends. The Highwaymen were singing in praise of and for farm folk, poor people, and anyone struggling to survive in the borderlands.

★

BY THE TIME Cash had moved beyond collaborating with Billy Graham to reach America's young people and, after the 1960s, started speaking to the economic plight of so many of his fellow citizens, it had become increasingly clear that he alone determined how his Christian witness informed his actions as a citizen. Cash may have been close to people like Graham, and was certainly influenced by them, but he remained his own citizen, his own Christian. Those songs about precarity, his empathy for farm folk, his public ridicule of a system designed to make hardworking people fail—all of these things set him apart from the majority of evangelical Christians who were then mostly consumed with fighting the so-called culture wars. Cash put as much faith in these culture warriors as he did in the gospel of supply-side economics.

Almost as if to clarify where he stood on such issues, Cash made his boldest religious-political statement in 1986, when he published his novel about the Apostle Paul, called *Man in White*. At first glance, one might imagine a novel about one of the apostles as the indulgence of a man who once towered over American music but now wanted to share what inspired him as a believer. But as much as any record Cash made, *Man in White* is a key to understanding Cash's politics of empathy, its roots in his faith, and how it played out in his public citizenship. Cash had been fascinated with Paul's story— how Saul, the persecutor of Christians, became Paul, the apostle of Christ—for years, and he read deeply on the subject. A lapse into drug addiction in the early 1980s fueled his obsession in much the way it had driven his concept album research in the 1960s. Instead of writing a straight biography, Cash decided to write a novel, but it is a thoroughly researched and learned piece of writing, perhaps one of his greatest achievements. In Cash's rendering, Saul is a violent zealot, fanatical in his defense of doctrine. Christ and his followers offend Saul because of their total disruption of what he claims to know is the will of God. Cash describes a scene in which Saul, fasting to purify himself, pledges to God that "under your hand I will destroy the wicked of the land." One did not have to strain to find contemporary parallels in America.

Cash writes about Saul being blinded by the light of Christ—the Man in White—on the road to Damascus in awestruck tones. There, Christ acknowledges how hard it is to "kick against the goad," against the seemingly immutable law and doctrine that determines, supposedly under God, what is right and wrong. But the voice of the Man in White tells Saul that this is why he has appeared to him: "to make you a witness of these things which you have seen and which I shall reveal to you." Saul realizes that he is blind, "blinded in order that I may see," and in his blindness he comes to recognize and regret the pain and suffering he has unleashed in the name of God. There is no way to read Cash's interpretation of these events and this revelation without concluding that *The Man in White* and *The Gospel Road*, produced thirteen years apart, grew out of the artist's primary motivation: to reach young people, to show that the violence done in God's name is not only wrong, it is unchristian. By the end of the novel, Saul (now Paul) has renounced violence and the ideas and laws with which he had been trained and become an evangelist for Christ based on personal witness. His faith sprang from the promptings of his own experience, not from what he was told to believe and, henceforth, his actions on behalf of Christ will follow suit. According to John Carter Cash, by the time his father had completed his research and writing on the book, Paul had become like a mentor and friend to Cash.[33]

The evidence of that was easy to spot. Cash expressed skepticism of anyone certain of the righteousness of their cause, prepared to resort to violence in support of an idea, whether they were anti-abortionists or anticommunists. Where most evangelicals (save for some of the *Sojourners* crowd) in the 1980s still supported American wars, covert and overt, against the backdrop of the intensifying "second Cold War" of the Reagan years, Cash refused to see American foreign policy in terms of black and white, good and evil. Dating to the start of the Cold War in the 1940s, evangelicals had lined up behind American efforts to contain the "godless," "atheistic" ideology of communism around the world.[34] To Cash, this second Cold War was just another culture war, and all that mattered to him was the likelihood of human suffering when this global struggle came to its inevitable, disastrous end.

Johnny Cash put peace ahead of almost all other political issues in the 1970s and beyond. Yes, he was still the guy who recorded the clumsy "Song of the Patriot" with Marty Robbins in 1980, declaring himself a "flag-waving patriotic nephew of my Uncle Sam." He also agreed to do a series of concerts (which never came to fruition) called "The Johnny Cash Freedom Train," a project aimed at raising money for veterans and their families. But just because he admired America's veterans and loved the flag did not mean he supported militarism.[35] By the late 1970s, he was vocal in his opposition to the buildup of nuclear weapons. Just as he had in his television show's Veterans Day monologue in 1970, when he recounted man's history of developing weapons from club to sword to gun to the atom and predicted a "final war" that would "lay to waste what man had come to be," in the following decade, as the United States and the Soviet Union continued to build nuclear weapons and delivery systems at a breakneck pace, Cash spoke out, suggesting, for the sake of provocation, that grade school children should decide on the nuclear arms race. "For one thing, I think if we left it up to the kids, there wouldn't be *one* [nuclear weapon] on Earth," he said. "I think it's insanity that humankind exists with one nuclear warhead anywhere in the world." Although many evangelicals had been willing to tolerate the build-up of nuclear weapons in the battle against the godless communists, Cash did not find himself alone in his stand against them. In fact, he may have been influenced by the 1978 "Call to Faithfulness" among a few evangelical leaders committing themselves against nuclear weapons. And just months after Jimmy Carter, the born-again president, had negotiated the second Strategic Arms Limitation treaty with the Soviets in 1979—sparking a whiplash of criticism for "selling out" to the Russians—Billy Graham himself came out against nuclear weapons, too. The differences between the United States and its enemies, he said, were not worth a nuclear war.[36]

Cash expressed his opposition to American military policy, and to those who would wrap themselves in the flag, most sharply during his Highwaymen years of the 1980s and early 1990s. Like his old friend and fellow Highwayman, Kris Kristofferson, Cash criticized the Reagan administration's support for the Contras in Nicaragua. "It bothers me that we're going to have 50,000 men on maneuvers off the coast of Central America in May [1987], and at the same time the Russian submarines are off the East Coast more than ever, conducting war games," he said. "I mean, let's face it, there's no winner in a war." But more than that, although he allowed that there might be some legitimate human rights motive for American intervention in another part of the world, the old Cold War (and evangelical) argument for containing communism did not move him. "I see these politicians get up and say, 'We can't have another communist country in the Western Hemisphere,' but who are we to say?" he asked Patrick Carr of Country Music. "Our whole thing is that we're free to choose our own form of government and worship as we please and say what we want, and I'm all American in that way; I think communism is a bad thing. But I can't tell another people who are hungry how to live." When Kris Kristofferson played the Bottom Line in New York City, Cash joined him on stage to perform Bob Dylan's "Masters of War" as a statement against Reagan's policies in Nicaragua. "We've got Johnny Cash on our side against the Contras!" Kristofferson shouted, as Cash returned to his seat. "Watch out, Reagan!"[37]

Rather than pump out recordings of his own antiwar songs in these years, Cash recorded a number of Kristofferson compositions that spoke to the same issues. As early as 1984, Cash recorded Kristofferson's "They Killed Him," an homage to Mahatma Gandhi, Martin Luther King Jr., and Christ, three "revolutionaries" taken before their time. It's hard to imagine Reagan fan Marty Robbins tapping his feet to that one. On Kristofferson's "Love Is the Way," Cash warns of warriors "waving their old rusty sabers" and preachers "preaching the gospel of hate," which only leads to us "killing each other." For both men, the only way forward is through love. But perhaps no song better summed up Cash's and Kristofferson's feelings for their country than "Anthem '84" off the second Highwaymen album. Written by Kristofferson, but sung by Cash, the song is a lament that their country has gone astray, a love letter to a wayward nation. Although the lyrics never mention America or even use the words "country" or "nation," when Cash sings to "you," we know it is to his homeland. When the narrator sings that he will always love his country, that he would never leave, even with all the "crazy things" it's doing, it's obvious that Kristofferson was writing about the Reagan administration's adventures in Central America. Although he believes that the country has, regrettably, traded its "compassion" for its "pride," Kristofferson believes that America can recover its earlier tradition of doing right, with God on its side. The song ends up being hopeful, but not before offering a blunt critique of the nation. It is the kind of complicated expression of patriotism that people with an "America: Love It or Leave It" bumper sticker struggle to understand. Both Cash and Kristofferson plainly love their country, but one way of expressing that love is by calling out its failures.

During Highwaymen concerts, the two liked to toy with their audience's sense of patriotism, too. As it happened, in the late 1980s and early 1990s, many Americans were outraged that the Supreme Court had twice ruled that the First Amendment to the United

States Constitution protected a citizen's right to express themselves by burning the American flag. Against this controversy, Kristofferson wrote a song, "Johnny Lobo," about John Trudell, a member of the American Indian Movement who had participated in the takeover of Alcatraz. According to Kristofferson, when Trudell burned an American flag on the steps of the FBI building in Washington, DC, in 1979, someone retaliated by setting fire to his home, killing his wife, three children, and mother-in-law. It is a serious, powerful song, but some Highwaymen fans grumbled, able to focus only on the burning of Old Glory. Cash would then come forward and talk about his love of all the freedoms guaranteed in the United States, including the right to burn the flag. That really set the audience off. The arenas would fill with howls and people booing, but Cash would quiet them. "Shhhhhh . . . ," he would say. "We've also got a right to bear arms, and if you burn my flag, I'll shoot you," Cash said, as the crowd thundered its approval. (The joke was on them because Johnny Cash never advocated shooting anybody, except in a song.) While the crowd continued to whoop, Cash used the microphone to talk over them: "But I'll shoot you with a lot of love, like a good American!" he would shout, eliciting another, somewhat confused roar. He might as well have finished with, "like a good Christian," however, because his evangelical worldview, his study of Paul, had led him to this point.[38]

By the 1990s, Johnny Cash's evangelicalism had broadened his politics of empathy. He engaged political questions now as almost an elder statesman, but as an elder believer, too. His earlier, more traditional ways of expressing his Christian belief had given way to a commitment to witnessing to the less fortunate, to charting his own path on the political problems that plagued the country. His long association with Billy Graham continued—he still appeared at the preacher's crusades even after making his first *American Recordings* LPs. But when the United States went to war against Iraq for the first time in 1991, Graham not only publicly approved of President George H. W. Bush's war against Saddam Hussein, he and his wife spent the night at the White House, watching the news reports of the bombings. Cash stayed home, drawing dark, brooding images of the oil fields burning in Kuwait. Instead of waving the flag, he seemed to drift again into a deep meditation on American violence.[39]

Epilogue

What matters to me, though, is when people get
an attitude about somebody and paint that person
all one color.

—NEIL YOUNG

On the same night that Odetta performed on *The Johnny Cash
Show* in 1969, Cash introduced what he jokingly called "our love
song for the night." "Delia's Gone" is a very old tune, mined from
deep in the American folk tradition, the kind of thing one could hear
in the Greenwich Village coffee shop where Odetta performed earlier
in the decade. But as Cash sang that he might have married poor
Delia if he had not shot her, a knowing smile crept over his face, as
if he knew he had violated decorum on national television. After his
performance, Cash tried to lighten the mood a bit by repeating that
this was a "love song," but the joke fell just as flat as it did the first
time. He never played the song on the show again.[1]

Twenty-five years later, when Cash released *American Recordings*
to critical acclaim, he led off the album with a reworked version of
"Delia's Gone," accompanied only by himself on acoustic guitar, an

even more spare and ominous rendering than his previous versions. The label released a video in which Cash acts out the murder and burial of Delia, played by supermodel Kate Moss, her apparently lifeless body tied to a chair and later carried by Cash to a lonely grave. Shot in monochrome, it looks like a scene from a B movie horror film, the kind you would see at the drive-in, hoping your date might squeeze you tight just to quit trembling. Cash, appearing a little unhinged, seems to be a bearer of all the qualities of the old, cruel America. The story ends with a shot of Cash trapped behind bars, haunted by "the patter of Delia's feet," likely to be tormented, as in the song, forever.

The video prompted so much criticism that MTV had to pull it. Cash responded by clarifying that the song—which is based on a true story from 1901—is "not an anti-woman song; it's just an anti-Delia song," but it didn't matter. Cash's newly crafted image as a loner outlaw prowling an indeterminate Southern Gothic landscape would prove hard to erase.

American Recordings went on to win the Grammy Award for Best Contemporary Folk Album, and two years later, *American II: Unchained* won Best Country Album. American music fans had rediscovered Johnny Cash (or found him for the first time), but the Cash they celebrated starting in the mid-1990s—the dark, dangerous, shot-a-man-in-Reno Cash—was as monochrome as the "Delia's Gone" video. Looking back now, it's easy to see that as his label and his fans began to shore up the foundation of his badassery, Cash's multifaceted standing as a public citizen, which had defined his work in the 1960s and 1970s, got buried underneath. In building up legends, we always keep it simple, straightforward, and legible—in a way that is acceptable to the highest number of tourists, who are, after all, just winding through this hall of heroes on their way to the gift shop.

It was Cash's collaboration with producer Rick Rubin that sealed his status as a towering figure in American popular culture. Without that last major comeback, his Sun years, the prison albums, his national standing during the television show's run, would have been cited as evidence that once, long ago, Cash had been in the same league as Jerry Lee Lewis or Glen Campbell. It would be easy to blame Rick Rubin for hiding Citizen Cash behind the Outlaw Cash. After all, when it came time to assembling the albums, Rubin looked for the material that best captured Cash's Man in Black image. *That* image, he said, had been buried beneath the Christian, family-man Cash of the 1970s and 1980s, but Rubin, the hip-hop impresario, knew that the OG Cash of "Cocaine Blues"—the Cash who dragged his mic stand across the foot lights of the Opry and flipped a bird at photographer Jim Marshall—*that* Johnny Cash, even in his sixties, would appeal to a younger audience. And he was right.

Rubin recorded Cash pretty much exactly as Cash wanted to be recorded, stripped of the ornamentation previous producers had tried, and that first *American Recordings* album sold more copies than any of Cash's records since *Man in Black* in 1971. At their best, some of the recordings possess the gravitas of the field recordings of John and Alan Lomax. You can listen to them and find yourself lost in another time. Rubin just let the tape roll, as if capturing some old oral tradition of song unavailable anywhere else, or from anyone else. He documents a chapter of American realism that is Johnny Cash himself, as the singer plays song after song of all the tunes he has collected since the 1930s, like he was Leadbelly recording them before they were lost altogether. "Listening to the record," Tony Tost wrote in his 33 1/3 book on *American Recordings*, "it is like overhearing history singing to itself."[2]

Although Johnny Cash infused his concept albums with a politics of empathy, he did not achieve the same effect in the *American Recordings* albums. Each album is comprised of a collection of songs, some gathered by Cash over the decades, some proposed by Rubin and others, but even though they are carried by Cash's aging baritone—which conveys a depth of experience—they lack the cumulative weight of the concept albums. As collections of songs, the *American* albums are certainly better than most of the albums he put out in the 1970s and 1980s, and given Cash's own declining health in this period, that he managed such creative output at all is simply stunning. He had mortality on his mind, and instead of politics, he focused on themes of love and hate, sin and redemption, darkness and light.

Cash couldn't have missed the political division that characterized American life during this period. Although President Bill Clinton promised a peace dividend following the breakup of the Soviet Union and the end of the Cold War, American-led international sanctions against Iraq following the first Gulf War prompted no small amount of protest (including from Cash's friend, Kris Kristofferson). At home, American companies moved more and more manufacturing jobs to Mexico, Central America, and Asia, while wages continued to stagnate. Only the personal computing revolution kept the American economy afloat. The 1980s crisis in the heartland continued as industrial farming forced growing numbers of family farmers off the land. Homelessness was rampant. And as the Clinton administration and Congress led the way with stiffer drug laws and sentencing guidelines, American prison populations soared—particularly among Black men. The most prominent of the Christian Right's ministers continued to rail against feminism, abortion, and gay marriage. Yet Johnny Cash remained uncharacteristically quiet on almost all these issues in his work.

But Cash continued to address political questions in interviews and, in 1997, his second autobiography. In that book, which came out after *Unchained*, and the second *American Recordings* album, Cash reflected on the enduring importance of the image put forth in his song, "Man in Black." Twenty-five years after he wrote the song, "apart from the Vietnam War being over, I don't see much reason to change my position today," he noted. "The old are still neglected, the poor are still poor, the young are still dying before their time, and we're not making many moves to make things right. There's still plenty of darkness to carry off." By 2002, when *American IV* came out, he had begun to rethink the image of himself that he and his label had projected in recent years, because the mainstream press, as one writer observed in *No Depression*, now lionized him as "an avatar of darkness—equal parts proto-punk and forerunner of the modern gangsta MC." That image clearly resonated with a lot of young people, but Cash did not like it that "a hardness and a bitterness and a coldness" seemed to define him in the eyes of some. As if to correct that impression, he listed off his heroes—"the poor, the downtrodden, the sick, the disenfranchised"—in a way that showed not a coldness of heart, but a warmth derived of empathy. "Ain't no end to street people," he lamented. "There's no end to the people of the margins, [and] there's no end to the people who can relate to that." Americans living "on the margins of economic situations and the law," he suggested, grew more numerous by the day, pointing particularly to the millions of his fellow citizens locked up in the nation's burgeoning prison industrial complex. As much as he loved his country, he did not deny its faults. "The raggedness of the flag is due to a lot of things that we've brought onto it ourselves," he concluded, a year after the 9/11 terrorist attacks, when such sentiment coming from anyone else could get them branded as unpatriotic.[3]

The prospect of the United States waging another long war troubled him most toward the end of his life. When the Bush administration started bombing targets in Afghanistan in response to the 9/11 attacks, Cash told Kris Kristofferson that he did not see the sense in "bombing a tribal people." And as the White House tried to concoct what turned out to be the lie linking Saddam Hussein and Iraq to Al Qaeda, Cash grew anxious about the prospects of a protracted war in the Middle East. "I fear for my grandchildren," he remarked to one reporter. "I fear what's coming down on them, how they're going to handle all the hell that this country is going through, if it goes to war. And it's going to be hell—it's going to be terrible what we're going to face if we go to war." As it happened, Cash found himself hospitalized in March 2003, just as the Bush administration, in the face of worldwide protests, launched a "pre-emptive war" in Iraq. As his daughter, Rosanne, later recounted, when Cash awoke from a two-week-long medically induced coma, he opened his eyes and immediately reached for the arm of the little hospital television set. "Did we go to war?" he asked once he could speak, the very first thing he said. When she told her father that, yes, the war had begun, he muttered, "No, no, no . . ."[4]

When Cash died on September 11, 2003, in a historical moment marked by political polarization, his friends and fans reflected on his life, including his public citizenship. "He represented so much that appealed to me—like freedom," Kristofferson remembered. "He was willing and able to be the champion of people who didn't have one." And although Kristofferson could see why some would be drawn to Cash for his wild side, "to me, he doesn't represent danger, he represents integrity," he said. Former vice president Al Gore, for whom Cash had campaigned in the past, said that the two men did not always agree on particular issues (like the death penalty, which Cash opposed), but Cash impressed him with his knowledge of social conditions and his desire to write laws and policies that would help the poor and disadvantaged. "You could always tell when he talked about what was going on in America, that he cared most of all for those who have a tough row to hoe." Maybe only Bob Dylan anticipated the trouble that would come in trying to pin down Johnny Cash. When Cash died, Dylan famously wrote that "in plain terms, Johnny was and is the North Star; you could guide your ship by him—the greatest of the greats then and now." But he warned of trying to classify him too precisely. "I think we can have recollections of him," Dylan said, "but we can't define him any more than we can define a fountain of truth, light, and beauty." If only the partisans had listened.[5]

No sooner had Cash "passed into the greater light," as Dolly Parton put it, did Americans start fighting over the right to claim him for their own political ideology. When the Republican Party held its convention in New York City in August 2004, renominating George W. Bush for a second term as president, police arrested nearly two thousand protesters who had organized dozens of protests over the war, civil rights, and climate change. But the cops also answered a call to corral protesters at Sotheby's on the Upper East Side, of all places. The American Gas Association, an industry lobbying group representing more than 150 utility companies, and Nissan Motor Corporation, the Japanese company that builds cars in Smyrna, Tennessee, decided to honor the Tennessee delegation of the Republican Party and Senator Lamar Alexander by hosting a posh party amid all of the artifacts from the June Carter and Johnny Cash estate, then on exhibit at the auction house. To anyone who saw Cash's image on the invitation to this soiree, it sure looked like the organizers and the Tennessee Republicans thought that Johnny Cash was one of them. A stunned Steve Earle reportedly said, "Johnny would be rolling in his grave" at the thought of being associated with the party of George W. Bush. And although Alexander and the Cash family went way back, the Cash children felt obliged to intervene. Lawyers for the family forced the withdrawal of the invitations with the singer's image, and Rosanne Cash issued a statement clarifying that the event should "NOT be seen as a show of support for the Republican agenda." In the meantime, a hastily produced web page, defendjohnnycash.org, called on protesters to gather outside Sotheby's to greet the Tennessee delegation. Jello Biafra, the punk politico and former lead singer of Dead Kennedys, reported on the protests for WBAI's *Democracy Now!* Biafra described Cash as "our Abe Lincoln," not the kind of guy who belonged to these "Republican fat cat scam artists" waging an illegal war, destroying homes and the environment with mountaintop removal in pursuit of fossil fuels, and overfilling the nation's prisons. "Johnny Cash spoke for the poor and under-represented," protest organizers said. "This administration speaks for the rich." As the Republican delegates stepped off their bus from Midtown and filed toward the entrance, the crowd chanted "grave robbers!" and

"Bush out of NYC! Cash hated prisons and so do we!" In life, Cash had transcended political polarization; in death, it seemed he would be pulled apart.[6]

★

IN THE INTRODUCTION to *The Best of The Johnny Cash TV Show*, released in 2007, the narrator says, "one man served as the ultimate ambassador, with a variety show that excluded no one and drew in everyone." The television show, the producers claim, "brought every family in America together," which is a gross overstatement of the popularity of a show that never broke into the top ten, and in a country in which not every family owned a television. Still, it's hard not to see where this is going. "I don't necessarily think that my father was ever turning to the left or that he turned too far to the right," his son, John Carter Cash, says in a way that makes you think he is trying to sell you something. "My father was truly apolitical." Johnny Cash may have been generally nonpartisan (he only ever publicly backed Jimmy Carter and Al Gore for president), but he would not have known how to be apolitical if the Lord commanded it. The conventional wisdom seems to be that "Johnny Cash," the brand, works best when its appeal is universal and its politics meaningless.[7] Yet Johnny Cash the man, as an artist, as a citizen, defined himself by his politics. At the peak of his fame and cultural power and in the midst of one of the most politically polarized periods of American history, he stepped forward as the nation's public citizen in chief. He has a lot more to teach us in our own moment if we stop talking about him like a light beer that everyone can enjoy.

Rare is the historical epoch that has not seen America polarized, but in recent years the insistence of media commentators and opinion makers that we must all be either liberal or conservative, right or left, red state or blue state, has built into a kind of sclerosis on the body politic. Come election time, most Americans will vote either Democrat or Republican, and pundits, covering these contests like sporting events, will fill in the map in two colors. But when you ask Americans a particular political question, the vast majority will, like Johnny Cash, respond based on their experience and understanding of the issue; what they won't do is respond by spouting a talking point from a party platform (or say, "I, as a liberal," or "I, as a conservative, believe . . .")[8] There have always been outspoken hardcore ideologues beating the doctrinaire drums, but as Cash found, experience, emotion, and empathy speak to more Americans, bridge the social and political chasms that have almost always existed in American life. A politics of empathy isn't necessarily "better" or "more effective" than a politics of ideology—but they can coexist (they *do* coexist), each with their own limits and appeal. It's just that, for our political sport commentators, mapping out the politics of empathy would require coloring outside the lines. And a new set of crayons.

Johnny Cash's politics transcended division precisely because it derived from a combination of his own experiences and an openness to follow his curiosity to the point of understanding the plight of others. Partisans do not, in contrast, distinguish themselves by self-reflection. They can get so wrapped up in their political identity and righteousness that they leave themselves no room for doubt, no open space in which to be wrong. Of course, sometimes they *are* right, but Cash seemed to devote himself to considerable self-reflection before voicing his views on an issue. He may not have opened certain spaces as much as he could have or should have—at least not to our liking—and we may wish that he had more forcefully shut down a space for discussion, but he was tolerant of a wide array of perspectives.[9] Nothing was as simple as black and white, red and blue, and there were no shortcuts.

In his last great composition, Johnny Cash left clues about the hard work a politics of empathy requires. "The Man Comes Around," the title song for the fourth *American Recordings* album, came out in November 2002, more than a year after the 9/11 attacks, and with the United States already at war in Afghanistan and making the case for war in Iraq. Cash, then in failing health, produced the capstone song of his career. "The Man Comes Around" is not an explicitly political song, but it is impossible to separate from its historical context—of a nation at war, of his concern for his family's and his country's future. Cash first started thinking about the song several years earlier, after waking from a dream while on tour in England. He dreamed of going into Buckingham Palace, where he found Queen Elizabeth II and a friend talking and laughing as they sewed or knit. When the Queen looked up, she said, "Johnny Cash! You're like a thorn tree in a whirlwind!" That image nagged at Cash, who felt like it might be biblical. Using a concordance, a reference system for the Bible, sure enough, he tracked down a passage about "waiting for God in the whirlwind" in the Book of Job. Much of the song is drawn from the Book of Revelation, with the Man coming around taking names, deciding, on Judgment Day, who will get to climb the golden ladder and hear the hundred million angels singing, and who will not.

At the risk of overthinking Cash's lyrical choices, one way to read his parting message in "The Man Comes Around" is to focus on that "thorn tree in a whirlwind" (or as he ultimately wrote it, "the whirlwind is in the thorn tree") image. To live a life of Christian witness, to follow a politics of empathy amid the chaos of a modern world—particularly as your country is launching a dubious, preemptive war—is to experience the whirlwind in the thorn tree. No one said bringing about a thousand-year reign of peace before the day of judgment would be easy. It could only be a prolonged battle. When he sings in the next line, "it is hard for thee to kick against the pricks," it is not only the thorn tree to which he refers, but to Christ's exact words to Paul (then Saul) on the road to Damascus. In the terminology of the time, the prick (or the goad, as Cash wrote in *Man in White*) was a primitive cattle prod, used to move the cows onward, in compliance. To "kick against the pricks" meant *non*compliance with official doctrine. In Cash's time, it is not hard to imagine him thinking that to "kick against the pricks" is to resist the easy path of saving one's own soul and, instead, to choose the divergent path of saving the social order. Although the premise of the song is in no small measure frightening, when Cash sings "it is hard for thee to kick against the pricks," it is not with the expectation that you will *not* kick. He fully expects you to struggle, to do the hard work required to satisfy the Prince of Peace. It is an acknowledgment of the pain that must be incurred in building a beloved community, but it is also a word of encouragement, for in the end, one *must* kick.

In a fractured republic, one can embrace the easy politics of polarization, saving one's soul and demonizing everyone else, or one can choose a politics of empathy—facing the whirlwind and kicking against the cattle prod. As Cash's children reminded the world when news cameras captured the image of a white supremacist wearing a Johnny Cash T-shirt in 2017 at the "Unite the Right" rally in Charlottesville, Virginia, their father repeatedly impressed upon them "you can choose love or hate." Cash told his children that he chose love. But the thing is, choosing love, choosing empathy, sometimes means going against the grain, against those who choose war and hatred, against those who set the terms of debate. And that means inviting the whirlwind.

Acknowledgments

I shudder to think about how long this book has been in the pipeline. If you can believe it, I started thinking about writing about Johnny Cash's politics when the *At Madison Square Garden* CD came out in 2002. I treated it as a side project for many years, culminating (I thought) in the publication of an essay about Cash's politics of empathy and the Vietnam War in *Popular Music and Society* in 2014. Only when the article won the journal's R. Serge Denisoff Award did it dawn on me that maybe I should write a book about Cash. I'm grateful to *Popular Music and Society* editor, Gary Burns, the journal's anonymous referees, and the Denisoff prize committee for prompting me to think a little bigger.

Both before and after the article published, I benefited from generous and critical feedback whenever I presented research on Cash—at seminars and conferences in the US, UK, Ireland, the Netherlands, and Germany. Catherine Lavender, Richard Lufrano, Samira Haj, Jonathan Sassi, Chad Montrie, Dean Bergeron, Daniel Kane, Lucy Robinson, Brian Ward, Dan Scroop, Dick Hebdige, Eithne Quinn, David Hesmondhalgh, Simon Hall, Dan Geary, John McMillian,

Brendan O'Malley, Tim McCarthy, Ian Lekus, and Jeremy Varon stand out in my memory as asking the kinds of questions that pushed me to sharpen my ideas over many years.

This book makes use of a lot of previously untapped archival material, all of which is made accessible by the talented librarians, archivists, and curators charged with preserving it. I viewed and took notes on all of the episodes of *The Johnny Cash Show*, his later television specials, and numerous other television appearances at four indispensable repositories, starting with the Museum of Television and Radio in New York, before it became one of the two Paley Centers for Media. The other Paley Center is in Beverly Hills, and I am especially grateful to Martin Gostanian for his assistance there. At the UCLA Film and Television Archive, Maya Montañez Smukler fielded endless requests, digitized programs formerly preserved only on tape, and directed me to the Paley and other libraries for other shows. Kathleen Campbell at the Country Music Hall of Fame in Nashville not only gave me access to episodes of *The Johnny Cash Show* unavailable anywhere else, but she also comped me on admission to the museum, and hooked me up with parking every day (in a city where parking is criminally expensive) when I was on a tight budget.

Also in Nashville, Joshua Bronnenberg gave me a personalized private tour of the Ryman Auditorium, geared toward helping me visualize the production of Cash's television show, and let me wander for hours, taking photos and notes. Similarly, at Historic Dyess Colony and Johnny Cash Boyhood Home, Aimie Mikhelle Taylor not only guided my tour of the Cash homestead, but she came in on a Sunday to talk about northeastern Arkansas history, politics, and culture. She opened the Southern Tenant Farmers Union Museum just for me, directed me to other off-the-beaten-path sites in Mississippi County and in Memphis, and to Arkansas history resources I would never have found on my own. When Aimie left Arkansas State University Heritage Sites, her successor, Adam Long, graciously fielded countless follow-up questions by email.

Thanks to the immutable laws of geography (and insufficient research funding), I could not always get to the archives I needed to visit, but help was always available on site. I'm grateful to Kaye Lundgren, Elise Tanner, Andrew McCain, and especially Cody Bessett at the Center for Arkansas History and Culture at the University of Arkansas at Little Rock (UALR) for assistance with all Cash related materials in the papers of Governor Winthrop Rockefeller. And thanks, too, to my old friend John Kirk for helping me navigate Arkansas from a distance and for fielding Rockefeller questions. Heather Dean and John Frederick at the University of Victoria's library made research in Saul Holiff's papers possible from six thousand miles away. Dorissa Martinez did the same at the Richard Nixon Presidential Library, sending me photocopies of every single mention of Johnny Cash in the administration's papers. My thanks to Tim Hodgdon for help with Cash fan club materials in the Southern Folklife Collection at the University of North Carolina (UNC) at Chapel Hill. And Matt Turi, also at UNC, labored mightily on my behalf to scour the STFU papers for all material related to Dyess. I thank Kris Bronstad at the University of Tennessee for guiding me through Howard Baker's papers, Zach Johnson and Philip Nagy at Vanderbilt for fielding inquiries about Lamar Alexander's papers and Cash's 1971 visit to the university, and Kevin George at the Center for Missouri Studies at the State Historical Society of Missouri for tracking down the elusive issue of *Overseas Weekly* that reported on Cash's 1969 Long Binh performances.

Thanks to the global health crisis, I had to suspend my usual habit of picking up books and records (for research only—really!) on trips to the States. When I desperately needed to hear Leon Bibb's *Tol' My Captain* LP (1960) and couldn't find a reasonably priced copy anywhere in Europe, my Philadelphia brother from another mother, Charlie Hattman, acquired and digitally recorded an original vinyl copy and then transferred the audio files, along with scans of the liner notes. It was a true transatlantic dust-to-digital experience.

Photo research always takes longer than I expect, but the following archivists, curators, and administrators made my life easier: Mark Thiel and Amy Cary at Marquette University; Jan Grenci at the Library of Congress's Prints and Photographs Division; Cody Bessett at UALR; Catharine Giordano at *Stars and Stripes*; Toby Silver and Tom Tierney at Sony; Kara Cravens and Barry Arthur at the *Arkansas Democrat-Gazette*; Kim Reis at Imagn/*USA Today*; Ryan Pettigrew at the Nixon Library; Adam Long at ASU Heritage Sites; and Josh Matas at Sandbox Entertainment.

On certain subjects, I needed to turn to certain experts. Thank you to fellow Cash historians Antonino D'Ambrosio, Colin Woodward, Mark Stielper, and Dan Geary for answering so many random questions you would have thought I was running a quiz show. I'm especially grateful to Colin for sharing his book manuscript, *Country Boy: The Roots of Johnny Cash*, which I look forward to seeing published. Thanks, too, to Dan Berger, who knows everything there is to know about American prison history, convict leasing, and chain gangs. When I needed to know more about Odetta, Matthew Frye Jacobson directed me to her former manager, Doug Yeager, and Ian Zack led me to Belinda McKeon, who went to the trouble of digging out a transcript of her Odetta interview on an old hard drive in the middle of the night. Toni Anderson traded emails with me about "Swing Low, Sweet Chariot." And Amanda Daloisio fielded all of my questions on theology and American religion. And speaking of religion, Scrivener evangelist Simon Middleton not only saved me from the eternal hellfire of disorganized notes, but he also answered even the dumbest questions after I converted.

Beyond research help, I'm grateful to Peter Richardson for his book proposal advice and to Thomas LeBien for introducing me to Zoë Pagnamenta, literary agent extraordinaire. Zoë not only guided me to Basic Books, but she and her colleagues, Alison Lewis and Jess Hoare, have advised and supported me beyond this project, too. I am lucky to have this awesome team on my side.

I'm grateful to Dan Gerstle for convincing me that a fuller political biography of Cash would make a better book than the smaller one I first proposed. When Dan moved on to another gig, Lara Heimert reassured me that she and the folks at Basic would not let me fall through the cracks; she was true to her word, supporting me in my darkest hour, when I needed it most and, later, she very kindly assigned me to editor Claire Potter.

Claire has been *Citizen Cash*'s most enthusiastic cheerleader, but more than that, she helped rein me in when I got repetitive or dived so deep into historical context that I couldn't find my way back to the surface. Claire's not afraid to get her hands dirty, either; by the time we got to the third round of revisions, it felt like we were in the trenches together, working shoulder to shoulder (from three thousand miles apart) and line by line. Her contribution to the book has been immense, but needless to say, any remaining errors of commission or omission are my responsibility alone. Thanks, too, to Abby Mohr for managing seemingly every last detail as the book became a reality. Copyeditor Brittany Smail not only possesses an eagle eye that saved me from countless errors and inconsistencies, but she imposed order on a tangled mess of endnotes—I am so grateful for her help. And my thanks, too, to Liz Wetzel and Jessica Breen, Basic's heads of publicity and marketing; senior publicist Ivan Lett; and marketing experts, Meghan Brophy and Kara Ojebuoboh—all of whom have been on the job, promoting the book even before we finished copyediting. And thanks to production editor Melissa Veronesi, who held my hand as I tip-toed through the minefield of correcting page proofs on, gasp, a screen!

It's a lot to ask of anyone, even your nearest and dearest, to read an unrevised manuscript, but I asked, anyway. My nearest and dearest, Kathryn Dale, read the whole damn thing; even after I dragged her across the Atlantic to live in three different countries, she is not only still speaking to me, but she reads my work. Dan Geary read the whole thing, too, and Jeremy Varon read most of it, and they're not even married to me. I am so grateful to all three for their insightful critiques and varied suggestions, which greatly improved the subsequent and final drafts.

Thank you to Rosanne Cash for offering encouraging words at the start of the book project, right when I needed it. At Université Grenoble Alpes, François Genton tapped ILCEA4 funds to help me make the trip to Nashville, Memphis, and Dyess. And my thanks to Maud Balme and Samuel Debionne who loaned us their mountain cabin in the Parc national des Écrins, where I wrote most of the first half of the book.

I'm blessed to have received steady support and encouragement from my extended family, from all of the Foleys and Dales. I regret that my Dad, who once tried to convince me that we were related to Red Foley (we're not), is not here to read this one. More than a few times, I've heard him, in my head, warbling his off-key version of "There Stands the Glass" while I've worked on the book. I cannot imagine why. In the meantime, I am grateful for the encouragement from my mom, Judy, and her partner, Lloyd, who always checked in on my progress from afar. My mother-in-law, Patricia, deserves special mention for clearing her desk in the basement every summer, so I can get in a few hours of work every day while the kids play, and for shipping research materials that I was unable to collect because of the health crisis.

Thanks to the pandemic, Kathy Dale and our daughters, Hattie and Ophelia, have gotten a sense of what it's like to be jailed with an ornery inmate who, when he's not chained to his laptop, insists on playing country music all the time. It's a wonder that they haven't yet written a song called "COVID Prison Blues." Instead, they've spent their time empathizing with others, raising money for frontline health care workers and the homeless, and making the most of the time we've spent together in close quarters. I wouldn't want to be in lockdown with anyone else (though we have really missed having big sister Emma around, too).

Just as I started working on this book, my brother Kurt died unexpectedly and much too young. I have tried to resist the temptation to relate the loss of my older brother to Johnny Cash's loss of his older brother Jack when they were just kids. For one thing, I realize now what a gift it was that I got to grow well into middle age with Kurt, enjoying many more years together than the Cash brothers got. Still, Kurt's death hit our family with a force that shatters; to say we're still picking up the pieces would be underplaying it.

Kurt loved music and books and films as much as anyone I've ever known. He haunted his Warwick, Rhode Island, library, and he was fond of making pilgrimages to storied sites of American music making. He reported back to me on Nashville and Memphis, Muscle Shoals and Chattanooga, Cleveland and Chicago, as if he led a scouting party (and he knew Los Angeles and San Francisco better than almost anyone). And like a grandma clipping coupons, he would send me envelopes full of tightly folded news clippings on anything he thought might be relevant to me and my work. Kurt would have read this book before anyone else. Mostly, he would have been proud of me in a way that I, as a little brother, would have relished.

Johnny Cash himself once wrote that there's no way around grief and loss: "you can dodge all you want, but sooner or later you just have to go into it, through it, and, hopefully, come out the other side." Cash knew from experience that "the world you find there will never be the same as the world you left." I dedicate this book in memory of Kurt because, in this world, that is where he lives on. But I would give anything to go back to that other world where we were once kids together, where he played guitar and quoted movie lines, and where, much later, the unexpected arrival of his neatly folded news clippings made my day.

Notes

INTRODUCTION

1. Alan Light, *Johnny Cash: The Life and Legacy of the Man in Black* (Washington, DC: Smithsonian Books, 2018), 22.

2. Robert A. Levine, "The Silent Majority: Neither Simple Nor Simple Minded," *Public Opinion Quarterly* 35, no. 4 (1971–1972): 571. It is worth pointing out that Levine was not alone on this front. As early as 1964, the political scientist Philip Converse had shown that, when asked, only a small minority of Americans could even define what it meant to be liberal or conservative. Even after the 1980s, when more Americans began to self-identify as liberal or conservative, they did so despite "a lack of attitudinal change." Alan S. Miller and John P. Hoffmann, "The Growing Divisiveness: Culture War or a War of Words?," *Social Forces* 78, no. 2 (1999): 721–752. More recently, Donald R. Kinder and Nathan P. Kalmoe have argued that the political polarization that seems driven by warring ideologies is disproportionately the work of political elites. The vast majority of Americans participate politically on the basis of group identity, beyond ideology. Donald R. Kinder and Nathan P. Kalmoe, *Neither Liberal Nor Conservative* (Chicago: University of Chicago Press, 2017).

3. I first used this term in 2013, when I published an article about Cash and the politics of the Vietnam War (Michael Stewart Foley, "A Politics of Empathy: Johnny Cash, the Vietnam War, and the 'Walking Contradiction' Myth Dismantled," *Popular Music and Society* 37, no. 3 [June 2013]: 338–359) but in recent years, as scholars and pundits have pondered our present political predicament, empathy has come into vogue as an oft-suggested remedy to polarization. These days, you can get a "Practice Radical Empathy" T-shirt or tote bag on The Bitter Southerner website, and even

Barack Obama talked about it on his book tour (Michiko Kakutani, "Obama, the Best-Selling Author, on Reading, Writing, and Radical Empathy," *New York Times*, December 8, 2020).

4. Johnny Cash, *Cash: The Autobiography* (New York: HarperCollins, 1997), 195.

5. For clarity's sake, I regard the summer replacement season (June through September 1969) as the first season; the January to May 1970 episodes as the second season; and the September 1970 to March 1971 episodes as the third season. Even among official sources, the numbering of seasons and episodes is inconsistent (for example, the summer replacement series is often treated as the first half of Season One, making what I call the third season the second season). Consequently, I have dropped season and episode numbers and list only the air dates in the following notes, which can be used to search for particular episodes at any of the repositories I used.

6. John Frook, "Hard-Times King of Song: Johnny Cash Makes Everyone Like Country Music," *Life*, November 21, 1969.

7. Mikal Gilmore, "Johnny Cash: September When It Comes," in *Stories Done: Writings on the 1960s and Its Discontents* (New York: Free Press, 2008), 197.

8. Jefferson Cowie and Joel Dinerstein, "The Role of the Popular Artist in a Democratic Society," in *Long Walk Home: Reflections on Bruce Springsteen*, ed. Jonathan D. Cohen and June Skinner Sawyers (New Brunswick, NJ: Rutgers University Press, 2019), 53. Cowie and Dinerstein claim that no other artist but Springsteen has "self-consciously claimed both to speak to a tradition of national values and the right to voice a nation's dissent," but as this book shows, Johnny Cash beat Springsteen to it.

9. Maurice Isserman and Michael Kazin, *America Divided: The Civil War of the 1960s* (New York: Oxford University Press, 1999). Isserman and Kazin, in their influential *America Divided*, first described the "civil war of the 1960s."

CHAPTER 1: A NEW DEAL FOR THE CASH FAMILY

1. Richard Goldstein, "Johnny Cash, 'Something Rude Showing'," *Vogue*, August 15, 1969; Christopher S. Wren, *Winners Got Scars Too: The Life of Johnny Cash* (New York: Ballantine Books, 1971), 242.

2. *The Johnny Cash Show*, aired August 2, 1969, on ABC.

3. *The Johnny Cash Show*, aired September 6, 1969, on ABC.

4. Wren, *Winners Got Scars Too*, 54.

5. Jeannie Whayne, *Delta Empire: Lee Wilson and the Transformation of Agriculture in the New South* (Baton Rouge: LSU Press, 2011), 12–15.

6. Van Hawkins, *A New Deal in Dyess: The Depression Era Agricultural Resettlement Colony in Arkansas* (Jonesboro, AR: Writers Bloc, 2020), 1; Whayne, *Delta Empire*, 3–4.

7. Donald Holley, *Uncle Sam's Farmers: The New Deal Communities in the Lower Mississippi Valley* (Urbana: University of Illinois Press, 1975), 7; David M. Kennedy, *Freedom from Fear: The American People in Depression and War, 1929–1945* (New York: Oxford University Press, 1999), 207.

8. Holley, *Uncle Sam's Farmers*, 11–13, 35; Nan Elizabeth Woodruff, *American Congo: The African American Freedom Struggle in the Delta* (Cambridge: Harvard University Press, 2009), 115.

9. Robert S. McElvaine, *The Great Depression: America, 1929–1941* (New York: Times Books, 1993), 59, 76, 147; Hawkins, *A New Deal in Dyess*, 7; Holley, *Uncle Sam's Farmers*, 3–4, 13; Kennedy, *Freedom from Fear*, 201, 208.

10. McElvaine, *The Great Depression*, 148, 150; Kennedy, *Freedom from Fear*, 205, 209; Robert S. McElvaine, *Down and Out in the Great Depression: Letters from the Forgotten Man* (Chapel Hill: The University of North Carolina Press, 2009), 74.

11. Woodruff, *American Congo*, 160; Sue Thrasher and Leah Wise, "The Southern Tenant Farmers' Union" *Southern Exposure* 1, no. 3 & 4 (1974): 16, 24; Holley, *Uncle Sam's Farmers*, 84.

12. Holley, *Uncle Sam's Farmers*, 85; Kennedy, *Freedom from Fear*, 209; Thrasher and Wise, "The Southern Tenant Farmers' Union," 19.

13. Kennedy, *Freedom from Fear*, 209; Whayne, *Delta Empire*, 203–204; Thrasher and Wise, "The Southern Tenant Farmers' Union," 24; *The Great Depression*, season 1, episode 5, "Mean Things Happening," written and directed by Dante James, Blackside Inc., 1993.

14. McElvaine, *The Great Depression*, 116; Hawkins, *A New Deal in Dyess*, 11.

15. Woodruff, *American Congo*, 188; Holley, *Uncle Sam's Farmers*, 33, 87; McElvaine, *The Great Depression*, 301.

16. Holley, *Uncle Sam's Farmers*, 36–37; Hawkins, *A New Deal in Dyess*, 15.

17. Cash, *Cash: The Autobiography*, 13–14, 15; Peter Guralnick, "John R. Cash: I Will Rock 'n Roll with You (If I Have To)," *Country Music*, July/August 1980, 44; *Johnny Cash! The Man, His World, His Music*, directed by Robert Elfstrom (1969: Continental Distributing).

18. Rosanne Cash, *Composed: A Memoir* (New York: Viking Penguin, 2010), 208–209; Wren, *Winners Got Scars Too*, 36–40.

19. Colin Woodward, *Country Boy: The Roots of Johnny Cash* (Fayetteville: University of Arkansas Press, forthcoming), 26; Light, *Johnny Cash*, 52.

20. Hawkins, *A New Deal in Dyess*, 8, 21, 49; Christopher Wren, "The Restless Ballad of Johnny Cash," *LOOK*, April 29, 1969, 71–72.

21. Frye Gaillard, *Watermelon Wine: Remembering the Golden Years of Country Music* (Montgomery: NewSouth Books, 2013), 102; Wren, *Winners Got Scars Too*, 40; Guralnick, "John R. Cash," 46.

22. "4-H Club Addressed by Mrs. Roosevelt," clipping from *Dyess Colony Herald*, June 19, 1936; Hawkins, *A New Deal in Dyess*, 29–30; Robert Hilburn, *Johnny Cash: The Life* (London: Hachette UK, 2013), 8.

23. "Hygienic Notes," *Dyess Colony Herald*, May 29, 1936.

24. Holley, *Uncle Sam's Farmers*, 44; Hawkins, *A New Deal in Dyess*, 26; *Historic Dyess Colony: Boyhood Home of Johnny Cash. Main Text for Administration Building Exhibit Panels* (Dyess, AR: Historic Dyess Colony, n.d.), 7; Cash, *Cash: The Autobiography*, 237–238.

25. Johnny Cash, *Man in Black: His Own Story in His Own Words* (Grand Rapids: Zondervan, 1975), 30.

26. Cash, *Man in Black*, 50; Johnny Cash, *Silver*, Columbia Records JC 36086, 1979, 33 1/3 rpm, liner notes.

27. Vivian Cash and Ann Sharpsteen, *I Walked the Line: My Life with Johnny* (New York: Scribner, 2008), 71; Danny Goldberg, "Johnny Cash Walks the Line . . ." *Circus* (March 1970): 24–26; Cash, *Man in Black*, 23; Daniel Durchholz, "The Last American Hero?," *Request*, June 1994, 75–76; Tara Cash Schwoebel, ed., *Recollections by J.R. Cash: Childhood Memories of Johnny Cash* (Jonesboro, AR: Arkansas State University, 2018), entries for January 13, May 28, May 31, July 22; David Horowitz, "Cash's In the Chips," *Commercial Appeal*, August 3, 1969, 26–28; folder 9, box 145, RG IV, Winthrop Rockefeller papers, Center for Arkansas History and Culture, University of Arkansas at Little Rock.

28. V. Cash and Sharpsteen, *I Walked the Line*, 71; Cash, *Cash: The Autobiography*, 236–237.

29. Cash, *Man in Black*, 34–35; George Carpozi Jr., *The Johnny Cash Story* (New York: Pyramid Books, 1970), 26; Cash, *Cash: The Autobiography*, 291; Hawkins, *A New Deal in Dyess*, 34–36.

30. "Lepanto Road News," *Dyess Colony Herald*, July 10 and July 17, 1936; Robert Echols, "Friendship," *Dyess Colony Herald*, July 3, 1936.

31. Miscellaneous clippings, *Dyess Colony Herald*, August 14, 1936; Clipping on religious life, *Dyess Colony Herald*, undated, 1936; Mrs. Robert Hargett, "Road 10-A," *Dyess Colony Herald*, October 9, 1935; Hawkins, *A New Deal in Dyess*, 25; Cash, *Man in Black*, 24–27.

32. Hawkins, *A New Deal in Dyess*, 31; Holley, *Uncle Sam's Farmers*, 40, 202; Woodward, *Country Boy*, 73–74.

33. Holley, *Uncle Sam's Farmers*, 46, 204.

34. Holley, *Uncle Sam's Farmers*, 207, 212; Hawkins, *A New Deal in Dyess*, ix, 39.

35. Donald Holley, "Trouble in Paradise: Dyess Colony and Arkansas Politics," *Arkansas Historical Quarterly* 32, no. 3 (1973): 209; Holley, *Uncle Sam's Farmers*, 89.

36. Monthly Report of Membership and Fees for Local 29, Dyess, February, March, and April 1940; Floyd Slayton to J. R. Butler, February 14, 1940; J. R. Butler to Floyd Slayton, January 20, 1940; Floyd Slayton to J. R. Butler, February 6, 1940; Floyd Slayton to J. R. Butler, February 14, 1940; Floyd Slayton to J. R. Butler, July 25, 1940; Floyd Slayton, "To the Farm Security Administration," undated, Southern Tenant Farmers Union Records, The Southern Historical Collection, Wilson Library, University of North Carolina at Chapel Hill; Holley, *Uncle Sam's Farmers*, 229.

37. Guralnick, "John R. Cash," 46.

38. "Across the road" can probably be interpreted broadly, meaning not directly across the road, on property that remained wooded for some time after the Cashes arrived in Dyess, but more likely down the road a stretch, on the other side, just off colony property. Adam Long of Arkansas State University Heritage Sites confirmed that a sharecropper shack once stood down and across the road from the Cash house, occupied at one time by a family named Wolf, but it is not clear whose land they worked. In addition, some of the abandoned Dyess farms were used, in time, by the Wilson and Stuckey plantations to house sharecroppers.

39. Michael Streissguth, *Johnny Cash at Folsom Prison: The Making of a Masterpiece* (Cambridge: Da Capo Press, 2004), 41–42; Johnny Cash, "Christmas as I Knew It," and "Ballad of the Harp Weaver," *The Christmas Spirit*, Columbia Records CL 2117, 1963, 33 1/3 rpm. Note that "Christmas as I Knew It" is credited not to Cash but to June Carter and Jan Howard, but it is clear that they were writing about Cash's family, as each of the children are named in the song and the shack "across the road" squares with his other memories of the place. The song was so important to him that it is the only song he put on two Christmas albums. See also *The Johnny Cash Family Christmas*, Columbia Records KC 31754, 1972, 33 1/3 rpm.

40. Johnny Cash, "Man on the Hill," *Songs of Our Soil*, Columbia Records CL 1339, 1961, 33 1/3 rpm; Johnny Cash, "All of God's Children Ain't Free," *Orange Blossom Special*, Columbia Records CL 2309, 1965, 33 1/3 rpm.

41. Wren, "Restless Ballad," 72.

42. *The Johnny Cash Show*, aired July 12, 1969, on ABC; *The Johnny Cash Show*, aired July 19, 1969, on ABC; *The Johnny Cash Show*, aired February 18, 1970, on ABC; *The Johnny Cash Show*, aired March 18, 1970, on ABC; *The Johnny Cash Show*, aired April 8, 1970, on ABC.

43. *The Johnny Cash Show*, aired February 11, 1970, on ABC.

44. *The Johnny Cash Show*, aired February 25, 1970, on ABC.

45. *The Johnny Cash Show*, aired April 15, 1970, on ABC.

CHAPTER 2: PATRIOTIC CHORES

1. *The Johnny Cash Show*, aired August 16, 1969, on ABC.

2. Bruce J. Schulman, *From Cotton Belt to Sunbelt* (Durham: Duke University Press, 1994); Charles S. Bolton, "Turning Point: World War II and the Economic Development of Arkansas," *Arkansas Historical Quarterly* 61, no. 2 (2002): 123, 133; Hawkins, *A New Deal in Dyess*, 52. A World War II monument in Dyess listed approximately 230 names of men who served during the war. The monument is no longer there, but an old photo, shared by Adam Long of the Arkansas State University Heritage Sites shows the names on the monument. Separately, Dr. Ruth Hawkins found that 433 draft cards were issued to Dyess men during WWII; it is not clear how many of those enlisted or were drafted.

3. Rosanne Cash quoted in *Country Music*, episode 3, directed by Ken Burns (PBS, 2019), DVD; Cash, *Cash: The Autobiography*, 50; Light, *Johnny Cash*, 52; Hilburn, *Johnny Cash: The Life*, 11; "Friends of Cash Share Good Times, Bad Times, Life, Love and Music," *Country Music* July/August 1980, 76; "Silent Night," *The Johnny Cash Family Christmas* Columbia Records KC 31754, 1972, 33 1/3 rpm.

4. Wayne W. Daniel "Hayloft Patriotism: The *National Barn Dance* During World War II," in *Country Music Goes to War*, ed. Charles K. Wolfe and James E. Akenson (Lexington: University Press of Kentucky, 2005), 84, 89, 90; William U. Eiland, *Nashville's Mother Church: The History of Ryman Auditorium* (Nashville: Grand Old Opry, 2014), 60; Bill Malone is widely credited for arguing that World War II nationalized country music.

5. Don Cusic, "Country Music and Progressive Politics: Singing Cowboys, FDR and the New Deal," *International Country Music Journal*, 2016, 121; Schwoebel, *Recollections by J.R. Cash*, October 14 entry; Michael Duchemin, *New Deal Cowboy: Gene Autry and Public Diplomacy* (Norman, OK: University of Oklahoma Press, 2016), 6–7.

6. Duchemin, *New Deal Cowboy*, 4, 5, 219–220.

7. Chris Willman, *Rednecks & Bluenecks: The Politics of Country Music* (New York: The New Press, 2007), 148–150; Charles K. Wolfe, "'Bloody War': War Songs in Early Country Music," in Wolfe and Akenson, *Country Music Goes to War*, 29–30.

8. Wolfe, "'Bloody War,'" 32; Maybelle Carter and the Carter Family, "Why Do You Cry, Little Darling?," Bluebird 33 0502, 1943, 78 rpm.

9. Cash, *Cash: The Autobiography*, 283–285.

10. John Howard, *Concentration Camps on the Home Front* (Chicago: University of Chicago Press, 2009), 126, 131.

11. Whayne, *Delta Empire*, 212; Woodruff, *American Congo*, 207.

12. Whayne, *Delta Empire*, 216; Merrill R. Pritchett and William R. Shea, "The Afrika Korps in Arkansas, 1943–1946," *Arkansas Quarterly* 37, no.1 (Spring 1978): 14.

13. Howard, *Concentration Camps*, 233–235.

14. Cash, *Man in Black*, 31–33; Cash, *Cash: The Autobiography*, 28; Dixie Deen, "Everything Ain't Been Said," *Music City News*, January 1966, 1, 3, 9.

15. Deen, "Everything Ain't Been Said," 9.

16. Cash, *Cash: The Autobiography*, 27–28; Cash, *Man in Black*, 50.

17. Cash, *Man in Black*, 48; Steve Turner, *The Man Called Cash: The Life, Love, and Faith of an American Legend* (Nashville: W Publishing, 2004), 155.

18. Schwoebel, *Recollections by J.R. Cash*, entries for February 19, 20, 23, 26, March 1, June 11, July 8; Light, *Johnny Cash*, 42.

19. For Cold War country songs, see *Atomic Platters: Cold War Music from the Golden Age of Homeland Security*, Bear Family Records BCD 16065, 2005, 5 CD box set; Charles K. Wolfe, "Jesus Hits Like an Atom Bomb: Nuclear Warfare in Country Music, 1944–56," in Wolfe and Akenson, *Country Music Goes to War*, 108.

20. Cash, *Man in Black*, 55–58; Peter Cooper, *Johnny's Cash and Charley's Pride: Lasting Legends and Untold Adventures in Country Music* (Whites Creek, TN: Blue Hills Press, 2017), 215–216.

21. Cash, *Cash: The Autobiography*, 59; Light, *Johnny Cash*, 44.

22. Cash, *Cash: The Autobiography*, 59; George Q. Flynn, *The Draft, 1940–1973* (Lawrence: University Press of Kansas, 1993), 112–113, 115.

23. All of the songs described in this section are featured on *Battleground Korea: Songs and Sounds of America's Forgotten War*, Bear Family Records BCD 17518, 2018, 4 CD box set, and *Atomic Platters*.

24. *Life* quote from Michael Sherry, *In the Shadow of War: The United States Since the 1930s* (New Haven: Yale University Press, 1995), 184–185.

25. Flynn, *The Draft*, 114; since the draft could not be mobilized so quickly, Truman called up more than 650,000 reservists and National Guard troops. Most were veterans of the Second World War, serving as "weekend warriors" on the home front. They

howled in protest. Draft calls increased proportionate to the howls. George Q. Flynn, "The Draft and College Deferments During the Korean War," *The Historian* 50, no. 3 (May 1988): 377–378.

26. Turner, *The Man Called Cash*, 33; Hilburn, *Johnny Cash*, 41; Sherry, *In the Shadow of War*, 185; Leonard Rifas, "Korean War Comic Books and the Militarization of US Masculinity," *positions* 23, no. 4 (2015): 619–631.

27. Turner, *The Man Called Cash*, 32–33; V. Cash and Sharpsteen, *I Walked the Line*, 52, 65–66, 176–177.

28. V. Cash and Sharpsteen, *I Walked the Line*, 59, 73, 242.

29. V. Cash and Sharpsteen, *I Walked the Line*. There are too many letters to list on these subjects, but those on pages 78 and 81 are representative.

30. Cash, *Cash: The Autobiography*, 69.

31. Cash, *Cash: The Autobiography*, 71.

32. Lizabeth Cohen, *A Consumers' Republic* (New York: Vintage, 2008), 126.

33. Hilburn, *Johnny Cash*, 69; Wren, *Winners Got Scars Too*, 83.

34. Colin Escott, "Son of Sam," in "Johnny Cash and the Story of Country Rock," special issue, *Mojo Classic* 1, no. 11 (2006): 22.

35. The draft finally caught up to Elvis in 1958, after he was a star.

36. Hilburn, *Johnny Cash*, 277.

37. Colin Escott with Martin Hawkins, *Good Rockin' Tonight: Sun Records and the Birth of Rock 'N' Roll* (New York: St. Martin's Press, 1991), 98; Peter Guralnick, *Sam Phillips: The Man Who Invented Rock 'N' Roll* (London: Hachette UK, 2015), 500–511; John Pugh, "The Rise and Fall of Sun Records," *Country Music*, November 1973, 26; Guralnick, "John R. Cash," 44; Hilburn, *Johnny Cash*, 66–67.

38. Durchholz, "The Last American Hero?," 24–30, 75–82.

39. Grace Elizabeth Hale, *A Nation of Outsiders* (Oxford: Oxford University Press, 2014).

40. Lester Bangs, *Psychotic Reactions and Carburetor Dung* (New York: Anchor, 2003), 327; Streissguth, *Johnny Cash at Folsom Prison*, 26–27.

41. Wren, *Winners Got Scars Too*, 97; Cash, *Cash: The Autobiography*, 144; Paul Ackerman, "A Man of Basic Truth, Says Carl Perkins," *Billboard*, May 23, 1970, C-3; James D. Kingsley, "Mr. Phillips Met the Appliance Salesman at 706 Union Ave," *Billboard*, May 23, 1970, C-16.

42. Marshall Grant and Chris Zar, *I Was There When It Happened: My Life with Johnny Cash* (Nashville: Cumberland House Publishing, 2006), 47; Cash, *Cash: The Autobiography*, 68; June Carter comments from *The Barbara Walters Special*, ABC-TV, 1983, UCLA Film and Television Archive; Wren, *Winners Got Scars Too*, 101; Light, *Johnny Cash*, 72; Escott, *Good Rockin' Tonight*, 104.

43. Wren, *Winners Got Scars Too*, 115–116.

44. Conrad J. Ward, "The Day I Met Johnny Cash," reprinted from *Gastonia Gazette*, October 31, 1971, 28, in *Man In Black: The Official Johnny Cash Society newsletter*, March 1972, folder 9, Southern Folklife Collection Fan Club Newsletters, 1952–1998, Southern Folklife Collection, Louis Round Wilson Special Collections Library, University of North Carolina at Chapel Hill.

45. Bill Geerhart and Ken Sitz, liner notes for *Atomic Platters: Cold War Music from the Golden Age of Homeland Security*, Bear Family Records BCD 16065 FM, 2005, 5CD+DVD box set.

46. John Loughery and Blythe Randolph, *Dorothy Day* (New York: Simon and Schuster, 2020): 263–265.

47. Grant and Zar, *I Was There When It Happened*, 86; Peter Lewry, *I've Been Everywhere: A Johnny Cash Chronicle* (London: Helter Skelter, 2001), 36; Naomi Allen, "World's Most Unusual Traveling Salesman," *The Legend* 2, 19–20, box 8, Southern Folklife Collection, Louis Round Wilson Special Collections Library, University of North Carolina at Chapel Hill; Johnny Cash, *Treasury Department US Savings Bond Division Presents: Guest Star*, aired May 24, 1961, on syndicated radio.

48. *The Johnny Cash Show*, aired December 16, 1970, on ABC.

49. *The Johnny Cash Show*, aired November 11, 1970, on ABC.

50. Richard M. Fried, *Nightmare in Red: The McCarthy Era in Perspective* (Oxford: Oxford University Press, 1991), 99.

CHAPTER 3: CASH AND BLACK LIVES

1. Today, that sign is gone, removed in 2018 in light of controversies over Confederate monuments throughout the South; but in Nashville in 1969, few in the country music community questioned the political import of a monument to defenders of slavery. To *Grand Ole Opry* performers and fans, the sign simply marked the construction of the balcony in 1897 for a reunion of Confederate veterans held at the Ryman.

2. Vera Hall recorded "Black Woman" with Lomax, appearing on *Jazz Volume 2: The Blues*, Folkways Records, FP 55, 1950; Rich Amerson recorded it for Harold Courlander, appearing on *Negro Music of Alabama Volume 1—Secular*, Ethnic Folkways Library P 417, 1951; *Music Down Home: An Introduction to Negro Folk Music, U.S.A.*, Folkways Records FA 2691, 1965, includes the Amerson version, but is worth examining for the extensive liner notes and lyrics to "Black Woman."

3. *The Johnny Cash Show*, aired August 30, 1969, on ABC.

4. Blaik Kirby, "The Country King Has a Cause," *Toronto Globe and Mail*, October 18, 1969, folder 17, box 1, Holiff Family Fonds, University of Victoria Special Collections and University Archives; Bob Lardine, "Johnny Cash," reprinted from *New York Sunday News* in *Strictly Cash: The Official Johnny Cash Society newsletter*, no. 32, November 1969–March 1970, 12, folder 9, Southern Folklife Collection Fan Club Newsletters.

5. Tom Dearmore, "First Angry Man of Country Singers," *New York Times*, September 21, 1969, 58; John Garabedian, "Singer Johnny Cash Fights the Voice of Hate," *New York Post*, October 6, 1966, folder 17, box 1, Holiff Family Fonds; Wren, *Winners Got Scars Too*, 184–185; Streissguth, *Johnny Cash at Folsom Prison*, 129–130; Colin Escott, "Ring of Fire," in "Johnny Cash and the Story of Country Rock," special issue, *Mojo Classic* 1, no. 11 (2006): 30; Bill Flanagan, "Johnny Cash, American," *Musician*, May 1988, 111.

6. Although other, all-Black colonies were established by the Resettlement Administration, including a few in Arkansas, the agency bowed to local norms in Mississippi County, even if administrators found them objectionable. "In none of our projects are we sanctioning any discrimination in regard to nationality, race, or creed," one RA memo read. "However, in localities where there exists deep-rooted prejudices they cannot be ignored." The RA pledged to follow "enlightened social practices" in its colonization projects, but conceded that "it is not our function to attempt to reform in a day age-old attitudes of the people" in those areas. There is no evidence that the recent spate of violence between planters and the STFU directly influenced this policy, but someone with enough knowledge of the area may have let it be known that an interracial colony of five hundred families would have been viewed as an affront to the racists of Poinsett and Mississippi Counties and almost certainly would have brought violence to Dyess. Hawkins, *A New Deal in Dyess*, 18.

7. Hilburn, *Johnny Cash*, 48.

8. I am grateful to Colin Woodward for sharing these findings and others from the manuscript of his forthcoming book on Cash and Arkansas. Colin Woodward, *Country Boy*, chapter 1.

9. Streissguth, *Johnny Cash: The Biography*, 4; Turner, *The Man Called Cash*, 15.

10. Woodruff, *American Congo*, 103.

11. Nancy Snell Griffith, "'At the Hands of a Person or Persons Unknown': The Nature of the Lynch Mob in Arkansas," in *Bullets and Fire: Lynching and Authority in Arkansas, 1840–1950*, ed. Guy Lancaster (Fayetteville: University of Arkansas Press, 2017), 54–55; Brent Staples, "When Southern Newspapers Justified Lynching," *New York Times*, May 5, 2018; Todd E. Lewis, "'Through Death, Hell and the Grave': Lynching and Antilynching Efforts in Arkansas, 1901–1939," in *Bullets and Fire: Lynching and Authority in Arkansas, 1840–1950*, ed. Guy Lancaster (Fayetteville: University of Arkansas Press, 2017), 151–153; Cherisse Jones-Branch, "'Working Slowly but Surely and Quietly': The Arkansas Council of the Association of Southern Women for the Prevention of Lynching," in *Bullets and Fire: Lynching and Authority in Arkansas, 1840–1950*, ed. Guy Lancaster (Fayetteville: University of Arkansas Press, 2017), 231.

12. Cash talks about levee camps from the stage when he introduces "I Still Miss Someone" on the *Strawberry Cake* album, for example; Matthew J. Mancini, *One Dies, Get Another: Convict Leasing in the American South, 1866–1928* (Columbia: University of South Carolina Press, 1996), 120; James T. Wooten, "Prison Road Gangs Fading Fast in the South," *New York Times*, October 23, 1971; Robert T. Chase, "We Are Not Slaves: Rethinking the Rise of Carceral States Through the Lens of the Prisoners' Rights Movement," *Journal of American History* 102, no. 1 (June 2015): 77; Douglas A. Blackmon, *Slavery By Another Name: The Re-enslavement of Black Americans From the Civil War to World War Two* (London: Icon Books, 2012), 467, 468, 471–472.

13. John A. Lomax and Alan Lomax, *Our Singing Country: A Second Volume of American Ballads and Folk Songs* (New York: Macmillan, 1949), 379; Goldberg, "Johnny Cash Walks the Line . . . ," 24–26.

14. Cash, *Cash: The Autobiography*, 60.

15. V. Cash and Sharpsteen, *I Walked the Line*, 131–135, 138.

16. David Welky, "'There Will Be No Discrimination': Race, Power, and the Memphis Flood of 1937," in *An Unseen Light: Black Struggles for Freedom in Memphis, Tennessee*, ed. Aram Goudsouzian and Charles W. McKinney Jr. (Lexington: University Press of Kentucky, 2018), 91; Laurie B. Greene, *Battling the Plantation Mentality: Memphis and the Black Freedom Struggle* (Chapel Hill: University of North Carolina Press, 2007), 242; Jason Jordan, "'We'll Have No Race Trouble Here': Racial Politics and Memphis's Reign of Terror," in Goudsouzian and McKinney Jr., *An Unseen Light*, 130–131.

17. Elizabeth Gritter, "Black Memphians and New Frontiers: The Shelby County Democratic Club, the Kennedy Administration, and the Quest for Black Political Power, 1959–1964," in Goudsouzian and McKinney Jr., *An Unseen Light*, 178–179.

18. Hilburn, *Johnny Cash*, 69–70; Wren, *Winners Got Scars Too*, 84; Guralnick, *Sam Phillips*, 502.

19. Clive Anderson, "Johnny Cash: The Sun Years," liner notes for *Johnny Cash, The Original Sun Albums, 1957–1964*, Charly Records B-916, 2017, CD box set; Johnny Cash, Rock and Roll Hall of Fame induction speech, January 15, 1992, Rock and Roll Hall of Fame, www.rockhall.com/inductees/johnny-cash; Light, *Johnny Cash*, 51; Flanagan, "Johnny Cash, American," 101; Cash, *Cash: The Autobiography*, 70.

20. Walt Whitman, "Song of Myself," *Leaves of Grass*, WhitmanWeb, University of Iowa International Writing Program, https://iwp.uiowa.edu/whitmanweb/en/writings/song-of-myself/section-33.

21. The record came out in 1959, which means that Cash almost certainly did not buy it, as he later remembered, at Home of the Blues in Memphis. By 1959, Cash had not only switched labels but he had moved his family to California.

22. Hilburn, *Johnny Cash*, 154.

23. Alan Lomax, *The Land Where the Blues Began* (London: Minerva, 1994), 473.

24. Cash, *Cash: The Autobiography*, 197.

25. Hilburn, *Johnny Cash*, 249, 28; Matthew Frye Jacobson, *Odetta's One Grain of Sand (33 1/3)* (New York: Bloomsbury Academic, 2019), 23.

26. Colin Escott, liner notes for *Johnny Cash, the Man in Black—1959–1962*, Bear Family Records BCD 15562 EH, 1992, CD box set; Blake Emmons, "Canadian Country," *Country Song Roundup*, undated, 35–36, folder 9, box 17, Holiff Family Fonds.

27. No one knows the exact origins of "Swing Low, Sweet Chariot," but Toni Anderson points to a couple of theories, one of which involves a slave named Wallace Willis who was sometimes called "Uncle Wallace." Cash no doubt came up with "Uncle Moses" from this theory of the spiritual's origins. For more information, see Toni P. Anderson, "'Swing Low, Sweet Chariot'—The Fisk University Jubilee Quartet (1909)," Library of Congress, www.loc.gov/programs/static/national-recording-preservation-board/documents/Swing%20Low%20article.pdf.

28. Benjamin Houston, *The Nashville Way: Racial Etiquette and the Struggle for Social Justice in a Southern City* (Athens: University of Georgia Press, 2012), 4–5.

29. Peter La Chapelle, *I'd Fight the World: A Political History of Old-Time, Hillbilly, and Country Music* (Chicago: University of Chicago Press, 2019), 117.

30. Hilburn, *Johnny Cash*, 229–230, 249; Cash, *Cash: The Autobiography*, 197.

31. John A. Lomax quoted in Benjamin Filene, *Romancing the Folk: Public Memory and American Roots Music* (Chapel Hill: UNC Press Books, 2000), 609.

32. Although workers of various types sang about John Henry for decades after he competed with a steel drill in the 1870s, the song only gained public prominence thanks to Carl Sandburg, the poet and raconteur, who picked it up in his travels. Fiddlin' John Carson recorded the song first, in 1923, having grown up as a white kid listening to Black work songs. After that, many artists recorded the song, including Leadbelly and Merle Travis, who included it on *Folk Songs from the Hills*.

33. Scott Reynolds Nelson, *Steel Drivin' Man: John Henry, the Untold Story of an American Legend* (Oxford: Oxford University Press, 2008), 137–141; Lomax and Lomax, *Our Singing Country*, 258–260; *Ridin' the Rails*, directed by Nicholas Webster (1974; Jerry Dexter Distribution, Rhino Home Video, 2005), DVD. For other versions of "John Henry" that Cash surely heard, listen to: Pink Anderson, Dave Van Ronk, Ramblin' Jack Elliott, Pete Seeger, Harry Belafonte, Sonny Terry and Brownie McGee, the Limeliters, etc.

34. Marci McDonald, "To You It's Country—to Him It's 'Johnny Cash Music,'" *Toronto Star* June 7, 1969, 51, folder 9, box 145, RG IV, Winthrop Rockefeller papers.

35. Lomax and Lomax, *Our Singing Country*, 380–381. See Jacobson, *Odetta's One Grain of Sand*, 20–21 on Odetta's version. Note that Leon Bibb's 1958 version combines cold, iron shackles with "hurts my pride," not cornbread and molasses. Meanwhile, Big Bill Broonzy's 1956 live version of "Take This Old Hammer" says Leadbelly wrote the song, but that they used to sing it up and down the river in the levee camps. "Take This Old Hammer" does not have the cold, iron shackles line. Neither does the Sonny Terry and Brownie McGhee version.

36. Cash had surely heard other versions of "Another Man Done Gone." Lorrie Collins, for example, recorded an almost rockabilly version in 1959, featuring pretty funky guitar, but she recast it so that it is mostly about a man leaving her ("I was his tagalong") for a business deal—not about a lynching or chain gang—which makes it into a somewhat Sun-sounding torch ballad. This adulteration of the original may have irked Cash, and made him want to honor the original. Pete Seeger also recorded a live version with Memphis Slim (of the *Blues in the Mississippi Night* LP) on *At the Village Gate, Vol. 2* in 1962, the same year as *Blood, Sweat and Tears*. He uses "he killed another man" about the man done gone—same as Vera Hall.

37. Norm Cohen, "'Casey Jones': At the Crossroads of Two Ballad Traditions," *Western Folklore* 32, no. 2 (April 1973): 77–103.

38. Cash recorded Leadbelly's "Pick a Bale of Cotton" the day after he recorded "John Henry" and released it as a single, but did not put it on *Blood, Sweat and Tears*. It certainly would have been a better fit than "Roughneck," but perhaps he or Don Law thought that "Busted" already covered the cotton farm experience.

39. Jacobson, *Odetta's One Grain of Sand*, 35–36; Flanagan, "Johnny Cash, American," 101; Sean Wilentz, *Bob Dylan in America* (New York: Anchor Books, 2011), 194.

40. *The Johnny Cash Show*, aired August 30, 1969, on ABC.

41. *The Johnny Cash Show*, aired April 22, 1970, on ABC.

42. *The Johnny Cash Show*, aired October 28, 1970, on ABC; *The Johnny Cash Show*, aired November 11, 1970, on ABC; Jeannie Sakol, "The Grit and Grace of Johnny Cash," *McCall's*, July 1970, 28, 110.

CHAPTER 4: COWBOYS AND INDIANS

1. "Down By the River," in "Johnny Cash and the Story of Country Rock," special issue, *Mojo Classic* 1, no. 11 (2006): 17–18.

2. "Down By the River," 17–19; Schwoebel, *Recollections by J.R. Cash*, August 5; Roy Cash, "Wild Western Outlaw," *Dyess Colony Herald*, May 29, 1936.

3. Duchemin, *New Deal Cowboy*, 6–7, 15.

4. To learn more about the original inhabitants of Northeast Arkansas, visit the Virtual Hampson Museum, http://hampson.cast.uark.edu/about.htm; Mary Landreth, "Becoming the Indians: Fashioning Arkansas State University's Indians," in *Team Spirits: The Native American Mascots Controversy*, ed. C. Richard King and Charles Fruehling Springwood (Lincoln: University of Nebraska Press, 2001), 46–49.

5. Wren, *Winners Got Scars Too*, 161; Bill Williams, "J. R. Cash—A Family View," *Billboard* May 23, 1970, C-10; Guralnick, "John R. Cash," 44.

6. Deloria, *Playing Indian*, 3, 184, 199n19.

7. Deloria, *Playing Indian*, 6–7.

8. Hilburn, *Johnny Cash*, 166.

9. Antonino D'Ambrosio, *A Heartbeat and a Guitar: Johnny Cash and the Making of Bitter Tears* (New York: Nation Books, 2011), 196; Streissguth, *Johnny Cash at Folsom Prison*, 31. Streissguth is one among many who see Cash as angling to expand his audience to include the folk crowd.

10. Rosanne Cash, in *We're Still Here: Johnny Cash's Bitter Tears Revisited*, directed by Antonino D'Ambrosio (2015, Kino Lorber), DVD; Grant and Zar, *I Was There When It Happened*, 102; Turner, *The Man Called Cash*, 107.

11. D'Ambrosio, *A Heartbeat and a Guitar*, 96, 120; Joy A. Bilharz, *The Allegany Senecas and Kinzua Dam: Forced Relocation Through Two Generations* (Lincoln: University of Nebraska Press, 2002), 54–55.

12. D'Ambrosio, *A Heartbeat and a Guitar*, 120.

13. Charles Wolfe, liner notes for *Bitter Tears* (revised), Johnny Cash, Bear Family Records BFX 15127, 1984, 33 1/3 rpm; Cash, *Cash: The Autobiography*, 197.

14. "Johnny Cash," ad, *Billboard*, August 1964, folder 3, box 1, Holiff Family Fonds.

15. "An Open Letter—To Johnny Cash," ad, folder 3, box 1, Holiff Family Fonds.

16. Carpozi, *The Johnny Cash Story*, 125; *Johnny Cash! The Man, His World, His Music*, directed by Robert Elfstrom (1969: Continental Distributing).

17. *The Johnny Cash Show*, aired July 19, 1969, on ABC; Peter Goddard, "Cash's Music as True and Simple as Always," *Toronto Star*, November 11, 1969, folder 14, box 1, Holiff Family Fonds.

18. Paul Chaat Smith, *Like a Hurricane: The Indian Movement from Alcatraz to Wounded Knee* (New York: The New Press, 1997), 25–30.

19. *The Johnny Cash Show*, aired February 4, 1970, on ABC.

20. *The Johnny Cash Show*, aired May 6, 1970, on ABC.

21. Richard M. Nixon, "Message to Congress," July 8, 1970, in *Public Papers of the Presidents of the United States: Richard M. Nixon, 1970*, 564–576 (Washington, DC: Government Printing Office, 1971).

22. *NET Playhouse*, season 4, episode 20, "The Trail of Tears," written and directed by Lane Slate, aired April 30, 1970, on NET, Paley Center for Media, Los Angeles.

CHAPTER 5: GOING TO PRISON

1. Cash, *Cash: The Autobiography*, 201.

2. *The Johnny Cash Show*, aired July 7, 1969, on ABC.

3. *The Johnny Cash Show*, aired August 23, 1969, on ABC.

4. Streissguth, *Johnny Cash at Folsom Prison*, 20–21.

5. Light, *Johnny Cash*, 62; Hilburn, *Johnny Cash*, 170–171; Cash, Man in Black, 153.

6. Merle Haggard and Peggy J. Russell, *Sing Me Back Home* (New York: Pocket Books, 1983), 172; Sylvie Simmons, "Jailhouse Rocker," in "Johnny Cash and the Story of Country Rock," special issue, *Mojo Classic* 1, no. 11 (2006): 36; *Johnny Cash's America*, directed by Morgan Neville and Robert Gordon (Sony BMG Entertainment, 2008), DVD; Streissguth, *Johnny Cash at Folsom Prison*, 41; "Remembering Johnny," *Rolling Stone*, October 16, 2003, 74.

7. "Transfusion Blues" and "Why Do You Punish Me (For Loving You)" on *Now, There Was a Song!* (1960); "Going to Memphis" on *Ride This Train* (1960); "In the Jailhouse Now" and "I'm Free from the Chain Gang Now" on *The Sound of Johnny Cash* (1962); several chain gang songs on *Blood, Sweat and Tears* (1963); rerecordings of "Folsom Prison Blues" and "Give My Love to Rose" on *I Walk the Line* (1964); "The Wall" on *Orange Blossom Special* (1965); several outlaw songs and Shel Silverstein's "25 Minutes to Go" on *Johnny Cash Sings the Ballads of the True West* (1965); "Austin Prison" and "Joe Bean" on *Everybody Loves a Nut* (1966); and "The Walls of a Prison" on *From Sea to Shining Sea* (1967).

8. Haggard had recorded "The Fugitive," "Branded Man," "Mama Tried," "Sing Me Back Home," and "Huntsville."

9. June Vosburg to Johnny Cash Society members, November 23, 1966, scab, 43, folder 8, Southern Folklife Collection Fan Club Newsletters; Mable Somland to Cash, Reba, and Johnny Cash Society members, October 18, 1967, Southern Folklife Collection Fan Club Newsletters; Ralph J. Gleason, "A Roving Poet with a Guitar," *San Francisco Chronicle*, November 6, 1966; Wren, *Winners Got Scars Too*, 198–201.

10. "Johnny Cash Show Smash Hit," *The Folsom Observer*, December 1, 1966, 1, reprinted in *The Legend*, 32, folder 8, Southern Folklife Collection Fan Club Newsletters.

11. Daniel Geary says Cash wanted listeners to "place themselves alongside the prisoners as an audience." Daniel Geary, "'The Way I Would Feel about San Quentin': Johnny Cash and the Politics of Country Music," *Daedalus*, October 2013, 68.

12. Geary, "'The Way I Would Feel about San Quentin,'" 68.

13. Wren, *Winners Got Scars Too*, 220.

14. To be fair, Law *did* make plans to record Cash at a state penitentiary in Kansas in 1965, but Cash's drug-fueled hijinks in California—including accidentally setting the Los Padres National Forest ablaze—and elsewhere made it impossible. He was too unreliable at the time.

15. Hilburn, *Johnny Cash*, 324–325.

16. Wren, *Winners Got Scars Too*, 222.

17. In fact, in January 1968, neither the inmates nor Cash could have known that no prisoner would be executed that year, nor in any of the subsequent eight years (while the state awaited resolution of constitutional challenges). At the time of the concert recording, the inmates undoubtedly expected executions to continue.

18. See Hale, *A Nation of Outsiders*.

19. Light, *Johnny Cash*, 117; Rev. Floyd Gressett to Reba Hancock, undated, ca. 1968, reprinted in *The Legend* 3, Johnny Cash Society, Box 8, Southern Folklife Collection Fan Club Newsletters; "Empathy in the Dungeon," *Time*, August 30, 1968, 48.

20. Hilburn, *Johnny Cash*, 333–334; Wren, *Winners Got Scars Too*, 222.

21. Cathy Kunzinger Urwin, *Agenda for Reform: Winthrop Rockefeller as Governor of Arkansas, 1967–71* (Fayetteville: University of Arkansas Press, 1991), 93–94.

22. Urwin, *Agenda for Reform*, 94.

23. A 1972 investigation again found that the three bodies Murton dug up did not die as a result of violence, but Murton continued to press his case. His memoir of the period, *Accomplices to the Crime: The Arkansas Prison Scandal*, served as the basis for the 1980 Robert Redford film, *Brubaker*, in which Redford plays the Murton character at a fictional Ohio prison. Urwin, *Agenda for Reform*, 96, 98, 99–100; Thomas O. Murton and Joe Hyams, *Accomplices to the Crime: The Arkansas Prison Scandal* (London: Michael Joseph, 1970), 136, 192–193, 215.

24. Urwin, *Agenda for Reform*, 101, 103, 104.

25. V. Cash and Sharpsteen, *I Walked the Line*, 212; Wren, *Winners Got Scars Too*, 224; Urwin, *Agenda for Reform*, 105–107.

26. One important difference is the absence of Tennessee Three guitarist Luther Perkins, who died in a house fire in early August, after falling asleep smoking. The recording of the Fayetteville Rockefeller campaign rally of September 17, 1968, still exists—this is the show Marshall Grant and Carl Perkins could not get to because of bad weather (their flight was grounded), and at which Bob Wootton, a nobody from Tulsa, showed up and offered to play Luther Perkins's guitar parts. To hear Cash calling out keys to Wootton and another Bob, plucked from the crowd to play bass, as they perform—with Wootton matching Luther's picking almost precisely—is thrilling. Wootton's guitar sounds fuzzier, distorted in a way that Perkins's guitar never did, but it is easy to see why Cash invited him along to play the Harrison rally two days later, as a kind of audition with the rest of the band.

27. The campaign paid Cash $4,000 per rally. Fayetteville and Harrison, Arkansas, expense vouchers, Winthrop Rockefeller campaign papers, Series II, courtesy Colin Woodward; Winthrop, Arkansas (misidentified as Murfreesboro) campaign rally, Tapes 742–746; Fayetteville and Harrison Rockefeller campaign rallies, Tapes 758–766, Winthrop Rockefeller collection, Center for Arkansas History and Culture, University of Arkansas – Little Rock; Urwin, *Agenda for Reform*, 103; "Rockefeller Calls for Investigation of Arkansas Prison Shootings," *Caroll Daily Times Herald*, October 15, 1968, 8.

28. Geary, "'The Way I would Feel about San Quentin,'" 66–67.

29. As evidence of how carefully crafted the album is, some of the attempts that Cash and his group made at relating to prisoners were left off the album, particularly those dealing with sex. On the complete recording, for example, we hear June Carter joke to the men to take their hands out of each other's pockets, and at another point, Cash starts shouting to a television cameraman that this is no place to be bending over—two jokes about homosexuality deemed, perhaps, too off-color for the listening audience. June also jokes that she and the Carter Family women are not one of those other kinds of girlie shows that sometimes came to prisons. "This is as sexy as we're gonna get," she proclaims.

30. Paul Hemphill, *The Nashville Sound: Bright Lights and Country Music* (New York: Simon and Schuster, 1970), 100; David Horowitz, "Cash's In the Chips."

31. Johnny Cash, interview with CBS News, date unknown, possibly before Madison Square Garden show in December 1969, YouTube video, www.youtube.com/watch?v=vKHkleiw7AQ.

32. Sarry Gordon, "Prisoners Go Wild as Cash Sings About 'When I Get Out of Cummins,'" *Arkansas Gazette*, April 11, 1969, clipping, folder 8, box 251, RG IV, Winthrop Rockefeller papers; Bill Lancaster, "Down on the Farm, Cash Sings for TV," *Pine Bluff Commercial*, April 11, 1969, clipping, folder 8, box 251, RG IV, Winthrop Rockefeller papers.

33. Lancaster, "Down on the Farm"; Tim Hackler, "Johnny Cash Sings at Cummins," *Arkansas Democrat*, April 11 1969, 3A, folder 8, box 251, RG IV, Winthrop Rockefeller papers; "Hello, Cummins Prison Farm, I'm Johnny Cash," *Arkansas Gazette*, April 13, 1969, 12A, folder 8, box 251, RG IV, Winthrop Rockefeller papers.

34. Gordon, "Prisoners Go Wild"; Lancaster, "Down On the Farm."

35. Gordon, "Prisoners Go Wild"; Lancaster, "Down On the Farm"; Sakol, "The Grit and Grace of Johnny Cash."

36. "King of Cummins," *The Pea Pickers Picayune*, April 18, 1969, 1, folder 7, box 257, RG IV, Winthrop Rockefeller papers; Sakol, "The Grit and Grace of Johnny Cash"; Woodward, "There's a lot of Things That Need Changin': Johnny Cash, Winthrop Rockefeller, and Prison Reform in Arkansas," *Arkansas Historical Quarterly*, 79, no. 1 (Spring 2020): 54.

37. Haggard and Cash wrote up a lighthearted segment for their conversation about the former's time at San Quentin for the episode that aired on August 2, 1969. When Haggard says he really enjoyed that show, Cash says he doesn't remember Haggard being on that show, and Haggard says, "I was in the audience." But the episode ran long, and the Screen Gems producers, not realizing the significance of what had

happened, picked up some extra time by cutting what they thought was too much chitchat between the stars. My thanks to Mark Stielper for clarifying this by email. Mark Stielper, email to author, October 5, 2020.

38. *The Johnny Cash Show*, aired January 28, 1970, on ABC.

39. Prison Reform show, October 20, 1970, reel-to-reel tape 1324, RG VII, Winthrop Rockefeller papers.

40. Dan Berger, *Captive Nation: Black Prison Organizing in the Civil Rights Era* (Chapel Hill: UNC Press Books, 2014), 238, 296, 317–318.

41. Berger, *Captive Nation*, 28.

42. Jonathan Silverman, "The Politics of Covers: Johnny Cash, Rick Rubin, and the *American Recordings*," in *The Honky Tonk on the Left: Progressive Thought in Country Music*, ed. Mark Allan Jackson (Amherst: University of Massachusetts Press, 2018), 96.

43. Berger, *Captive Nation*, 359–362; Heather Ann Thompson, *Blood in the Water: The Attica Uprising of 1971 and Its Legacy* (New York: Vintage, 2016), part II.

44. Johnny Cash, comments on Attica, KATV Little Rock, October 1971, MCR-1152, Pryor Center for Arkansas Oral and Visual History, https://pryorcenter.uark.edu /videoplayer.php?c=2&dir=projects/KATV/MCR-1152&video=MCR-1152_x264 &title=KATV%20MCR-1152&playhead=685#player.

45. US Congress, Senate, Subcommittee on National Penitentiaries, *Hearings on S. 2383, S. 2462, S. 2955, S. 3185, S. 3674 to Amend Parole Legislation*, ninety-second Congress, second session, July 25–27, 1972, https://archive.org/stream/parolelegisla-tio1972unit/parolelegislatio1972unit_djvu.txt.

46. Michelle Alexander, *The New Jim Crow: Mass Incarceration in the Age of Colorblindness* (New York: The New Press, 2020).

47. Albert Nussbaum, "When Johnny Cash Visited Leavenworth," *Sunday Gazette Mail*, October 7, 1973, reprinted in *Ring of Fire: The Johnny Cash Reader*, ed. Michael Streissguth (Boston: Da Capo Press, 2002), 80; Bob Battle, "Johnny Cash With a Helping Hand!," *Strictly Cash: The Official Johnny Cash Society newsletter*, no. 48, ca. fall-winter 1975–1976, folder 9, Southern Folklife Collection Fan Club Newsletters.

CHAPTER 6: A DOVE WITH CLAWS

1. *The Johnny Cash Show*, aired January 28, 1970, on ABC.

2. Carpozi, *The Johnny Cash Story*, 127.

3. *The Johnny Cash Show*, aired January 28, 1970, on ABC.

4. On how the Vietnam-era draft made Vietnam a "working-class war," see Christian G. Appy, *Working-Class War: American Combat Soldiers and Vietnam* (Chapel Hill: University of North Carolina Press, 1993); Lawrence M. Baskir and William A. Strauss, *Chance and Circumstance: The Draft, the War, and the Vietnam Generation* (New York: Random House, 1978); James W. Davis and Kenneth M. Dolbeare, *Little Groups of Neighbors: The Selective Service System* (Chicago: Markham, 1968). For a longer view of the Selective Service, see Flynn, *The Draft*.

5. John Buckley long ago identified "Home and Family" as one of eight basic themes of country music. John Buckley, "Country Music and American Values," in

All That Glitters: Country Music in America, ed. George H. Lewis (Bowling Green: Bowling Green State University Press, 1993), 200. Penny Lewis, *Hardhats, Hippies, and Hawks* (Ithaca, NY: Cornell University Press, 2013), 51–53, does the best job of summarizing working-class attitudes about the Vietnam War. On "feeling and relating," see Aaron Fox, *Real Country: Music and Language in Working-Class Culture* (Raleigh: Duke University Press, 2004).

6. Johnny Cash to Saul Holiff, July 14, 1965, folder 9, box 1, Holiff Family Fonds.

7. Cash, *Cash: The Autobiography*, 216–217; Cash, *Man in Black*, 172. Jan Howard later appeared as a guest, with Bill Anderson, on *The Johnny Cash Show*, aired January 13, 1971, on ABC.

8. Report by Jackie Whittenberg, undated newsletter, ca. 1968, folder 8, Southern Folklife Collection Fan Club Newsletters.

9. "Roll Call" did appear on the 1969 compilation album *More of "Old Golden Throat."*

10. Of course, he was also well paid, grossing $2,500 a day over thirteen days of shows in Okinawa, Taiwan, Manila, Vietnam, and Tokyo, and $1,250 for each show in excess of two per day, for a total of $33,750. The accounting is hard to follow, but it looks like, after expenses, he was due close to $23,000 and then had to pay Saul Holiff, his manager, $4,575. Cash still net more than $18,000, which, in today's money is nearly $126,000. Saul Holiff, January 1969 income and expenses, folder 5, box 3, Holiff Family Fonds.

11. Cash, *Man in Black*, 176–177

12. "Johnny Cash Wows the Troops: 'Folsom Prison' Brings Down House," *Overseas Weekly*, March 1, 1969, 7, folder 504, Ann Bryan Mariano McKay Papers, State Historical Society of Missouri.

13. Larry Linderman, "*Penthouse* Interview: Johnny Cash," reprinted in Streissguth, *Ring of Fire*, 154; "The New Johnny Cash," *Amusement Business*, June 7, 1969, 1, 8–9, folder 17, box 1, Holiff Family Fonds; June Carter Cash, *From the Heart* (New York: St. Martin's Press, 1987), 30.

14. Cash, *Cash*, 218; Johnny Cash, liner notes for *The Legend*, Columbia Records CXK93000, 5CD+DVD box set, 85; Hemphill, *The Nashville Sound*, 101; Gilmore, "Johnny Cash," 182–183.

15. Hemphill, *The Nashville Sound*, 101; Dearmore, "First Angry Man of Country Singers," 42; Wren, *Winners Got Scars Too*, 77.

16. On the *Smothers Brothers Comedy Hour*, see David Bianculli, *Dangerously Funny: The Uncensored Story of "The Smothers Brothers Comedy Hour"* (New York: Touchstone, 2009) and Aniko Bodroghkozy, *Groove Tube: Sixties Television and the Youth Rebellion* (Durham: Duke University Press, 2001); on *Glen Campbell Goodtime Hour*, I'm relying on various episodes viewed at the UCLA Film and Television Archive.

17. For data on draft resistance, see Michael S. Foley, *Confronting the War Machine: Draft Resistance During the Vietnam War* (Chapel Hill: University of North Carolina Press, 2003); also see *The Boys Who Said No!*, directed by Judith Ehrlich (InSight Productions, 2020), www.boyswhosaidno.com.

18. Cash, *Man in Black*, 172; Bill Miller, *Cash: An American Man* (New York: Simon & Schuster, 2005), 54–55.

19. See, for example, the magisterial Bear Family Records box set, . . . *Next Stop is Vietnam: The War on Record: 1961–2008*, Bear Family Records BCD 16070, 2010; it includes more than just country music (there's blues, soul, and rock as well), but it provides a good range of songs, well-known and not so well-known. See also Doug Bradley and Craig Hansen Werner, *We Gotta Get Out of This Place: The Soundtrack of the Vietnam War* (Amherst: University of Massachusetts Press, 2015).

20. Ernest Tubb, "It's for God, and Country, and You, Mom" and "It's America (Love It or Leave It)" (both 1965); Stonewall Jackson, "The Minutemen (Are Turning in Their Graves)" (1966), by Harlan Howard; Dave Dudley, *There's a Star-Spangled Banner Waving Somewhere* (1965); Autry Inman, "Ballad of Two Brothers" (1968); Hank Snow, "A Letter from Viet Nam (to Mother)" (1966); Marty Robbins, "Private Wilson White" (1966).

21. Cash, *Cash: The Autobiography*, 216–217.

22. See, for example, Rachel Lee Rubin, *Merle Haggard's Okie from Muskogee (33 1/3)* (New York: Bloomsbury Academic, 2018).

23. Tom Wells, *The War Within: America's Battle over Vietnam* (Berkeley: University of California Press, 1994), chapter 7; Charles DeBenedetti, *An American Ordeal: The Antiwar Movement of the Vietnam Era* (Syracuse: Syracuse University Press, 1990); Melvin Small, *Antiwarriors: The Vietnam War and the Battle for America's Hearts and Minds* (Wilmington: Scholarly Resources, 2002), chapter 6.

24. Richard M. Nixon, *RN: The Memoirs of Richard Nixon*, 2nd ed. (New York: Touchstone, 1990), 408–411.

25. Marci McDonald, "Cash Sure Is 'Makin' it Okay'," *Toronto Daily Star*, November 11, 1969, 30; Jack Batten, "Johnny Cash Deserved Record Gardens Tribute," *Toronto Daily Star*, November 11, 1969, 30.

26. At least as far as we know from *Johnny Cash at Madison Square Garden*, which is not an archival recording but a commercial release put out by Columbia/Legacy in 2002. It is almost certainly not the complete concert.

27. The performance is captured on *Johnny Cash at Madison Square Garden*, Columbia/Legacy CK 86808, 2002, compact disc. Alfred Aronowitz, "A Man Called Johnny Cash," *New York Post*, December 8, 1969, reprinted in liner notes to the compact disc. Note that in Tom Smucker's *Village Voice* obituary/tribute to Cash, Smucker describes this sequence as Cash following the "patriotic tear jerker 'Remember the Alamo' with the anti-war tear jerker 'Last Night I had the Strangest Dream.'" Smucker then remarks, "And it works," but asks, "How did he pull it off?" What Smucker misses is that although "Remember the Alamo" is clearly a patriotic song, the introduction drawing the parallel with the Vietnam War is what makes it work with the antiwar anthem. Tom Smucker, "Cowboy and Indian, Sinner and Believer, Patriot and Protester, the Man in Black Walks His Final Line," *Village Voice*, September 12, 2003.

28. Aronowitz, "A Man Called Johnny Cash"; Carpozi, *The Johnny Cash Story*, 10.

29. Indeed, for a performer who was allegedly so single minded about keeping his diverse audience, he had a funny way of showing it. On television, especially, Cash seemed willing to experiment—and fail publicly—in a way that few artists could match. His public declaration of his faith and, at times, privileging of gospel

music—moves that his producers blamed for declining ratings—were not the deci-sions of an artist concerned only with satisfying his audience. On the contrary, he seemed quite willing to lose some of his audience.

30. Jonathan Silverman, *Nine Choices: Johnny Cash and American Culture* (Am-herst: University of Massachusetts Press, 2010), 132–134. Silverman concedes that "one cannot know" whether the "dove with claws" line "was a strategy to appeal to many audiences." But it does not "require speculation." It requires a careful examination of all of the evidence, circumstantial and contextual included. I have not found a single quote, from any document or interview attributed to Cash, his managers Saul Holiff and Lou Robin, or anyone at Columbia Records indicating that Cash's alleged strad-dling on the question of the Vietnam War had anything to do with his concern about audience. On the country music audience and the war, a September 1970 national poll showed 55 percent support for withdrawing from Vietnam by the end of 1971; broken down by region, the country music strongholds of the Midwest and South showed 56 percent and 49 percent support, respectively—hardly a significant difference from national attitudes. George Gallup, *The Gallup Poll: Public Opinion, 1935–1971*, Vol. 3 (New York: Random House, 1972), 2266–2267.

31. *The Johnny Cash Show*, aired January 21, 1970, on ABC.

32. Hubert Saal, "Johnny on the Spot," *Newsweek*, February 2, 1970, 84–85; Cleve-land Amory, "The Johnny Cash Show," *TV Guide*, April 4, 1970.

33. Richard M. Nixon, letter to Johnny Cash, February 2, 1970, on display at Sotheby's auction of the Johnny and June Carter Cash Estate, New York City, August–September, 2004.

34. Wren, *Winners Got Scars Too*, 14; Peter McCabe and Jack Killion, "Interview with Johnny Cash," *Country Music*, May 1973, reprinted in Streissguth, *Ring of Fire*, 137–138.

35. *The Johnny Cash Show*, aired February 18, 1970, on ABC.

36. *The Johnny Cash Show*, aired March 18, 1970, on ABC.

37. Folder Evening at the White House—Johnny Cash, Friday, April 17, 1970, box 125, White House Special Files, Staff Member and Office Files, President's Per-sonal Files, Richard Nixon Presidential Library and Museum, Yorba Linda, Califor-nia; Folder Evening at the White House—Johnny Cash April 17, 1970, box 6, White House Central Files, Staff Member and Office Files, Lucy A. Winchester, Richard Nixon Presidential Library and Museum, Yorba Linda, California; Folder April 17, 1970 Evening at the White House—Johnny Cash, boxes 21 and 112, White House Central Files, Staff Member and Office Files, Sanford Fox, Richard Nixon Presidential Library and Museum, Yorba Linda, California.

38. Wren reports that Cash told reporters at the White House that "Welfare Cadil-lac" was "not the kind of song I'd like to do" (Wren, *Winners Got Scars Too*, 11). In a 1975 interview, Cash said he didn't want to sing "Okie from Muskogee" because it was Merle Haggard's song, and that he didn't want to perform "Welfare Cadillac" because he'd heard it once and did not like it (Linderman, "*Penthouse* Interview," 154–155); Finally, in Cash's 1997 autobiography, he's more vague. He claims the song request came in too late, and he just wasn't prepared to sing them, though he implies if they had come in on time, he might have refused them anyway (Cash, *Cash: The Autobiography*,

211–212). Haggard later sang "Okie from Muskogee" when he performed at the Nixon White House (Nixon, *RN*, 539).

39. In Arkansas, especially, the press congratulated Cash for refusing to sing the songs requested by Nixon. "Congratulations, Johnny Cash," *Baxter Bulletin*, April 2, 1970; "Johnny at The White House . . ." *Osceola Times*, April 2, 1970; "A Song He Won't Sing," *Pine Bluff Commercial*, April 1, 1970; all clippings in folder 9, box 145, RG IV, Winthrop Rockefeller papers.

40. Wren, *Winners Got Scars Too*, 11, 16; Nan Robertson, "Cash and Country Music Take White House Stage," *New York Times*, April 18, 1970, 33. In January 1970, Nixon had a 65 percent approval rating on Vietnam; by April 12, it was 48 percent (Gallup, *Gallup Poll*, 2236, 2244).

41. Recording of Johnny Cash Show's Evening at the White House, WHCA SR #P-700418, CD-R, White House Communications Agency Sound Recording Collection, Richard Nixon Presidential Library; "Johnny Cash at the White House," White House Staff Super 8 Collection, Compilation Disc 3, 1970—Disc 1 of 2, DVD-R, Richard Nixon Presidential Library; Dan Rather report for CBS News, Weekly News Summary, 4/18/1970–4/24/1970, White House Communications Agency Videotape Collection, DVD-R, File ID: WHCA 3690, Richard Nixon Presidential Library. Note that although some of this concert can be heard on Columbia's 2011 release *Bootleg Vol. III: Live Around the World*, the complete concert included a number of other songs performed between "What is Truth" and "Peace in the Valley." The commercial release runs the two songs together, including the discussion of the war, which makes it seem like a sustained engagement with the subject of the war across several minutes when, in fact, Cash brought up the topics of war and dissent separately.

42. "Nixon Puts 'Bum' Label on Some College Radicals," *New York Times*, May 2, 1970.

43. Some profiles came out in the months after the Cambodian invasion that still quoted Cash as supporting the president, but they were based on pre-Kent State interviews. See for example Sakol, "The Grit and Grace of Johnny Cash"; on the Christmas 1970 episode of *The Johnny Cash Show*, Cash reflected, with his family, on the events of the past year. When they recalled the White House trip, Cash said to his father that Nixon was "a mighty nice man." *The Johnny Cash Show*, aired December 25, 1970, on ABC.

44. *The Johnny Cash Show*, aired May 6, 1970, on ABC.

45. *The Johnny Cash Show*, aired September 23, 1970, on ABC.

46. *The Johnny Cash Show*, aired September 23, 1970, on ABC; *The Johnny Cash Show*, aired October 21, 1970, on ABC; *The Johnny Cash Show*, aired November 4, 1970, on ABC.

47. On the draft lottery, see Flynn, *The Draft*, 243.

48. *The Johnny Cash Show*, aired February 17, 1971, on ABC.

49. *The Johnny Cash Show*, aired March 10, 1971, on ABC.

50. *The Johnny Cash Show*, aired March 17, 1971, on ABC.

51. Emphasizing the cost to Americans always resonated with the broader public more than appeals based on sympathy for Vietnamese civilians. Even the murder of

hundreds of civilians at My Lai did not guarantee American public sympathy. In 1971, "The Battle Hymn of Lt. Calley," by C Company featuring Terry Nelson, sold more than a million copies. The song defends William Calley, the only officer held accountable—and then, only briefly—for the My Lai massacre.

52. For a range of studies on those subsets of the antiwar movement, see Marian Mollin, *Radical Pacifism in Modern America: Egalitarianism and Protest* (Philadelphia: University of Pennsylvania Press, 2006); Amy C. Schneidhorst, *Building a Just and Secure World: Popular Front Women's Struggles for Peace and Justice in Chicago in the 1960s* (New York: Continuum, 2011); Shawn Francis Peters, *The Catonsville Nine: A Story of Faith and Resistance in the Vietnam Era* (New York: Oxford University Press, 2012); Murray Polner and Jim O'Grady, *Disarmed and Dangerous: The Radical Lives and Times of Daniel and Philip Berrigan* (New York: Basic Books, 1997); Amy Swerdlow, *Women Strike for Peace: Traditional Motherhood and Radical Politics in the 1960s* (Chicago: University of Chicago Press, 1993). Indeed, among the thousands of letters that pediatrician and peace activist Dr. Benjamin Spock received during the war—many of which urged support of the troops by bringing them home alive, in one piece—a number of writers criticized Spock and others for failing to privilege the deaths of American GIs over the killing of Vietnamese civilians. See Michael S. Foley, ed., *Dear Dr. Spock: Letters About the Vietnam War to America's Favorite Baby Doctor* (New York: New York University Press, 2005), 64–65, 141–142, 194, 241; in particular, letters 43, 105, 152, and 201 express sentiment similar to Cash. Letter 201 expresses a heartache that sounds much like Cash's.

53. June Vosburg, "Cash Country," *Man in Black: The Official Johnny Cash Society newsletter*, no. 5, February 1971, folder 9, Southern Folklife Collection Fan Club Newsletters; *Strictly Cash: The Official Johnny Cash Society newsletter*, undated, ca. 1972, folder 9, Southern Folklife Collection Fan Club Newsletters.

54. June Vosberg, "Cash Country," *Man in Black: The Official Johnny Cash Society newsletter*, April–June 1973, 7, folder 9, Southern Folklife Collection Fan Club Newsletters; McCabe and Killion, "Interview with Johnny Cash," 137.

55. Tony Tost, *Johnny Cash's American Recordings (33 1/3)* (New York: Bloomsbury Publishing USA, 2011), 70; Johnny Cash, *American Recordings*, American Recordings 9 45520-2, 1994; Johnny Cash/Willie Nelson, *VH1 Storytellers*, American Recordings CK 69416, 1998; Hilburn, *Johnny Cash*, 542.

CHAPTER 7: GOD AND COUNTRY

1. *The Johnny Cash Show*, aired March 25, 1970, on ABC.

2. *The Johnny Cash Show*, aired April 8, 1970, on ABC.

3. *The Johnny Cash Show*, aired November 18, 1970, on ABC; Hilburn, *Johnny Cash*, 397.

4. Johnny Cash, liner notes for *American II: Unchained*, American Recordings 9 43097-2, 1996, compact disc.

5. V. Cash and Sharpsteen, *I Walked the Line*, 81, 144, 165; Cash *Man in Black*, 69.

6. Dixie Deen, "Everything Ain't Been Said," *Music City News*, January 1966, 1, 3, 9.

7. It also prompted him to perform Christopher Wren's song "Jesus was a Carpenter" at the White House, the recording of which appears as the last song on *Hello, I'm Johnny Cash* (1970). A writer for *LOOK* magazine, Wren shortly thereafter wrote one of the best biographies on Cash, *Winners Got Scars Too*.

8. *The Johnny Cash Show*, aired March 4, 1970, on ABC; *The Johnny Cash Show*, aired May 13, 1970, on ABC; *The Johnny Cash Show*, aired January 13, 1971, on ABC.

9. Eileen Luhr, *Witnessing Suburbia: Conservatives and Christian Youth Culture* (Berkeley: University of California Press, 2009), 55.

10. Miller, *Cash: An American Man*, 294.

11. Miller, *Cash: An American Man*, 7; Robert Booth Fowler, *A New Engagement: Evangelical Political Thought, 1966–1976* (Grand Rapids: William B. Eerdmans Publishing Company, 1982), 115, 189; Luhr, *Witnessing Suburbia*, 20–21; Christian Smith, *American Evangelicalism: Embattled and Thriving* (Chicago: University of Chicago Press, 1998); Sara Diamond, *Spiritual Warfare: The Politics of the Christian Right* (Montreal: Black Rose Books Ltd., 1990), 212–213.

12. Fowler, *A New Engagement*, 116–117.

13. Fowler, *A New Engagement*; Dorothy Gallagher, "Johnny Cash: 'I'm Growing, I'm Changing, I'm Becoming,'" *Redbook*, August 1971, 61, 172–182.

14. David Stanton, "How Johnny Cash Became a Minister of God," *Strictly Cash: The Official Johnny Cash Society newsletter*, October–November 1972, 7–9, folder 9, Southern Folklife Collection Fan Club Newsletters; Richard Beck, *Trains, Jesus, and Murder: The Gospel According to Johnny Cash* (Minneapolis: Fortress Press, 2019), 160–161; Luhr, *Witnessing Suburbia*, 82–82; Hilburn, *Johnny Cash*, 421; "A 'Religious Woodstock' Draws 75,000," *New York Times*, June 16, 1972, 1; "Challenge to Change World Ends Explo '72," *Fort Worth Star-Telegram*, June 18, 1972, 1.

15. Fowler, *A New Engagement*, 54–55.

16. *The Johnny Cash Show*, aired June 7, 1969, on ABC; *The Johnny Cash Show*, aired June 14, 1969, on ABC; *The Johnny Cash Show*, aired June 21, 1969, on ABC; *The Johnny Cash Show*, aired July 12, 1969, on ABC; *The Johnny Cash Show*, aired July 26, 1969, on ABC; *The Johnny Cash Show*, aired August 2, 1969, on ABC; *The Johnny Cash Show*, aired August 9, 1969, on ABC; *The Johnny Cash Show*, aired August 16, 1969, on ABC; *The Johnny Cash Show*, aired August 23, 1969, on ABC; *The Johnny Cash Show*, aired December 2, 1970, on ABC; *The Johnny Cash Show*, aired September 23, 1970, on ABC; *The Johnny Cash Show*, aired March 24, 1971, on ABC; Cash, *Cash: The Autobiography*, 137; *Mother Maybelle Carter's Scratch*, directed by Gregg Mogford (Mebcon Production, 1990).

17. And it is a remarkably weak record, too, showing a post-television-show lack of focus, weighed down in particular by Cash and Carter's unhinged performance of Chris Gantry's "Allegheny," a song about a guy promising to drag his thieving half-Cherokee mail-order bride back home by her hair. That they included a couple of Christian songs on the album did not offset the damage of a man plotting revenge on "his woman."

18. Fowler, *A New Engagement*, 202–205; Sakol, "The Grit and Grace of Johnny Cash"; Dorothy Gallagher, "Johnny Cash: 'I'm Growing, I'm Changing, I'm

Becoming'"; June Carter Cash, *Among My Klediments* (Grand Rapids: Zondervan Publishing Company, 1981), 96, 100–102; Light, *Johnny Cash*, 134.

19. Cash, *Cash: The Autobiography*, 228–229; David Stanton, "How Johnny Cash Became a Minister of God," *Strictly Cash: The Official Johnny Cash Society newsletter*, October–November 1972, 7–9, folder 9, Southern Folklife Collection Fan Club Newsletters; Light, *Johnny Cash*, 167.

20. Hilburn, *Johnny Cash*, 411.

21. George Vecsey, "Cash's 'Gospel Road' is Renaissance for Him," *New York Times*, December 13, 1973, 62; Richard Maschal, "A Man 'For the People,'" *Washington Post*, February 16, 1973, B5; *Mornings with Siegel*, WLAC-TV, Nashville, August 20, 1975, Paley Center for Media, Los Angeles; David Stanton, "How Johnny Cash Became a Minister of God." 7–9.

22. Patrick Carr, "Johnny Cash's Freedom," *Country Music*, April 1979, 25.

23. Peter McCabe, "Johnny Cash vs. Merle Haggard: The Saga of Country Music," *Argosy* 281, no. 1 (January 1975): 13, 25–28; *Heartworn Highways*, directed by Jim Szalapski (1976: Light in the Attic, 2016).

24. *Mornings with Siegel*, WLAC-TV; Nick Tosches, *Country: The Twisted Roots of Rock n Roll*, rev. ed. (New York: Da Capo, 1996), 136.

25. Cash, *Man in Black*, 153; California Department of Corrections, "Johnny Cash at Soledad," 1980, California Audiovisual Preservation Project, Internet Archive, https://archive.org/details/car_000167; Gilmore, *Shot in the Heart*, 344, 346, 349.

26. A partial list of benefits includes concerts for the children and widows of policemen killed on duty in Nashville and in Port Richey, Florida; for Farrow Manor Baptist Children's Home in Senatobia, Mississippi; for an Apache school in Arizona; for the Maybelle Carter Retirement Center in Madison, Tennessee; an eye bank in North Carolina; SOS Children's Village in Jamaica, among many others. A partial list of charitable donations: homes for autistic children; a battered women's shelter in Nashville; adult literacy programs; and the endowment of a burn research center in memory of Luther Perkins. David Horowitz, "Cash's In the Chips"; June Vosburg, "Cash Country," *Man in Black: The Official Johnny Cash Society newsletter*, March 1971, folder 9, Southern Folklife Collection Fan Club Newsletters; *Mornings with Siegel*, WLAC-TV; Grant and Zar, *I Was There When It Happened*, 188–189; Flanagan, "Johnny Cash, American," 98, 111; All-Star Tribute to Johnny Cash, TNT, aired April 18, 1999, YouTube video, www.youtube.com/playlist?list=PL263F0CAC9363E9B5.

27. Robert K. Oermann, "Superstar Cash Still Speaks for the Hearts of Americans," *Nashville Tennessean Showcase*, April 26, 1987, 14.

28. In fact, the "movements" to roll back taxes were not as grassroots as they appeared, and as numerous studies later showed, any benefits went disproportionately to commercial property owners and landlords, while public services suffered from the reduced revenue. See Isaac William Martin, *The Permanent Tax Revolt: How the Property Tax Transformed American Politics* (Stanford, CA: Stanford University Press, 2008).

29. *Johnny Cash Spring Fever*, CBS, aired May 7, 1978, Paley Center for Media, Los Angeles.

30. Michael Stewart Foley, *Front Porch Politics: The Forgotten Heyday of American Activism in the 1970s and 1980s* (New York: Hill and Wang, 2013), chapter 8.

31. "Singers Offer Talent, Advice for Ironic Plight of Farmers," *Des Moines Register*, September 23, 1985, 2A; "Country Music Can Compete Against its Rock Music Cousin," *The Hanford Sentinel*, October 26, 1985, TV-3; "Rain Fails to Dampen Farm-Aid Spirit," *Baltimore Sun*, September 23, 1985, 4B.

32. *Sojourners* ran an entire issue on the farm crisis, "America Foreclosed," in October 1986; *Christianity Today* followed with Rodney Clapp, "The Fate of the Soil," October 2, 1987, 14–15.

33. Johnny Cash, *Man in White* (Nashville: Thomas Nelson, 2008), 89–93, 100–101; John Carter Cash, afterword to *Man in White*.

34. Darren Dochuk, *From Bible Belt to Sunbelt: Plain-Folk Religion, Grassroots Politics, and the Rise of Evangelical Conservatism* (New York: W. W. Norton & Company, 2010), 412–413.

35. Stephen Miller, *Johnny Cash: The Life of an American Icon* (London: Omnibus Press, 2005), 294.

36. *The Johnny Cash Show*, aired November 11, 1970, on ABC; "It's Great to Be Alive," interview with Johnny Cash by Glenn Jorgenson of River Park treatment center in South Dakota, ca. late 1970s, YouTube video, www.youtube.com/watch?v=rhuSVkoi5Jo; "A Change of Heart: Billy Graham on the Nuclear Arms Race," *Sojourners*, August 1979, https://sojo.net/magazine/august-1979/change-heart.

37. Robert K. Oermann, "Superstar Cash Still Speaks for the Hearts of Americans," *Nashville Tennessean Showcase*, April 26, 1987, 14; Patrick Carr, "Cash Lives," *Country Music*, March/April 1989, 41; Flanagan, "Johnny Cash, American," 104, 106.

38. The Highwaymen, *The Highwaymen: Live—American Outlaws*, Columbia 88875100002, 2016, 3 CD+DVD box set.

39. Stephen P. Miller, *Billy Graham and the Rise of the Republican South* (Philadelphia: University of Pennsylvania Press, 2011), 3, 212; John Carter Cash, *House of Cash: The Legacies of My Father, Johnny Cash* (San Rafael, CA: Insight Editions, 2011), 90.

EPILOGUE

1. *The Johnny Cash Show*, aired August 30, 1969, on ABC.

2. Tost, *Johnny Cash's American Recordings*, 184.

3. Cash, *Cash: The Autobiography*, 63; Bill Friskics-Warren, "Johnny Cash," *No Depression*, November–December 2002, 83, 94.

4. Jason Fine, "Johnny's Final Music," *Rolling Stone*, October 16, 2003, 73; Rosanne Cash, interviewed in *We're Still Here: Johnny Cash's Bitter Tears Revisited*, directed by Antonino D'Ambrosio (Kino Lorber, 2015), DVD.

5. Peter Cooper and Tim Ghianni, "Requiem for a Music Legend," *Nashville Tennessean*, September 16, 2003, 1; "Remembering Johnny," *Rolling Stone*, October 16, 2003, 74–75.

6. Chris Willman, *Rednecks & Bluenecks: The Politics of Country Music* (New York: The New Press, 2005), 253; *Democracy Now!*, aired September 1, 2004; Peter Rothberg, "Johnny Cash was NOT a Republican," *The Nation*, August 24, 2004, www

.democracynow.org/2004/9/1/rnc_protesters_rush_to_defend_johnny; John Nichols, "The Man in Black Bloc," *The Nation*, September 1, 2004.

7. *Best of Johnny Cash Show*, directed by Michael Borofsky, executive produced by Lou Robin and John Carter Cash (Sony Pictures Television, 2007), DVD; see also, *Johnny Cash's America*, directed by Morgan Neville and Robert Gordon, written by Morgan Neville, executive produced by John Carter Cash and Lou Robin (Sony BMG Entertainment, 2008), DVD.

8. See Foley, *Front Porch Politics* for countless examples of Americans mobilizing around political issues based not on ideology or political identification but on the promptings of their own experience.

9. My analysis here got a boost from a timely column: Molly Worthen, "The Trouble with Empathy," *New York Times*, September 4, 2020.

Permissions

The author is grateful for permission to quote from the following songs and texts:

COCAINE BLUES
Words and Music by T.J. ARNALL
and WILLIAM LEE NICHOLS
© 1979 UNICHAPPELL MUSIC INC.
and ELVIS PRESLEY MUSIC INC.
All Rights Administered by UNICHAPPELL MUSIC INC.
All Rights Reserved

TELL HIM I'M GONE
WORDS AND MUSIC BY JOHNNY CASH
© 1963 (RENEWED) CHAPPELL & CO. INC. (ASCAP)
All Rights Reserved

ANOTHER MAN DONE GONE
New words and new music adaptation by Vera Hall
Collected and arranged by John A. Lomax, Alan Lomax and
Ruby Pickens Tartt
Additional lyrics by Johnny Cash
TRO- © Copyright 1959 (Renewed) and 1966 (Renewed) Ludlow Music, Inc.,
New York, NY International Copyright Secured
Made in U.S.A.
All Rights Reserved Including Public Performance For Profit
Used by Permission

Index of Song and Record Titles

Index

337

MICHAEL STEWART FOLEY is a historian of American political culture. He is the author or editor of seven other books, including the prizewinning *Confronting the War Machine: Draft Resistance During the Vietnam War*, *Front Porch Politics: The Forgotten Heyday of American Activism in the 1970s and 1980s*, and the 33⅓ book on punk band Dead Kennedys' political masterpiece, *Fresh Fruit for Rotting Vegetables*. He has served as historical advisor on a number of films and television shows, including *Mad Men*, and his writing has appeared in the *New York Times*, the *Guardian*, the *Boston Sunday Globe*, and the *Daily Beast*, among other news outlets. He is Professor of American Civilization at Université Grenoble Alpes in France.